PENGUIN BOOKS
THE LAST TIME I SAW TIBET

Bimal Dey was born in 1940 in Kolkata. He travelled to Tibet on foot in 1956, at the age of sixteen; this journey is the subject of his travelogue *The Last Time I Saw Tibet*. From 1967 to 1972, he undertook a 230,000 kilometre journey around the world on an ordinary bicycle. He has also been to the Arctic Circle and Antarctica a number of times. A yoga teacher of repute, he lives in France and is associated with a number of social welfare projects in Africa and in India.

Malobika Chaudhuri runs Mono Translation Bureau, a multilingual translation agency, in Kolkata. She has translated several novels of Saratchandra Chattopadhyay for Penguin.

The Last Time I Saw Tibet

Bimal Dey

Translated from the Bengali by
Malobika Chaudhuri

PENGUIN BOOKS

PENGUIN BOOKS
Published by the Penguin Group
Penguin Books India Pvt. Ltd, 11 Community Centre, Panchsheel Park,
New Delhi 110 017, India
Penguin Group (USA) Inc., 375 Hudson Street, New York, New York 10014, USA
Penguin Group (Canada), 90 Eglinton Avenue East, Suite 700, Toronto,
Ontario, M4P 2Y3, Canada (a division of Pearson Penguin Canada Inc.)
Penguin Books Ltd, 80 Strand, London WC2R 0RL, England
Penguin Ireland, 25 St Stephen's Green, Dublin 2, Ireland
(a division of Penguin Books Ltd)
Penguin Group (Australia), 250 Camberwell Road, Camberwell,
Victoria 3124, Australia (a division of Pearson Australia Group Pty Ltd)
Penguin Group (NZ), cnr Airborne and Rosedale Roads, Albany,
Auckland 1310, New Zealand (a division of Pearson New Zealand Ltd)
Penguin Group (South Africa) (Pty) Ltd, 24 Sturdee Avenue, Rosebank,
Johannesburg 2196, South Africa

Penguin Books Ltd, Registered Offices: 80 Strand, London WC2R 0RL, England

Published as *Mahatirther Shesh Jatri* by Paribrajak Prakashani 1982
First published in English by Penguin Books India 2007

This translation copyright © Penguin Books India 2007

All rights reserved

10 9 8 7 6 5 4 3 2 1

ISBN-13: 9-780-14310-124-6   ISBN-10: 0-14310-124-2

Typeset in *Minion Regular* by SÜRYA, New Delhi
Printed at Baba Barkhanath Printers, New Delhi

CONTENTS

❧

Preface to This Edition   vii
Preface to the Original Edition   xi

A Farewell to My Roots   1
On the Way   26
A Tibetan Family   39
The City of Yatung and Dungkar Gumpha   44
Phari   51
A Nocturnal Journey   57
Kiangphu Gumpha and Lama Tshering Jong   63
To Gyatse   65
On the Eternal Pilgrimage   74
The Pilgrims' First Offering   77
Meditation on the Arya Tara   89
From Gyatse to Samding Gumpha   100
The Dorje Pamo   109
The Language   113
My First Glimpse of the Sangpo   115
The Chaksam Gumpha   116

On the Threshold   123
The Drepung Gumpha   125
Lamas and Learning   131
A Tibetan Tale: History and Faith   134
Lhasa and Jokhang, the Core Temple   140
Lhasa   148
Potala, the Royal Palace   151
Lama Lamdup   161
Norbulingka, the Dalai Lama's Summer Palace   164
The Dalai Lama   167
Lhasa: The Last Days   175
Gearing Up for Kailashnath   179
In Search of the Route to Kailash   184
The Exorcist of Sangpo   185
A Night of Terror   193
Strangers Become Friends   196
Shigatse   198
The Panchen Lama   203
On the Way to Kailash   206
The Sage of Pasaguk   210
Tradum   217
At the End of My Tether   225
A Few More Steps to Heaven   228
Heaven, at Last!   233
My First Night at Mansarovar   238
Kailashnath   246
Kailash Baba   254
Tibet's Eternal Flame: Milarepa   267

Afterword: Lhasa Once More in the New Millennium   279

PREFACE TO THIS EDITION

☙

IN THE 1981 preface to *The Last Time I Saw Tibet* I had written: 'In 1956, the doors to Tibet were almost closed to foreigners, most certainly to Indians . . . Somehow, that year, the government of Nepal managed to obtain permission from the Chinese embassy in Kathmandu for a group of pilgrims to travel into Tibet . . . Later I heard that that group of ours was the last group of pilgrims that was allowed in. It was the last time that I—or any of us—were to see Tibet.'

I had also written: 'Since 1958 Tibet became virtually inaccessible. But I have been praying for the situation to change. The doors to heaven cannot under any circumstance be barred; every human being has the right to go on a pilgrimage of Kailash— the Almighty is not the particular property of any country. Kailash is a holy pilgrimage site for all of humanity.'

My prayers have been granted—the path to Kailash has once again been opened. In the past few years almost fifteen thousand pilgrims from India have travelled to Tibet. They have circumambulated Kailash and bathed in the holy waters of the Mansarovar. For this I and thousands of pilgrims and those with wanderlust offer our heartfelt gratitude and respect to the Indian and Chinese governments.

On 6 July 2006, my joy knew no bounds. That day, in Gangtok, Pawan Kumar Chamling, the chief minister of Sikkim, announced the reopening of the Nathu La pass. Nathu La! The name resounds across the continents, and every cell in my body reverberates with a strange thrill. Finally, the ancient link between two great nations—India and China—has been re-established.

The Nathu La pass is of historical importance. In ancient times this was part of the Silk Route. Of course in the course of time the Silk Route has changed its path a number of times. But the basic route lay from Europe, particularly Venice, through Tehran or Istanbul (in olden times its name was Constantinople) and other ancient cities like Samarkhand and Tashkent, to Lhasa, and through the Nathu La pass to Siliguri and Kolkata. Many foreigners believe that the Nathu La pass was the gateway to the Silk Route for the Mongols between Gangtok and Lhasa. For us, however, it is much more: it is the gateway to the original route to the ultimate pilgrimage of all, to Kailash and Mansarovar.

A separate visa is not granted for going to Lhasa, the capital of Tibet, from India via Kailash and Mansarovar since it is not on the route. Pilgrims to Kailash travel from Nainital or Almora to Lipulake and Taklakot and take the Gurla pass to reach Mansarovar and Kailash. But one can reach Lhasa directly from Nathu La by following the course of the Brahmaputra river. One has to go to Nathu La via Gangtok. From Kolkata the Nathu La pass is 550 km and from Lhasa, it is 460 km; it is at a height of 14,910 ft (4545m).

Nathu La was the border post between India and China on the ancient Silk Route. Local people call it the Dalai Lama's path because this is the route he took when he came as a refugee to India. Nathu La is called Yadu on the Tibet side. The people there refer to it as a salt route. This is because sea salt would reach Lhasa from Midnapore along this route.

This historic Nathu La pass has reopened now, and can there be greater cause for happiness than this? For me, this is the pilgrimage route to Jokhang and Potala.

For the past few decades I have been wandering all over the world. I have seen that human society exists through a process of creation, destruction and renewal. No border of any country is permanent. There have been far-reaching changes in so many parts of the world. Humanity was divided and a wall constructed through the middle of a city in Germany; but this Berlin Wall was also destroyed, without bloodshed, thanks to the combined onslaught of humanity. In Europe many countries have united now, as had happened with the states in America. At the other end of the world, the Palestinian Wall had been constructed and then broken. While moving along, this is what I have realized—mankind as a whole wants amity, peace and unity. When all seek the same effect, it is then that there can be a sense of true freedom. That is what is known as global harmony.

It is in the spirit of harmony that India and China have today united at the Nathu La pass. In the past, at the Tibetan border, there was a massive signpost which stated: 'You are under enemy observation now'. This has now been replaced by a board which proudly states: 'Please come here. We are very good friends'.

1956 was not the last time I saw Tibet. I have gone back several times. And will again. The only difference is that back then, in 1956, it was Tibet; now it is China.

France, 2006   **Bimal Dey**

PREFACE TO THE ORIGINAL EDITION

꿎

IN ATTEMPTING TO put down some thoughts for the preface to this book, I seem to be having a difficult time. The book was based on a diary, if you can call it that. It began with some stray sheets of white paper, and graduated to a notebook—when I could lay hands on one. For the better part of the time it was just stray thoughts jotted down on bits of paper. I smiled to myself even as I read through them and tried to put them in some sort of order. However, I was able to find a pattern that threaded through them—and the credit for that goes to those whose blessings have been my mainstay.

In 1956, the doors to Tibet were almost closed to foreigners, most certainly to Indians. On 23 May 1951, according to a directive of the Central People's Government of China, the Peaceful Liberation Army of the Beijing government began to gradually spread through Tibet. Even after political ties were severed, however, some options were left for pilgrims. Somehow, that year, the government of Nepal managed to obtain permission from the Chinese embassy in Kathmandu for a group of pilgrims to travel into Tibet. That was how I had managed to get into Tibet. Later I heard that that group of ours was the last group of pilgrims that was allowed in. It was the last time that I—or any of us—were to see Tibet.

Many years have passed since then. There have been

innumerable changes in the life of the 'Silent Monk'. Some strange attraction had pulled that runaway boy from one end of the country to another. Now, inspired by the pristine spirit of Tibet, he set off to traverse the whole world.

In 1967 I set off on my travels with an old bicycle and only eighteen rupees in my pocket. My capital was the inspiration I had derived from Kailash. After travelling through Asia, Africa, Europe, America and Australia, I returned home in 1972. There was wonderment from my family and friends and various sections of the media. Some assumed I was a born traveller, some thought I was extremely courageous, while there were others who reflected on all the experiences that I had had. But of all of them, how many thought of asking—what have you gained from your travels?

I have indeed seen a lot—the Himalayas, the Alps, the Rocky Mountains—but of them all the Himalayas reign supreme. I have come across a lot of lakes—from Lake Geneva to Titikaka, but there is nothing to surpass Mansarovar. Beautiful scenery has come my way many times, and similarities between diverse climes have struck me time and again. Lake Geneva can be compared to Mansarovar. From Italy Mont Blanc looks very like Kailash. However, nothing abroad comes even close to the spirit that is an inherent part of the Himalayas. In Europe, wherever the scenic beauty is commendable, bars have flourished, and in America there are the 'souvenir stalls'; but in India the scenario is altogether different. Since time immemorial India has been aware that where there is beauty, there is divinity. So, in every beautiful segment of the Himalayas, temples, gumphas and chaityas have grown.

In each inhabitant of the Himalayas I have seen a reflection of the divine. Even the extremely poor villagers along Lhasa and Kailash reflect the spirit of Shiva. These are the thoughts that lay hidden in the torn pages of my twenty-four-year-old notebook. Have I been able to impart those feelings? I had let my thoughts flow in those pages, but never ever thought that a book would come of it.

The revered Gopinath Kabiraj had once blessed me and said, 'If possible, put down on paper all your thoughts, feelings and experiences about Tibet.' Alas, he is with us no more, but a feeling of being sanctified remains with his memory. In this context I should also mention that in 1975 Swami Shivanandaji Maharaj, founder of the Kamakhya Umachal Ashram, also greatly inspired me. My respectful salutations to him. I must also mention Swami Yogeshwarananda Saraswati Maharaj, the head of Shivananda Yogashram. Though he is a personal friend, I must express my gratitude to him for helping me as regards the publication of this book. I also remain indebted to the chairman of the Shivananda Yogashram sangha, Srimat Swami Devananda Saraswati Maharaj—my respectful salutations to him.

A number of others have influenced me as well. I met the Dalai Lama in Dharamsala, and in Sonada the same year I met Kalu Rimche. The next year in Mont Pelblanc I had the honour of meeting Geshe Repten. Then, in Rumtek, I conversed with the Karmapa. (Presently they are all Tibetan refugees.) Despite my best intentions, I was just not getting the time to organize matters when another strange incident took place. In Gangtok I suddenly met Dongaldada, my guide in Manas and Kailash. What a coincidence!

In 1979, a particularly good friend in Santiniketan, Gora Sarbadhikari, took me to a truly great yogi. At first sight my heart leaped up in joy—I thought that he was my lost sadhu baba. There was a physical resemblance between them and their natures seem to be similar as well. On a sudden meeting it would seem that he was a young man in the guise of a venerable sage! He was known as sadhu baba too. I did not ask him any questions about my sadhu baba, but said to myself that he was the knowledgeable mentor who had first guided me. It is keeping him in mind that I began this book. His presence was necessary for this book and it is his blessings that have given me the necessary impetus to complete it. I have mentioned nothing of this matter to him—I know he is omniscient.

This book cannot be placed in the same genre as any other travelogue. My intention was never to visit Tibet in particular—running away from home was what was on my mind. All the events that later unfolded happened because the Almighty so willed.

Since 1958 Tibet became virtually inaccessible. But I have been praying for the situation to change. The doors to heaven cannot under any circumstance be barred; every human being has the right to go on a pilgrimage of Kailash—the Almighty is not the particular property of any country. Kailash is a holy pilgrimage site for all of humanity.

The book is nothing extraordinary, but it contains some accounts of the wondrous spiritual experience I had, which I would like to share with the world at large.

France, 1981 **Bimal Dey**

A FAREWELL TO MY ROOTS

❦

I DID NOT fall into the clutches of a godman as might have been surmised in the circumstances. On the contrary, it was I who had found him by the wayside, indisposed and ailing, and volunteered to look after him. What was more, his constant refrain, after he recovered, had been, 'Go back home where you belong!'

There was, of course, no question of my heeding his advice. Smiling to myself, I had mused, 'It wasn't with the intention of turning back that I left home in the first place, was it?'

Gaya had, in fact, been on my mind as my holiday destination before I boarded the train that would bring me all the way here from my hometown, Ichhapur. A ticketless traveller, I had been moving about quite happily. The little money I carried had long been spent on some spicy puffed rice on the train. And that was when I had met the godman, my sadhu baba.

Though Gaya might not have been a particularly prepossessing town, it had a charm all its own, having evolved at the juncture of heaven and hell, as it were, from a curious amalgam of elements that encapsulated both the sins of the present and the urge to atone for future transgressions. I would spend a great deal of time with Hindu and Buddhist religious men and quite enjoy myself in their company. The rumour went that their company was conducive to spiritual upliftment. I would much rather affirm, however, that physically too, great benefits were to be derived from consorting with them.

There were many who came here in quest of enlightenment and still others who sought to set their souls free. Why had I come? I really couldn't pin down the reason. I was in pursuit of neither enlightenment nor spiritual release. I rejoiced in all I observed and in whatever I gleaned from my observations. The very atmosphere of this place exuded an aura of freedom that was intoxicating.

The sadhu baba from Gaya had refused to take me seriously. According to him, I was not yet matured and needed to return home in order to further my education and allow myself to be propelled towards a future that dazzled with promise. Being a half-baked fakir could never lead to anything of consequence, he had maintained. And so he had repeatedly tried convincing me to go back home. But how could I relinquish what I had gained? I could never tell the sadhu baba that it was the aura around him that drew me irresistibly to him. He spoke with an accent reminiscent of the speech patterns common to Kolkata's Marwari community. Apart from his mother tongue, he was perfectly fluent in Nepalese and Bhutia. From his attire, one might have taken him for a Tibetan lama. He could spout the scriptures and knew the Buddha's teachings by heart. His knowledge of Hinduism was profound. From the little I had learnt about him, I gathered that he was at least seventy years old, had no refuge of his own to retreat to and had spent many years in a monastery at Sarnath.

I had first met him on the roads that ran past the dharamsala. I had told him everything about myself—that I was an orphan with no younger siblings to provide for, no ties to sever, no education, no financial assets—nothing.

Sometimes, I addressed the sadhu baba as 'Baba' or 'Sadhu Baba'. Or, if I happened to be in a particularly exuberant mood, I called him 'Guruji', my spiritual mentor. We conversed in a language that accommodated both Hindi and Bengali, but our exchanges were limited. He had put up in a room at the dharamsala. His meals consisted of little more than boiled vegetables, cooked over the fire, stoked in a makeshift oven fashioned from three bricks. The expense incurred in preparing these meals was minimal. All one needed to do was purchase a bundle of sticks. Everything else was given to us free of cost. The job assigned to me entailed grocery shopping for the sadhu baba each morning.

Shopping without any cash to pay for the goods was a

disconcerting experience indeed. I had to approach vegetable sellers for whatever handouts I could manage; to put it baldly, I begged. Sometimes, I would have to wander about the entire morning just for a single piece of vegetable. It was easiest to procure potatoes and flour and I had volunteered to take on this responsibility. If I mentioned to Guruji that I was going begging, he would fly into a rage. As he saw it, this wasn't begging at all, but merely an exercise in humility and self-effacing courtesy.

After twenty-two days had gone by in this manner, I returned exhausted one morning from my shopping errand to find Guruji engrossed in a discussion with three other lamas. Instead of disturbing him, I busied myself preparing the meal, glancing frequently into the room where they were gathered. I felt the three men might be Sherpas or Nepalese. In fact, they looked rather like the sadhu baba himself.

In a short while, the meal was ready: five pieces of bread, four boiled potatoes and a little boiled spinach. According to the instructions I had received, everything that had been obtained from the market would have to be consumed. If there was a surplus, it would be given away—no leftovers were hoarded for the following day. The three lamas shared the meal with us. Needless to say, both Guruji and I went without food that day.

When the meal was over, Guruji rose to his feet, as did the three other men. Then touching his small pouch to my forehead, he murmured, 'May you live long. May God's blessings be with you and keep you in fine fettle.'

I was startled at this sudden shower of blessings and asked him, 'What does this mean?'

His tone was detached as he replied, 'It means goodbye.'

This sudden announcement left me speechless with shock. Even moments ago, he had said nothing about it. Taken completely unawares, I was left gaping. He departed without even a glance in my direction, leaving me in a pitiable frame of mind. My blood boiled, fuelled by rage and hurt. Grinding my teeth in fury, I hurled the earthen cooking pot on to the road outside, smashing it to pieces. Then looking at the people around me, I ranted, 'So much for that worthless sadhu! An ungrateful wretch, if ever there was one, a fraud I nursed through the agonizing pain of arthritis! Now that he has found his own kind, just look at the way he has shrugged me off! Finer feelings are quite beyond him!'

Contemplating the shattered earthenware, I concluded that everything was now over for me in Gaya. I had not had a proper meal the day before; nor, for that matter, had I done so that day. The lamas, after all, had shared our meal. And compounding it all was my sudden parting with the sadhu baba. Overcome by a spell of dizziness that made my legs go numb, I collapsed in a heap beside the broken earthenware. Was this to be the final outcome of all the care I'd showered on the sadhu baba? Within a few minutes, however, I managed to pull myself together. Realizing that there was no one around to console me, I ran along in the direction in which the sadhu baba had headed. Soon, I had managed to catch sight of the four lamas.

Approaching the sadhu baba from behind, I caught hold of his small, knotted bundle. His expression seemed to suggest he had been waiting for me. What a charming smile played on his face, a perfect blend of reassurance and ease! Looking at me, he said, 'I know you're feeling unhappy. But everything in this universe is an illusion. Don't allow yourself to become so wrapped up in it. I am going far away. If the place were close by, I would have taken you with me.'

The weariness brought about by my emotional turmoil seemed to fade away as I asked,'Where is that "far away"?'

'Gangtok.'

'Forgive me, I misunderstood your intentions,' I replied and humbly prostrated myself at his feet. He proceeded towards the station and I went off in the direction of the river.

Another couple of days went by.

Ever since the sadhu baba had left, the word 'Gangtok' kept reverberating in my ears. I had been to Siliguri and Darjeeling a number of times and knew that one would have to travel to Gangtok, the capital of Sikkim, via Siliguri. What would it be like travelling there? No sooner had the thought occurred to me than I set off. My happiness suddenly welled up from hidden depths.

Three days later, I had reached Siliguri and from there had made my way atop a truck to the Indian border at the foothills of the Himalayas—Teesta Bazaar, a small town bustling with army personnel and trucks loaded with a variety of goods. The Teesta river flowed solemnly by. There was no one at all crossing the border and neither the military nor the police bothered me with questions. They were keeping an eye out for goods and foreigners. As far as they were concerned, Indians did not fall into that category. Having crossed the bridge on foot, I was overwhelmed with joy. It was foreign soil, after all!

Also proceeding towards Sikkim was a host of trucks, buses, jeeps and land rovers. Some were headed for India; others were going further up. Lepchas, Bhutias and Sikkimese nationals thronged the streets. I discovered that the road climbing up was the easiest route, leading straight to Gangtok. One could also make it on foot over a period of three days or more. The people here seemed not to have a very clear concept of distance in miles.

During my last two days in Gaya, I had earned about three rupees in a hotel, washing dishes and carrying tea up to the rooms. So far, I had spent no money on transport. I had only spent it on food. I had some loose change left over. Entering a small tea shop, I had a cup of hot, strong tea with two pieces of hand-rolled unleavened bread. Then I set off for Gangtok.

What scenic splendour lay before me! There was that distinctive fragrance of trees growing at high altitudes, the sheer beauty of the hills and forests around me. It seemed as though fatigue could not possibly conquer anyone walking along such roads, even if the journey were endless. The horizon lay in the distance, barely visible. The Teesta raged along, dangerous in its turbulence, wrecking many lives around it as it went. It was the month of April and still quite cold. I wore a light shirt and half-pants—quite inadequate in such climatic conditions. Despite that, I barely felt the cold, so desperately eager was I to reach my destination.

Along the route, truck drivers would frequently lean out and ask if I wanted a lift. Each time, my smiling response was the same: No. I had heard that to travel on the roof of a lorry, one had to pay a mere pittance. But I could not afford even that. So, what other option had I?

The beauty of the Himalayas was like a magnet drawing the beholder ever closer. After nearly four hours had elapsed, it became increasingly apparent that the task of making it on foot to my destination wasn't quite as easy as it had seemed. But in a way, I was fortunate: There was no dearth of drinking water along the route. A little search would reveal rippling streams that pierced the heart of the mountains and provided succour for the traveller. I walked along, panting and pausing to rest every so often.

At this point, luck favoured me. A lorry stopped close by. The driver who seemed to be from Bihar asked,'Where are you headed?'

'Gangtok,' I answered.

'Hop in,' was his prompt response.

'I haven't any money at all,' I confessed.

He laughed. 'Looking at you, that's obvious!'

I realized that sheer kindness had prompted him to help me out. He explained that I would have to travel on the truck's roof. The plastic sheet covering the goods piled there could tear any moment. It would be my job to keep an eye on things. If the rope actually broke, I would have to thump on the roof and let him know. Both of us stood to gain by this arrangement: The driver could concentrate on his driving and I got a free ride to Gangtok. Such trucks usually carried a helper, a general handyman for taking care of odd jobs. In this case, however, the helper had had to remain behind for an errand near the Teesta Bridge. The driver was, therefore, obliged to take me along in his place.

The zigzags in the hill road forced the lorry to a crawl. But wherever the road straightened out somewhat, the driver forged ahead, full throttle, adding to my misery as I perched on the roof with an icy wind whipping past my ears. Finally, matters came to such a pass that even when the truck moved at a leisurely pace, the cold seemed unbearable. About an hour later, I thumped on the roof and forced the truck driver to a halt. I told him apologetically that it was impossible for me to withstand the cold on the roof. If he were kind enough to let me off, I would walk the rest of the way.

Sympathetic to my plight, the driver smiled and said, 'All right, but we've come more than halfway. You can sit in the truck for the rest of the journey.' Stopping at a wayside Bhutia tea shop, we had a hot glass of tea each before proceeding on our way. We reached Gangtok around four in the afternoon. Thanking the driver profusely for the ride, I walked to the Big Bazaar.

When I had run away from home nearly a month back, I had never dreamed of reaching Gangtok. An ambience that was entirely new to my experience prevailed here. As I gazed at the market and the people milling around, it seemed as if I had arrived at some place that was far, far away from the world I had known. My knowledge of Hindi would probably carry me through. But looking at the Sikkimese around me, I did not feel they had much use for Hindi.

My first job was to find the sadhu baba. In actual fact, it was certainly not as easy as I had imagined. Searching for a particular sadhu in Gangtok was rather like looking for a needle in a haystack. Gradually, dusk descended and lights flickered on like fireflies in the surrounding darkness. Meanwhile, I had asked dozens of people in the market place about the sadhu baba, but none was able to point me in the right direction. Without a specific name to go by, finding him in this town that housed hundreds of lamas would be an impossible task.

The market at Sikkim was rather like the one at Darjeeling, crowded with people from the hills. There were virtually no Bengalis around. I spent the night in Diwali Bazaar in front of the fire at the den for drivers. There, a Lepcha even treated me to tea and bread.

The next morning, I continued my search for the sadhu baba. Buddhism being the predominant religion in Sikkim, Hindu temples were unknown here. All around me were stupas and monasteries. Instead of referring to him as 'Sadhu Baba', I began inquiring after my 'Guru Lama'.

The Sikkimese were a cheerful, straightforward and easy-going lot. They were all eager to be of assistance. Being unfamiliar with their language did not turn out to be as much of a hindrance as one might have imagined. There was always somebody or the other in the bazaar who spoke Hindi. I came to know Anchu, a simple young lad my age who was keen to help me out. The bazaar itself served as his home. He worked as a porter of sorts, loading goods into trucks and unloading them from others. When there was no work, he would perch on the railing that flanked the road and watch the world go by. He knew everybody in the bazaar. It was difficult for any stranger arriving in Gangtok to escape his notice. Anchu talked to me in an endearingly mellifluous mix of Hindi, Lepcha and Nepalese. That I belonged to Kolkata seemed to be the defining factor in my identity. Anchu promised to help me in every possible way. Having shared tea and bread, the two of us set out from the bazaar. Just behind it ran a narrow road that climbed steeply up.

High above, nestled in beautifully picturesque surroundings

that were not only a visual delight but also balm for the soul, lay Gangtok. A view of the Himalayas from the Mall in Darjeeling was rather different from the glimpse one could get of them from Gangtok, a town that was not perched atop a hill, but had grown lengthwise along the flanks of the mountain itself and was virtually devoid of level roads. Exquisite in its beauty was the Kanchendzonga, Gangtok's main attraction. It seemed as though an artist had painted in a white mountain above an entire range of verdant green ones.

We gradually moved further up and arrived at a point where one of the summits had been levelled flat. From this vantage position that afforded an unimpeded view, whichever way one faced, Sikkim appeared ever more beautiful. Walking on, we arrived before a wooden edifice with a beautifully carved exterior. It looked like a palace and was painted in bright hues. Those carvings, in particular, attracted and held one's attention.

'This is the royal palace of Sikkim,' Anchu volunteered.

The lad was known here, it seemed. Noticing him at the gate, the guard asked him a question to which Anchu offered a smiling response. Then crossing a small courtyard, we went up and stood right in front of the house. Peering in, we noticed a massive image of the Buddha right away and I realized that this was a Buddhist temple. The Sulakhang Temple, it turned out, where the king came to offer his prayers. We entered and touched a lamp lit near the Buddha.

Emerging from the house of worship, we walked a few steps ahead and came to a smaller adjoining temple. Anchu pointed to it and said, 'A great many lamas come here from all over the world. There's a good chance of your coming across your guru here.

Delighted, I clutched his hands and exclaimed, 'You are a true friend!'

Entering the place with the lad, my first impression was of a dharamsala, a kind of resting place for lamas. That was the purpose it was serving at the moment. Some of the lamas were in meditation. Others chanted loudly. A few ate, while others were busy packing their belongings. In other words, it seemed like a veritable fair ground for lamas. I studied each one of them carefully, hoping to find my beloved Lamaji. There were at least a hundred and fifty odd lamas around. It was from that very point that I took up my investigation. I asked Anchu to leave and promised to meet him in the evening at his usual haunt after conducting an extensive, if futile search for my sadhu baba. And should I be lucky enough to find the man, I would inform him of it. Anchu advised me to wait around. The king provided a free noon meal for the lamas and mendicants were also invited to join them. I agreed to his suggestion. The boy went off, leaving me there.

I was accustomed to brick and cement edifices along with the stone temples that occupied pride of place at Indian pilgrimage centres. That was probably why this Buddhist temple belonging to the royal palace intrigued me so greatly. It resembled a wooden pagoda, rather similar to the one at the Jain temple in Kolkata. Its delicate wood carvings and beautiful colours were remarkable indeed.

Among the groups of lamas, I came across a couple who understood Hindi and explained my problem to them. They were all prepared to come to my aid, but could not figure out how they could be of help. Gradually, word of my quest spread. Soon, everybody there had come to know that I was searching for my guru. In less than half an hour, all the two hundred-odd lamas there were ready to help me. It had not occurred to me that preoccupied as they were with their prayers and their own work, the lamas would be so concerned over my problem. I found their anxiety over my plight and their affection for me really touching.

'What is the name of your Guruji?' they asked. 'Where does he live? How old is he? What is his faith? Of which Buddhist sect is he a follower? Which *gumpha* does he belong to? Is he a Lepcha, Bhutia or Nepalese?'

I could answer none of their questions. In Gaya, I had addressed him as 'Sadhu Baba' or 'Guruji'. He wore the garb of a Buddhist sage. His features suggested that he was from the hills. When he left Gaya, there were three other lamas with him. That was it. Beyond that, I had no information at all.

Inevitably, disappointment stared me in the face. I was reassured, however, that since my intentions were pure and honest, I would surely be successful in my quest. All of a sudden, the Tibetan bugle sounded. Startled, I looked in the direction from which the solemn sound had thundered out, making everything appear to quake. The noise reverberated along the peak of the

Kanchendzonga and the Himalayan ranges. The bugle fell silent after sounding only once, but the echoes it set off continued to undulate like waves. This caused a stir among the lamas who gathered their utensils together and rushed towards the field. One lama asked me, 'You do want to eat, don't you?'

Another lama also asked me to join them for lunch on the field. But the problem was posed by the lack of extra utensils. Each one had come prepared with his own plate or bowl. No plantain leaves or plates to eat off were handed out before the meal was served.

Glancing at me, one of the sadhus asked, 'Don't you have anything at all?'

'Nothing whatsoever,' I replied.

'How, then, will you receive anything at all? Only when one gives, can one receive. How will you receive without giving?'

It seemed as if his question contained some hidden truth, but at that moment, I was not in a position to judge if, indeed, it did.

Aware of my plight, one of the lamas handed me an aluminium bowl and indicated that it would serve my purpose. I looked at it. Yes, it would certainly do, but it was absolutely filthy. Just running my fingers along the inside was enough to turn my hand a dirty black! The lama suggested, 'Hold out the bowl and eat your fill.'

There was a kind of mixed vegetable curry and rice, which everybody ate with relish. It wouldn't have been fair, after all, to expect more from a free meal. Once lunch was over, I was stunned to see that the question of washing up simply did not arise. Everyone just put their used plates into their bags once they were done. I had heard that Tibetans were not particularly fussy about hygiene and cleanliness. And now, I was seeing it for myself!

As evening approached, I felt light-hearted and carefree. Chiding myself again for my earlier despondency, I derived consolation from the thought that it mattered little whether I found the sadhu baba or not. At least my quest to find him had brought me to Gangtok. Whose presence could possibly match the magical experience of travelling to Gangtok from Gaya—the majestic Himalayas, the brightly coloured ornamentation of the royal palace, the sanctity of the Buddhist temple? Far from losing something, I had gained much instead. Perhaps, the sadhu baba had deliberately mentioned Gangtok to me. He might well be a long way from this place. Maybe, he had wanted to trick me into coming here? And that was why he had mentioned Gangtok? Possibly, he had never intended coming here in the first place.

Whatever the reason, coming to Gangtok had benefited me. Running away from home this time had proved to be a far richer experience than ever before.

I had been left with no option but to run away after being cooped up for six intolerable hours a day in school. I had repeatedly asked my elder brothers, 'What is the point of studying at all?'

And every time, I had received the stock reply: 'You must grow up to be a worthy human being.'

I not only found this answer repetitive, but rather uninspiring as well. Was a life confined within four walls indispensable for evolving into a worthy human being? It seemed to me that students were brought up expressly for the purpose of providing their teachers with a pretext for venting personal and social frustrations. Instead of being introduced to the history of our own region and climes, we would be taught the history of England. My heart would rise in silent rebellion against all the diktats imposed at home and school. All I received for my pains was a few hard slaps. As a result, I turned still more intractable. And that was when I ran away from home.

As I sat there in the courtyard of the temple, stray thoughts washed over me. I contemplated the strange hand fate had dealt me. I could just as easily have been the biddable boy and not stepped out of home, I mused. Danger and difficult problems would, in that case, not have come my way. Considering the distance that separated me now from home, I was awestruck by the journey I had just completed. To any normal person, my present environs would have been deemed to lie beyond the scope of anything remotely resembling civilization. At night, I slept outdoors and spent the day in the company of coolies and beggars. I ate no regular meals. Hunger gnawed perpetually at my innards. My head became immured to hard surfaces from resting on bricks and stones. But despite it all, my joy and enthusiasm had ebbed not a whit.

In the evening, I slowly came down from the forest. Finding Anchu was no problem at all. Studying my expression, he grasped right away that I had been unable to locate my guru. I made it clear to him that even if I didn't find my guru, it wouldn't be a problem, because I had really grown to love Sikkim. If I managed a refuge of some sort, I could simply stay on. Anchu was amazed at what I had to say. After all, Gangtok was huge and sprawling, crowded with houses, markets and roads. And there was the sky, encrusted with stars. Yet, I didn't have a place to lay my head. Anchu couldn't quite figure out what exactly my words implied. If you did not have blankets to cover yourself at night, you needed a fire. To his mind, fire and food were essential for survival. If a person had both at his disposal, he needed little else. And he was so right. Thinking over it carefully, I realized that fire and food were, indeed, indispensable.

Gradually, I came to know Gangtok a little better. There were any number of Buddhist monks and lamas living there. Dotting the town were *chaityas* and gumphas or Buddhist temples. The gumphas had a characteristic peculiar to them. They were not content with merely being a place for offering prayers at the temple; they also provided accommodation for lamas. Consequently, dharamsalas or boarding houses had grown up around them. Sikkim was home to almost seventy of these viharas and most of them were located within approximately forty miles of Gangtok. On level land, a distance of forty-odd miles meant little; but in these hilly tracts overgrown with forests, it was quite a distance. The Nepalese, Bhutia ('Bhotia' to locals) Gurkhas, Lepchas and Tibetans easily walked these long distances. The only access to remote villages from Gangtok and other cities was by foot. Sikkim's royal family followed the Buddhist faith. For the average citizen, the Kanchendzonga was a sacred peak. The name probably meant the resident 'Goddess of the Poor'. From wherever you might find yourself in Gangtok, the Kanchendzonga was clearly visible. Perched atop the highest peak, she was the ultimate hope for the weary traveller, guiding him in the right direction.

Another five days went by. By now, I was quite familiar with the roads and alleyways of Gangtok. While exploring them, I had also run into some Bengalis. I had been particularly careful about avoiding their company. Befriending them would have meant my having to return home. I searched all the gumphas and temples around the city with a fine toothcomb, in case my guru was there. I stayed with Anchu and ate my meals with him. I gave him a hand lifting and carrying luggage and in my spare time taught him a few words of English and Bengali The cold no longer bothered me. Whenever cars drove in from Kalimpong, Siliguri or Darjeeling, Anchu would run after them to bag their passengers as clients. Since I was not a local like him, I had no right to board buses to look for clients. The head had, in fact, warned me repeatedly that there was no way I could become a member of their group. But helping Anchu was a different matter.

No sooner had a bus from Teesta Bazaar arrived than we all ran towards it, as was our habit. Just before it entered the garage, a whole bunch of Sherpas literally pounced on it. Anchu climbed up from the rear, while I took up my position by the window to help him unload the luggage. As the bus came to a halt, the passengers slowly began to get down. Catching sight of one of them, I stood there stunned! Then I moved forward for a better look. Sure enough, just as I had imagined, it was him. Found, at last! I jumped up with joy, ran to him and blocked his way. He enfolded me in an embrace. Bliss!

'I have found Sadhu Baba!' I yelled out to Anchu. 'Look, here is the treasure I had lost.'

Anchu immediately climbed down from his perch and I introduced him to the sadhu baba.

A little later, the three sadhu babas who had accompanied Guruji also got off the bus.

My sadhu baba, however, was not at all surprised to see me. He did not even ask how I had come to be there. But it was clear from his expression that he was, in fact, very happy to see me. In his bid to bring the sadhu baba up to date about my current situation, Anchu volunteered details of where I had put up and what I ate. Needless to say, the members of the sadhu baba's entourage were amazed to see me. They just could not fathom how I had managed to find the sadhu baba in the midst of teeming thousands. Yet again, I repeated the ancient adage to them, 'Where there is a will, there is a way.'

My meeting up with the sadhu baba this time seemed even more incredible to me. In Gangtok, in the presence of these elderly lamas, it did not feel right to address him as 'Sadhu Baba'. So, from that moment onwards, he was 'Guruji'. He carried no luggage, but the other lamas had a large trunk with them. Anchu offered to carry it. I urged him to allow me to lend a hand, in case he got out of breath. Without a rope to strap it to my back, I had to enlist Anchu's help in carrying the trunk.

From Gangtok we started climbing up, proceeding along the main road itself. It was quite broad and clean and looked just like the main thoroughfare that led from the bazaar to the Mall in Darjeeling. Anchu took the lead, walking along with a swaying gait, and we brought up the rear. It had been clear to me from my experience in Gaya that conversation with Guruji during the journey was out of the question. He preferred not to speak while walking. So we moved ahead in almost complete silence. Guruji had probably mentioned his destination to Anchu, because the lad had moved far ahead of us. Pausing occasionally, before resuming the journey, it took us about an hour to reach a Buddhist temple standing atop what must have been Gangtok's highest hill. The temple's local name was Echey Gumpha. The others lay beyond the outskirts of the city. From this vantage point, the entire city of Gangtok, particularly the royal palace and the adjoining temple, was clearly visible. The view of the Kanchendzonga from this angle was still more imposing.

Almost as soon as we reached the gumpha, a score of boys came running up and crowded around Guruji. They seemed close to him. Half a dozen elderly lamas also came forward to greet him. In these new environs, I was rediscovering the man I had regarded as a mendicant of sorts when I had first come across him in Gaya. Anchu left, promising to return. Guruji asked me to stay back. Basking in his reflected glory, I interpreted his request as a sign of the greatest good fortune to have visited me.

Echey Gumpha stood on the summit of a hill in a lovely glade sheltered by pine and fir trees. The dharamsala was almost entirely constructed of wood, small rooms rising from a hardwood foundation. Arrangements had been made for me to stay with Guruji himself. A terraced garden had been laid out around the gumpha. Right next to it was a cardamom grove. There were twenty-six children in the gumpha, aged between ten and fifteen. Of the eight people running the establishment, two were senior lamas occupying the position of gurus. The remaining six were ordinary lamas. The children were acolytes—trainee monks— known as *daba*. To put it briefly, everybody at the gumpha, be it in a teaching capacity or in administration, was a lama, whereas the students were dabas. The latter were all clad in saffron and the ambience of the place was simply magical. Never before had I been blessed with the good fortune of spending time in such ethereal surroundings. Compared to Gaya, this place was truly heavenly. We were not expected to go out and beg every morning. On the contrary, we devoted ourselves to prayer. Unlike in Gaya, Guruji needed no nursing either; he had recovered completely from his earlier indisposition. During the day, I was entrusted with a new chore that involved a thorough scrubbing down of the prayer area in the temple and giving it a fresh coat of paint. Actually, a pair of lamas handled this chore; I merely assisted them. Here, I gradually learned all about the various manifestations of the Buddha. I also came to know about the tantrik occult images, for the branch of Buddhism of which these lamas were adherents was Tantrik-Buddhist. I was a stranger to both. Not being able to converse with most of the people here because of the language barrier no longer seemed that great an inconvenience.

Within a few days, I discovered another aspect of Guruji of which I had been unaware: He was a renowned Buddhist *bhikshu*, a well-known sage. His ancestral home lay somewhere near Sikkim. At one point, he had been associated with a sangha here, but had moved away since and was now truly free of all bonds. Though a Buddhist lama, he was greatly enamoured of Hinduism. He believed that Tathagata, the Buddha, had merely enhanced the Vedas. Buddha had been born on Indian soil and it was from that sacred soil that Buddhism had sprung. It was from India that the words of the Lord had spread to the world at large. So, for Guruji, India was the world's most sacred pilgrimage centre.

This time, Guruji had come from Gangtok to lead a group of lamas to Lhasa. The three lamas in his entourage had left some gumpha in Tibet about a year ago to go on a pilgrimage and seek knowledge and enlightenment along the way. They were about to go back and would be returning in a month or so. Gaya, Sarnath, Benares, Kolkata, Siliguri and this gumpha at Gangtok were the places where they gathered and went over the preparations for their anticipated journey. Though the sadhu baba had not shared any of this information with me, I had no problems at all gathering it from others.

Within ten days or so, eighteen more lamas had arrived. Everybody was supposed to be meeting at the monastery which a great many people knew as the Echey Monastery. I did some mental calculations and realized that there were still another eight days to go. This meant that once the period was over, I would, yet again, have to bid Guruji farewell. A wave of despair swept over me at the very thought. Then I told myself that this time, at least, it would not come as a shock; I was getting time to prepare myself for the inevitable parting.

Strolling around the courtyard of the monastery, that evening, I asked Guruji, 'Are you going to Lhasa?'

'Yes,' was Guruji's terse reply.

'I shall accompany you.'

He smiled gently at my words and said, 'Now, if it had been anybody else, I would have refused outright. But you are not one to pay heed to any words of discouragement and there is none to stop you either from having your way. But let me think over the matter and I'll let you know how I feel about it.'

'Where lies the problem?' I countered.

'There are a great many problems.' He looked at me and continued, 'The very first obstacle is that you are neither a sadhu nor a lama. Other than such people, I am unwilling to include anyone in the group. The reason is the Chinese soldiers who patrol the borders of Tibet these days. They are unwilling to let anyone through, apart from lamas. Secondly, you do not know the language. These are the primary difficulties. Everything else can be worked out.'

'But Guruji,' I retorted, 'I know not a word of Nepalese, Bhutia or Gurkha. Yet, I haven't managed too badly. I face no difficulties at all.'

Guruji heard me out before saying, 'It is no use arguing now. Let me think it over.'

I had not forgotten the help extended by Anchu when I needed it. Whenever there was time on my hands, I would go and meet him in the bazaar. Or he would come over at night. He wouldn't spend too much time with us in the gumpha, though. The solitude and ambience of a place of worship made him feel claustrophobic. He felt that this place was listless, somnolent. It was the market place, the bazaar that was truly vibrant. As Guruji was fond of him, he would sometimes invite him to have a meal with us.

I told Anchu in the course of conversation about the trip to Tibet. He was amazed at what he heard and asked, 'What is there in Tibet?'

Guruji explained to him that Tibet was like a pilgrimage centre. Even if one discounted that aspect, as a country too, it was wonderful. Anchu heard him all right, but kept his mouth shut in Guruji's presence. Looking at me, he said, 'If there is ever any way of doing so, if God wills it, I will go to Kolkata one day. To Anchu, Tibet was like a desert. It was infinitely better to go to Kolkata than die on a trip to Tibet. After all, there was a lot of fun in it and money too, of course.

I would get up at seven in the morning and after saying my prayers, go into the kitchen. There I lent a hand in preparing the meals. It was easy enough to make rolled, unleavened bread over a coal fire, but a special skill was required if it was prepared over a wood fire. I did my best to master it. I had just managed to get a firm grip on the wood, when Guruji came up to stand beside me. Placing his hand on my head, he said, 'Step out. There is something I have to tell you.'

Asking the lama next to me to take over my duties, I followed Guruji along the narrow, winding hill track leading towards the forest. He pointed to a boulder and said, 'Sit there.'

Settling down, I gazed up at him.

He looked back at me and said with a smile, 'I am setting you a task. Please pay attention to what I have to say. Today, you will remain by this boulder all day. You are not to go anywhere else. You can take a break for your afternoon meal. But you will stay here for the rest of the day. Tell me, are you ready for that?'

I nodded instantly.

'You are to focus your mind on your family all day. You will reflect on nothing but your home and your friends and relatives. Be careful not to overlook anybody. Think about them all and try to mentally communicate with them.'

'All right.'

He patted my head affectionately and said, 'Come here again tomorrow morning after you've had your tea and snacks. We'll have a talk.'

I did as he had advised. But instead of settling myself on the boulder, I began to look around me. In my imagination, I seemed to be flying off to Tibet. I did not know a thing about that country, but the very name had the power to pull me close like a magnet.

Oh, no! What was I thinking about? I steeled my mind to do as Guruji had advised. Instead of allowing my thoughts to travel quite so far as Tibet, it was better to abide by Guruji's instructions and turn them homewards.

It was as though my mind were prepared for the task ahead. As I concentrated on thoughts of home, the first person to come to mind was my grandmother. This was followed by thoughts of each of my siblings and, subsequently, by those of my friends from the locality where I had lived. I ruminated about the endless debate that must be taking place at home over where I might have gone and what I could possibly be doing. I remembered my schoolfriends and those belonging to our neighbourhood. But I failed to notice anything special about the thoughts that flitted through my mind. What did keep occurring to me, however, was the idea that if only I could get my family and friends here, if I could persuade them just once to breach the boundaries they had laid down for themselves and savour the immortal beauty of this place, the difference between us would surely melt away. They believed I was a vagabond and a good-for-nothing. If my heartfelt appreciation of the wonders of this universe marked me out as a fool, then, please, God, might I always be reborn as one! Could the joy a wandering minstrel experienced in communing with his flute ever be found within the confines of a school?

Guruji had asked me to concentrate my thoughts on my home all day, but I was at a loss, wondering whom I could bring to mind. With the exception of my grandmother, I had no ties at all with those at home. My parents had died when I was a child and I had been brought up by my brother and my sister-in-law. In fact, being an orphan had turned out to be not a misfortune, but the greatest blessing in my life. Perhaps, that was why I had fewer ties than I would have if my parents had still been living. So, I was definitely not the sort to sit on the boulder and brood for hours. Despite repeated attempts to do so, I could think of no person on whom I might focus my thoughts. Neither did I relish the prospect of sitting quietly on the boulder; it seemed such an appalling waste of time. I was reluctant, however, to disobey Guruji. Why had he insisted on my thinking about home? Had something happened to my grandmother? Even if it had, what could I possibly do? There was no dearth of people to look after her.

The next day, at the appointed time, the two of us—master and disciple—sat down near the boulder. Smiling, he asked, 'So! Are you still thinking of home today?'

'No,' I replied.

'Tell me if you feel like going home,' he went on, 'I will arrange for your ticket and have you sent over.'

'Ticket?' I was surprised. A man who survived by begging for alms would pay for my train ticket from Gangtok to Kolkata!

Guruji probably gauged my thoughts. He continued in the same vein, 'Yes, indeed, buy a ticket. You will return home in a manner befitting a gentleman. Don't you worry. I have money.'

'No, I do not want to return home. I want to go to Tibet with the rest of you. You needn't worry about me. I'll be able to keep up with you and reach our destination as well,' I tried reassuring him. 'Have you understood?'

'I understand, son,' he replied. 'Get ready.'

That was wonderful news! I put my arms around his waist and hugged him. Emotionally, I said, 'Fine. Then prepare me for what lies ahead.'

Thinking it over, he said, 'Right. Then listen to me carefully.'

'I will treat your advice as the motto of my life.'

'Today, try sitting on this boulder for as long as you can manage,' Guruji began. 'If your body starts aching, get up and move about a bit. Then come back and take your seat here once again.' He paused for a while, then continued, 'Today, you will direct your thoughts somewhat differently. Listen to me attentively. You may sit on the boulder in whatever position you choose. There is no hard and fast rule. Looking straight ahead, you will concentrate on the distant horizon where the mountains seem to merge into the sky. Right?'

'Right,' I agreed.

'Always look straight ahead. Focus your attention on the sky. As you gaze at it, tell yourself that these vast open spaces are infinity. They lie beyond petty joys and sorrows. Contemplate the mountains and reflect, "They are immense. They exist. They are bound by limits".'

Once more, Guruji explained his thoughts and instructions to me before saying reassuringly, 'If it all seems unbearably dull to you or if you encounter a lot of problems, come over and see me.'

'Fine. Your instructions will be complied with.'

Guruji paced about in the forest for some time, then went off towards the market. Perhaps, he had some errands to run. 'God Bless Guruji,' I thought. Spreading my mat on the boulder, I took my seat. Infinite … limitless… I began to ponder over the words and tried to find an expression that would describe the sky. Perhaps the expression, 'Infinite space', was true to some extent, but what did 'beyond joys and sorrows' mean? A little later, I made an attempt at logical analysis. It was, indeed, true that the infinite, boundless spaces of the sky were devoid of sorrow. Real grief was tied down to the existence of the body. Hence, the limits of sorrow lay between the human body and the world at large. The body was physical matter, destined for death. The infinite and boundless sky should not be subject to corporeal sorrows. Petty physical problems were inconsequential, merely fit to be ignored. I was deep in contemplation. Philosophy was not a subject I had studied. Nor was I familiar with a single word pertaining to religion. If I were keen on following Guruji's instructions, however, I would have to reflect on such matters.

The topic today was quite absorbing, unlike the boring one I had been asked to focus on the day before. I continued to contemplate the issues Guruji had raised as I either sat on the boulder or rose, occasionally, to walk around the forest. The welcome warmth of the morning sun on my body, along with the beauty of the Himalayas, visible through the gaps between the trees, made me feel carefree and at peace.

Why would I have to probe beyond happiness? The way I understood it, its opposite was sorrow. Or, perhaps, both were intimately linked. If one made its presence felt, the other would follow. The very fact of seeking happiness automatically paved the way for sorrow to make its appearance, so inextricably were the two intertwined. Perhaps, that was the reason why Guruji had described the sky as eternal and had declared its great spaces to be beyond all joys and sorrows?

All morning, many such thoughts passed through my mind. I observed that far from burdening my heart with despondency, these reflections inspired me to probe deeper into my consciousness. In no time at all, the day had moved on and it was time to be summoned for a meal.

Later, I prepared myself for a second round of serious contemplation. That mountain in the distance—how colossal were its dimensions! It seemed to occupy a greater part of the world. Guruji had described the mountain as gigantic, but confined by certain boundaries. Our bodies too, had their limitations, but our minds could, in all likelihood, be channelized towards immortality. Seated on the boulder, my body remained chained to its physical existence. My eyes, ears and other senses registered awareness of my surroundings, but my thoughts remained unshackled and free. They roamed wherever they desired, even soaring up to feel the infinite blue expanses of the sky.

On the third day, Guruji issued fresh instructions. 'Imagine that your mind is the sky, your thoughts the clouds wafting across it,' he began. 'Contemplate your thoughts as you would the clouds floating by. Put yourself in the position of a silent spectator and try to follow the trajectory of your thoughts as they move from their source to their goal, the way clouds travel across the sky.'

Like an obedient child, I continued to follow the instructions Guruji had left me, as I had on the previous days.

On the fourth day, Guruji asked me, 'Any problems?'

'None whatsoever,' I replied.

'Do you find it very boring to be on your own in the forest?'

'I don't.'

There was never any question of my suffering from deprivation of any kind. Along with everyone else, I put in an appearance for the midday meal as soon as the bell rang out. Lunch over, I made my way to the designated spot in the forest. The entire day passed in solitude. At night, I would return to the monastery and after evening prayers, go to sleep. This had almost become a routine. I realized, however, that there must be a purpose behind Guruji's instructions and chose not to question him in any way.

He said to me, 'You do not have to go to the forest today.' Then whispering conspiratorially, he asked, 'Do you really want to go to Tibet?'

'Definitely!' I replied, firm in my resolve, 'but if you are dead against the idea, I won't accompany you. If you can just give me directions to my destination and the basic information I may need to make my way, I'll be able to manage on my own.'

Having heard my answer, Guruji put forth the crucial question: 'Why do you want to go to Tibet?'

I had not expected this question from him because of my assumption that being a wanderer himself, he would surely be well aware of the answer. I did not have a ready reply to his query, but I could see that Guruji expected one, so some response would have to be offered. 'Do you know the reason why the clouds skimming the peak of the Kanchendzonga behave in that manner?' I asked him.

The moment I had uttered those words, Guruji changed the topic. 'Help the lama with the painting job today,' he said. 'Tomorrow, I will have fresh instructions for you.'

'As you wish, Guruji.' I replied.

On the fifth day, Guruji woke me up before daybreak and said, 'Go and complete your ablutions.'

It was a long time to sunrise and abandoning the warmth of the blanket that had covered me was something of a trial, but I really had little choice. After I had washed myself in the cold water of the tank, I presented myself before Guruji who led me to the temple where a lamp fuelled by ghee always burned. After trimming the wick and ensuring that the flame would burn brightly, Guruji laid out the mat and offered his respectful prayers to the Bhagavad. I did the same. Then he asked me to take a seat on the prayer mat laid out at the side. Here, on the long seat, prayer mats were always laid out, so that those wishing to meditate could do so at will.

'Observe the Lord Tathagata's facial expression carefully,' Guruji told me.

In the muted glow of the lamp, that massive image was almost a blur. Moreover, since the lamp burned continuously, year after year, the room had acquired a sooty patina. The Lord Tathagata's image too, was so monumental that from such close quarters, it was practically impossible to bring the whole of it into focus. So, I gazed intently at his face. The light from the lamp fell directly on his eyes. The pinpoints of blue standing out from the whites of the eyes glistened and burned; that was where I directed my gaze. It seemed as though he were staring at me.

At that moment, Guruji's voice reached my ears. 'Now, slowly close your eyes,' he whispered. 'Don't move your body at all. Just sit quietly and try to absorb the Lord Buddha's heavenly aura. The glow emanating from him is gradually spreading through your body. Hold this posture for a while. Simply concentrate on Tathagata's glowing visage. Now, chant aloud, "*Om Mani Padme Hum, Om Mani Padme Hum, Om Mani Padme Hum...*". Then repeat them silently to yourself. Do not allow them to go astray. Articulate the words and listen to them in your mind.'

In accordance with Guruji's instructions, I chanted the holy words to myself. Despite my prolonged efforts to do so, I failed to hold on to the words; they kept eluding me, slipping away beyond reach. A time came when the words began to clash with my thoughts. While I fervently wished to hold the words in my mind, my thoughts persistently dislodged them. It seemed as though my random thoughts waged a perennial battle with each other.

Once again, I heard Guruji's voice: 'Keep your mind free and receptive. If thoughts enter, welcome them. Struggling to keep them out will defeat the purpose. You must tame them with love. No thought is ever negative in itself. Do not try and judge whether your thoughts are good or evil. Without resorting to haste, try letting the holy words gently take over your thoughts.'

I changed position, shifting around a bit before sitting still once more and tried to focus my mind on the magical words: '*Om...*'

A long stretch of time passed in this manner. Suddenly, my mind seemed to come awake, as though from a stupor. I felt as though I had fallen asleep where I was. I saw that Guruji was no longer with me. Sunlight was peeping in through the door. The haze enshrouding me seemed to dissipate. The door faced west; usually, the sun only streamed through late in the day, before dusk fell. I did not know whether I should get up. My body seemed extraordinarily light, my mind weightless, lighter still than the floating clouds. What an incredibly strange and beautiful sensation it was! I began gazing at the statues again in silence.

Guruji appeared at this point. Smiling, he asked, 'How do you feel?'

'Very well,' I replied. 'My body and mind feel so light; I almost believe I could fly!'

Guruji laughed. 'Now you may get up,' he told me. 'Go and have something to eat. Nauka is waiting for you.'

I rose to my feet, bowed respectfully before the Lord, then did the same before my guruji. He clasped me to his breast.

'Are you going to initiate me into the Buddhist faith?' I asked him.

'The main goal is to get to know the Lord,' he answered. 'Losing sight of that in the observance of the method and the means would be pointless.'

'Guruji,' I said, 'I'm really keen on knowing about this: The manner in which I prayed or meditated today—is it a part of the Mahayana division of Buddhism or the Hinayana? I have heard that the Bajrayana tradition is a prevailing influence in Buddhism.'

'All divisions lead to the ultimate truth,' was his response. 'Henceforth, always chant these words. Whenever you do, make sure that no break occurs in the rhythm.'

Guruji's directives would be obeyed. Emerging from the temple, I noticed that much time had elapsed since afternoon had ceded to twilight. It was quite beyond my imagination how swiftly the hours had passed. I felt as though I had been rooted to the same spot for twelve hours from four o'clock in the morning.

The following morning, Guruji informed everybody that I had been initiated into the Buddhist fold. All smilingly acknowledged their acceptance of me as one of their own. In the evening, one of the lamas from the monastery tonsured my head. From that moment onwards, I was instructed to wear saffron robes like the rest of them and became a part of the brotherhood. The formalities were taken care of without a fuss. The path of truth was really a very simple one. Outward show was eschewed. What was called for was piety and devotion.

Guruji instructed the teacher to introduce me to the Tibetan alphabet. Since time was running out, I would have to be really quick in grasping what I was taught. Thus began my lessons in Tibetan. I had no name yet to identify me as a member of the brotherhood; Guruji had not bestowed one on me. So, everybody at the monastery would address me as 'Hey you!' or 'You there!'

The day marked out for the scheduled journey to Tibet passed by. In the meantime, all the lamas who were to set out with Guruji had gathered at the monastery. Guruji had indicated earlier that we would be travelling towards the beginning of March. It was almost mid-March. Yet, there was no sign of anybody making a move. Finally, I was compelled to approach him to seek an explanation for the delay.

I learnt from him that it was becoming increasingly difficult to cross the border into Tibet. In the past, no permits had been required. There were no borders worth the name. But since 1950, the residents of Nepal, Bhutan and Sikkim were required to obtain prior authorization for visiting Tibet. This was handed out from the embassy in Kathmandu and available exclusively to lamas who were travelling to Tibet as pilgrims. The question of an Indian being allowed to do so simply did not arise.

'But I am an Indian, Guruji,' I told him. 'They will certainly not permit me to travel to Tibet.'

'That's true,' he confirmed, 'they will stop you right at the border. However, I will tell them you are my disciple and that you belong to Sikkim.'

'But Guruji, I am unfamiliar with the language spoken in Sikkim. And a mere glance at me will make it quite clear that I do not belong to these parts.'

Placing a reassuring hand on my shoulder, Guruji said, 'Don't worry. I have thought everything through on your behalf. Now, listen carefully to my plan. You are aware that I have a gammy right leg. So, along with your own luggage, you will have to carry my blanket. It might seem an absurdly easy task on the face of it, but when you have walked some distance carrying it, you will realize what I mean. If you shoulder this burden, it will be of immense help to me. Our permit is valid for fifty-two people. Certainly no more than thirty people will be travelling in our group. From the time of the Chinese occupation of Tibet, the lamas do not risk travelling there, even if they want to. No specific names are indicated in the permit. So, I can take whomsoever I want with me. You will accompany me as my disciple and wherever there are Chinese soldiers around, remain silent. I will tell them you are a lama who has taken the vow of silence. You will, therefore, not be required to speak and I will handle whatever exchanges are necessary. Remember, you are accompanying us as the monk who has taken a vow of silence.'

At these words, I could not contain my feelings and jumped for joy. Enfolding Guruji in an embrace, I exclaimed loudly, 'Long live Sadhu Baba!' I humbly prostrated myself before him and began repeating the words, '*Guru Kripa Hi Kebalam*—the Guru's mercy is the only truth.'

'Now, do curb such excessive displays of emotion, my boy,' Guruji remonstrated. 'Make an effort, instead, to harness your sentiments to the tenets of Buddhist philosophy. *Om...*'

'*Om...*,' I repeated, chanting along with him.

ON THE WAY

ON 8 APRIL 1956, the required authorization came through, causing much pleasurable excitement among the lamas. An official from the Chinese embassy in Kathmandu arrived in Gangtok to personally deliver the much-awaited document. He had already heard of Guruji. The latter's name had been put forward as that of the guide chosen for the journey. That, in fact, was when I came to know his real name: Guru Geshe Repten—unquestionably, a Tibetan surname of great distinction. The lamas had jointly applied to the Chinese embassy in Guruji's name for permission to travel to Tibet. And here was the response. The gentleman, a Nepalese employee of the embassy, sought Guruji's permission before taking several counts of the number of pilgrims about to undertake the journey. Then having fingerprinted them all—taking care to record the impressions of all five digits—he took his leave. Whatever dues the visiting lamas had run up during their stay in the Echey Monastery were settled. It was hardly any amount at all—just a few paise per person a day.

That very evening, new blankets and shawls arrived for us all from the royal palace of Sikkim. The king of Sikkim always made such provisions for all travellers heading for Kailash or Lhasa. That very night, Guruji proffered his last bit of advice. He alone in the entire group had visited Tibet before. For the others, it would be a maiden voyage. There was no end to all the joyous celebrations and the sheer excitement generated by our anticipation of the unknown.

The following day, we rose at the crack of dawn in preparation for departure. Each one of us carried very light luggage along with a heavy outfit suitable for extremely low temperatures, prayer beads and a stick. The luggage itself consisted mainly of a blanket, some ordinary flour and a special kind of flour made from barley. In addition, each person carried at least five to six kg of salt, for the latter was a very expensive commodity in Tibet and would become increasingly so, the further up one climbed.

Group prayers over, we set out from the monastery. Once outdoors, Guruji pointed to the mountain in the distance and said, 'There lies Chumbi valley. We have to climb up to the summit of the mountain that flanks it. At the top lies the mysterious world of Tibet, and along with it, the ultimate in pilgrimage centres— Kailashnath and Mansarovar. A number of people from the monastery had accompanied us outside to see us on our way. Before bidding them farewell, we joined them in prayer again:

'Without profound wisdom, one cannot meditate.
Without meditation, one cannot gain wisdom.
Oh Lord of the World, in your infinite kindness,
Lead us along the path of profound wisdom.
Lead us to where lie the Buddha, Religion and the sangha.'

Needless to say, everybody at the monastery knew Tibetan. It was on this foundation that the system of proffering prayers had grown. Guruji introduced me to everyone by my new name: Gelang Lama.

We set out on our journey, bidding farewell to each and every member of the monastery, from the oldest to the youngest. On the way, we met Anchu. Embracing me and lapsing into his usual hotchpotch of different tongues, he said, 'Don't forget me.'

I too, gave him a gentle pat of reassurance on the back. He knew I had been forbidden to converse with anyone on the way.

The monastery where we had spent the night was located a short distance from Gangtok. From here, we moved on towards Nathu La. Along with my own luggage, I was carrying Guruji's blanket and an aluminium pot that had been added on. The entire lot did not amount to even 10 kg. Climbing down the mountain was no problem at all. What did prove a hindrance was the garb we sported. Not that it was heavy. It was more complicated than that, a cross between a man's garment and a woman's, topped by a bulky woollen sweater and a shawl.

Four hours later, we had reached level land. We moved ahead at a steady pace, flanked by military camps on both sides. Guruji had been firm in his directive that we were neither to speed up our pace nor engage in conversation during the journey. We halted for the afternoon meal. Gathering together dry twigs and branches, I lit a fire so that lunch could be prepared. So far, we had been following a descending path and none of us were, therefore, really tired. We relished the steaming hot rice and boiled potatoes before setting off again.

The time had now come for us to move uphill. I was the youngest of the group and Guruji, the oldest. Most of the lamas were between forty and fifty years old and all were from the hills. Mountains were very much a part of their lives, their heart and soul. Keeping in step with them, I began to make progress as well. Like Gangtok, this region too was dotted with beautiful groves of pine and fern. That familiar dank smell of moisture-laden rocks hung in the air. We had left the main road of Sikkim behind us and were moving along towards Nathu La ('Nathu' meant 'name'; 'La' signified 'danger'), the path that lay wedged between two mountains. Jilap La was yet another pass of this kind. From where we now found ourselves, a path branched off in its direction. On our way, we passed the prosperous village of Karponang.

The higher we climbed, the more spectacular seemed to be the changes that Gangtok and the entire range of the Himalayas went through. In fact, the latter appeared to present themselves in a different light altogether. We moved along the forest path that ribboned its way around the mountain. The environs and their ambience were a delight, an experience in itself. The physical exertion we put ourselves through during our climb was made bearable by the bitter cold. But it was difficult to escape the feeling of fatigue that slowly seeped through us. From the way we dragged our feet, it was apparent that we were all beginning to tire.

As evening drew near, Guruji told us we would be covering another short stretch before calling it a day. And sure enough, an hour's trek brought us to a little village or, rather, a sort of post suitable for an overnight halt. Guruji informed us that the place was called Chengu or Changu. No sooner had we stopped in front of a wooden house than some men came out to meet us. After Guruji had made some inquiries in their language, the men led us to a room on the second floor. Arrangements were made for our group of thirty-two lamas to somehow cram themselves into two rooms. It was clear that this was where we would have to spend the night.

The next day, we set off at daybreak as usual. Nathu La was only another eight miles from Chengu. It takes a day and a half to reach this point from Gangtok by the usual route, but a short cut had allowed us to make the journey in a single day. Navigating our way ahead was becoming really difficult now. The narrow road zigzagged its way up, flanked on both sides by military camps standing cheek by jowl. From this point, the view of the Kanchendzonga was more beautiful than ever.

Suddenly, a soldier approached us and blocked our way. 'Don't go any further,' he advised. 'Return to wherever you came from.'

We were amazed. Guruji was quite at home in English and explained to the soldier that we were pilgrims heading for the Tashi Lumpa and Mansarovar.

At this, the soldier laughed out loud. 'All pilgrimages have been halted,' he told us. 'Just go back, will you?'

Guruji advised us to ignore him and carry on. As soon as we started off, the soldier blocked our path again and said, 'Go ahead if you insist. Further ahead is the border, where you will be stopped by soldiers and harassed no end!'

We refrained from getting into an argument with him and continued to move ahead. About half an hour later, we were brought up short by a barrier erected across the road. A felled tree laid across the road served as a makeshift line of demarcation. About half a dozen Jat soldiers, originally from Punjab, caught sight of us and moved forward to intercept us. Guruji was ready for this eventuality and explained to them that letting us pass through would not in any way imply that they had been lax in their duties. We had all the necessary papers. Having heard Guruji out, they took us to a camp nearby and presented us before an officer. He scrutinized our papers carefully and permitted us to move on. The border was still a long distance away.

Three whole hours later, the road dwindled to a narrow trail. The mountain before us seemed to thrust itself out like a wall. Guruji called a halt. We were impatiently waiting for this very command and as soon as the words were uttered we all promptly sat down on the road to rest.

After half an hour's reprieve, we set off again. No sooner had we rounded the bend ahead of us than we found ourselves in a huge military camp. At least a hundred-odd soldiers moved in our direction, their guns cocked. The thought might well have flitted through our minds that they had been lying in wait for us. The message was clear that we were now at the border separating India, Sikkim and Tibet.

Given their quick reflexes and ready response to our arrival, one could not help lauding the Indian armed forces. A wooden house by the road constituted the border post and it was there that we were herded. An officer asked us to be seated. His accent seemed to indicate that he was from Bengal. Even though I felt impelled to talk to him, there was no way I could allow myself to do so. A little slip risked ruining my whole journey. The officer was very polite and cooperative. He assured Guruji that he had heard of our journey from official sources. There was no problem whatsoever; all our papers were in order. His exchanges with Guruji were in Hindi. He escorted us all to the army canteen and introduced us to the quartermaster there. In a short while, a huge container of tea was brought in and served to us with bread and vegetables. The gesture came as a pleasant surprise and we showered blessings on them all when we took our leave.

At long last, the much-awaited opportunity was at hand for me to catch a glimpse of the dangerous Nathu La—the highest mountain pass and the most terrifying of mountain hazards. What an awesomely beautiful aspect of the Himalayas it offered! Five miles to the south lay another pass: Jilap La. In the far distance, Sikkim and the Kanchendzonga were resplendent in their beauty. Facing us was the path to the Chumbi valley. Moving further ahead, we came upon a deep ravine; it was as though someone had suddenly swept aside the mountain at that spot. And right afterwards, we came upon a dangerously turbulent mountain stream. We began to descend with the utmost caution—there could be a landslide any moment. We noticed a huge mound of small stones at the side. Guruji explained that while crossing this point, pilgrims would add a stone to the pile; it was a way of showing respect to the deities presiding over the Himalayas. Each of us added a stone to the heap as we passed. I prayed, 'O Almighty Ones! Please bless us and ensure that we reach our destination safe and sound.'

Before us unfolded the awe-inspiring vista of the great Chumbi valley. We moved on, leaving behind my motherland, India. As far as geographical demarcations were concerned, we were now on Tibetan soil.

Traversing eight miles on level land was no problem at all, but in steep, mountainous terrain, it was tough going indeed. Initially, we would stop to rest every half an hour. Then we began halting every fifteen minutes or so. The pebbled path was now rising more sharply than ever before. The higher we went, the more resplendent was the beauty of the Himalayas. Even Sikkim appeared to grow ever more alluring, the various mountain peaks rising up like giant waves in the ocean. The mountains in the distance appeared to have descended straight from the clouds. Climbing from one elevation to another, we had traversed the different phases of the Himalayas before arriving at this point. As dusk gradually set in, we admired the crimson embers of the sinking sun.

We gathered in the shelter of a large boulder to recharge our batteries. Before entering the Tibetan village, Guruji addressed us all, outlining the final guidelines for the journey.

'We will soon be reaching the first village that lies inside the Tibetan border,' he explained. 'Even before we step into it, we are likely to encounter the Han—Tibetans call the Chinese "Han". Understandably, they will subject us to a gruelling session of interrogation to verify whether we are genuine lamas or not. Be prepared for your patience to be sorely tried, but don't lose your composure.'

We resumed walking again and had almost reached level land when we were stopped short by the first checkpoint. Nearly all the sentries at the border were Tibetan, barring a couple of Chinese soldiers. With wireless sets strapped to their backs, the soldiers ordered us to halt. The Tibetan guards approached with a query in their own language. In response, Guruji presented our travel papers. The Chinese soldiers started minutely scrutinizing our release papers—authorization documents issued by the Chinese embassy in Kathmandu. Along with them were Guruji's personal identity papers and those issued by the Government of Sikkim, containing effusive testimonials and good wishes for a safe journey. The Tibetan soldier translated the Tibetan documents, word for word, into Chinese for his Chinese counterpart. The latter, in turn, listened very attentively to whatever was read out to him. Then getting in touch over the wireless with his superior officer in our presence, he proceeded to convey all the details to him.

We waited there for almost an hour, hoping in vain for an answer from the senior officer. Gradually, the day waned and was swallowed by dusk. But no confirmation of the order to proceed came through. Guruji had cautioned us: 'Be careful! Don't lose your patience.' And silence reigned over that motley crowd of thirty-two lamas, four Tibetan guards and two Chinese soldiers. Not a word escaped anyone's lips.

About an hour later, the phone rang and with bated breath, we awaited the response that had come through, delivered in Chinese. The guards carefully listened to the instructions that were issued. A while later, they explained that we would be allowed to go through, but not before being subjected to a thorough search. The news of our impending release gladdened our hearts. The soldiers made good their promise. We were searched, but a careful scrutiny of our clothes and belongings yielded nothing suspicious and they were forced to let us go.

We had obtained permission to enter Tibet! Our joy knew no bounds. Thanking the soldiers, we set off again. Well, set off we may have, but another peril lurked in the darkness that had descended, for we had virtually no light to guide us by. Before we could even gauge what was happening, we were surrounded and set upon by what we suddenly realized was a pack of dogs. They barked wildly, ready to tear us to pieces if we so much as took a step forward. My Buddhist incantation momentarily consigned to oblivion, I cried out in Bengali, 'Ma Tara, save me!' Then, jolted into recalling my new avatar as the sage bound by a vow that denied him the luxury of speech, I hastily relapsed into silence. It didn't seem likely that anyone had heard me. Encircled by the dogs, we stood in a guilty huddle, like thieves caught in the act.

Shortly afterwards, lights began to glow in the darkness.

Thank God! There seemed to be a village not far from where we stood and some of its residents were approaching. As soon as the first few appeared, Guruji explained to them, 'We are pilgrims on our way to Lhasa. We have undertaken the journey to pay our respects to the Wondrous Guru Chenreji.'

The dogs gradually calmed down. Guruji had a talk with the locals before whispering to me, 'They had taken us for Chinese soldiers. That's why nobody had emerged when the dogs started barking. From now on, be very careful. Instead of addressing me as "Guruji", call me Geshe Repten.'

'Right,' I replied in the same undertone.

With the villagers leading the way, we crossed a little bridge and entered the village. Passing through a massive wooden door, we cut across what appeared to me to be a small field. In the muted glow of the lamp, only the path was barely visible. The rest lay in darkness.

A short while later, the villagers brought us up to the veranda of a monastery called the Kargid Gumpha, where they asked us to wait. It was bitterly cold. Moreover, we were exhausted and cramping from acute hunger pangs. I was not sure how the other lamas felt, but I, for one, was in what might be described as a truly pitiable state. Guruji implicitly understood how I felt. I did not have to utter a word of explanation. No sooner had we reached the place than he asked the villagers whether some food might be available. Who could tell how late the hour was? No, we were told, all the shops were closed and no food was available at that hour. But thanks to the Buddha's mercy, a local tea-shop owner was prepared to make some tea for the lamas—for a price, of course! In Tibetan, tea is known as *chang* and is prepared with large quantities of tea dust, butter and salt.

When one is famished, anything in the form of food or beverage is welcome. In a short while, the tea-shop owner sent for his son and daughter to prepare chang in our presence. This was no mean task, as there were thirty-two people to serve. We spread out our blankets in the adjoining field and stretched out on them gratefully. Geshe Repten was truly to be admired. Despite the rigours of the journey, he had remained on his feet. It was not merely a question of physical stamina, but of sheer will power. And his was incomparable.

A portable wood stove was lit. A large tin of hot water was placed on it. Beside it, in two equally gigantic tin containers, the owner's daughter pounded and crushed what appeared to be pieces of brick! Unable to contain my curiosity, I went up and tried to smell the aroma emanating from the tins. The girl laughed in amusement at my enthusiasm and said, by way of explanation, 'Chang!' It smelled like tea. Probably, the tea had been frozen into blocks for convenient storage. The block of chang or tea was as hard as a brick. After she had finished grinding the tea, the girl poured the boiling water over it and began stirring the mixture with a long stick. After nearly half an hour of this, the mixture was placed back on the fire. Then what looked like a bowl of flour was sprinkled on the tea. It was stirred some more before butter and milk were blended with it.

As soon as the tea had been consumed and paid for, the tea shop owner packed up his belongings. As the stove was still burning, however, he left it behind for the lamas, along with some extra wood. We placed the stove in the centre of the veranda and, without further ado, lay down around it, huddling under our blankets.

I do not know how long we slept, but our slumber was deep indeed. I woke up to much clamour and shouting and found that it was nearing daybreak. We were surrounded by a group of Tibetans. Prodding us awake with their bayonets was a couple of Han or Chinese soldiers. I was probably the first among those in my group to wake up. Guruji was lying closer to where the soldiers stood. To prevent him from being poked by bayonets, I had no option but to rouse him. Almost as soon as he opened his eyes, he took measure of the situation.

A mere glance at the people milling around was enough to tell us that they were desperately poor. They looked as though they came from Sikkim or Bhutan. The clothes they wore might have been filthy, but they themselves were robust and well built. Both men and women wore their hair long. It didn't seem as if their children had ever run a comb through their hair or washed it, for that matter.

Guruji urged us to get ready to set out for the town of Chumbi which we needed to reach as soon as possible. After leaving the monastery, Guruji explained the matter to us in greater detail. After we had passed the checkpoint the previous evening, the soldiers manning it had informed their senior officers over the wireless that a group of lamas had crossed the border and would be reaching Chumbi very soon. Accordingly, the police station there had made preparations for our arrival. When the whole night went by with neither sight nor sound of us, the soldiers there had set off to look for us. It was they who would soon escort us to their checkpoint where our actual conversation with Guruji would take place.

'The name of the place is Chubitang,' Geshe Repten told us. 'Please note carefully that this monastery is a very ancient one and usually serves as the first overnight halt for pilgrims.'

These days, of course, the number of pilgrims had dwindled to a mere trickle. It was, indeed, a shame, that having to accompany the border security force to the police checkpoint prevented me from exploring the Kargid Gumpha. This monastery was somewhat different from others of its kind in Tibet. Instead of a lama serving as the titular head of the gumpha, which was the norm in most such establishments, a descendent of Sikkim's royal family was the supreme authority here. The acolytes or student lamas were known as *trapa*s in this region.

About an hour after leaving the monastery, we caught a glimpse of Chumbi. Though Tibetans looked upon it as a city, to my eyes, even a small village in Midnapore would have occupied a larger area. Innumerable government-run camps dotted the roadside and among the personnel manning them were Chinese soldiers. Geshe Repten had already pointed out to us which of the men were Han and which Tibetans. The distinction was now only too apparent to us. It was obvious from the gait of the Tibetans that they belonged to this land. There was a rhythm to their movements that was typical of this part of the world. The Chinese soldiers, on the other hand, seemed like foreigners. An aura of menace, of oppression hung about them. It was completely at odds with the ambience of their environs.

Chumbi turned out to be a prosperous old village. It was, in fact, one of the oldest in Tibet. Its main attraction was the market which consisted of a few houses sitting on a kind of wooden platform and three rows of shops, the usual traditional ones: a handful of tea shops, about half a dozen little stores selling groceries and a huge leather and cured meat shop. By the wayside were many smaller shops. The vegetable market was tiny.

The walls of the police station in Chumbi were made of cement and stone and the building had a wooden balcony. The very look of the building seemed to shriek out that it was more than a hundred years old. There was a pair of armoured jeeps parked in front of the house. Armed sentries stood about. Asking us to remain seated outside, Guruji went in with the Chinese soldiers for our papers to be checked. We continued to wait by the roadside from where the mountains seemed to recede and fade into the distance. At this point, the valley was very wide. The houses here, built of local stone and wood, were undistinguished by any particular architectural feature. There was a marketplace right in front with the flavour of a fair. The few shops there sold groceries. I observed the locals in the tea shops and those selling woollens and garments. The morning sunlight felt very pleasant on my skin.

Nearly an hour went by before Geshe Repten returned to tell us that we would have to be exceedingly patient. The soldiers would examine each of us individually and also subject our belongings to a thorough scrutiny. We were categorically forbidden to object to anything they might choose to do and were urged to cooperate in every way possible. Or else they would assume we had something to hide. Our behaviour should make it clear that we had nothing at all to be secretive about. Our exemption papers had come from the Chinese embassy in Kathmandu. Gradually, the afternoon drew to a close. We began making arrangements to eat by the wayside for want of a more suitable place. There was nothing particularly problematic about that, for all it entailed was eating flour mixed with water and a little salt— enough for sustenance.

Having, perhaps, found no grounds for suspicion after interrogating some of the lamas, the guards gradually reduced the duration of each bout of questioning, until no more than half an hour was spent on each of the remaining members of the group. All of a sudden, four Chinese officers came out and demanded that we spread out our belongings on the road; it would make it that much easier for the guards to go through them. We obeyed their orders and, needless to say, there was nothing there to hide: a mug, a plate, rags for cleaning up, a quantity of flour, salt, potatoes, rice and lentils, prayer beads, woollens, clothes, shoes, a vest, a shawl and a blanket. How could these objects possibly arouse suspicion? The way those items were arranged along the road, we might well have been selling them by the wayside.

Having carefully scrutinized everything—even our sticks—the officers began to search our non-existent pockets there and then. The Chinese officers were accompanied by five Tibetan soldiers who began to ask every lama absurd and pointed questions. One of them came to an abrupt halt right in front of me. The moment I caught his eye, I averted my gaze and clutching the beads firmly in my hands, began chanting the Buddhist incantation. The soldier did not budge. Looking me up and down with a very suspicious expression, he asked me a question. I could not understand a word of what he had said. Then he grasped my hand and, perhaps, repeated his query. This time, he was not to be fobbed off. I pointed a finger at Geshe Repten, indicating that the question should be put to him.

In a barely audible whisper meant only for my ears, Guruji explained in Hindi, 'They are reluctant to accept that you are a lama from Nepal who has taken the vow of silence. Keep your wits about you. They will make every effort to verify your claim. Seek the blessings and protection of Tathagata, the Buddha.'

Soon, Geshe Repten was sent for. He went inside and returned after being interrogated for half an hour. Then it was my turn. In great trepidation, I entered the office, silently sending up a prayer for divine protection.

A quartet of Chinese officers and a couple of their local Tibetan assistants awaited me. A graver atmosphere in the room could hardly have been imagined. As soon as I entered, a remark was tossed at me. I remained mute. They repeated what they had said earlier. My response was utter silence. Then a Tibetan repeated the comment yet again, this time in an almost angry tone of voice. I remained wordless. It was clear that my unbroken silence was beginning to cause them some discomfiture. In the meanwhile, I had managed to gather my wits about me. My legs had been trembling and I willed them to be steady. After all, these men couldn't swallow me whole, could they? At the very most, they would send me back. Fine, I would go back. How did it matter?

What was there to be so afraid of? Failing to elicit any response from me, the officers began concocting all sorts of tales about me. One of the Tibetan soldiers went out of the room and returned a little later with a young Tibetan. The latter began by scrutinizing me from head to foot. Then staring at me, he asked in perfect Hindi, 'What is your name?'

His accent and speech pattern betrayed the fact that he had probably worked as a porter for sometime in the marketplace at Gangtok. His gestures too, were crass. Receiving no reply from me, he declared, 'You have come from Darjeeling. You are no Nepali.'

I silently mused that he had hit the nail on the head. From my appearance alone, he had gauged right away that I was not from Nepal. This time, the man became truly enraged at my silence. Uttering an obscenity, he demanded, 'Give me your name.'

The Chinese soldiers looked at him, gave him some advice and departed, leaving the two of us alone in the room. Now that he had me all to himself, the man brought his face very close to mine and said, 'I know that you are not a Nepali. Give me your name.'

I knew only too well that once I disclosed my name, everything would be over for me. Suddenly, I had an idea. I pretended to count my beads twice very rapidly before touching his head with them in a threatening way. Then, adopting a tone of voice that would suggest I were casting an evil spell, I uttered the incantation, '*Om Bhur...*'

That did the trick! He leapt a foot backwards and began muttering something to me in Tibetan. I could not understand a word of what he said. But from his behaviour, it was apparent that he was petrified. Adopting a benevolent air once more, I began peacefully counting my beads. The four officers I had seen earlier entered the room and having failed in their quest to extract an incriminating response from me, somewhat reluctantly asked me to leave. I was safe. The trick I had resorted to was also one Guruji had taught me. In the course of a conversation we once had, he had told me that Tibetans were ardent believers of the occult and psychic sciences.

The Tibetan who had been called in to interrogate me left and showed no sign of returning. The officers sent for Guruji once again. Pointing at me in a rather agitated way, they began saying something in their language. From what I could make out, Guruji was earnestly trying to convince them that I was, indeed, a bonafide lama. Left with no choice, the officers examined the rest of the lamas before allowing us to proceed. An entire day had gone by.

A TIBETAN FAMILY

AS EVENING APPROACHED, we had some light tea again. This was nothing but tea prepared with salt and butter. It was extremely cost-effective and served in containers at least seven times larger than the regular ones in which tea was served back home. Sorting out our belongings, we set off once again. Villagers—little children, young men and elderly ones too—gradually began clustering around us.

As we walked along, a strange sight met our eyes. While a great many of the local people stuck their tongues out at us, others prostrated themselves at our feet! Guruji explained it as the Tibetan way of showing respect. There were others, though, who had adopted the Indian way: that of prostrating themselves.

The firewood we bought here consisted of little twigs, rather like small sticks of sandalwood. I had seen similar twigs being used as fuel in Assam and North Bengal. The view from here was absolutely stunning. The Himalayan peaks on either side and even the rolling expanse of snow seemed to lie far below us. A continuous swathe of dense fir forest blanketed the mountainside. The path ran ahead, leaving a mountain stream behind it. In these beautifully pristine surroundings, only the local inhabitants appeared to be filthy. But they were clearly an exceedingly cheerful and amiable lot. Every once in a while, they would burst into loud peals of laughter and reveal their simple and easy-going nature.

A Tibetan boy of about sixteen or seventeen had been following us right from the town's checkpoint. He had been pestering Guruji with queries about where we intended to spend the night. Ignoring him completely, we had moved on. But two other people joined him from the bazaar. They wanted to organize our evening meal and arrange for the provisions required to light the fire we would need. Guruji consulted with us before bargaining with them. It was finally agreed that we would pay a sum of thirty rupees for a large room for the night, a fire to warm ourselves by and an evening meal for the thirty-two people in our group.

A while later, we were standing before a palatial house where the three boys asked us to wait. One of them went round to the rear to enter the house through the back door and open the front door for us. No sooner had he done so than a dog leaped out at us, barking furiously all the while. Luckily for us, the other boys were able to catch hold of it at once and bring it to heel. We entered the house in the fading light and stood in the courtyard, from where we could catch a glimpse of the interior. The house, an attractive wooden structure standing on a cement foundation, was, undoubtedly, old. But it hadn't yet lost its air of distinction. On reaching the upper veranda, we found an elderly woman waiting there, lamp in hand. Her aristocratic lineage could be traced in the wrinkles that lined her face. She greeted us all by prostrating herself fully on the floor. This was the owner of the house and we were duly introduced to her. The woman's husband had died a long time ago. Her three sons and two daughters now lived in Sikkim. She was the sole member of the family clinging to their ancestral property. Her nephew, Thangmey, was the one who had followed us all the way from the market.

Overjoyed at the prospect of having holy men as guests, she opened out three rooms for us—two large and one small. Two of those rooms were situated close to each other. The other one was further down. We noticed the huge fire that had been lit in the courtyard and all the lamas slowly gravitated towards it. In such bitterly cold weather, there could have been no greater friend than the warmth of that fire.

At long last, I had Guruji to myself in the room. He reassured me that I could now speak. I heaved a sigh of relief. Finally, I could speak freely! First of all, I wanted to discuss all that had happened at the border. 'Do you remember,' I asked him, 'that you had once told me how Tibetans felt about cursing? When that wretched interpreter was harassing me no end, I had clutched my beads and recited the Gayatri mantra aloud, causing him to take to his heels in terror! Mercifully, the idea had occurred to me at the opportune moment. Otherwise, who knows what might have happened?'

Listening to me, Guruji smiled slightly before saying, 'It is truly your good fortune that you were not asked for your *Idm*.'

'What is Idm?'

'That is the core incantation handed down by a mentor to his disciple.'

'*Om Mani Padme Hum* is not Idm, then, is it?'

'Every Tibetan is familiar with that incantation; it is not meant for any particular individual. The Idm is categorically restricted to a communication between the mentor and his disciple. Indian Hindus and Tibetan Buddhists are very similar in this respect.'

'Time—*Mahakaal*—is regarded as a deity by Tibetans and it is accordingly worshipped. There are other Tantrik divinities like Bhuvaneswari. Can their names be taken to be Idms?'

'You're right there. In any contingency, they may serve as the base or root incantation.'

'Now, let us come to another point. Guruji, everybody here addresses you as Geshe Repten. Will you object if I continue to call you Guruji?'

'That's all right. You may, if you wish to.'

'I have another request, Guruji. You are aware that the good fortune of being allowed to go on such a pilgrimage is rare. It certainly does not visit one twice in a single lifetime. So, if you could, while talking to the other lamas, intersperse your conversation with a few words in Hindi, it would make it easier for me to follow. They all come from Nepal or, at least, understand Nepalese. But they know I am from India. Since they have put up with me so far, I am sure they will not raise any objections.'

'I will try to accommodate your request,' was Guruji's answer. 'However, only when both of us are alone in a room will you speak. On all other occasions, you will remain silent. That is the only way to ensure that our journey is completed without complications coming in the way.'

We were conversing in this manner, when the sound of heavy footsteps on the stairs caused us to lapse abruptly into silence. 'Even disciples sworn to silence and solitude are permitted to talk to their mentor,' Guruji reassured me. 'That is not counted as a transgression. Even if someone did overhear you, it would not invite censure.'

The door opened and the elderly woman stepped in, accompanied by a young girl. They bowed low before us. Then sitting by the door, they said something in Tibetan, to which Guruji responded. Looking in my direction, Guruji explained, 'The girl is Thangmey's sister—the woman's niece.'

The woman apparently wanted Guruji to shower such blessings on the girl as to ensure an entire lifetime of bliss for her. It would be impossible to find as nice a girl as her niece, she claimed. All she wanted was for the girl to have a happy married life. Guruji blessed the girl and they left the room after respectfully bowing before him. The girl was comely. Her face radiated the glow of youth. 'How old is she?' I asked Guruji.

'Who knows?' he replied. 'She might be fourteen or twenty-four, for all I know. I didn't get a chance to look at her properly. Let us go downstairs and see what they are cooking. You need to know a little about local dietary habits.'

Guruji and I joined the rest of our group by the stove and he began to recount to the others the details of what was happening at present. Thangmey and his brother prepared the meal, while their aunt and sister handed the necessary ingredients to them from time to time. This was the first peaceful day we had enjoyed after entering Tibet. Fuel was extremely expensive here. So, as long as wood burned in the stove, the question of lighting lamps did not arise. Finally, the meal consisting of *thukma*, a Tibetan dish, was ready. Potatoes had been boiled in hot water till they were soft enough to mash. Then long sticks prepared from flour had been tossed into the pot and allowed to simmer for quite sometime. Later, small pieces of cured lamb meat had been thrown in as well. After the mixture had been boiling for a while and had released a lovely aroma, a dollop of butter and a pinch each of salt and turmeric had been added, along with some fragrant herbs. In the West, it would, perhaps, have been described as a kind of stew.

My hunger pangs aroused, I felt as if I had not eaten for days. Suddenly, a thought struck me. I asked Guruji, albeit in a whisper, 'There is meat in there. How do we accept that food?'

Guruji replied that Tibetan lamas were not vegetarian. Eating flesh was perfectly acceptable. While Guruji was still in the midst of his explanation, Thangmey's sister came in and asked the lamas to be ready for their meal. We went to our rooms and returned carrying our plates and bowls. It was the first time, since our departure from India, that we were sitting down to a proper meal. After communal prayers were over, we settled down to eat.

Oh, it was simply wonderful! This, then, was thukma—so easy to prepare, so divine to taste, like nectar! We could ask for as many helpings as we wanted. There were no restrictions on the quantity served to each of us. After the meal, we returned to our respective rooms. In the centre of the room, provisions had been made for a fire to be lit. So, it was quite warm. All that we needed to do was lay out the blanket. After thanking Thangmey's aunt profusely for her hospitality, we turned in for the night.

The next day, we rose relatively late. Guruji had made it a point not to wake us up, assuming that if we were all well rested, the journey would be a lot easier for us. It was, probably, around 9 a.m. that we gradually emerged from under our blankets, one by one. The prospect of using water from the stream to wash in didn't bear thinking about. The ice on the surface had barely melted a few metres by then.

Around ten-thirty in the morning, we prepared once again to set forth. Guruji handed Thangmey's aunt forty rupees for all she had done for us. Her face wreathed in smiles, the old woman repeatedly requested us to avail of her hospitality again on our way back. Guruji bestowed his blessings on her. Thangmey and his siblings accompanied us to the main road. Here, we were compelled to bid farewell to them and move on.

THE CITY OF YATUNG AND DUNGKAR GUMPHA

AROUND 10 A.M., we had tea of better quality in one of the last tea shops on the outskirts of Chumbi. It hadn't tasted that good the first day. But now, the tea didn't seem quite so undrinkable. We had enjoyed a wholesome meal and enough rest to continue our journey with renewed enthusiasm. The landscape before us was spectacular. The peaks of the Chomolhari range rose in front of us while in the background, the Kanchendzonga loomed large, a reassuring presence. The mountain stream looked lovelier still, with clusters of wild flowers sprouting along its banks. Groups of young children, engrossed in plucking the blossoms, turned to gaze at us in wide-eyed wonder as we passed. They were probably unused to seeing such a large group of lamas travelling together! The sun gradually rose in the sky. Given the beauty of our surroundings, the travails of covering long distances in mountainous terrain were of no consequence whatsoever. I carried some firewood along with my personal luggage. It hardly weighed anything at all—a mere 5 kg. Pausing for the occasional breather, we began making good progress. For the path along which we travelled wasn't the typical uneven hill track. Though we had skipped lunch, carrying on, regardless, did not seem an imposition at all. Guruji had explained to us that the greater the distance we managed to cover, the more convenient it would be for us in the long run; the more we saved on our supplies, the more secure we would be, for the eventuality of rations falling short would be that much less likely.

Towards evening, we reached the town of Yatung. Just before entering it, we crossed a beautiful bridge and noticed a huge military camp to our left. It was apparent that it was manned by Chinese soldiers. There was also a checkpoint here, but after going through our papers, the officials let us proceed without a fuss. Yatung was an appealing little town. By appealing, I mean that it was the only place we had passed after Chumbi that could in any way be described as a town. So far, we had not come across any traffic. There was, therefore, little danger of being run over by a car! From the houses, the marketplace, and everything else there, Yatung seemed to be a prosperous little place. We noticed a number of new wooden houses and the Indian goods prominently on display in the shops. The town also boasted a police station and a tax office.

Meanwhile, blocking Guruji's way was a Tibetan family engaged in vociferous sales patter, as its members tried persuading him to buy woollen caps and socks. Gesturing at our feet, they sought to convince him how cheap wool was out here. If the cold were to be fended off—and we certainly weren't appropriately shod for the harsh local climatic conditions—it was best to buy from them, they contended.

Despite his best efforts to be on his way, Guruji found it impossible to do so. Ultimately, he had no option but to ask the other lamas if they were interested in buying socks. Though not particularly keen, everybody finally agreed to do so. There was no doubt, of course, that we were all chilled to the bone. Seven of the lamas among us had nothing by way of footwear but shoes made of cloth. The Tibetan family trying to sell its wares had no fixed abode. They were gypsies. Throughout the winter months, they knitted socks, blankets, sweaters, caps and other woollens and sold them during the summer. There was no doubt that their stuff was of pure wool. They sheared sheep and converted the handspun wool into coarse garments. Realizing that we were pilgrims, the head of the family wanted to make a quick profit all around. He would sell his goods at rock-bottom prices, thereby generating sales and adding to his stock of good deeds. He was amiability itself as he insisted, 'If I could afford to do so, I would have gifted everything to you as a token of my respect.'

We were being offered thirty-two pairs of full-length Tibetan woollen socks dirt cheap, at a mere ten rupees for the lot! The lamas were initially reluctant to accept the goods at such a low price, for nobody was willing to take advantage of the man's simplicity and large-heartedness. But the gypsy smiled as innocently as he had before and said adamantly, 'No, I do not want to take a paisa more for the socks. You are all lamas and pilgrims too. I consider it my great good fortune that you will be going on your pilgrimage wearing socks you bought from me. As you are well aware, there are virtually no pilgrims these days.'

We pressed him to accept an additional two rupees for the socks, over and above the price quoted, showered blessings on him and went our way.

Guruji asked us to wait for him behind a mound of earth before going off to make inquiries about where we could spend the night. He returned to inform us that accommodation for the night wasn't as much of a problem as the fact that nobody could make provisions for all of us to stay under one roof. If it had been a matter of lodging a couple of people, it could have been managed, but there were no hotels or guest houses around capable of housing thirty-two lamas at one go. None of us were willing, however, to be separated from Guruji even for a night. We were, therefore, compelled to move on.

Guruji remarked, 'A little distance away lies an ancient monastery. I am acquainted with the head lama there. If he is present, we will have no problems finding accommodation for the night. And since we can cook our own food, we will be able to save on expenses.'

Leaving the road behind us, we began to go up into the mountains. About an hour later, we caught sight of a monastery perched among the rocks along the mountainside. Guruji drew our attention to it and said, 'See how beautiful it looks! That is the Dungkar Gumpha. If the Lord Tathagata is willing, we will be able to spend the night there.'

We all sat down together in one place for a short rest and Guruji took the opportunity to tell us about the gumpha. In Tibet, Buddhism had several branches, of which the main one belonged to the Geluk-pa sect. One of its adherents, Goang Lobsang Choden, had set up the Dungkar Gumpha. Here, a practitioner of the occult, locally known as Krulep, was in charge of conducting the prayers. And it was here that young children were admitted for training as future lamas.

The chaityas, known in this region as chorten, were the first structures we noticed on drawing close. We passed them, murmuring all the while, '*Om Mani Padme Hum...*'. Right before us was a massive wall, probably part of a fort. We moved on towards the main door. Hardly had we gone a few steps than we felt as though we were being attacked by tigers! For barking ferociously and lunging at us was a pair of dogs posted near the main door to guard it. Thankfully, they were chained or we would have found ourselves in a good deal of trouble! We did not have to wait long. A group of novice lamas or trapas came rushing out and pacified the curs. Observing that we were also dressed in the garb of lamas, they greeted us respectfully and stood aside to let us pass. They asked Guruji if he wanted to enter the monastery.

Of course, we did! It hardly resembled a monastery, though, and looked more like a fort, an architectural wonder nestled in the mountains. At long last, we had, it seemed, reached a true vihara. Having gone some way inside, we came to the courtyard which was surrounded by rooms assigned to the novices. At one end was an office. Some trapa had, in all likelihood, already conveyed news of our arrival, for before we could reach the office, an elderly lama with a surprised expression and an air of authority about him approached us and asked, 'May I know who you are? Could you tell me where you would like to go?'

They were matter-of-fact queries. Guruji informed him briefly of our plans, then asked, 'Is Guru Chu-Minjen here? He knows me.'

'That's wonderful! Guruji has gone to Geligong. Didn't you meet him on the way?'

No, Guruji told him, we had not come across him. He then came to the point: could we all stay here overnight? The gentleman could make no reply to that query. After all, Guru Chu-Minjen was the chief. In his absence, nobody had the authority to take a decision of this kind. We would have to wait until his return. Keeping our luggage in the office, we started exploring the monastery more thoroughly. I asked Guruji, 'From the time we left Gangtok, we have crossed a number of chorten (stupas). Could you explain what it all means?'

Acknowledging my question with a nod, Guruji replied, 'Chorten basically means "voluminous". Different people and sects interpret it in different ways, but the basic meaning remains the same. Chorten is a symbol of this corporeal world of ours. When a great man or a religious person passes away, a chorten is built to honour his memory. You have seen this kind of structure in India, marking the spot where a person has been cremated or buried. Whenever you come across such a structure, always keep it to your left and grant it due respect. A chorten is also the symbol of religion, of the sangha and the Buddha. Whatever be its form, never neglect it. A chorten represents a temple and is a living entity in that it contains all the five elements and something beyond them. Like the other gumphas, this one too contains a temple and has arrangements for the accommodation and education of lamas and trapas. A completely separate house is dedicated to the study of art. At present, there are fifty-five students, but if required, arrangements can be made to house two hundred. This is only so far as the juniors are concerned. The Dungkar Gumpha is a meeting place for lamas of the highest order. They congregate here from all over the world for meetings and discussions on education and the dissemination of our faith. The meditation rooms here are situated in a beautiful locale; no matter which direction one faces, the incomparable beauty of the Chomolhari and the Himalayas is there before one's eyes.'

When dusk was almost upon us, a kind of bugle sounded and everybody rushed away at once. That was, probably, the signal for everybody to gather together. All of a sudden, a low, intense buzzing filled the air, as though a stone had been tossed at a beehive. I realized, then, that it was the sound of the lamas praying in unison.

Guru Chu-Minjen arrived long after this. The boys here seemed to be adept at passing on messages. For Chu-Minjen knew of the presence of strangers at the monastery even before he himself had arrived. As soon as he reached the office, he caught sight of our guruji in the lamplight. The two embraced each other in the manner of brothers coming together after a very long time. Once the euphoria of the meeting had died down, Geshe Repten introduced us, one by one, to Chu-Minjen. When asked whether we could stay there for a day, the latter consented right away, adding that we could spend as many days there as we liked. Taking us to the kitchen, he pointed to the huge utensils and said that we could cook there. The fuel and everything else we might need had already been provided. Then, introducing us to a person called Jonker, he said, 'He will extend every possible help to you. Now, let us go to the temple. You can complete your evening meditation there.'

Through narrow, winding alleys, we made our way to a huge house. By the dim light of the lantern, I could not clearly make out the etchings and decorations on its wooden door. Owing, perhaps, to the intense cold, it was not the practice to take off one's shoes before entering a Buddhist temple in Tibet. Nor was it necessary here. A row of lamps burned brightly in front of us and in the glow cast by their flames, the gigantic image of Abalokiteswara smiled serenely. This image was their ultimate god. Of his four hands, the lower pair reassured his devotees and showered benediction on them. The other pair held a lotus and a streak of lightning. Flanking the idol on both sides were innumerable other images. My gaze travelled to the large shelves right next to them. They were packed with huge tomes, each with wooden covers wrapped in coloured fabric to protect them, perhaps, from the soot deposited by all those lamps. Drawn irresistibly to the books, I moved forward to examine them.

As soon as I made to touch them, the chief approached, smiled at me gently, and asked me something in Tibetan. Unable to comprehend his words, I merely stared up at him. Holding my gaze, he asked me in perfect Hindi where I hailed from. In any other situation, I would have had no qualms pretending to be bound by a vow of silence. In an ambience such as this one, however, pure and unsullied as it was, I could not bring myself to lie; that was an option I reserved for the Chinese soldiers. I answered the chief's question honestly: 'I'm from Kolkata.'

He was very happy to hear that. Gesturing towards Geshe Repten, I suggested to the chief, 'You can ask him for the details. He knows everything about me.'

Guruji introduced me to Chu-Minjen in an undertone. The latter was overjoyed to hear about me and observed, 'It is of great benefit to a person if he is able to undertake a pilgrimage when he is young. It will serve him well later in life, particularly if he is fortunate enough to have as his mentor as experienced and erudite a person as Geshe Repten. Did you know, the two of us were together in Ladakh for four years?'

I asked him: 'Do these books contain texts of the Mahayana sect?'

'Wait, let me show you,' Chu-Minjen offered. He proceeded to take down a large tome and grasping it firmly in both hands, placed it on a wooden shelf. Then he launched into his explanation. The book was enormous—two-and-a-half feet long and a couple of feet wide. Executing a reverential bow before the book, he declared, 'This is our Tibetan Upanishad, our sacred religious text. The Buddhist norms have been translated from Indian Sanskrit books known as Kangiour. This kind of tome can only be found in large monasteries. All the books stacked here are numbered. One hundred and eight of them constitute the Kangiour. In other words, each Kangiour consists of one hundred and eight parts. Each of those parts constitutes a single book.'

Looking at the huge hand-printed volumes in amazement, I asked, 'How do you manage when they have to be transported from one place to another?'

He offered a slight smile in response before saying, 'That does, indeed, pose a problem. Four of these books, two on either side, are slung over the back of a donkey, which is, in turn, pulled along by a lama or trapa. Of course, one has to be constantly alert that no disrespect is shown to the books in any manner.'

'Can junior lamas read these tomes?'

'No, as a matter of fact, they cannot. Appropriate preparation is required for that. After they have lived in the monastery for fifteen or sixteen years, we gradually teach them the simplified form of Tangiour.'

'Tangiour? What is that?'

'It is a rudimentary version of Kangiour, also composed in the Tibetan language. Allow me to show you what lies in the next room.'

Once there, he lit a pair of lamps and asked us to look around. It turned out to be another cavernous room with wooden walls crammed with books. Chu-Minjen resumed his explanation, 'All the books here are Tangiour. The room has been specially constructed to house them and is divided into two hundred and twenty-five sections. If you count the alcoves, they will add up to that precise number. The trainee lamas or trapas are not permitted to touch these books. Their top and bottom covers are made of wood. The unnumbered pages of each book, separate and unbound, are arranged sequentially, one after the other. All those who come to peruse these tomes handle them with the utmost respect and care.' Looking at me, Chu-Minjen added, 'These texts are far more difficult than either the Ramayana or the Mahabharata.'

Both the gurujis left after showing us around the main temple. Having derived a feeling of reassurance and security from their presence, we settled down for our meditation session.

The following morning, I noticed that none of the inmates of the monastery ate a meal. They were accustomed to no more than two meals a day: one in the afternoon, the other just before evening set in. We joined them and Guru Chu-Minjen led us to the second temple to have a look. It was even more resplendent than the first. The edifice had probably been hewn out of the mountainside. Though there was broad daylight outdoors, no light penetrated the interiors, for the temple had but one door and no windows. Inside were images of various deities and demons. The third temple was also filled with idols. Due, perhaps, to the lack of space, they had all been placed there together. Colourful decorations and symbols also adorned the temple. The etchings on the gold lamps in all three temples were striking indeed. These places of worship had been constructed in such a manner as to make it impossible for anyone to enter them without specific directions to guide them in. An individual would have been quite at sea if he had tried making his way into one of these temples alone.

We joined the students for our midday meal. After thanking everybody for their help and hospitality, Geshe Repten announced that once the meal was over, we would be on our way.

PHARI

WE STARTED OUT as planned. It had grown really late by the time we set out. Guruji warned us that we would have to cover as much of the distance as we could possibly manage that day. We would probably be halting briefly to prepare and eat our evening meal. We would then continue on our way.

Our halting point was a dilapidated house where I prepared the bread we would all be eating. Then, having added some salt to it for seasoning, we relished it. The trek was a rather long, monotonous one. Halting three or four times on the way for a rest, we caught a glimpse of Phari around dawn.

Right on the outskirts of town stood a tea shop. We called out loudly for the owner, but it was his middle-aged wife, instead, who woke up and opened the door to a large group of lamas. It was a blessed morning for her and an extremely fortunate one at that. She bowed low in deference to our stature as holy men and asked us what we desired. Tea, of course, we told her. Asking us to wait, the woman hurriedly roused her husband. She had no alternative, for catering to so many people wasn't something she could have managed single-handedly. Amazingly, within minutes, three men emerged from the room. They were probably siblings sharing the same spouse.

Tea and a little flour mixed in warm water—that was all we needed before preparing to move on again. By the time we had arrived at the tea shop, we had all reached the end of our tether and were badly in need of sustenance and rest. Guruji reassured us that we would be heading towards the gumpha visible from this place. After spending the morning there, we would set out again in the evening.

In front of the gumpha were huge flags attached to tall bamboo or wooden poles. It was difficult to miss those poles. They were landmarks of sorts, indicating the direction one should follow to reach the gumpha. Little pieces of coloured cloth inscribed with prayers were strung up high from these poles, rather in the manner of the paper chains that served as decoration during the festival season in Kolkata. Moving along a narrow path, we came up against the ancient wall of the gumpha, constructed, apparently, from local stones and clay. There was no entrance as such; a gap in the wall served the purpose of a doorway. It opened out into a vast courtyard, the way the entrances of certain houses did in prosperous villages in Bihar. A covered veranda ran all the way around. There was nobody in sight from whom we could have sought permission to use it and Guruji advised us to take shelter in its shade and rest.

It must have been well past noon when we woke up. A number of trapas surrounded us and moved away respectfully as soon as they saw we were awake. Among them was an elderly lama belonging to the gumpha. When we introduced ourselves, he was overjoyed and welcomed us warmly.

After some conversation with the lama, Guruji decided that in return for our meals—the gumpha would serve us *tsampa*, a kind of broth—he would pay ten rupees and also hand over some salt as a gift. Later, I told Guruji that ten rupees was a mere trifle for tsampa served to thirty-two people and was roundly rebuked for my remark. 'Of course not!' was his reply. 'Ten rupees is a lot of money! Tsampa is barley water blended with flour and some pieces of cured meat. Barley is grown locally and, therefore, dirt cheap.'

We set out to explore the town. Right after leaving the gumpha, we took a right turn and headed in its direction. At first glance, it looked to be the largest one in the region. The closer we moved to the heart of Phari, the more extensive the area the villages seemed to cover. The town appeared to sprawl over a wide area—all along the valley, the houses were increasingly spread out. We strolled around aimlessly. On entering the town, we noticed the yaks wandering loose on the roads. The animals looked like a cross between a cow and bullock. In front of a meat shop, a group of men were busy playing a game by tossing coins on the ground. It was here that we saw young local girls for the first time. Their hair was tied back tightly and their dress was the *banku*, a kind of long chemise. Elderly men and women wore nearly identical clothes. Since there were no schools to speak of other than the one within the gumpha, parents had no option but to enrol their offspring there. As far as schooling was concerned, young girls faced the same situation. As soon as they were a little older, however, their parents would receive marriage proposals for them. As a result, we hardly saw any female acolytes or trainee nuns. In fact, there were, probably, very few women in Tibet which, perhaps, was the reason why several brothers married one woman, thereby fulfilling a social obligation.

Phari was locally known as Phari Jong—'jong' meaning a fort. The town had developed around the fort which served as its nucleus. The fort itself had initially risen around a monastery. Phari was Tibet's main trading centre with Sikkim, Bhutan and Siliguri. Over the years, business relations had developed between India and Phari. The latter was better known as the Trade Centre and an Indian government representative was stationed here.

There was little doubt that the city was filthy. There was no sewerage to speak of. Neither was there a properly constructed toilet. All the fields and open spaces around seemed to serve as a substitute. Urban folk, however, found it very difficult to adjust to the lack of even basic facilities, particularly when the need was urgent. It was obvious that the unofficially designated spot for all garbage to be dumped lay either right outside the door or the kitchen window of every dwelling. It was the reason why so many houses had huge mounds of rubbish piling up in their immediate vicinity. Close to the one crossroad in town was the post office; all mail from Lhasa and Pema Chowki on the Indo-Tibet border was sent here. Once a week, this post office served as the main one in the area. To its left was a raised dais, standing almost ten feet high. It was made of small wooden blocks placed haphazardly atop each other and surrounded by a tattered wall of jute. Immediately below it, a virtual hill of human excreta rose from the ground. The slightest inattention on anyone's part could lead to a really nasty accident!

A voice greeting me in Hindi made me spin around in surprise. Well-wrapped in a blanket, a man stood behind us, smiling pleasantly. It was obvious from his physique and the manner in which he was dressed that he was no Tibetan. Guruji looked at him and greeted him. I too, gave him a gentle smile. Ignoring Guruji, the man looked straight at me and observed, 'You look very young. Are you from India?'

I was wondering whether or not to reply, when Guruji answered on my behalf. 'We are from Nepal,' he told him by way of explanation. 'This boy is my disciple.'

'Oh! No wonder I thought he was from India! So, which destination do you plan to travel to?' The man was beginning to get familiar.

'We have set out on a pilgrimage,' Guruji answered.

'What places do you plan to visit?'

'Who can tell? For the present, we are on our way to Gyatse.'

'You are lucky that you belong to Nepal. These days, Indian monks have virtually stopped coming to Tibet.'

Guruji now began questioning him in turn. 'Are you from India?' he asked him. 'What are you doing here?'

'I operate a business in woollens here. I buy woollens from

here and send them to India and purchase a few commodities from there and sell them here. I don't own the business; I work on behalf of my employer who lives in Sikkim.'

The man was friendly. Originally from Samastipur, India, he had been living here for four years. Once a year, he went back home on vacation. In the course of our conversation, he informed us that business these days was suffering badly. All trade was gradually being taken over by the Chinese. Powerless, the lamas could not, despite their wishes, defy the might of the Chinese. The man continued with a sigh that if the situation remained unchanged, he would be forced to wind up the business and return home. The Tibetans were gradually moving closer to the Indian border in anticipation of some help. But the situation was grim, very grim indeed. As ascetics, how could we be expected to know about it? It had to do with politics. The man ended with a flourish and invited us for a cup of real Darjeeling tea, not the stuff that was locally available.

We accompanied him to his house. It was built of local stone and earth. The doors and windows as well as the balcony were made of wood. Right in front of the door, a great many young children played with small pieces of stone arranged in rows. As soon as we entered the house, a Tibetan man stuck out his tongue and greeted us with due respect. We entered an untidy room on the second floor. Our host hastily swept the bed clear of the articles cluttering it and made a place for us to sit. Then, opening an old tin of barley, he showed us his priceless treasure of Darjeeling tea. Lighting a stove, he put some water on to boil. I was itching to talk to him and Guruji was familiar with my impulses. Smiling gently, he gave me permission to do so and I heaved a sigh of relief. 'Be very careful, though,' Guruji warned me.

I went right up to the stove and told our host, 'My name is Bimalananda. Actually, I am a Bengali.'

The man almost jumped for joy. 'A Bengali from Kolkata!' he exclaimed.

Throwing a damper on his effusive enthusiasm, Guruji put forward his disclaimer: 'Yes, but for the purpose of this journey, he is a monk from Nepal who has taken a vow of silence. That is what the documents claim.'

The man nodded in acquiescence. 'Yes, of course,' he said, 'I understand. You have done the right thing, Babaji. But be very careful that nobody guesses the truth. The people of Gyatse and Shigatse are not well-disposed towards Indians.'

Shibshankar Tiwari was the man's rather striking name. He repeated rather regretfully that if the situation had been anything like it used to be in the past, he certainly would not have let us go so easily, especially since young ascetics like me were hard to come by. In the course of our conversation, Shibshankar Babu also mentioned that beyond the town's fort stood a checkpoint that was extremely tough to get through.

Having heard him out, Guruji said, 'It makes no difference to us. We are ascetics. God is our strength. If He wills it, we will go ahead. If not, we will return.'

The man pressed two five-rupee notes into my hand and insisted that I accept them. Without any hesitation, I said, 'Fine, I will, since you are so insistent.'

Blessing the man, we took our leave. But this did not deter him from accompanying us right up to the crossroad. Then stopping in front of a big shop, he asked me, 'Is there any shopping you need to get done?'

I looked at the shop then. It was huge and sold a variety of groceries, sweets and meat. Pondering over the matter, I finally replied, 'If you could get me a few notebooks and pens, it would make me very happy.'

Right away, he bought me three notebooks and a couple of pencils. For Guruji, he purchased a torch.

Instead of remaining in a single group, we broke up; it would make things less difficult for us all at the checkpoint if we weren't quite so conspicuous. There would be at least five thousand soldiers manning that point. We progressed cautiously, trying to walk as much like the average Tibetan as we could possibly manage. Our only source of security and reassurance were the prayer beads we held and the power of the incantation to the Buddha. The Chinese soldiers loved stretching out their welcome over hours and it determined the speed of our progress.

A NOCTURNAL JOURNEY

WE HEADED TOWARDS central Tibet, that is, in a northerly direction. The Chomolhari peak seemed to be slowly moving towards us as we progressed. With evening approaching, it began to grow colder. As the snowy peaks of the Chomolhari range (15,420 feet) turned to a magical gold in the glow cast by a dying sun, a painfully sharp chill seemed to stab right through us. No sooner had the sun dipped behind the horizon than our bodies grew numb from the cold. The wind too blew in stronger gusts. It was not something we were prepared for. Even while crossing the Nathu La pass, the cold had not seemed quite so bitter.

Unfolding our blankets, we wrapped ourselves tight in them and were even forced to don the woollen socks we had bought on the way. But having put on the socks, we were confronted with yet another problem. The socks were so thick, that getting our feet into our shoes became virtually impossible. We needed sturdy Tibetan shoes for the purpose. A handful of us began to shiver uncontrollably. Taking in the situation at a glance, Guruji allowed us to light a fire. We sought shelter behind a large boulder. It dawned on me at long last why we had been asked to carry fuel. I cannot put into words what a blessing that fire was for us all.

But where divine intervention was at hand, could any problem stand up to it? In the fading light of dusk, we came upon a tent standing by the wayside. Actually, it was less of a tent than a sort of canopy, open on all sides and erected to protect those who took shelter beneath it from the searing rays of the sun. A careful survey made it only too clear that even if our group were to just stand beneath it, shoulder to shoulder, there wouldn't be enough place for us all; the question of sitting under it simply did not arise. On seeing us approach, two men—nomads from the look of them— emerged from the tent, coughing all the while, and Guruji began speaking to them. Even with my limited intelligence, it seemed to me for the first time since I had met Guruji that he had taken leave of his senses. Where there was no place in the tent to even stand upright, how did the question of taking shelter there arise? I observed, however, that every single lama in our group was silent on the subject. Had I not been playing the part of a lama sworn to silence, I would definitely have raised a storm of protest.

I could not follow the conversation Guruji was engaged in with the two men, but within a short while, a fire was lit again. One of the nomads put water on to boil in an old aluminium pot. Belonging as they did to this region, these men were familiar with its climatic conditions from childhood and could predict from the chill of the blowing wind how sharply temperatures were going to dip. They told us that it was only to be expected that we would feel chilled to the bone—it had not been a sensible idea to set out in the cold so soon after the noon meal. Only if one started out in the morning and walked continuously, right through to the evening, did the body work up enough heat to successfully withstand the cold.

The water had warmed up in the meanwhile and into it were tossed some herbal roots, along with butter. The roots were boiled for quite sometime. We sipped the concoction like tea and warmed our feet by the fire. This liquid tasted like boiled water into which some ginger had been thrown and it worked like magic, infusing us with fresh energy.

I realized, later, that selling tea to travellers was what this nomadic family specialized in. Of course, what had been prepared for us with herbal roots was extremely expensive and beyond the means of the poorer people in this area. The three rupees charged for at least forty mugs of water, some expensive herbal roots, a little tea and butter served to thirty-two of us seemed amazingly cheap to me. But Guruji insisted that we had paid a criminally high price. I can vouch for the fact, however, that never has there been as potent a drug for generating heat in the body!

Before proceeding on our way again, Guruji told us of an amazing trick to prevent ourselves from losing our bearings during the nocturnal trek ahead. He said that we would have to move in a northerly direction. Since the path was dark and full of potholes, Guruji pointed to a brightly gleaming north star and directed us to follow it blindly. Even if we got separated for some reason, so long as we followed his instructions, there would never be any question of getting lost.

By now, we were well into the night. Nobody could tell the exact time, though, for none of us were wearing watches. We neither had an instrument to read the temperature nor a clue as to how many more miles we needed to cover. But Guruji declared that we were right below the Chomolhari mountains. From here, the mountain track climbed up. Another mountain would have to be crossed, the last of the Himalayan range. And then we would enter the level land of Tibet.

Silence reigned supreme. The area we were travelling through was almost completely bare of vegetation. A flimsy wall of darkness seemed to surround us. Occasionally, we could make out the silhouette of huge boulders and continued to move ahead, stumbling over small pebbles and stones as we did so. In the utter quiet that encircled us, our very breathing was audible. It was cold all right, but the sky overhead was clear and spangled with stars that seemed to light up our path. We walked on, our eyes trained on those stars all the while. We had lost track of the number of hours we had been on the move when, all of a sudden, a melodious voice reached us. It was the familiar one of our beloved guruji. We came to a halt and, along with Guruji, serenaded the silent goddess of the night. Guruji informed us that we had reached Tangla, which lay very close to the Chomolhari peak. This was the steepest section of the journey. Once we had navigated it, it would be downhill all the way. We would be arriving in Tungla within another hour or so.

After a brief rest, we moved on. The stars gradually dimmed in the sky; it was clear that dawn was fast approaching. We had walked the entire night as though in a trance. Gazing at the stars, we had all but forgotten our weariness. This kind of experience was possible only if complete silence were maintained throughout. Only if one felt that sense of oneness with the stars did the strength come to disregard physical exhaustion. Nothing proved my claim quite so irrevocably as our nocturnal trek. Tibetan sages and pilgrims were well versed in this skill. Had we been unfamiliar with it ourselves, it would have been quite impossible for us to cross the Chomolhari mountains in so short a span of time.

The moment we left the mountainous terrain behind us, dawn broke over the horizon revealing a portion of the landscape that was simply beautiful to behold. The sun's rays turning the pristine snow to gold was a visual treat to be treasured, rather like the sunrise visible from Darjeeling's Tiger Hill.

After leaving Phari behind us, we had passed through a number of smaller places which had served us as overnight halts. On the sixth day of our trek, as afternoon drew near, we reached Samada, a small town. We had, so far, moved through Tuna, Ram and Dosen, of which only the last could be described as a town. Moreover, I could not help noticing that proper roads in this area were few and far between.

Samada, like Dosen, was, indeed, a town. But compared to Phari, it was tiny. I had not, so far, noticed any signs of electrification on the roads. All I had seen by way of traffic were some jeeps driven by Chinese soldiers. The locals had probably never seen lorries, motor cars or buses, let alone trains. As we were about to enter the town, a large white house festooned with multicoloured paper and cloth appeared ahead of us. Drawing closer, we noticed that a portion of the area in front of the house had been enclosed and covered with cloth. Some sort of festival was evidently being celebrated here. A large group of people sat in front, along with a band of musicians and a few beggars. The moment they spotted us, they stood back deferentially, amiable smiles lighting up their faces, and stuck their tongues out in greeting. We returned their greetings and moved on.

We had barely left the house behind us when some men came running after us. One of them approached and greeting us respectfully, asked, 'Would you please follow us to the house? The owner requests your presence.'

'Why, what is the matter?' Guruji asked him. 'Is some sort of festival on?'

'Yes, it is my sister's wedding and my father would appreciate your presence there.'

An exchange of glances was all it took for us to decide right away to make our way back to the house.

Our host was waiting for us at the door. He prostrated himself before us and taking the cue from him, the others followed suit. He laid out a mat for us on the road itself. At a gesture from Guruji, we all took a seat.

The man introduced himself as a local landowner. His elder daughter's wedding was taking place and owing to what he considered his great good fortune, he had been blessed with the arrival of so many holy men together. This would certainly prove to be auspicious for his daughter. It was very rare for a person to have such a bounty of blessings bestowed on him. He requested us, therefore, to stay back for a while. Guruji was urged to partake of the afternoon meal that would be served and, in return, to bless our host's daughter with good fortune throughout her life. I could not have guessed at that moment what the other lamas thought of it, but to me, it seemed a golden opportunity. It was the first occasion on which I had seen a well-to-do Tibetan family. There were smiles and cheerful expressions all around. The men wore loose garments, while the women were clad in a manner similar to that of Sikkimese women. They wore what went by the name of banku. A small, light wooden frame that looked rather like a cage supported their elaborate hairdos. The clothes these people wore were possibly an indication of their aristocratic lineage, for they were poles apart from the attire of the man on the street and were probably worn only during festivals or special occasions.

The head of the household approached us a short while later. Guruji listened attentively to what he had to say, then nodded his assent. A temporary tent had been set up behind the house and arrangements for cooking were being made there. That, in fact, seemed to be the nucleus of all the merrymaking. Young girls laughed and joked among themselves. Young children ran about. The elderly were engaged in discussions and sought to lend a helping hand in the activities.

We were given to understand that chang was being organized for us from the market. An extremely popular cold drink in Tibet, it didn't contain even a trace of tea. It was even more avidly sought after during festive occasions and celebrations. Made from barley, it was mildly intoxicating, but drinking it was not frowned upon. Quite often, every member of the family joined in for a taste of the brew.

The head of the household came out to inform us that a light meal of sorts was ready. At the same time, he humbly appealed for our consent in the matter of keeping our *padodak*. We had arrived from the land of the Buddha and it was not an opportunity they were likely to come by often. He hoped and prayed we would agree to his request. That so many holy men had gathered there at the wedding, quite by chance, was a sign that the wishes of the god, Chenreji, were being fulfilled, he contended.

We looked at Guruji, uncomprehending. He explained that we were regarded as truly holy men since we had come from India. The Tibetan was seeking our permission to retain the water with which our feet had been washed. It was, like the water of the Ganges for us, deemed sacred. Withholding consent in this case was naturally out of the question, but I did not feel entirely happy about the matter. Unless the Almighty or a true spiritual mentor bestowed the sacred water, the whole affair seemed unethical. For among all these holy men, I was the only imposter, the sole fraud.

A little later, an enormous tin container of water was carried in. Guruji instructed us all to take off our shoes. A simple enough request, but in that bitter cold.... However, his wishes were ultimately complied with and Guruji was the first to dip his feet in that icy water and wash them. The others followed suit. Then it was my turn. It seemed that my very veins would burst from the cold! Somehow, I managed to stop myself from flinching and carefully washed my feet in that water. It had been almost a month since I had actually washed my feet with water. A woman waiting beside me gently wiped them and, blessing her, I took my seat on the mat she had laid out. My feet seemed about to freeze. But in a while, and to my great surprise, the blood began to circulate more freely than it had earlier and they warmed up in no time at all. Perhaps, this too, was an experience we needed to go through. Gradually, all the members of the household came up to touch our feet reverentially. Finally, it was the turn of the bride and her younger sister. The girl was beautiful and clad in silk, with a kind of belt around her waist. Most Tibetan girls wore this extra layer— a rather practical way of keeping warm. I had observed something similar in Bhutan and Sikkim. A number of men sported westernized hats. Apart from that, men and women were dressed almost identically in a loose garment with voluminous sleeves. It was only in summer that they rolled up the sleeves. The girl prostrated herself before each lama in turn and received his individual blessings.

Having left the festivities and moved on, we entered Samada at last. It wasn't a bad place at all from the look of it; at least, it was a lot cleaner than Phari! The houses too, were beautiful and constructed mostly of stone and clay. Of course, the doors, windows and hanging verandas were made of wood. To the left was a small military post. We noticed several women drying sheep's wool by the roadside and, depending on how much they required, stuffing it into large baskets. Observing so many lamas together, people around us began running up to touch our feet respectfully.

About two hours after our departure from Samada, we arrived at a palatial gumpha. Pointing to it, Guruji informed us that we would be staying there for the night. Of course, if arrangements could not be made for us, we would have to return to Samada.

KIANGPHU GUMPHA AND LAMA TSHERING JONG

❧

AS WE APPROACHED, the dogs began to bark. Hearing the commotion, an elderly gentleman emerged from the gumpha. Owing to his failing eyesight, it took him a while to recognize Guruji. This was Lama Tshering Jong and once upon a time, he had been the assistant lama of the gumpha. Two years ago, the chief lama had left and Lama Tshering Jong had succeeded him.

The gumpha was a small one with tall clay walls atop which stood a lightly carved wooden structure. The place appeared to be positively ancient. We went in and all the important conversation was conducted in a large hall. Initially, the lama was hesitant about putting up so many people and seeing to their meals. Guruji explained to him, however, that we would not be putting him to any expense; everybody carried his own food and all we sought was a lighted fire and a shelter. We were even willing to pay for the fuel. Besides, we would also make a token payment of five rupees. Despite his initial reluctance, the lama ultimately gave in.

As the day wore on, it began to get increasingly chilly. The cold here was quite intolerable. If the temperature dipped any further, staying the night here would pose a serious problem. So, while there was still time, Guruji asked Lama Tshering Jong if he could organize a room for us; it would be of immense help. Tsheringji was probably waiting for this opportunity and agreed to the request. For this privilege, we would, of course, have to pay an additional three rupees.

We were led to an old temple belonging to the monastery. A lamp glowed on the premises and a number of ancient bench-like structures stood about. Tsheringji explained that this place of worship was a very auspicious one. Thirteen years ago, it had been the main temple. But a new structure had subsequently come up and the Lord Buddha's image had been moved there. Apart from that, everything else had been left very much the same. It was decided that we would stay there and prepare our meals in the monastery's kitchen.

My eyes were irresistibly drawn to the colossal image of the Tibetan god, Job Jung. I realized that it also reminded me of certain aspects of Hinduism. However, there seemed to be nothing peaceful about that image. I had observed this in some form or the other in almost every gumpha we had visited. But since I was sworn to silence, it was impossible for me to ask questions. I could only speak late at night or in virtual isolation. This, then, was the opportunity to seek explanations about it from Guruji.

After the meal was over and everybody had gone to bed, I urged Guruji to tell me something about the history behind this image. He had never dissuaded me from asking such questions; on the contrary, he had been very encouraging and had provided answers to my queries in a language that was simple and easy to follow. Guruji now launched forth into his explanation.

The image in question, he declared, depicted the union of Shiva and Shakti or strength and presented it before the common man. While Nature or Prakriti symbolized our individual souls, Shiva represented the soul of humanity itself. This was the Hindu interpretation as opposed to the one upheld by Tantrik Buddhism, the occult-based religion of Tibet. According to this branch of Buddhism, a strong tie existed between the Buddhist faith and the influence of the occult. For a clear perception and understanding of its intricacies, one would have to meditate and study the subject in depth.

TO GYATSE

꩜

THE FOLLOWING DAY saw us on our way once more. The large town we had passed through at night on our way to Samada was Dosen. We had noticed a beautiful lake nearby—Ram Sarovar, one of the many names by which it was known. It was reputed to be as auspicious and picturesque as Mansarovar itself. Lama Tshering Jong of Kiangphu Gumpha had asked us whether we had offered our prayers at Ram Sarovar. In fact, we had not, for Guruji would not allow us to linger there because of the bitter cold. Tshering Jong was particularly keen that the moment we set out, we should, like all pilgrims passing through the area, make it a point to pray at the temple by the lake. We decided to abide by his suggestion. Guruji admitted that he too had wanted to spend a night there, but had refrained from doing so because of repeated warnings that Han soldiers stationed at the spot did not look kindly on pilgrims. It was the reason why he had been forced to navigate it only after nightfall.

Once we had left Tangla behind us, the path became less arduous. But it was still a mountain trail and, for someone from Kolkata, difficult enough to tackle. At that particular point, we were crossing over the Himalayas and although we were engaged in a continuous process of ascent and descent, the average height of the terrain we passed through remained over 11,000 feet.

For the past couple of days or so, we had been physically and mentally invigorated and were getting quite acclimatized to the cold. Some of the members of our group were slightly asthmatic while others had to contend with coughs and colds, but on the whole, everybody seemed to be feeling a great deal better. Once we had passed Tuna, the landscape grew spectacularly beautiful, with nothing but snow-clad mountains all around. The icy white peaks seemed to be engaged in a play of colours with us. The Himalayas were no longer an obstacle. We had crossed them and were now on the other side. Back home in Kolkata, we would have been preparing to celebrate the advent of spring. But here, an endless celebration of the eternal snows appeared to be in progress. There were no forests in this area; trees could not survive in such an unforgiving climate. When the weather grew warmer, grass would sprout and cover the entire area.

With no option in sight, we resumed our journey north. There was a brief halt in the afternoon, for the wood we used for fuel was all but over. We also picked up some food from Samada. As we stopped in front of a local house, crowds gathered around us and people greeted us with beaming smiles and extended tongues. They included both the young and the elderly. When they came to know who we were, they touched our feet in respect. When we asked for some hot water to soak the barley, they hastened to get it ready for us. If each of the families present arranged for water that would suffice for half a dozen of us, it would cover the needs of the whole group. The children remained seated before us.

We shared our simple meal with the villagers who were elated at the very prospect of doing so with such a large number of holy men. One would have thought they were in heaven itself. The meal over, we were on our way once again.

We spent that night in a small shanty room and the following afternoon, reached a prosperous village. On entering the Khanma village, a member of the local police force approached us. Greeting us respectfully, he asked, 'Are you coming from Gangtok? Are you pilgrims from Nepal?'

We had no choice but to admit the truth. We suspected he might be taking us to the Han police station for questioning. 'Please follow me,' he told us.

About half an hour later, we reached a small bungalow where a man who resembled a lama greeted us with a smile. We were immensely relieved. After he had prostrated himself, all the others followed suit. Guruji and the rest of our group blessed them. The man, whose name was Soren Thape, humbly welcomed us into the village. He informed us that news of our arrival had already been intimated to him from Gangtok by a telegram. The revered king of Sikkim had requested him to look after us. His brother worked for the monarch in Sikkim and it was he who had sent the message. It was news that gladdened our hearts, but it certainly would not do for dignified lamas like us to jump for joy. So, accepting the news with equanimity, we raised our hands and blessed the brother in faraway Sikkim.

Soren Thape explained that the bungalow was Indian property. In a bid to maintain trade relations between India and Tibet, many such bungalows had been constructed along the route linking Gangtok and Gyatse. As there were few tourists at the time, the bungalows were rarely occupied. Thanks to the influence of the Han, there were virtually no pilgrims either. So, the bungalow to which we had been led could be regarded as village property. Soren Thape was the highest authority in the village and in charge of all matters pertaining to law and order. The village population had risen to almost four hundred. Barley was farmed in summer and there were plenty of sheep too, from which wool of excellent quality was obtained. Soren Thape invited us to stay in that bungalow as long as we desired.

Built in the old British style, it was a beautiful bungalow made of local clay and stone. Once upon a time, it had had a garden enclosed by a fence, but that had now been converted into a playground for children. During the summer, it probably served as a sheep pen. Our host had the ancient locks opened with a great deal of difficulty and allowed us to examine the rooms. For us, these were princely arrangements indeed! It was the first time after our arrival in Tibet that this kind of hospitality was being lavished on us. From the look of the beds and carpets, it did not seem as if anyone had entered the room for five years or more; there was a thick layer of dust everywhere. We put our luggage down and proceeded to make ourselves comfortable there.

Soren Thape lived some distance away. He repeatedly reassured us that we would not have to put up with any inconvenience; the village people would keep a constant vigil to ensure that. And there was news that brought us still greater joy: We would not need to cook! The villagers would take turns in preparing our meals for us. Bungalows like this one had been full of retainers at one time. But due to the lack of visitors, looking after guests like us fell to the villagers themselves.

Guruji said he believed it was safe for me to speak if I wanted to. Meanwhile, I had managed to grasp a few words of Tibetan, but had been unable to put them to use. What was the harm in my making the attempt, now that Guruji had given me permission to speak? Leaving the bungalow, I set out by myself. It was a small village, but a peaceful and charming one, with no barriers at all enclosing it. The houses were built close to one another. Roads had developed and boulders had been arranged to flank them like borders. The bungalows did not have the usual wooden veranda. Timber was probably a very expensive commodity in the area. People came out of their houses and greeted me respectfully.

As all the villagers had come to know of our presence by then, they turned out to pay their respects. A great many of them, particularly the young ones, asked a lot of questions. Unfamiliar as I was with the language, I was unable to answer them. I returned their greetings with a smile and moved on. In a short while, all the villagers came to know me.

As evening approached, the villagers came to meet us. Many of them had been to Sikkim. We sat on the veranda, surrounded by them, and tunefully chanted aloud our prayers. We prayed, first in Pali, then in Tibetan. Though I did not understand the latter, I found it immensely appealing, especially when the words were slowly and clearly enunciated.

We had no particular plans and the villagers found the mere presence of holy men a stimulant. With sunset, darkness descended all of a sudden. I noticed, then, that some of the Tibetans were crowding around a number of large pans they had collected so that they could warm themselves by the heat from the burning embers these contained. Initially, I felt they had gathered for the very purpose of warming themselves. Our presence merely served as a pretext. Gradually, it seemed that people had congregated just for idle conversation. Everybody appeared to be a member of the same family. Occasionally, one person or the other would rise to his feet and ask Guruji a few simple questions:

'How long did it take you to reach our village?'
'Are you going to take a look at Chenreji?'
'Will you be staying with us for long?'

The focus of the women's questions was somewhat different:

'How many sons will I give birth to?'
'Will my daughter marry well?'
'Will my son be cured of his ailment?'

As the night progressed, Guruji asked the villagers to approach him individually so that he could hand over with his blessings a few grains of rice from our own stock. This greatly pleased them. The time had now arrived for them to return home. At this juncture, Soren Thape walked up to Guruji and whispered something in his ear which brought a little smile to his lips. Looking at me, he said, 'The villagers know you are Indian and declare that they have never seen an Indian ascetic so young. They regard your presence in their midst as highly auspicious. They would be grateful for some sort of message from you.'

'Fine,' I answered, 'but what do I say to them?'

'Whatever you wish.'

With this reassurance from Guruji, I said, 'Very well. Please interpret into Tibetan whatever I say to them in Hindi.'

He agreed and I addressed the crowd:

'My dear brothers, sisters and respected elders! It is unfortunate, indeed, that I do not know your language. But before I visit you again, I will make it a point to learn Tibetan. I would like to tell you how pleased we are with the kind of hospitality you have extended to us. To think that I have found my brothers and sisters so far away from my homeland! My Guruji's blessings have brought me here and a more beautiful country I have yet to see! To be on a great pilgrimage and be given the opportunity of seeing you all on the way makes my journey truly worthwhile. With your simplicity and generosity, you are like Lord Shiva in the Himalayas. I pray for your welfare.'

I fell silent once the prayer was over and the villagers returned home.

That night, they brought us rice and lentils. After a long interval, it was an experience we enjoyed very much. Urged by the villagers, we had to stay on the next day as well. Our very presence made them happy and they would linger around us all day. One of our duties was to visit every Tibetan household there. It was considered auspicious and a sign of great good fortune to be visited by a lama and even more so, if the lama partook of a meal in that home. That evening, I received one such invitation to dinner. Soren Thape had taken Guruji and the other lamas on a visit to the various households. I had been invited to the Dorje house, which was nearby.

When I arrived there, I noticed that a large mat, probably made of dry straw, had been laid out on the floor. I was to take my seat there. Mrs Dorje appeared at once and, aware of my unfamiliarity with the language, led me by the hand to help me sit comfortably. Taking her filthy dress from the peg it had been hanging on, she laid it on the mat like a cover and asked me to take my seat. Then looking at her husband, she addressed him in their language. She seemed to be rebuking him for asking a holy man to sit on a bare mattress! Not that it made much of a difference to me. But her eagerness to please was so touching that I smiled and blessed her.

The bedroom had a small veranda running along it and installing me there, Mrs Dorje went in. From its very structure, it was apparent that this served as the kitchen; it had no other door or window. As soon as the stove was lit, thick smoke poured into the room. Mrs Dorje put some water on to boil, a prelude, no doubt, to showering hospitality on her guest. I observed the proceedings intently. A quantity of Chinese frozen tea was crumbled up and put into the boiling water. I had no idea what the ingredients in that beverage might be, but as I raised the cup to my lips and bore the onslaught of a noxious stink, I managed to hide my immediate feeling of revulsion. The Tibetans were a sensitive people and any offence I might cause them inadvertently could well translate into problems during the pilgrimage. There was no window either through which I could throw my tea away unobserved. Besides, it had been served with the good wishes of the entire family. How could I possibly show disrespect to their hospitality which they had gone out of their way to bestow on me despite their impoverished state? Perhaps, they preferred their tea to taste this way? I tried making allowances as I held this silent conversation with myself, but had to force myself to take a second sip. Seeing no way out of the impasse, I lovingly called out to the youngest child in the family, seated him on my lap and held the cup to his lips. Amazingly, no one uttered a word of protest. When the boy too averted his face, I called out to his older brother. There were no further problems after that. Even the women approached me and sipped tea from my cup. To them, it was something like partaking of blessed food. Finally, when the cup was empty, I handed it to Mrs Dorje and declared, 'That was excellent!'

No sooner had I uttered those words than she got up and poured some more tea into my cup. This was appalling! Though I had used nothing but words of praise, I was to be allowed no reprieve! She then indicated through gestures that I was to finish everything that was in my cup and not give it away again to the others. Everybody around trained their eyes on me. I was being forced to swallow a bitter pill indeed! The bamboo cup in which the brew had been served could hold at least four to five times the quantity of tea served back home in an ordinary cup. After finishing the tea, I thanked them all profusely, going to great lengths to conceal the violent revolt my stomach was engaged in.

While the Dorjes sat around me, I had so much to say to them. But unfortunately, there was no way I could communicate. True, Sadhu Baba had permitted his disciple to break his vow of silence. The consent had been given, but not the means. I looked at the members of the Dorje family gathered around me with devout expressions on their faces. Even the daughters seemed older than I was. I was almost young enough to be one of their offspring. Just to while away the time, I exchanged occasional smiles with their youngest son. Then it occurred to me that, perhaps, they wished to hear me recite some prayers or chant incantations. So, I closed my eyes and, in a most reverential manner, recited aloud some poetry I knew by heart, composed by our great Rabindranath Tagore. When I had finished, Mrs Dorje ushered everyone out, but remained steadfastly seated at my feet along with her eldest daughter who had helped her mother to prepare the tea. Then the lady herself also left. Only her daughter remained behind. Why, I wondered silently.

The girl drew even closer and sat facing me. Her face was as pure and serene as the Chomolhari mountains. The Bimal I had left behind at home began to awaken. Why? The girl glanced shyly at me and said something I could not decipher. I placed my hand on her head in a gesture of benediction and tried to get across the message: 'May God bless you. Please forgive me, but I do not understand a word of what you are saying.'

The silent ascetic in me had vanished. I rediscovered myself— a sixteen-year-old Bengali boy sitting across a young Tibetan girl. What was she seeking? What were their customs? And how could I help? The blood seemed to surge through my veins. It was a long time since I had faced such a situation. What would be the right response? Despite good intentions on my part, whatever I said or did might provoke adverse reactions. The slightest mistake on my part and the entire group of holy men might face innumerable problems. I suppressed my curiosity and remained detached. Then in order to determine the appropriate course of action, I closed my eyes and began to concentrate on the Buddhist incantation.

Observing me meditate, the girl began talking. It did not seem to matter at all to her whether I understood or not; she continued in full spate. Sometimes, she would look up at me and then continue murmuring. She appeared to be disclosing her innermost thoughts. But God only knew what they were. Then, like one did before deities, she prostrated herself before me and gazed up at me. After a prolonged period of silence, she left the room. Gradually, her family members came in, one by one. I remained for a while before leaving for the bungalow where we had put up, accompanied all the way by the entire Dorje family. Guruji would probably be there and I had assumed that some sort of explanation would be forthcoming from him. He had not yet returned, however. Hence, I turned to bid a pleasant farewell to the entire Dorje family.

This was one of Tibet's high-altitude regions. Phari Jong lay nearly 15,000 feet above sea level. Tuna too, stood at almost the same height. Though the Khangma or Niyang valley, as it was also known, lay at a relatively lower altitude than either Darjeeling or Gangtok, it was still located at a great height. Had it not been for trade with India, these villages would have scarcely developed, for agriculture of any sort was virtually impossible in these climatic conditions. People in this area usually earned their living by herding cattle and, during the rather brief summer, cultivated a little barley and wheat, ruined, for the most part, by frost before they could be harvested.

I awoke at dawn the following day to find Mrs Dorje and her daughter waiting by the fire in the centre of the room. For no reason at all, my curiosity was kindled. Why had they turned up at this hour? Had they found something wanting in my behaviour the day before? As was my habit, I rolled up my blanket and rubbing the sleep out of my eyes, made my way to Guruji. He was still not up. I waited there till he woke up. In the meantime, no sooner had our eyes met than Mrs Dorje and her daughter greeted me in the customary manner. Instead of going up to them, I waited for Guruji. Noticing me waiting by his side, his first question was whether I had had a good night's sleep. I humbly informed him that a lady was waiting for him outside. He immediately went out to meet the visitors and I followed him. Mrs Dorje carried a large pot that had been kept all this while in the corner of the verandah and handed it over, saying that it contained tea for us all.

Tea once again and that too, so early in the morning! No sooner had the word been mentioned than I began feeling queasy again. Somehow, I managed to conquer the feeling. Inspired by the great esteem in which they held us, these poor people had brought us this gift. We ought to accord the gesture due respect. The Buddha would be pleased. After heating the tea, Guruji and I took our seats in front of Mrs Dorje. She pushed the burning-hot vessel towards us and announced, 'I have come to hear you speak.'

Guruji then made it clear that it was for me that the remark was intended. I then seized the opportunity of explaining to him at length all that had transpired the day before, right from the tea session to being secluded with the girl—everything. I also remembered to add that though I had wanted to, I could not understand a word of what the girl had said. Guruji listened silently to it all before addressing the duo in a quiet voice. The girl began chewing awkwardly on one end of her dress and exchanged occasional glances with me. After the conversation had come to an end, Guruji explained the entire matter to me. The Dorje family had been greatly honoured by my visit and charmed by my behaviour. In keeping with Tibetan tradition, when ascetics or holy men visited private homes, it was customary for young girls in the family to discuss various issues with them and seek their advice. They also begged forgiveness for any sins they might have committed. That was precisely what the eldest Dorje daughter had done despite her awareness that I did not understand a word of what she was saying.

We too, remained silent for a long time. Then I requested Guruji to say a few words, anything at all, on my behalf. He refused. How could any answer be given, he asked me, without knowing what the question was? Particularly in cases like these, one should conduct oneself with due seriousness and not behave like a child. I laughed to myself at that. Had he conducted himself with due seriousness in accepting me as his disciple? And what about the time he had instructed me to play the role of a monk sworn to silence? Of course, it was not my place to sit in judgement on him. Now my main duty was to solve the problem at hand.

Mrs Dorje and her daughter were waiting for a reply. They might not leave until they received one. What a dilemma to find oneself in—crushed between pangs of conscience and the experience of being a fraud! It was I who would have to reply, it seemed. Guruji was merely willing to act as interpreter. I gazed at the girl's innocent face; it did not seem fair to deceive her by feeding her just any old story. Perhaps, this too, was some sort of a test for me. Suddenly, an idea occurred to me and I asked Guruji to convey it to them. Looking at the girl, I said, 'Somem [that was her name], even if I could not understand a word of what you were saying, the Great, All-knowing Buddha understood. Depend on him and move forward in life; you will definitely be blessed. I give you my word that I will pray for you in the largest temple in Tibet.'

No sooner had Guruji conveyed my words to them in their language than they both prostrated themselves before me, their faces radiant with smiles.

ON THE ETERNAL PILGRIMAGE

THANKS TO SOREN Thape, we had been given the opportunity of recharging our batteries and had also come to know the villagers well. Along with four other distinguished citizens, Sorenji was both eager to extend every sort of help to us and in a position to give us sound advice, for they were all thoroughly familiar with the roads in the area.

So far, there had been no discussion with Guruji about the route we were to follow. All I knew was that we were going to

Tibet. And now, we had reached Tibet. Guruji shouldered the entire responsibility of deciding on our destination, the places where we would halt overnight and the kind of meals we were to eat. All we were required to do was move on. Hence, discussing these matters with the village authorities was an exciting prospect for me.

In the course of our conversation, I came to know for the first time that we were to go to Gyatse. Then travelling eastwards, we planned to reach Lhasa. If the lamas remained in good health and spirits there, we would return via Shigatse, a town that had grown along the banks of the Brahmaputra. From there, we would make our way to a new destination: Kailashnath and Mansarovar. Subsequently, we would embark on the return journey to India through Almora.

There was a direct route to Lhasa from Khangma that Guruji had planned to take. But Sorenji told him it was imperative for us to halt at Gyatse. A telegram had arrived from the police station there with instructions for us to report to the staff manning it.

In Tibet, a gumpha was evidently a holy place, just the way temples were in India. For years, pilgrims had been visiting the famous places of worship including the temples in Lhasa, Shigatse and Kailashnath. Though all were equally revered by the lamas, Kaliashnath, in particular, occupied a special place in their hearts. Even five years ago, Indians had been allowed free access to these sites, but it was becoming increasingly difficult now. The Han followed no religion at all and regarded their political leaders as their deities. Though they had not imposed any restrictions on pilgrims so far, no Indian, whether in the capacity of pilgrim or traveller, was permitted to enter the country.

The air had changed radically from the time we had arrived in Sikkim. After crossing the Nathu La pass, it had been chilly and humid. But from Tangla onwards, the breeze had died down completely and a dry, bitter cold pervaded the atmosphere. If we had not had a fire to warm ourselves by at night, it would have been impossible for us to come this far; we would have had to give up our quest there and then. Having taken a fortnight to cross the Himalayas, we had been in the kingdom of the snows all this while, surrounded by small valleys and mountain streams born from the melting snows. The heat of the sun took the edge off the chill for a while, but no sooner did evening descend than it crept back and invaded our surroundings again.

As we moved further north of Chumbi valley, we entered a terrain that was increasingly bound by snow. If there was human habitation on this route at all, it was entirely due to the existing trade relations between India and Tibet. The mountain stream that followed us ran further north and merged with the Brahmaputra. If one moved along the banks of this river, one would come to Gyatse. Since we had to travel through that town, we could not, even if we wanted to, avail of the shorter route from Khangma to Lhasa.

A number of people gave us sound advice about breaking up into smaller, inconspicuous groups instead of travelling in a large one that risked attracting attention. There was a Han post some distance away and the general feeling was that officials there might harass us needlessly. As we had come from India, they might even take us for spies disguised as lamas.

The second piece of advice we received involved avoiding the larger gumphas as far as possible. There were Han soldiers even in the temples of Gyatse and on sighting a foreigner, they were liable to ask a great many probing questions. Our goal was Lhasa and since we had permits to go there, we did not anticipate problems. The villagers there wanted us to linger awhile, but we felt it would be less risky for us to move on and cover as much of the distance as we could manage.

After spending three nights there, we were compelled to bid farewell to the villagers. Before we departed, several of them brought out huge containers of water to wash our feet. For their unfailing hospitality, we showered our heartfelt blessings on them. Having recited our group prayers, we set off once more with the villagers accompanying us part of the way. The Dorje family too, was with me as part of our entourage. For some reason, my eyes continually strayed to Somem. I felt as though I had given her nothing at all. Suddenly, I remembered having some extra prayer beads with me and, on an impulse, handed them to her as a parting gift.

THE PILGRIMS' FIRST OFFERING

AS WE PROGRESSED further the following morning, the mountains on either side appeared to be closing in on us. The Niyangchu river no longer seemed interminable. We finally reached a point where the entire Niyang valley, with the river coursing between the two mountains, had merged into a world veiled in mystery. Although the route to Nathu La had been an ascending one, unlike the path we were now traversing, it had been very similar in every other aspect.

With its serpentine curves, the great river appeared to flow into the nether world. Our curiosity piqued by our surroundings, we experienced a sudden spurt of interest in all that lay before us. The azure expanse of sky overhead and the mountains flanking us on both sides seemed to be bound by a continuous wall running along the river at a height of at least 3,000 feet. This was the terrifying course the Niyangchu river had forged for itself after waging a millennia-long battle with the obstacles in its path. We were awestruck by the impact of its turbulent beauty and it took us a while to recover from our daze and pay our respects to it. The river with all its pent-up force leaped off a sheer cliff and crashed down below, splintering from the impact into a sea of white foam and branching off, eventually, into a myriad streams. Struck by the rays of the sun, countless little rainbows sprang up, arching over the watercourses that fanned out. It was as though innumerable beautiful nymphs serenaded some unseen god. Ancient images of the Buddha in shades of red, blue, yellow and green had been carved out of the mountainside. Of them, the main one was that of Padma Sambhava. Etched into the rocks were the words, 'Those who move on without showing me due respect are doomed.' Understandably, it was a mandatory halting point for all pilgrims, the first place, in fact, where they paused for prayers on the way to Kailashnath.

Padma Sambhava, another manifestation of Lord Buddha, could be called the child god of Tibet. His image was to be found in nearly every Tibetan gumpha, however minor. He had actually been a Kashmiri pundit, invited by the king of Tibet to propagate the Buddhist faith and popularize it in the country. One could well claim that it was he who had been primarily responsible for establishing Buddhism in Tibet and had introduced elements of the occult into the faith. Having grown aware of the depth of his knowledge and of his keen insight into the occult sciences, the Tibetans had humbly bowed to his will. In certain monasteries and temples of Tibet, Padma Sambhava occupied a position superior even to that of the Buddha. The common man in Tibet knew him as Guru Rimpoche. He was also known as Padmasan Baba to a great many pilgrims going to Kailashnath from Sikkim or Bhutan.

Padma Sambhava had divine powers. Owing to his prowess in occult practices, he was regarded as the supreme authority in that domain. It was on his advice that King Tri-Sron-De-San of Tibet had established the country's most important vihara and chaitya towards the end of the seventh century.The rockface bore several other images besides that of Padma Sambhava. Those representing Dhyanibuddha, Manjushree and Abalokiteswara depicted them all in meditative postures. There was nothing comparable anywhere else in the world. Our gaze fell on a row of chaityas beside it. The road ran ahead and right beside it was this beautiful pilgrimage spot, Niyangchu-chorten, so named because of the chaitya and the stream in its vicinity.

We discovered another small gumpha or, rather, what looked like the ruins of an ancient temple. We put our belongings there and prepared for worship. We would be halting there for an hour, Guruji informed us. This meant that by the time we got through our worship and the attendant rituals and finished cooking and eating our meal before setting out again, it would be evening. The Buddha had three principal manifestations: the Dhyani (Meditative) Buddha, the Dhyani Bodhisattva and the Manasi Buddha, known in Tibetan as O-Pa-Me, Chenreji and Shakya Thoop respectively. In Sanskrit, they were known as Amitabha, Abalokiteswara and Shakyamuni. In Tibet, all viharas and monasteries were divided into these separate categories, not accounting for the several other branches besides. The Panchen Lama, for instance, was known as the Amitabha Buddha, while the Dalai Lama was a form of Abalokiteswara, his local name being Chenreji. We planned to meet both the Panchen Lama and the Dalai Lama before moving on to Kailashnath.

The Lord had said, 'It is the body which is primarily responsible for all sorrow; the mind merely finds an expression. Underlying every sorrow is its foundation—a reason. If sorrow is to be eliminated, the reason underlying it must be destroyed as well.'

We had traversed the remote and inaccessible Himalayas and reached the roof of the world—Tibet. Nowhere else could we have breathed air more unpolluted nor trod on soil so sacred. Though we did find the extreme cold hard to bear, nowhere in the world could we have enjoyed the luxury of this serene, unbroken silence. In this holy land, I would have to meditate and discover whether any kind of sorrow afflicted me, and if so, what lay behind it. Was this sorrow supernatural, divine or intellectual? Think, meditate with all your soul, I urged myself. If you truly want to delve deeper, Padma Sambhava himself will appear and extend a helping hand.

The erudition of the lamas was so impressive that they could well have been described as philosophers. All this while, Guruji had been playing the role of a guide. But this morning, he had assumed the mantle of our mentor. Ensuring that everybody was seated on the riverbank, he explained briefly what needed to be done. The heat of the sun was gradually intensifying. Close to the river, we had discovered a warm-water stream; and almost at the river's edge was a kind of well in which water had accumulated. Dipping my hand into it, I was astonished to discover that even in this extreme cold, the water could be warm; its temperature was at least a couple of degrees higher than that of the human body. It was as though someone with our needs in mind had provided it for us. But before thinking of a wash, we sank deep into meditation.

Once the session was over an hour or so later, we stripped completely and dived into the lake. Nearly a month and a half had gone by since I had last poured water over my body. The feeling was one of sheer bliss. I could scarcely imagine that here we were, in the land of the snows, surrounded by snow and ice, and yet, we were bathing without a stitch on us! Guruji urged us to bear in mind that another opportunity to bathe might not come by very easily.

Gyatse, also popularly known as Gyanse or Gyachhe, was not

far away. While moving along the mountain path, Guruji suddenly asked us to halt and reminded us that we would soon be approaching Gyatse. The Han post would have to be crossed and we should prepare ourselves for the exercise in patience that lay ahead. We should all pray to the Almighty for help to get us through this last barrier successfully.

Guruji's words were a source of great strength and reassurance for us. In a short while, we would be entering Gyatse, one of Tibet's most culturally rich cities. Since ancient times, it had been among the three Tibetan cities renowned for their art and commerce. It occupied third place after Lhasa, the country's capital, and Shigatse. The revered Dalai Lama came from Tibet. The Panchen Lama, a manifestation of Shakya, lived in Shigatse, and Gyatse, famous for its Buddhist antecedents, was an extremely popular pilgrimage centre. After we had crossed the barrier of mountains, our eyes were drawn to a spot at their foot. It seemed to us as though gold from the heavens had suddenly spilled over on to this patch of level land. This, then, was Gyatse! The rays of the morning sun glanced off the golden roofs of the city. From our vantage point at a far greater height, the place appeared simply magical, like a dream.

Guruji explained to us how Gyatse was neatly divided into two sections. From where we stood, we could see innumerable houses with paths and roads between them. This constituted one quarter. It was the second one, enclosed within high, protective walls, that we were heading for. It housed the holy temple and various other religious edifices. The largest golden roof visible from where we stood belonged to the main temple. It was, as Guruji observed, an immortal creation inspired by the Buddhist faith and an outstanding example of authentic Tibetan architecture.

Then it was time for us to descend. We reached the gates of the city within half an hour. To our right lay several shanties. Behind them stood gypsy tents. A number of yaks and donkeys explored the adjacent field in search of grass. Apart from being quite a large group of people, we were dressed in the colourful robes of lamas. That was bound to attract attention. The sight of us brought the yaks to an abrupt halt. Some sheep bleated out a noisy welcome in their own language. But the most vociferous greeting came from the guard dogs that charged at us, forcing us to stop in our tracks. As was typical of them, these dogs did not attack if we remained perfectly still. They usually left us alone and went their way after a while.

What a welcome, right after entering the city! This seemed more like an ill omen to me. The loud barking of the dogs had drawn people out and they began to gather around us. As was customary, they greeted us with a prominent display of their tongues. After crossing some shanties, we entered the main city. Flanking the road on either side were houses made of brick, mortar and clay that belonged, evidently, to Gyatse's affluent residents. There were wayside tea stalls and stalls selling snacks. The shops with woollens and groceries on sale appeared to be doing well too. We also spotted a meat shop in an alley. All the houses here had roofs rather similar to the ones back in India.

The road meandered through the centre of the market. We stopped at a large tea stall located towards the peripheries of the market. Unlike our Indian pilgrimage centres, Gaya and Puri, where aggressive touts virtually fell upon visitors in their eagerness to offer their assistance for a price, nobody here disturbed us in any way. Outside the tea shop, two young women concentrated on mixing butter with tea. At large tea stalls like this one, it was the practice to employ people exclusively for this purpose. We entered and each of us had a glass of tea for which we paid. This city resembled a small Indian town, but for the fact that there was no traffic. We had already come across a few Indians on the road. They had greeted us and moved on. The road was paved with stones, not bricks, tar or cement. Suddenly, we were intercepted by three Han soldiers accompanied by a local Tibetan guard. After greeting us, they asked, 'Where are you coming from?'

'From Nepal,' we replied.

'Have you come via Sikkim?'

'That's right, via Gangtok, Pema Chowki and Phari Jong,' Guruji explained to them.

The Tibetan guard explained the situation in turn to the Han soldiers. It was very easy to distinguish between the Han and Tibetan army staff. The former sported a kind of khaki uniform, just like their Indian counterparts. They wore full-length trousers with a shirt, a jacket, belt boots and a cap. They also carried a gun. The Tibetans, on the other hand, wore a capacious garment with loose-fitting trousers. Over it went a very bulky pullover. The overall effect was so heavy and constricting, one wondered how they could possibly break into a run, if the need arose. The Han soldiers were far shrewder. Much shorter than the Tibetans, their complexions had a yellowish cast to them.

They asked us to follow them. It went without saying that another bout of police interrogation was in store. This was probably the last time we would have to contend with such a problem. Once we had left Gyatse, we would have nothing more to fear. Taking another road, we reached the outskirts of the city. There we noticed temporary structures fashioned from wood and tin and row upon row of tents housing soldiers.

We were led to the tent occupied by the post's seniormost officer. It stood in the middle of a large field where a military parade was in progress. A temporary headquarters had been set up beside the tent by laying out a table and a chair. As we approached, our eyes were drawn to a short, rotund man who looked like a miniature soldier. When we were quite close, the soldiers saluted him and we realized that this person was the highest authority in the area. The man approached and greeting us with a smile, asked, 'Which of you is the leader?' He had asked the question in Tibetan and it was obvious that he knew the language well.

Taking out our papers, Guruji replied, 'I am their guide. We have all come from Kathmandu's Swayambhunath Gumpha. To avail of the shorter route, we have come via Sikkim. We are going on a pilgrimage and plan to return as soon as we possibly can.' Guruji informed him of our intentions as clearly and concisely as possible.

The man carefully scrutinized the papers and asked in a grave voice, 'The paper mentions fifty people ... where are the rest?'

'They didn't come.'

'Why not?'

'The extreme cold finally deterred them from accompanying us.'

'Hmm... Have any of you ever been here before?'

'I alone am familiar with the route. I have led pilgrims here a number of times in the past. It is the first time for the rest of them.'

'Hmm... What are you carrying with you?'

'A little food and some extra clothing.'

Having heard Guruji out, the man called out to someone. Immediately, the soldier presented himself, his gestures as mechanical as a puppet's. Then following his master's commands, he began rummaging through our luggage. Needless to say, he failed to find anything incriminating and was forced to let us go.

Though he cast several suspicious glances my way, the man did not ask me any questions. The fact that I was so young could well have prompted him to let me go. After almost an hour's walk, we came to our destination and entered the blessed land.

Encircled by boundary walls was a palatial temple standing in grounds that also accommodated several other temples of different sizes. The moment we entered the compound, we saw a small chaitya and put down our luggage there. At the sight of our group, some young lamas came running and began talking to Guruji who informed them that we were pilgrims. They went off right away and within fifteen minutes or so, the news had reached everyone. Two elderly lamas approached us and greeted us respectfully. They asked us how long we expected to stay and where we intended going subsequently. After introductions had been made, they said, 'Please follow us so that you can be introduced to our head lama. He is the highest authority here.'

After passing numerous places of worship, we were finally brought to a large temple. The lamas asked us to wait there and one of them suggested, 'Do feel free to have a look around while I check whether Thampo is available or not.'

The second lama remained with us.

Having explored the place for the third time, we sat down. We gazed in wonder at the colourful temples that dotted this sanctified area, enclosed from all sides. The lama returned, panting from his exertions. Accompanying him were three more lamas. The gentleman informed us that the head lama, the Revered Thampo, was waiting for us in his room. Some distance from the main temple stood a large, imposing white house. Along its length ran beautifully carved wooden balconies painted in bright shades of red and yellow. Around the doors and windows were etchings in yellow and red. The stairs we climbed led to a large hall. In one corner, on a wooden couch, sat Thampo, the head of the monastery, along with some other lamas. He rose to greet us cordially and with great warmth asked us to be seated. Guruji conveyed to him the messages from Swayambhunath Gumpha and the king of Sikkim. Thampo assured us that he would make all arrangements for our accommodation and meals for a couple of days. We needn't worry at all. Then he asked to be introduced to all the lamas, one by one.

Guruji spoke of me. 'He is my disciple,' he said. 'For the duration of the pilgrimage, he is bound by the vow of silence. After the pilgrimage is over, he will become a full-fledged lama. For now, he has been initiated into the difficult trapa mode.'

The Revered Thampo paid close attention to Guruji's words. Then sending a searching glance my way, he commented, 'He does not look like a Nepalese. Well, perhaps, his parents are Indian. Of course, there isn't much of a difference between the north Indians and the Nepalese. It's only because he is so young … or else, escaping detection by the Han would have been extremely tough. They detest Indians.'

'You are right,' Guruji conceded. 'We had to go through intensive grilling at the post. It was simply because he was a pilgrim and such a young one at that, that they did not stop him.'

Thampo blessed me. 'Be a good human being,' he exhorted. 'May the Buddha protect you.' Finally, entrusting a fellow lama with the responsibility of looking after us, he announced, 'We will meet at the temple again this evening.'

We were put up at the guest house there and arrangements were made for us to have our meals with the lamas. That day, the lamas and trapas were asked to congregate and we were introduced to them all. Since I was the youngest member of our group, all attention was naturally focused on me. Everyone was amazed that despite the arduous journey we had undertaken all the way from Sikkim, I was not yet exhausted. After introductions were over, we entered the dining hall. There, everybody surrounded Guruji and began to flood him with innumerable questions about me. Which sect did I belong to, they wanted to know. Since when had I been part of the monastery? How had he chosen me for the pilgrimage? Which level of spiritualism had I attained? Did I have any special characteristics that distinguished me from others, and so on.

The following day, I woke up before dawn. I could barely contain my eagerness to explore this sacred city thoroughly by daylight. I looked out through the small window of the dharamsala. It was not yet light. I would have to curb my impatience for a little while more. I was really keen on watching the sunrise. So, after tossing and turning for a while, I got out of bed. I glanced out of the window again; this time, the view was far more distinct. There was nothing further to hold me back. Wrapping my blanket around me like a shawl, I set off. As I was also in the garb of a lama, there was nothing about me to attract unwarranted attention. Almost as soon as I had stepped out, I came across a lama. The man approached and raising his hands in respectful greeting, asked, 'Where are you headed?'

I smiled and replied, 'Kumbum.' That was only because no other name had come to mind.

The lama led me in that direction. I had planned on moving about alone in the silence of dawn, enjoying the tranquillity of my surroundings and admiring the scarlet with which the rising sun splashed the sky. But that was not to be, for the lama just refused to leave me alone. We went and stood by the Kumbum Chaitya. I have no idea what I would have done if he had not been with me, but in his presence, I was compelled to enact the role of a genuine lama. Had I not, there would have been much talk. It was so bitterly cold that I almost froze. I prostrated myself on the ground and offered my salutations nonetheless. Then I moved towards the prayer circle. Rotating the prayer wheels as I went, I began to circumambulate the temple.

After completing seven rounds, I moved in the direction of the main door. The lama accompanied me like a devotee. He was, in all likelihood, a guard, because his appearance suggested that he had been up all night. He had a very charming smile, nonetheless. On reaching the main door, I found it locked. But the two small doors at the side were not and at least a dozen dogs lay sleeping just outside them.

The sky had lightened a great deal. From the other side of the boundary wall, I could hear a cock crow. But the sun kept out of sight and the sky failed to acquire that golden tinge I was so familiar with. I was disheartened. Moving alongside the boundary wall, I suddenly caught sight of the sunrise. True, it was not quite as spectacular as the one I had seen from Darjeeling's Tiger Hill, but standing on the roof of the world and witnessing the advent of the Sun God was a different experience altogether. Soon after the sun had risen, the silvery light began playing on the snowy peaks. I joined my palms together and reverently offered my heartfelt salutations.

I then proceeded to complete the appropriate yogic exercises. The lama continued to observe me respectfully. A steady descent brought us back to the place where we had been put up. I found that everyone was nearly on the verge of leaving. Swiftly, I put away my blanket. I did not have to explain the purpose of my brief excursion to Guruji—the lama did the needful. Guruji announced, 'This morning, everybody at the Gyatse Monastery and the Vihara Samiti will be felicitating us. We have to be there.'

Within the same boundary walls stood the sanctified monastery where all the resident lamas stayed. There were no Buddhist nuns on the premises. Some women devotees would be coming from the city and the chairman of the Gyatse Corporation would also be there to welcome us.

We reached a big wooden bungalow and went up to its veranda where we proceeded to wait. The veranda looked on to a large field where people were beginning to congregate. In a short while, we were joined by a group of musicians in colourful attire. They were dressed in the garb of lamas and wore tall hats and intricately embroidered woollen shoes that looked like long stockings. They blew on some conch-like instruments and played a variety of tunes on their pipes for nearly a quarter of an hour. All the local people gathered in a crowd behind the lamas. On the veranda stood a huge throne-like chair where the Revered Khampo took his seat.

An instrument rather like the shehnai was played to welcome the pilgrims. When the music had died down, we were introduced to the general public by the Revered Khampo. Then the chairman of the Gyatse Corporation shook hands with us and warmly welcomed us. At the end of the prayer session, all the trapas and lamas came up individually to greet us. This continued for almost an hour. The greetings that the lamas extended will live forever in my memory. I was utterly charmed by their spiritual largesse and eternally smiling faces. Moreover, the fact that so many people lived within the boundary walls of this city was truly remarkable.

Then the local public began showering their devotion and greetings on us. Almost everybody prostrated themselves before us and all wanted to have at least a glimpse of us.

The closing item was another round of music played by the temple orchestra, after which its members departed. The session ended with our expressing heartfelt thanks to the Revered Khampo and offering communal prayers in his presence. The whole event had covered nearly two-and-a-half hours.

From a distance, the Kumbum Chaitya resembled a temple. In fact, it looked like Kathmandu's Swayambhunath Temple with the Buddha's two eyes painted near the top. Within the stupa lay the interred remains of the late monk, the Revered Dorje Chang. If correctly translated, 'Kumbum' means 'the temple of a hundred images'. The basic foundation was one hundred and eight cubits long and just as wide. The upper segment was painted a deep yellow; white was the predominant shade in the lower portion which was multicoloured. There were prayer wheels everywhere, of course, as well as a great number of images. The walls were decorated with images carved in stone, rather like that at the Sun Temple in Konark. In spite of so many images decorating its surface, the contours of the stupa remained flawlessly symmetrical.

On top of the dais were the eternal Meditating Buddha and images symbolizing the six senses. The Kumbum Monastery was a four-storeyed architectural marvel containing seventy-four temples where the devotee and his devotion had become one, and the world, as we knew it, had transcended to a different level. Rejecting the different points of view that existed, Lord Tathagata had established a dream temple on a higher plane than the material world where those very differences held sway. The reason underlying human sorrow and misery was beautifully depicted through the representations of the various deities.

In Gyatse—a veritable kingdom of temples—everything appeared sacred. From morning to evening, the trapas could be seen going back and forth. Theirs was the predominant presence in this sector of the city. As there were no schools, parents had no option but to send their children to the monastery for their education. There, heads tonsured and clad in saffron robes, they were imparted religious instruction. Later, these young trapas would become lamas. And from among the latter would be chosen the venerated leaders of the country. They were the ones who later entered society in the domain of trade, commerce, religion, politics or the arts.

Girls were not quite so fortunate, however. Not all monasteries had arrangements for women's education. The women picked up a little learning from their guardians and had to be content with that. Putting the little that they imbibed to good use, they went about managing shops, buying and selling goods or tending to agriculture. A visit to the market would have given the impression that it was the women who managed the kingdom and everything pertaining to the material world, while the men merely turned into ascetics and wandered from place to place.

On our second day there, something else caught my appreciative gaze. I noticed that the lamas used shawls of no more than two or three different colours and wore hats that covered their ears. Initially, I had presumed that either the unavailability of colours or an aversion to a combination of too many had resulted in this choice. A shade of fawn was visible everywhere. Careful observation revealed, however, that this shade contained traces of red, yellow and saffron. On delving deeper, I discovered that it all came down to a matter of different sects. Here, three divisions had merged to form one. The first was the Geluk-Pa, headed by the Dalai Lama, the second, the Shakya sect of which the Panchen Lama was the chief. The third was the Sa-Lu sect which had no predetermined guru, but was guided by certain ideals.

In Gyatse, each of these different sects had a religious leader and a business and commercial head. The Revered Khampo, the appointed representative from Lhasa, was the religious leader of Gyatse and supervised and controlled all activities from his position of authority. He was far better known and held greater administrative powers than the municipal representative who was the commercial and business head. But according to many, since the advent of the Chinese, the power of the Chairman was increasing by leaps and bounds.

We stayed in the guest house and had our meals with the different sects. Accommodation for the lamas was to be found in the city's upper section. The thirty-two members of our group were scattered throughout the city. We went wherever and whenever we pleased; we were all totally independent. Guruji had given us complete freedom. I had to be a little careful, however, because among the eight hundred sages here, I was the solitary member sworn to a vow of silence. Everybody focused his attention on me. Silence was the best and most difficult path—and it was the one I had chosen. The tiniest lapse on my part, the slightest familiarity with my fellow lamas or too great a sense of ease in the company of others could lead me to relax my guard and inadvertently blurt out a response. That would not only bring dishonour on our group, but would also cause our pilgrimage to come to an abrupt halt.

The ambience of the city within the boundary walls was perennially solemn. The atmosphere was pure and unsullied, utterly devoid of levity. The ancient market at Gyatse, on the other hand, was a busy one and seemed to represent another world altogether. From morn till night, it resounded with the hustle and bustle of commerce and overflowed with the sounds of jollity and laughter. Everything was available at this strange market—from old toothpaste and frayed pairs of used socks to ivory tusks and Chinese dragons. There was also an Indian tea stall and light Indian snacks were on sale. Everything was available, so to speak, but none of it was fresh, not even the vegetables on offer.

MEDITATION ON THE ARYA TARA

ON OUR SECOND night there, we were savouring the silence in the hall when a trapa came up to Guruji and announced, 'The Revered Khampo would like to see you.'

Guruji followed him out. We remained seated. The hall was generally used either as a meditation chamber for lamas or for various religious programmes. Innumerable *thangkas* adorned the walls. The etchings in wood largely featured dragons and on the dais were countless images of deities, both male and female. The lamp fuelled by ghee burned continuously, but the light cast by it was so dim that it was virtually impossible to see anything at all. As in other temples throughout Tibet, the hall was devoid of windows and within its confines, day was almost indistinguishable from night. By the weak light filtering in through the door during the day, the artwork that lent the room its beauty could barely be discerned.

Guruji returned almost an hour later, looking rather perturbed. He seated himself in the centre of the hall and spoke of the new problem that now confronted us. Though Tibet was ostensibly an independent kingdom, it was the Han who policed its borders and administered its foreign affairs. The Han military force in Gyatse monitored all matters pertaining to foreigners. Well before we reached Gyatse, they had interrogated us. It seemed that one of their representatives had arrived to see the Revered Khampo with a batch of fresh directives. Firstly, the pilgrims would not be permitted to remain in Gyatse for more than a week. Secondly, if any religious programme were to be organized in the city, prior permission would have to be obtained from the military chief. Thirdly, only groups of three would be allowed to travel to Lhasa at a time. While the first two injunctions did not pose a problem, the third threw us into a quandary. What it amounted to, basically, was that we could not travel together as a group.

We had planned to stay for three days and set out very early on the morning of the fourth. But now that the Han had started taking an unhealthy interest in us, it was best to move on as soon as we could. Looking at me, Guruji said, 'I understand your desire to accompany me. But that will not be possible, because Khampo asks that you remain behind for a few days more.'

The question of my raising any sort of objection did not arise. Guruji would be the first to leave Gyatse; I would be the last. Needless to say, this time, I would be entirely on my own.

That very night, Guruji divided us into separate groups and explained the route we would be taking. He would set off first. We would follow at intervals of one-and-a-half hours or so. The very next day, sixteen lamas would set out and the day after, sixteen more would follow.

In this monastery, everybody was summoned for meals twice a day: once around 10.30 a.m. and the second time around 4.30 p.m. The concept of early morning and late evening meals did not exist. Our food consisted of rice, lentils and mixed vegetables of some kind. As soon as our meal was over, we bade Guruji farewell. All the senior lamas of the monastery offered prayers to ensure his safe journey.

About half an hour after Guruji had departed, the Revered Khampo sent for me. He invited me to take a seat next to him and having offered him my respectful salutations, I did so. In the meantime, I had picked up some Tibetan and could understand a little of the language, but could not speak it at all. I was startled when Khampo addressed me by my name; since we had left Gangtok, no one had called me by that name. I gazed at him in wonder. Could he be omniscient? Khampoji addressed me by my name once more and began speaking in fluent Hindi. 'Listen to me, Bimal,' he began, 'I know everything about you. I am impressed by the manner in which you have managed to make your way here from Gaya. I salute the courage and powers of endurance you have displayed. You may talk to me quite freely.'

Bashful, I touched his feet in a gesture of respect and murmured, 'Please forgive me.'

All of a sudden, I felt humbled in the presence of this towering personality. I could not decide what precisely I should say to him. Khampoji himself eased the situation for me by volunteering, 'I have been to Gaya thrice and have stayed in Sarnath for ten years. I am acquainted with a great many people in Kolkata. Since you have managed to come so far, there is no reason for you to worry; Lord Tathagata will protect you.' He then called out loudly for a lama and asked him to fetch two cups of tea. I had imagined that senior lamas who had renounced everything even abstained from drinking tea. In a short while, steaming hot tea arrived in two glasses and was served with some salty biscuits.

While we sipped our tea, Khampo outlined his plans to me. Although I was in the company of Nepalese lamas, several people in Gyatse apparently suspected that I was Indian. They found it difficult to accept my assumed identity as a Nepalese lama. For his part, Khampo thought very highly of Indians. He had, therefore, decided that the two days I remained in Gyatse would provide me with a good opportunity to learn something of worth. It would not do to while away the time merely gazing at temples and lamas. In Gyatse, arrangements were available for initiation at various levels. Khampo would teach me one useful process.

'Are you familiar with any Sanskrit incantation?' he asked.

'Certainly,' I answered.

'Which one?'

Having spent much time with ascetics and holy men, I was familiar with a large number of incantations, including the powerful Gayatri mantra.

Khampo was amazed at that. 'Really!' he exclaimed. 'Are you a Brahmin? Have you gone through the sacred thread ceremony?'

'No, sir, I haven't,' I replied. 'And nor am I a Brahmin. The mere fact of being a man entitles one to transcend this plane and attain a higher one; the Gayatri mantra is merely a step in that direction. I do not believe in the caste system. That divinity is inherent in man is the only reality I accept.'

'I am glad to hear you say so. That is as it should be. Let's hear you chant the incantation aloud, then.'

I complied by taking up my position and beginning to speak. After a while, Khampoji asked me to stop. He seemed very pleased. Once again, he loudly called out to the lama who had brought in the tea. The man was given some instructions. Khampoji then started talking to me about Kolkata. In his opinion, the city was simply fascinating. What amazed him most were the trams. He had apparently seated himself beside the driver and carefully observed how such a vehicle was operated. That the movements of a tiny wheel could actually propel so many people along the street! The more he thought about it, the more awestruck he became.

Listening to him, I asked, 'You do know that trams are operated by electricity?'

He laughed with the infectious spontaneity of a child. 'Oh, yes!' he exclaimed. 'That is precisely what astounds me the most! The fact that so much power can be transmitted through those thin wires seems unimaginable!'

Our conversation came to a halt as we noticed a lama at the door. Suddenly, Khampo turned grave. He called the lama and introduced me to him: 'This is the second chief lama of the Geluk-Pa sect. He has been to Darjeeling and Kalimpong and has also stayed in Sarnath. You will spend two days with him during which he will teach you certain things.'

I bowed down to touch the lama's feet as a mark of respect. It would have been nice to spend more time talking to Khampoji, but that was not to be. The very fact that he had made time to talk to me and had done so spontaneously despite his busy schedule had placed me eternally in his debt. Of course, I refrained from putting my feelings into words.

After respectfully taking my leave, I accompanied Therepa, the other lama, to wherever he was taking me. He was probably between forty and fifty years old. Though not particularly cheerful, his expression wasn't sombre either. He spoke in a blend of Hindi and Tibetan-influenced Nepalese, but I had no problem following him.

We entered an ancient temple with cold, dank interiors. Therepa lit a lamp and asked me to wait. In the dim light, I could make out several images of deities, both male and female. In alcoves stood row upon row of Tibetan books. Therepa arrived a while later carrying a pair of thick blankets. Thick blankets had been piled too, on top of some wooden planks in the corner. We seated ourselves on them, side by side. Now, I wrapped myself in the blanket I had been handed, covering my head and body. Although this temple had quite a large door, it might as well not have been there, for the boundary wall of another temple stood right in front of it. It blocked the view totally and any sunlight that might have penetrated remained a distant dream. Leaving the warmth of the beautiful sunlight outside, we entered a dark cavern.

Lama Therepa addressed me: 'Now, we will meditate on the Goddess Tara.'

My heart leapt with joy; the Goddess Tara was another incarnation of the Goddess Kali; what harm could come from choosing her as the focus of our meditation? From childhood, I had been familiar with the Kali temple in my locality and approved of Lama Therepa's words. Unable, however, to suppress my anxiety, I asked, 'You are Buddhists, aren't you? So, how is it that the Goddess Tara finds a place in your temple?'

'We are Buddhists who practise the occult sciences. Later, if there is time, I will explain it all to you. Now, let us meditate.

'The common man lay all responsibility for his present and future at the feet of deities. Lamas, on the other hand, had to ascend from one plane of existence to the next through their own efforts and the exercise of will power, overcoming all impediments on the way. In order to sever ties with the material world, it was necessary to attain nirvana.'

'I have heard of nirvana innumerable times,' I observed, 'Would you care to explain it to me?'

'Certainly,' Therepa replied. Then, translating a verse, he began, 'Lamas like us reside in a world that exists on a level completely distinct from the one containing this temple, sky, path, mountains and the people you observe around you. Instead of calling it a state of mind, we prefer to say that we transcend to another world by divesting ourselves of every remnant of ego. There, the world as we know it does not exist. That other plane is devoid of water and atmosphere, for the need to breathe is irrelevant. There, the stars do not cast any light; there is neither sun nor moon; darkness too, is denied entry. It is a world of eternity that transcends beauty and ugliness, happiness and sorrow, time and place. It is a world that is immortal.'

Lama Therepa lapsed into silence and closed his eyes in a bid, perhaps, to grasp the essence of that world mentally. After a long while, he opened his eyes again and asked, 'What mantra or hymn are you familiar with?'

Feigning incomprehension, I remained silent. I do not know what message was conveyed, but he changed the subject. 'You will have to sit here quietly and gaze at Ma Tara,' he told me. 'Remain sitting there and do not rise till I return.' The lama then rose to his feet and left.

In compliance with his instructions, I remained sitting there. I gazed at Ma Tara, but my mind kept returning to the various manifestations of Lord Buddha. Nearly half an hour later—or could it be an hour?—the lama returned and asked me, 'Is it a problem for you to sit in silence?'

'No, sir,' I replied, 'it isn't.'

He sat beside me and began to speak. 'You are aware,' he observed, 'that there is great similarity between Mahayana Buddhism and Hinduism. It is not just Ma Tara who is a reincarnation of the Hindu goddess Kali. Even our Prajnaparamita is compared to the Hindu goddess Saraswati. The Buddhists have Arati, while the Hindus have Aditi; another form of power wielded by the Buddha is Tara. Shiva and Manjushree, Indra and Bodhisattva Vajrapani are the same. No matter how we do so, to attain salvation or nirvana is our prime goal.'

'You know a great deal about Hinduism!' I remarked.

'Oh, no!' he replied, 'I know nothing about Hinduism. But to understand Buddhism, we have had to study it all. I will tell you certain things about Ma Tara. Listen carefully. As in Hinduism, where Shiva's strength is Uma, Kali or Parvati, Ma Tara is the strength of Lord Abalokiteswara in the Buddhist faith. Before aspiring to the divine, one has to attain the strength it demands to move to the ultimate state of being. Ma Tara assures her devotees of true freedom, the resolution of all problems and the circumvention of every peril. The Tibetan Ma Tara has two forms, of which one is green and the other white.' Here, the lama paused, probably giving me time to digest all that he had said. Then he resumed his explanations. 'We will now concentrate on the Green Tara. For ordinary men like us, it takes a very long time to attain enlightenment and demands great patience and innumerable prayers on our part. Before worshipping the Lord, one has to meditate on his various manifestations. Close your eyes. I will talk to you about him. And you will try and visualize him.'

'All right.' I shifted about a little, wrapping the blanket a bit more firmly around myself.

Lama Therepa looked at me and resumed speaking. 'Think of the sky,' he said, 'just the sky. It has no colour; it is merely a vast expanse of space, devoid of moon or sun, light or darkness. Now, imagine the growing presence of a green mountain in that mighty space. It is an incandescent green; try and hold on to that colour. It gradually builds up to take on the image of a woman. That is the image of our Bhagavati Tara. Now, open your eyes and find her facing you, this gentle and protective goddess, Ma Tara.'

Following the lama's instructions, I carefully looked at the image of the goddess in the lamplight. Then I closed my eyes and heard him speak again. 'Once more, use your imagination and try mentally conjuring up the goddess as I am describing her to you— resplendent, gloriously clad and bejewelled. Focus your mind totally on her and meditate.'

Unblinking, I stared at the reassuring Goddess Tara. After a prolonged period of meditation, it seemed to me that she was slowly disappearing from view. In spite of my desperate efforts to do so, I could not hold on to her form, even in my imagination. My entire body shivered violently from the cold. We prostrated

ourselves before the goddess and emerged from the temple to find
that it had, indeed, turned bitterly cold.

'Will you be sleeping here tonight or with your companions?'
he asked me.

'I have been with them and will continue to be with them for
a very long time.' I replied. 'But, perhaps, I will never ever get an
opportunity to be with you all again. With your permission, I wish
to sleep here.'

'You are so right! You can sleep here, if that is what you want.
Two or three others sleep here too and as the stove burns through
the night, the room is always warm and you should have no
problems.'

After spending some more time with me, Lama Therepa left.
I had presumed I would be spending the night in his company, but
it was not to be. I remained behind in the kitchen. Instead of
joining the other lamas for the night, it would be a different
experience altogether if I slept here beside the oven. So, I returned
to the dharamsala to inform my fellow lamas about my intentions
and to take leave of them.

Both Lama Therepa and sunrise arrived almost simultaneously.
Meanwhile, I had already drunk two cups of tea and was wide
awake. Lama Therepa had been entrusted with the responsibility of
overseeing my spiritual growth. I asked the lama to thank the
Tibetans for the tea. He feigned surprise and said, 'If you have
already had the tea, they will naturally have to be thanked. I had
planned a meditation session on the goddess on an empty stomach;
but the oversight is mine; I should have forewarned you.'

We set out and after circumambulating the main stupa seven
times, came to the last one. There, I was asked to carefully study
the images carved on it. After a while, we left the Kumbum stupa
behind us and took a descending path. Therepa reflected for a
while before saying, 'That temple was isolated, but dank. Let us go
to the Maitreyee Temple.'

We walked down to an ancient temple with beautiful etchings.
The lama explained to me that Maitreyee was the Future Buddha.
This would be followed by Manasi Buddha and Shakyamuni
Bodhisattva. The last manifestation of the Buddha had appeared
before Ashangamuni and had been offered many insights into the
mysteries of the occult. We were certainly going there, but our
focus would be on the goddess. All the forms of Buddhism

received equal recognition; it was simply the focus and the method of meditation that varied in each case.

Entering the temple, we took our seats on a dais near the door. Without wasting time on introductions, the lama came straight to the point: 'Now, close your eyes. Say to yourself:

O Goddess, be merciful and allow me to open my heart.
Ma Tara, free me from superstition;
Ma Tara, free me from fear;
Ma Tara, free me from maladies.
O Goddess, I seek shelter at your feet; I surrender myself to your will; I surrender myself to the sangha and the monastery.'

After an hour's postprandial rest, we were back at the Maitreyee Temple. Before sitting down to our meditation session, the lama said to me, 'You are young and need not, therefore, rigidly adhere to some of the more painful norms of meditation.'

'What are these painful measures?' I inquired.

'They seem simple, initially. But the higher you ascend, the more difficult it becomes to abide by the stipulated norms. For example, the first few are as follows: One must abstain from telling untruths, drinking alcohol, indulging in promiscuity, carrying out abductions and taking life, whatever be its form. The second level of strictures stipulates that one should abstain from eating untimely meals, sleeping on a comfortable bed and using perfume and garlands, that one should suppress all desire for dancing and music and refrain from accepting gold or any form of money. These constitute the most common pitfalls of the average man.

'Now, stand up, then sit back on your heels and pay obeisance to the goddess by touching your forehead to the ground. Each time you do so, remember the goddess from the very depths of your heart.'

I obeyed his instructions, taking the name of the goddess each time. By the time I completed my task, it seemed as if I had been thus engaged forever. Ultimately, when I sat down, he continued, 'Now, try to visualize the holy word, *Om*, written on your forehead. Focus your mind on your throat and try to imagine the word, *Ah*, written there. Then let your mind travel to your heart and look for the word, *Tom*, there. Now, the Om on your forehead is white, the Ah is red and the Tom in your heart is blue.'

I tried to think in terms of colours as the lama had instructed. Sitting in silence, I lost track of everything around me and wandered about in a dream world of my own where the snowy Himalayan peaks became the playground for Shiva and Shakti or strength. My trance was broken by the lama's mellifluous tones: 'Ma, free me from superstition; Ma, free me from fear; Ma, free me from maladies. Lead me to the path of the Buddha, to the path of religion and to the path of the sangha.'

On the fourth day of my sojourn at Gyatse, I bade farewell to all the lamas in our group. I was the only one who would remain behind. My departure would be deemed inauspicious until I had completed learning what had been set out for me. I had no objections to that, but without Guruji around, I felt very isolated and lonely.

Khampo placed his hand on my head and asked, 'So, how are you liking it with us?'

'Very much,' I answered with a smile. Then, I remained by him and refrained from speaking.

After a while, he got up abruptly and said, 'Follow me.'

We went round to the back of the house and climbing up a narrow alley, reached a palatial house that looked like a temple. On the upraised dais in front was a fearsome image. We paid our respects to it and stood before it. Khampo looked at me and asked, 'Can you tell me who that is?'

Staring intently at the image, I finally answered, 'It looks so familiar. But I can't seem to come up with the name.'

'This is an image of Eternal Time,' he told me, 'a very powerful presence indeed. You will remain here alone for some time and pray to the god for the realization of your hopes. Then come back to see me.'

With that, he left me on my own.

What could I ask for? What was there to ask for, anyway? So far, I had got everything without having to ask for it. Perhaps, what I longed for would not be beneficial for me? But then, Khampo had directed me to ask for something. I felt intimidated at the very thought of asking that fearsome image for anything at all. Eventually, all I did was remain sitting there without asking for anything. After I had spent quite some time there in silence, I rose and retraced my steps along the path that had brought me there and went back to Khampo's house.

He remained sitting for most of our time together and asked me to take a seat beside him. From his room, he administered all the proceedings of the sanctified area covered by the temple and its surroundings, including four educational institutions, the temple and its immediate environs and the roads, the priests and the three thousand residents. Khampo oversaw everything. Before 1950, he had been the sole caretaker of the whole of Gyatse. Now, as he grew older, the responsibilities were naturally being taken off his shoulders, little by little.

'Khampoji, why did you initiate me?' I asked.

'To ensure your becoming a true Tibetan lama so that no one could ever harass you again. Furthermore, this religion will guide and protect you throughout your sojourn in Tibet. If not now, you will understand this later. I have initiated you in accordance with my own wishes. I have informed your mentor about it. However, may your journey be trouble-free and may you be blessed.' Khampo touched my head affectionately and said, 'You may assume that the reason for this initiation is the fact that I have taken a liking to you. May Lord Tathagata bless you, and Goddess Tara always keep you free of sin.'

I spent a total of five days in Gyatse, leaving the city very early on the morning of the sixth. Khampo sent Desheng Wangdi, a man from the city, to act as my escort. He would accompany me till the next village, Gobshi. I had learnt a great deal in Gyatse. It was a spiritual gain certainly, but my material gains could not be discounted either: A brand new pair of Tibetan shoes, new saffron robes and two rupees in cash. This was the outcome of Khampo's largesse. There could be no gift more valuable in this bitterly cold land.

FROM GYATSE TO SAMDING GUMPHA

❧

WANGDI WAS ABOUT thirty years old and quite an amiable fellow. He wore his hair long like a girl and was dressed like a Lepcha. His village, Gobshi, where he ran a small grocery shop, was about eighteen miles away on the road to Lhasa. Every fortnight or so, he had to come to Gyatse to purchase goods. He had a mule with him to carry back the load. All his goods along with my own belongings were placed on its back. Wangdi was an inveterate smoker and also carried a bottle of country liquor with him. Nothing could be more appropriate in this severe cold for keeping both mind and body fresh and alert.

From Gyatse onwards, the Niyeru river ran alongside and gave the region its name: Niyeru Plateau. The temples of Gyatse were still clearly visible and the fort atop the hill stood out even more prominently. I had longed to visit the latter, but could not do so because of the journey I had now embarked on.

The wide plains of Gyatse were hemmed in to form a narrow valley. It was the first time I would come across arable land in this area. As in our own country, the land on either side had been ploughed. The thaw had set in. If we took the same route back, we would surely get to see Tibetan farmers tilling the land with the help of yaks. Though the road was a temporary one, paved with stones, it was in navigable condition. As we moved on, we frequently came across mules, yaks and donkeys carrying loads, their masters close on their heels. These wayfarers glanced at me oftener than they did at Wangdi.

We stopped near a stream in the afternoon. Wangdi anxiously tried making arrangements for his mule to munch on grass soaked in icy water. I took the opportunity of spreading my blanket on some ice-cold stones for a short rest. Then, after we had eaten our meal of dry bread and flour, mixed with cold water from the stream, we carried on.

As evening approached, we reached the village of Gobshi. No more than a thousand people inhabited it. The river flowed about a hundred and fifty feet below us. The houses were constructed of mud and an assortment of local stones. We stopped in front of one and knocked on the door. The moment we did so, our summons were answered and I caught sight of four people—an elderly woman, a young girl and a couple of young men. When Wangdi had introduced me, they put out their tongues in respectful greeting. The woman seemed the happiest to see us and positively beamed when she heard about me. She was Wangdi's mother. The young men were his siblings and the young girl was his wife. His two children were asleep.

A portion of this dwelling served as a shop. After Wangdi's brothers had unloaded the luggage from the mule's back, the lantern was placed in the centre of the room and everybody settled down around me. Their conversation with me was extremely limited. God only knew what Wangdi had said about me! That it was positive and in my favour was only too apparent. A little later, we all made our way to the kitchen. Thanks to the permanent haze of smoke, it was very dark. We settled down on small wooden seats by the fire. Everybody in the house had already eaten their evening meal. The food now being prepared was meant for us and consisted of a delicious broth in which cured lamb meat had been tossed in. Since we were exhausted, arrangements were made for us to go to bed as soon as the meal was over. The next morning, I awoke to the sound of Wangdi's children at play. Still in bed, they were playing with their father.

From now on, I would be entirely on my own. I had a three-day journey ahead of me. I had made a note of the exact places where I would be halting overnight. Guruji had written the names down for me. The lamas would be waiting for me at the Samding Gumpha. From Gobshi, I was to head for Samding via Ralung, Karo La, Jara, Nagatse and Tramaluk.

This time, the road running along the top of the mountain was rather narrow; the river could be seen flowing far below. Sometimes, the road rose in a sharp incline; at others, it sloped down. Every now and then, I passed deep ravines; a single misstep and all would have been lost. I could set my own pace, slowing down or speeding up at will. But I had learned by then that it was wiser to travel at a leisurely pace; it helped to conserve one's energy for the long trek that only came to an end when night closed in. Occasionally, I caught glimpses of vegetation; I had probably read about those very trees in textbooks back home. I could see houses perched on the mountainside. There was no dearth of people on the roads either. The path was very uneven and the valley narrowed down still further.

It was almost evening when I reached Ralung, a picturesque mountain village situated at a height of 14,025 feet. One advantage of being in Tibet was that I could ask for directions from any number of people. They came crowding around as soon as they saw a stranger. Seeing me in the garb of a lama, many assumed that I belonged to that region. But a closer look stopped them momentarily in their tracks, after which they approached warily, shooting a few brusque questions at me. Perhaps, they wanted to verify whether I was a foreigner or truly belonged to those parts. Luckily, there were no Chinese soldiers on this route. Had there been, I would have found it difficult to extricate myself from their clutches on my own.

Pausing before a shop, I asked, 'Can you tell me where the gumpha is located in this area?'

Everybody attempted to answer my query at the same time, gesticulating and offering directions. Unfortunately, I could not decipher a word of their rapid delivery. Finally, a man emerged from the shop and silencing the others, asked me, 'You want to go to the gumpha? Fine, it's not very far from here. If you go straight down this road, you will come to it; it's on this very route.'

I bade everyone a smiling farewell and had already moved on, when three or four voices called out loudly, 'Trapa! Trapa!' I stopped in my tracks and turned. I was told that someone was calling me from behind. I walked back to discover that it was the same person who had given me directions to the gumpha. He asked me if I wanted some tea and I gladly accepted.

The man entered his house at once, while I remained outside with the villagers. Meanwhile, the sun had set and a heavy darkness, knifed through by a murderous chill, shrouded the environs. A hot cup of tea in such surroundings was like manna from heaven. There was some money in my pocket, but the thought of treating myself to some tea had not occurred to me. All I could think of was the moment when I would be able to lie down for a while and rest.

A little later, a woman emerged from the shop. The tea had already been prepared. She merely reheated it and poured it into a glass. I handed her some money and asked her to deduct the price of the tea. Stepping back at once, she adamantly refused to accept payment. I was about to set out again, when the man asked me to wait and engaged in a long conversation with his wife. He told me that while the gumpha was not far off, the journey by night was hazardous in the extreme. The village dogs were unfamiliar with strangers who looked like me and could prove to be yet another peril. If I so desired, I could spend the night there. A fire burned in the stove virtually through the night, so the cold would not be a problem. At first, I hesitated a little. But the thought of spurning their sound advice did not appeal to me and I agreed to stay the night. I was touched and overwhelmed with gratitude at their concern over a pilgrim from an alien land.

Suddenly, I remembered the extra salt I was carrying in my bag. An extremely expensive commodity in Tibet, it could be sold if the need arose. When Guruji had set out from Gyatse, he had left some bits of firewood and the bag of salt in my custody. Since my hosts declined to accept payment for their hospitality, I thought it advisable to leave behind a gift for them. After I had finished my meal, I took out some salt and placed it in a little bowl. Both husband and wife were delighted with it and accepted the gift without a fuss. In the light of the lantern, their faces glowed with joy. I prepared for bed by laying out my blanket. As I was about to lie down, the woman handed me a table clock and somehow managed to communicate that she was keen to know whether I could make it work or not. Everything seemed to be in order, except for the fact that the clock had not been used for a very long time. As soon as it was wound, it began working perfectly and the woman could barely contain her delight. Much to their amazement, I even set off the alarm. At the sound, the woman started giggling like a young girl. As she later explained, the clock was a gift from her brother who had brought it from Siliguri. But since it was so precious, she would almost always keep it locked inside a box. Though her brother had obviously explained to her how the gadget worked, the woman had never been able to summon the courage to touch it. Realizing that I was exhausted, she placed the charcoal stove in the centre of the room and the three of us went to sleep around it.

The following day, a hot cup of tea awaited me as soon as I had risen and my hostess even took the trouble of seeing me off personally. Hardly anybody else was up at that hour. Stepping outdoors, I was rendered speechless by the sheer beauty of the Himalayas around me. Observing my bemused expression, the woman volunteered, 'This mountain is known as Nojin Kang Sang. Right below it flows the Sangpo river, known in your country as the Brahmaputra.'

Silently offering my salutations to nature's bounty, I set off once again. Originating in Tibet, the Brahmaputra was fed by the melting snows when the thaw set in. Just to imagine that I was a witness to the source of the Brahmaputra made my heart go wild with joy. Tibet's sacred Nojin Kang Sang mountain and the Chomolhari range converged at a place called Karo La. It was a mere three-hour trek away and we would have to pass it on our way to Lhasa. The Nojin Kang Sang stood at 24,000 feet. Snow kept piling up on the mountain; it was what we knew as a glacier. If it became top-heavy, the entire upper section could collapse and come tumbling down. The clouds hitting against the natural barrier created by the peak released moisture in the form of heavy snowfall. And the sunlight contributed its own share to the creation of an extremely turbulent stream—the source of the water that fed the Brahmaputra. After spending quite some time admiring the view, I set off in the direction of the Ralung Gumpha.

A mile's walk away, around a bend in the path, lay a small village that looked fairly prosperous. All the houses were topped with temple-like domes and stood surrounded by small patches of well-tended agricultural land. The river was not too far away. How serene was the ambience of these environs! Pointing out the village to me, the woman said that it was the Ralung Gumpha and the path we were on led straight to it.

To call it a village would be doing it a mild injustice, however, for it was a Buddhist vihara, pure and simple, that had evolved into its present form from the seven small houses around it. Innumerable prayer flags fluttered from tall pillars. Right before me were some sheep and donkeys that stared at me in amazement.

As was usual in Tibet, the dogs came rushing in my direction to greet me in their own fashion. Then two young lamas approached and asked, 'Are you the monk from Gangtok who has taken a vow of silence?'

Smiling, I nodded. I did not have to ask any questions. The lamas gave me the directions I needed. All the pilgrims had passed through this point and some had even spent the night here. If I set off at once, I could reach the Samding Gumpha that very night. That was where my fellow lamas awaited me.

The lamas took time in explaining it all to me in faltering sentences. It was clear to me that they assumed that sworn as I was to silence, there was no question of my uttering a word. They even explained the route to me. If I set out now, around the time evening approached, I would apparently come across a vast lake to my left known as the Jomdrok Sarovar. The road that emerged from the side and ran in a northerly direction would lead to the large Buddhist vihara known as the Samding Gumpha. Having gleaned from them the information I needed, I did not tarry. I joined them in offering my prayers at the huge temple and having turned the prayer wheels and circumambulated the temple, I departed.

The road gradually began to climb. It seemed that this path I was travelling along ended right on the snowy peaks of the Nojin Kang Sang. It was freezing in the shade and blazing hot in the sun. The sky was a brilliant blue, unmarred by a speck of cloud. Against this backdrop, the mountain peak rose like a proud sentinel. Since morning, there had been no wind, but the further I ascended, the stronger the gusts became. From the time I had left the gumpha, I had been on my own. But now, I found myself being joined by a pair of donkeys. There were apparently more donkeys and sheep way behind, though they were not visible to me. In all likelihood, the man who tended them was also accompanying them. The going was undoubtedly tough, but there was a certain pleasure in walking along this road. Had this land of the gods not been so bitterly cold, I would have remained here forever. The higher I went, the more laboured my breathing became. Then came a point where I had to pause for a rest every few paces. When I had reached a still higher elevation, the wind miraculously died down all of a sudden, probably due to the altitude of the spot. Leaving behind the two donkeys, I reached the Karo Pass. Here, I felt as if I were standing on the very summit of the Himalayas. It is impossible to put into words the effect the landscape had on me. There was nothing but snow all around. It was as though someone had scattered vast quantities of white cotton wool everywhere. I was overwhelmed by a sensation of lightness; the magic of the place was, perhaps, working on me too. It was that very magic which had, down the ages, drawn pilgrims like a magnet from every corner of the world to this place. Everybody was in search of this particular manna from heaven.

I was ignorant of the guiding forces that had carried me through to this point; I was merely a witness to this ethereal world where harmony reigned supreme. Was I truly worthy of appreciating the beauty of all that had been bestowed on me so easily, without my having to strive for it? In heartfelt gratitude to the omnipotent, omniscient and all-pervasive Divine Being, I prostrated myself to lay at His feet the spontaneous feelings that flowed from within.

A short while later, two herdsmen arrived with a flock of sheep and on catching sight of me, stuck their tongues out in respectful acknowledgement of my presence. They asked me a question, but since I was masquerading as a monk sworn to silence, any kind of verbal response on my part was impossible. Noticing a huge mound of stones at the side that supported a very tall pole for prayer flags, I followed the example of the Tibetans and picked up a pebble which I added to the growing pile.

After spending about an hour there, I continued on my way. Not far from Karo La, the road was enveloped in snow and ice. Since the rays of the sun did not reach the slope here, the snow took much longer to melt. With careful steps, I navigated the road glazed with a scattering of snow that looked rather like icing. The ascent had been inordinately difficult, but the descent seemed to demand no effort at all.

Coming down from Karo La, I arrived at a small village dotted with large stone dwellings that were, for the most part, farmhouses. There were sheep, yaks and pigs in abundance—a virtual zoo! They had all been tethered together by the wayside. I carefully stepped around them before moving ahead. At the centre of the village, I came across a tiny tea shop, where the young owner was absorbed in conversation with fellow Tibetans around a blazing fire. Acknowledging their greetings and conveying my own without uttering a word, I asked them through gestures whether there was a place they could recommend where I could rest. They seemed to understand my sign language. The owner led me to a corner of his shop and showed me some raw ingredients from which he could prepare me a meal, but indicated clearly that I would have to pay for it. I showed him the money, reassuring him silently that he had nothing to worry about.

Not long after, I ate a hot meal and happily handed the tea-shop owner two rupees. His eyes lit up with joy, but, unfortunately, he had no change. After all, I had paid in Indian currency and he would have to return the change in the same currency. All he had, however, were local or Chinese coins. I explained to him that he could return the change in whichever currency was available. Having learnt that the name of this village was Jara, I set out again.

Once I had left the village behind me, the snowy peaks to my right seemed to disappear behind another small mountain. The path descended steadily and, an hour later, opened out into a vast expanse of level land. Here lay the great Jomdrok Sarovar.

It was vast indeed and anyone who has seen Chilka Lake would have an idea of its immensity. The lake threw up a reflection of the clear blue skies. What caught my attention right away were the thousands of multicoloured prayer flags strung from poles that sprouted all over, in preparation, it would appear, for a forthcoming festival. The houses in the village were constructed of local stone over which a coating of cement had been applied. The roofs were made of tin. All the doors and windows had beautiful etchings in wood around them. The melting snow from the surrounding mountain peaks fed this vast natural reservoir from where a turbulent stream, nourished by water from numerous minor lakes and streams, branched off to merge with the Sangpo river of Tibet that flowed into our own country as the Brahmaputra.

The road I was travelling by led right into the village. Almost as soon as I entered it, I came across a large chaitya containing an image of Chenreji. After paying my respects there, I stayed on, admiring the temple. I noticed that most of the houses in the village had their doors and windows closed. Suddenly, I was surrounded by a gaggle of small urchins. Although their speech was incomprehensible to me, it was obvious that they were not beggars. Drawn by the sight of the children clamouring around me, a few young men also moved closer. Their accent was so thick, that try as I might, I could not decipher a word of what they were saying. One of them asked me to follow them and I did so, surrounded by the group of children. The further I progressed, the greater was the number of children who latched on to the hordes around me. After moving past a few houses to my left, I noticed between thirty and forty lamas lined up along the road. No viharas or monasteries appeared to be located close by. A great many questions vied for attention in my mind: Were they all waiting for me? Who had informed them of my arrival? Perhaps, it was the custom for the villagers to greet visiting lamas in this manner. Approaching still closer, I realized that all of them were waving their hands at me in a bid to attract my attention. As I neared them, my heart was beating so fast, I thought it would burst! I forgot all about my vow of silence and exclaimed aloud, 'Sadhu Baba!'

I stared at my guruji in amazement for sometime. He affectionately patted me on the head and back, restoring my composure somewhat. I imagined I had reached Samding, but simply could not figure out how I could have done so in such a short span of time. After all, it was a long way to evening. Sitting by the fire in a room in the village, Sadhu Baba explained everything to me. This was not Samding, as I had erroneously assumed, but the village, Nagatse. Samding was further north. Though we were supposed to be meeting there, it was in dire economic straits. So, for a few days, Guruji and his entourage had rented an old house in Nagatse from its owner who lived in Lhasa. The owner's brother had the key and had permitted the lamas to use the house without charging any rent as a way of enhancing his stock of worthy deeds.

Earlier, when Guruji had reached Samding and discovered that it would be impossible to make arrangements for lodging and feeding thirty-two lamas, he had returned to Nagatse right away. After a short rest, I set out with Sadhu Baba in the direction of the lake. Evening was about to set in. The water body was as vast as an ocean, the opposite shore invisible to the human eye. I felt as though I were standing on the sea beach at Puri. We chanted our prayers together and returned to the village. Sadhu Baba cautioned me, 'Be very, very careful. Remember, you are bound by the vow of silence. Do not utter a single word! The entire village knows you as the Silent Monk.'

I felt I had got back my own people after a long, long time; that itself was enough to thrill me. Even if I had to abide by my vow of silence for a million years, I told myself, with Guruji by my side, nothing was impossible.

The house where the lamas had put up was a single-storeyed one with thick stone walls. It was surrounded by a stone boundary wall. It was apparent that the property belonged to an aristocratic family, for the kitchen too, was huge. The terrace of the house looked like a pagoda, encircled by a wooden border, the way houses belonging to the landed gentry of the hilly tracts tended to be. All the lamas had taken shelter in the kitchen and were merely awaiting my arrival. And that very night, the decision was made to leave for Samding early the following morning.

THE DORJE PAMO

THE EVENING DESCENDED on Nagatse in all its splendour. The colours of the setting sun touched the snow-clad summits and created a kind of magic that seemed to transform the entire world. Once the sun had gone down, everybody retreated to the warmth of their homes. The severe chill ensured that not a soul remained outdoors, not even by a burning fire. After our evening meal was over, Guruji told us a truly absorbing story about the Samding Gumpha.

Samding, from which the ancient monastery takes its name, is a Tibetan word that means 'meditating mountain'. It is likely that the serenity of the mountains surrounding the gumpha inspired its name. Divided into two sections—one for men, the other for women—the Samding Gumpha was probably the largest of its kind for women in Tibet. Here, the women belonged to sects, just like the men. The monastery's ultimate authority—in other words, the guruji—was the Dorje Pamo, a Buddhist nun. The first Dorje Pamo had been known as the mother of all Tibet. In this country, there seemed to be no dearth of souls worshipped and revered as an incarnation of the Buddha. Any powerful lama regarded as the manifestation of the Buddha inspired a similar response. The Buddha had travelled widely to disseminate his religion and to expound the principles that served as its foundation. His spirit had always assumed a male physical form. It was solely in the Samding Gumpha that the Buddha had been reincarnated in the physical form of a woman—the Dorje Pamo. According to historians, the first female manifestation of the Buddha had appeared five hundred years ago. That first Dorje Pamo was gifted with extraordinary occult powers and regarded as the Earth Mother. Of the stories that abound of this remarkable individual, the following is the most widely known.

Samding Gumpha had always been intended for both men and women, though at the outset, the latter had been relegated to a position of subservience. During that era, the country was in turmoil, as Chinese Tartars pillaged and plundered their way through it. Apprehending mistreatment at the hands of these barbarians, a large number of learned lamas had sought shelter at the gumpha on the assumption that hidden as it was in the lap of the Himalayas, this monastery, at least, would be safe from the depredations of the marauders. They were mistaken, however. The Tartars were a cunning and ferocious lot and did not spare Samding. Without warning, they set upon the peace-loving residents of this village, killing, raping and looting as they went. Most of the villagers died defending themselves. The women who managed to escape their clutches ran to the gumpha and sought shelter there.

At the centre of the monastery was a large courtyard surrounded by the boundary walls of stone houses. When the Tartars came to know that almost everyone had taken refuge in the monastery, they attacked it. In fact, the walls of the gumpha still bear signs of that onslaught. Persistent though they were in their efforts to break down the monastery doors, barred from inside, the Tartars failed in their attempt. Ultimately, they brought out a massive hammer and began breaking down the door. Terrified by the noise of that assault, all the women inside the monastery approached the head lama, threw themselves at her mercy and beseeched her to intervene and extend her protection to them. She, for her part, assured them that there was no reason to be afraid.

The noise rose to a crescendo when the Tartars realized that the beautiful young women from the village were almost within reach. Their bestial yells were far more repugnant than the cries of animals. Finally, the Tartars broke open the doors and rushed in. To their utter bewilderment, however, not a soul was in sight. A herd of pigs with a white sow in their midst happily wandered about in the courtyard. Assuming that the village was deserted, the Tartars left. That white sow was actually the Dorje Phagmo or, as she was more commonly known, the Dorje Pamo; the rest of the animals were, in reality, the other lamas and people from the village. By virtue of her magical powers derived from the Buddha, the Dorje Pamo had saved the people of Samding from the brutal Tartars by transforming them into pigs. Ever since, the ancient lama of this temple is known as the Dorje Pamo.

The next morning, having bestowed our blessings on the villagers, we were on our way to Samding. During the daylight hours, the path seemed very easy to traverse and I began repeating to myself all the mantras I had been taught invoking the Goddess Tara. If I could master them, Guruji had promised, I would never have to endure any physical hardships in life.

After walking along the Jomdrok Sarovar for almost two hours, we reached its northernmost point, where the lake ended. Some temples were visible at the spot. As soon as we entered the village, a strong stink of fish assailed us. It was just as if we were in a fish market, but we could not spot anything even remotely resembling one. The main temple was located inside the gumpha itself. We passed through a pagoda-like door set in the boundary wall and went in. At the sight of us, some Buddhist nuns fled, scattering in all directions. A male lama approached us with the query, 'Are you pilgrims from India?'

'We are,' Guruji answered. 'Please inform the head lama of our arrival.'

The lama called out loudly to the others and was answered by some young women wearing the garb of lamas. Their heads were tonsured. They greeted us respectfully and our lama explained the matter to them. There were only fifty-six lamas at this gumpha.

The women here took the holy orders and remained at the monastery for about ten years. Then they set out for different villages to serve the people. From there, we made our way to a temple and I began to carefully examine my surroundings. The lake was not visible from this point. Peace reigned. Although some semblance of cultivation was, perhaps, possible in the summer, the thaw had only just begun to set in at this altitude. Apart from the main temple, there were a few smaller places of worship and a number of dharamsalas for the lamas. Every once in a while, a pungent whiff of fish odour wafted towards us. Villagers and lamas began to gather around us.

A short while later, an elderly woman approached us, flanked on either side by two relatively younger Buddhist nuns. They wore the same garb as their male counterparts and their heads were tonsured despite the severe cold. When they reached us, Guruji introduced us all. This extraordinary woman with a maternal air happened to be this gumpha's highest authority—the Revered Dorje Pamo. One by one, we prostrated ourselves before her and offered our respectful salutations. The young female lamas also paid us their respects. Since I was the youngest, I naturally attracted a great deal of attention. As soon as these ceremonies were over, auspicious bugles were sounded from both sides of the door. And this was how our welcome was conducted for nearly five minutes at the Samding Gumpha. As their honoured guests, we were welcomed once more in the traditional manner. The village was a small one and the only place worth visiting was the Samding Gumpha. In the main temple stood the colossal image of a hundred-armed Buddha.

At last, we came to a room right at the back of the temple. My heart surged with happiness, for I had discovered something new. 'In the room we are approaching now, you will find rows and rows of boxes,' Guruji began. 'They contain the mummified mortal remains of all the Dorje Pamos, starting from the first one. In fact, they are the remains of the Dorje Pamo you met; she casts aside one body and enters the other. On assuming a new physical manifestation—in other words, on being vested with the authority of the Dorje Pamo—she enters the room once to survey all the bodies she has inhabited in the past. She has to remain here in complete solitude for three days during which she meditates at length on certain predetermined issues. When she emerges from that mental state, she is already vested with supernatural powers.'

We entered the room which seemed to be cold as death. In the dim glow of the lamp, virtually nothing could be discerned and we had to content ourselves with a mere glance at the boxes containing the mummified remains. It was forbidden to even talk in the room. If I had not been with the pilgrims, I would have asked for permission to remain in that room for at least one night. There must be some inherent secret of the occult hidden there, I told myself.

Having spent nearly an hour wandering about here and there, we entered the village. Approaching the lake from the rear of the village, we came to a huge centre for preserving fish through a process of salting and drying. As soon as the bell sounded, we were led to the kitchen. Gradually, everyone else congregated there as well. The veranda was nice and sunny and we seated ourselves there in double rows. The women sat facing us. The responsibility for preparing the meal was entrusted to a different group every day. Those who cooked the meal served it as well. The meal consisted of a hotchpotch of various kinds of vegetables, salted and dried fish, lentils and rice. It was delicious and one couldn't help but be appreciative of the cooking. After finishing our meal and paying our respects to the Revered Dorje Phagmo, we handed her an ivory miniature of the Buddha and set out right away.

THE LANGUAGE

MEANWHILE, I HAD mastered a few words of Tibetan. If the language were spoken slowly, I could even follow it. What appealed to me most, though, were the prayers chanted in Tibetan. Though not particularly tuneful, their ascending cadences seemed to touch the mountain peaks. Though they were actually in prose that was recited in rhythm, the feelings underlying those prayers were so pure and intense, that the moment they were articulated, they seemed to take on the form of poetry. I was the Silent Monk certainly, but laboured under no restrictions as far as hearing was concerned. So, I listened to those prayers all the time. Speech, however, was forbidden to me and, therefore, despite my desire to practise my scant knowledge of Tibetan, I had no opportunity for doing so.

Each word in Tibetan consisted of two syllables. Deer, for example, was *khassa*, but it was pronounced kha sa. Similarly, *dharchak* or *dharchok*—flag—was pronounced as dhar chak or dhar chok. Of course, there were several exceptions to the rule as evident in monosyllabic words like *nya* (fish), *bha* (cow) and *ham* (fox). Thus, even a short sentence in Tibetan took ages to complete.

So far during my travels, I had come across few people who could count up to a hundred. Those who could count up to two hundred or more were rarer still. The average shop owner could usually manage up to ten or, at the very most, twenty. To add or subtract one sum from another, I had frequently seen them resort to the use of small pebbles or stones. The numbers sounded very appealing in Tibetan. When the children swayed rhythmically as they memorized their numbers, it sounded as though they were reciting poetry.

Watches were virtually redundant gadgets in Tibet. The wealthy did own them, but they served as symbols of prosperity more than anything else. To read the time, Tibetans usually relied on the crowing of the cock at dawn and the movement of the sun during the day. The following are some points I have noted down in my diary:

Chak-tang-po: The first cockcrow at dawn
Chak-neei-pa: The second cockcrow at dawn
Thong-rang: The first light of dawn

Familiarity with the above timings was mandatory at any gumpha, because on them depended its routine and regulations. As in our own country, there were seven days in a week: Ja-Ningma (Monday), Ja-Daba (Tuesday), Ja-Mingma (Wednesday), Ja-Lak-Pa (Thursday), Ja-Phurpu (Friday), Ja-Pasang (Saturday) and Ja-Pem-Pa (Sunday).

MY FIRST GLIMPSE OF THE SANGPO

FROM TRAMALUK, A continuous ascent brought us to the region's highest peak where the last obstacle to our pilgrimage lay—the Khamba La or Khamba Pass, situated at a height of 17,000 feet. We had had to contend with three such passes so far: Nathu La, Pharir Tang La and Karo La, in that order. But Khamba La was, undoubtedly, a departure from all the rest and had its own distinctive features. Here, the views flanking the pass presented a study in contrasts. On one side stood the Chomolhari range, along with other snow-capped Himalayan peaks. On the other lay the Sangpo Valley. From this vantage point, the Jomdrok Sarovar appeared ever so strange. The natural beauty of this region defied description; mere words wouldn't have sufficed to do it justice. The very life force of the serene, solemn and sacred Himalayas lay here.

From Khamba La, we descended to Patsi village. Our group dispersed for the night and somehow managed to find sleeping accommodation spread over three different houses. We reached the banks of the Sangpo river the following evening. A welcome reprieve awaited us there. The dry and unforgiving mountain chill had given way to a temperature that was positively civilized, so mild was it in comparison to what we had endured earlier! A large expanse of yellow sand marked the Sangpo's banks and quite a number of houses flanked the river on either side. Our gaze was drawn to the road across the river where a number of lorries plied. After a long pause there, we returned to our own world.

As the sun dipped below the horizon, we finished our prayers and poured holy water from the river on our heads. Flowing from west to east, the watercourse was calmer at this point and reminiscent of the Ganga at Rishikesh. We would have to cross the Sangpo before proceeding to Lhasa—a mere two days away on foot.

THE CHAKSAM GUMPHA

WE PROCEEDED IN an easterly direction along the banks of the Sangpo. The path had been constructed out of sand and pebbles from the riverbed. From here to Lhasa, no more mountains would have to be scaled. After covering part of the distance, a few temples appeared far away to our right. They were barely concealed by some leafless trees, a futile attempt at camouflage, it would seem. This, we were told, was the Chaksam Gumpha. Guruji announced that we would be spending the night there. His words miraculously rejuvenated our flagging spirits in seconds. All semblance of fatigue vanished without a trace.

Leaving the Sangpo behind us, we took a turn and made for the small hill in the distance. Without warning, danger more fearful than Tibetan dogs reared its head in the form of Chinese soldiers. It had not occurred to us that their tents could be hidden behind the mound. Roaring like beasts, they rushed towards us. We had had some experience in the past of their particular kind of hospitality, but that had been relatively civilized. I did not know what to make of this version.

Guruji was prepared for all contingencies and somehow succeeded in explaining to the soldiers that we were lamas travelling to the Chaksam Gumpha. They let us proceed, of course, but followed us all the way there. We knocked on the main door of the monastery and were greeted by the lama who answered our summons. As soon as we entered the place, we discovered that apart from our group, there were no other guests.

Sitting around the fire in the dharamsala, we thanked Guruji again and again. That we had been able to overcome innumerable difficulties and were actually on the verge of reaching Lhasa was entirely to his credit. To have reached the Sangpo was virtually akin to reaching Lhasa.

Chaksam was a palatial monastery with almost seven hundred inmates. Had they been authorized to do so, nearly another three hundred people could have been accommodated in the dharamsala. The latter was so huge, in fact, that our group occupied no more than three of its rooms located at one end. This particular gumpha was famous for the way it celebrated certain Tibetan festivals.

The monastery stood in picturesque surroundings. From this vantage position, the view of the Sangpo river and of the level land around was equally stunning. The Buddhist Temple, the Padma Sambhava Temple and the prayer rooms were beautifully decorated. The woodwork, the triangular structure of the walls and the images of the various deities were decorated with exquisite etchings. At Gyatse, the lamas had always accompanied us wherever we went and explained whatever we needed to know. But here, everything seemed so bare and empty. Lamas were present; yet, they did not seem to be there at all.

The following evening, the lamas responsible for running the dharamsala informed us rather apologetically that they regretted bringing us ill tidings, but the Chinese had sent on information about us to Lhasa. So, until the authorization for us to move on arrived, we were to kindly remain there and not make any attempt to cross the Sangpo river. This bit of news astounded us, because we had been under the impression that in Tibet, the word of the Dalai Lama was law. In reality, however, it was the word of the Chinese that mattered. They were the actual masters. The Chinese, or rather, the Chinese controlling Tibet had taken us for Nepalese pilgrims and allowed us in; this route was strictly barred to all Indians. With so many restrictions in force, it would be impossible for us to enter Lhasa. Besides, no matter how many questions the Chinese might have for us, replying to them was to be avoided at all cost. Despite our travails, our strength of mind had not been eroded in the least. If we could have come this far, we reasoned, we would certainly succeed in reaching Lhasa too.

We became acquainted with a young lama, the assistant administrator of the Chaksam Gumpha. The man approached us himself and asked us about the route we intended taking and at which points the Chinese soldiers were stationed. As the Silent Monk, I had to refrain from speaking, though I knew the answers to his queries—everything was recorded in my diary. All the other lamas remained silent. Guruji had strictly forbidden us from entering into such discussions with anyone, because we could neither have determined what that person's actual views were nor gauged how our own remarks would be interpreted.

Unable to elicit any responses to his overtures, the man tried being still more familiar. 'You are our brethren,' he said, 'I can, therefore, confide in you. Ever since the Chinese invasion in 1950, we have been allowed virtually no freedom. Many of our people have moved to India and Nepal. There are Chinese soldiers all around Lhasa. Immediately beyond its borders, there is some measure of freedom, but Chinese representatives are trying to introduce their policies in every sphere of our lives. Earlier, there were no soldiers in this area of the Sangpo. It's been just five or six days since they set up camp here. The ferry is anchored not far from here and it is the business of these soldiers to keep a strict vigil on passengers. They are unwilling to understand how this constant surveillance can be detrimental to our meditation. We have lodged a strong protest with Lhasa's PLA or Peoples' Liberation Army and the Preparatory Committee, but there has been no response from them so far. The Chinese Army is seriously disturbing the peace here. Now, since you have come from the border area, what do you have to say about the situation?'

'We are ordinary pilgrims,' Guruji replied. 'We did come across soldiers at certain points, but were not inconvenienced by them in any way so far. We do not distinguish between Tibetan and Chinese soldiers.'

That morning, a strange haze of heat hung over the place and Guruji suggested, 'Let us bathe in the Brahmaputra and offer our prayers there.'

At that time of year, small white flowers bloomed by the Brahmaputra (the Sangpo in Tibet) and gathering some, we reached the banks of the river. Our robes and socks were filthy; they would have to be washed. We fashioned temporary loincloths and stepped into the water. No sooner had my toes touched the water than I leaped up—that was no water! It was molten ice! It was impossible for me to think of bathing in it. Pneumonia would be the inevitable result. For the other lamas, it was less of a problem. They came from Kathmandu and were used to bathing in the icy waters of the Bagmati. I sat for a while on the bank and tried to summon up courage for the plunge, persuading myself that it was great good fortune to be able to bathe in these sacred waters. And if, in the process, I were to die here, it would be a blessed death. Besides, all the lamas were bathing. If I did not, it would surely prove beyond doubt that I did not come from cold climes and betray my real identity.

We were now at a height of 12,000 feet. The atmosphere was strange. The glaring sun scorched the patch of sand on the banks. All around us were snow-clad peaks, but they seemed unreal in the searing heat. The sight of Guruji gave me courage; if he could venture into the freezing water at his age, it would be unseemly on my part to abstain from a bath. I first wet my feet, then my elbows, and gradually became acclimatized to the cold. Giving myself some more time, I finally plunged into the crystal-clear waters.

We began praying together and with heartfelt devotion made an offering of the flowers we had collected. Tunefully, the lamas began reciting from the holy scriptures: 'O Benevolent Almighty! We appeal to you to free us from the labyrinth of earthly compulsions. By resorting to hatred, we cannot nullify hatred. It is only by immersing ourselves in the river of love that hatred can be vanquished....'

While the Vajradhara Temple at Chaksam was huge, the colourful thangkas and intricate workmanship of the Sahasrabahu Temple were worth noting. The Chaksam temples were known for a special feature—the rats infesting it. It was common belief in Tibet that when lamas died, their souls hid among the rat population there. It was, apparently, the reason why the rodents refused to leave. Setting traps to exterminate them or using other measures to drive them away was, therefore, out of the question.

Guruji would read aloud to us every day from the sacred scriptures. On the morning of the fourth day, we were released. In other words, the permission to travel further was sent on to us by the Chinese authorities in Lhasa. We received the news at nine in the morning and set out at once. By ten, we were approaching the banks of the Sangpo.

No matter how tranquil its waters might seem, the Sangpo was notorious for the strength and unpredictability of its currents. After covering part of the distance, we came across a few Tibetan villagers washing in the river and bathing, their voices raised in joyous song. The women happily frolicked in the freezing cold water that had so intimidated me. Most of them were young and bare-breasted, for before taking their baths, they had taken off their blouses and placed them on the boulders by the bank. Noticing our group, they stuck out their tongues in respectful greeting, as was the custom. But so innocent were they, that they seemed untroubled by even a semblance of self-consciousness. Perhaps, innocence of this kind was only possible in these regions. Only where the heart was pure, could freedom from the sense of shame or embarrassment reign supreme.

Moving on, we came to the jetty from where one could board the ferry—the only means by which the locals could reach the opposite bank—and found a great many people waiting for the very same purpose. Rather like the Tibetans who waited for days on end in Siliguri for their religious mentor to arrive, we too, waited for the ferry that would help us cross the river. Laden with passengers and luggage, the boat approached from the direction of the opposite bank. It wasn't exactly a boat, but a waterborne vessel of a certain kind and it seemed to be carrying across an entire village! And what did it not contain, starting from yaks, sheep and donkeys to pigs, hens, luggage, grass, fodder and, of course, people too! Since the advent of the Chinese, that is, after 1950, this waterborne transport had greatly improved. In the past, boats would be made of yak skin and could accommodate no more than ten passengers. Sometimes, only a single crossing and, occasionally, two could be managed in a day. But at present, the ferry made four trips a day and could even accommodate a fifth, if required. Apart from the usual vessel, there was another big military boat for the soldiers that even the Tibetan army officers could use.

It was the first time since we had arrived in Tibet that we were using any form of transport. For with the exception of the ferry for crossing the river, we had used no transport whatsoever, undertaking the entire journey from Gangtok to Lhasa on foot. Of course, those who had the means arranged for ponies or horses. Yaks and donkeys were also available to carry luggage.

Taking almost an hour to cross the Sangpo, we entered a whole new world. Having left the Himalayas behind us, we were about to touch the sacred soil of Lhasa. We thanked the Lord for allowing us to reach our destination in sound body and mind before starting out on foot again. The experience turned out to be a completely different one this time, as we made our way over soil that was, for the most part, sandy. For we had taken a short cut that ran through level land known as the Ki Chu Valley. A right turn would have brought us to the main road again. But the path we had chosen would save almost three hours and avoid the confluence of the Ki Chu and the Brahmaputra rivers from where the main road actually turned off. Once in a while, we would come across arable land and a few houses. It seemed very likely that the soil was fertile, for the area was well populated. The roads were crowded with people. At the end of a two-day trek without pause lay the holy land of Lhasa.

We halted at a small village called Chusul. Almost all the houses here were made of stone and plants and shrubs grew here and there, the way they did in small Sikkimese villages. A large group of little boys had started trailing us and it was from them that we found out whether twigs for firewood would be available. One of them, about eleven years old, offered to show us the way.

We followed him to a house by the river and knocked on the door. In Tibetan houses, if someone was home, the front door was usually left open. So, it was obvious from the closed door that nobody was in. Observing our group of thirty-two lamas assembled there, a crowd gathered, wondering what the matter could be. We explained that the matter was very simple indeed: we were pilgrims looking for a place to cook our meal.

A man came forward and said, 'Why didn't you say so? The owner of the house is not here. Please wait here while I make arrangements for fetching firewood.'

Peeping from behind a tree, some older girls watched us prepare our meal—just lentils, rice and flour mixed with hot water. Food, however, was merely necessary for sustaining the body. Our hearts, on the other hand, were replete with joy. Sheltering behind a big boulder by the river, we cooked in the vessels we carried with us. We also invited the villagers to share our meal. Four young children and two elderly persons accepted; the rest kept their distance. Having finished our meal and thanked the villagers, we prayed to the Almighty before setting out again.

Soon after dusk had descended, we reached the large village of Nethang. Guruji observed that he was quite familiar with these villages and that nothing had changed in the last twenty years. We stopped in front of a house and knocked on the door. It was the village gumpha and could be better described as a dharamsala or guest house, because all the lamas passing through used it as such. We noticed a chaitya between two houses to our left. An elderly lama came out to greet us. Having heard us out, he confessed that all the firewood in stock had been used up and the funds allotted from Lhasa to buy more had not arrived from the capital either. The village grocer was also hounding them for payment, but the money to pay him would arrive within a couple of days and there was no cause for worry. The lama made no move to ask us where had we come from nor how long we would be staying.

Though night was fast approaching, there was no sign of a lantern being lit. Nor was there light of any other kind. In the semi-darkness, the lama pointed to two rooms and said, 'Sleep there for the night; if it is at all possible, I will see whether any arrangements can be made for you.' With that, he disappeared into the darkness. Though we had been given two rooms, we used only one; huddled together, the cold seemed more bearable. No dinner was available that night and we were so exhausted that sleep overtook us easily.

We awoke very early the following morning and what I craved the most was food. My stomach seemed to be a yawning abyss; I had never ever experienced hunger so acute! The previous day, during our long trek, we had drunk from the waters of the Ki Chu; that too, was one of the reasons why we were now famished. As soon as it was light, we set off in search of a tea stall. Silently, we managed to slip out. Completing our prayers before the chorten, we started searching for a tea stall at random in an area that was probably the bazaar. Spotting a woman passer-by in the throes of a violent coughing fit, we asked for help. She pointed to a door some distance away and suggested we knock to rouse the people sleeping inside. After we had been doing so for quite some time, an irate voice wanted to know the reason for such a racket. Then answering the door and noticing so many lamas together, the man put out his tongue in respectful greeting and asked what he could do for us.

Having learnt that we wanted some tea, the man hastened to do the needful and humbly informed us that everything was organized; all we had to do was mix the butter. The tea was, however, extremely bitter and none of us could manage more than a sip or two. Observing our discomfiture, the man said, 'Oh! I understand you are not used to taking tea prepared in this manner. I usually throw some medicinal leaves into the tea. The villagers here suffer from chronic stomach ailments and the concoction does them a lot of good!'

ON THE THRESHOLD

WE CAME TO the banks of the Ki Chu again and started following the main road. The watercourse had now acquired the form of a mountain stream and roared the loudest at this point, for creating obstacles in its path and causing the river to crash through in violent protest were huge boulders that had tumbled down from the mountain rising straight up from its bank. From Nethang village, we began to move eastwards. Earlier, we had been heading north. Shortly after rounding the corner, an unimaginable scene unfolded before our eyes. All this while, the vast valley of the Ki Chu had remained hidden behind a wall of rock, but now, the vista that lay revealed before us sent us into a sort of trance from which it took us some time to emerge.

In the far distance, the rays of the morning sun glanced off the bright roofs of some temples perched on the mountainside, making them flash like countless miniature suns. On the smooth rockface of the mountain rising alongside was a huge painting of the Buddha from which the very essence of his spirit seemed to emanate with force and pervade the environs. We prostrated ourselves and paid our humble respects to that wondrous spirit. We then seated ourselves by the road to cleanse our minds and souls, for to obtain the Lord's blessings, we needed to be sanctified. Then we began our group prayers:

'Only when the reason for our earthly bonds,
Bonds of chores and weariness, are done away with,

Comes freedom.
From earthly cravings come bonds;
With true knowledge,
Freedom is possible, the great space
Show us the path to Nirvana
Through Knowledge...'

The smoothly polished mountainsides bore innumerable paintings depicting the images of different deities, male and female. In the face of such beauty, every trace of our weariness seemed to melt away. The monastery and temples of Lhasa, visible in the distance, seemed to be celestial visions come down to earth for us. Here, we realized, lay a mysterious part of the universe.

A little further on, we were forced to come to a halt. For on a raised platform in the middle of the river was a colossal image of the Buddha. Instinctively, we prostrated ourselves before it and paid our obeisance. The rarefied spiritual world in which we now found ourselves seemed to belong to another dimension altogether. I expressed my gratitude to the Lord for having been allowed to come this far in my journey. Not that it was so difficult to traverse the path I had chosen. Yet, how many people had come all the way here? I had succeeded in doing so only because I had chosen to run away from home and cut myself off from my roots.

Sitting on the riverbank, with the water rippling around me, I was lost in contemplation of such matters, when a sudden thought disturbed my concentration. Was my achievement instilling in me feelings of superiority, of inordinate pride? Immediately, I checked the inclination.

It was late afternoon by the time we completed our prayers. There was a place close by, strongly reminiscent of Rishikesh and Lachhmanjhula in India, where meals were available. We made our way to the palatial temple before us. Here was a city dotted with innumerable small temples. The domed main temple along with the many pagoda-like houses drew the eye of every traveller who passed this way. Here was the world-famous Drepung Monastery— the largest living monastery and vihara of our times! Nalanda and Taxila, renowned universities of a bygone era, now lay in ruins. But this monastery, built along the same lines, was still flourishing. It would be evening by the time we arrived at the Drepung Gumpha.

THE DREPUNG GUMPHA

WE SLEPT SOUNDLY at the dharamsala, untroubled by cares, for we were almost on the verge of attaining our goal. The following morning, we awoke to very loud noises coming from the direction of the veranda. Making our way there quickly, we came upon two Tibetan lamas, crowned and garbed in multicoloured robes, blowing vigorously on a pair of enormous bugles. We had seen flutes like this at the Gyatse Gumpha, but I do not recall seeing anything similar back home. The call of those bugles seemed to bounce off the surrounding terraces and come to a halt. We exchanged greetings and smiles with the two lamas. From the veranda itself, Lhasa seemed to unfold before my gaze and the first landmark that caught the eye was the Potala—the Revered Dalai Lama's palace. What a mesmerizing sight that was, half-hidden in the cradle of the mountain!

Right from the morning, we were kept busy at the gumpha. A government official from the foreign ministry had already made inquiries about us. All foreigners headed for Lhasa would have to register themselves with that department and furnish such details as the duration and purpose of their visit and the next destination they planned to travel to. Apart from providing the answers to these questions, the names of all the lamas had to be noted down. So, officially, I came to be known as 'Lama Mouni Baba'.

We were then summoned to the office of the gumpha's secretary. The chief secretary, a rather overbearing person, lived some distance away from our dharamsala in a beautiful bungalow shaped like a pagoda. He took each one of us by the hand and with a deep inclination of the head, welcomed us to the Drepung Gumpha. Needless to say, he was a busy man, and it was, therefore, his secretary who took down our names for the record. Then the chief secretary asked us, 'Would you like to have a cup of tea?'

Of course! This was what we had been hoping for.

The promised beverage was brought in within a few minutes and, to my utter amazement, turned out to be just like the kind served in Kolkata. Even the cups and saucers were delicate pieces of crockery made of porcelain. It was only too apparent that we were in the presence of one of the highest and most respected authorities in Lhasa. What surprised us still further were the biscuits that accompanied the tea! As we ate, the chief secretary chatted with us, asking us about our journey and how we had fared so far. Looking at me, he observed, 'That you have come so far despite your youth must be the reward for the good deeds of your previous incarnation.'

Having spent some more time in our company, he handed over to his colleague the responsibility of looking after us. It was this assistant who would show us around the Drepung Gumpha.

In Tibetan, Drepung Gumpha literally meant 'a mountain of rice'. And if one gazed at this dazzling white monastery from a distance, it did, indeed, live up to its name! It had changed somewhat in recent times, but the main temple and surrounding houses still retained their original character. We paused in front of a house and the assistant explained, 'It is not merely Tibetans, but foreigners too, who come here to study. In ancient times, a palatial gumpha called Sridang had existed in the Indian state of Orissa. Subsequently, it had fallen into disuse. The Drepung Gumpha has been constructed along similar lines. There are some Nepalese students living in this house. Let me introduce you to them.'

The building resembled the guest house of the gumpha in Darjeeling and as we drew closer, the sound of prayers and chants came to our ears. After we had met some of the students and introductions had been made, the others emerged, one by one, to pay their respects to us. From their conversation, it was clear to me that each and every lama in our group was erudite and well known. Guruji introduced us all. He told the group that I belonged to a village called Raxaul on the Indo-Nepal border.

There were four centres of learning around the main temple at the heart of the complex. The general architectural style of the buildings here was based on the pagoda. The roof and walls of the temple were of a golden hue and all around the balcony, doors and windows were decorations in bright red. This part of Tibet stretched across level land and since winter was about to give way to spring, the surrounding area and the gardens would soon blaze with an abundance of colourful blossoms.

The name of the first university was Loseling Kham and it was here that lamas from the east came to study philosophy and Tibetan culture. The second, third and fourth universities were the Gomang Tratsang, Deyang Tratsang and Ngakpa Tratsang in that order. The word 'tratsang' probably meant 'residential educational centre'. The number of students admitted to the university from the country's different regions was predetermined. The Overseas Department was meant for foreign students from countries like Nepal, Bhutan and Sikkim, but they were segregated from the Tibetan students.

The Drepung Gumpha had almost 10,000 students—all residential boarders—on its rolls. It was Santiniketan on a large scale—right in the midst of Lhasa! And had I not seen it with my own eyes, it would have been difficult to believe that such a thing was possible. Each academic head was known as the Khempo. Of them, the most senior in terms of years and erudition was the highest authority of Drepung, rather like the vice chancellor of Calcutta University. There were also two administrators known as the Shalingo who were responsible for maintaining peace, order and discipline among the students; they could be described as the guardians of Drepung.

All pilgrims, that is, those who stayed at the dharamsala were extended hospitality gratis for three days. Subsequently, the stay could be extended for four additional days with permission from the appropriate authority. If one wanted to stay on for a still longer period, religious instruction from resident priests was mandatory. As a general rule, pilgrims halted here for a day or two at the very most. After taking our afternoon meal, we set off again to explore the rest of the complex.

When evening was about to approach, we met the chief secretary again who, for reasons that eluded our comprehension, introduced us to the Chinese representatives. After all, they were only too well acquainted with us! Due to a number of reasons, almost all foreign tourists had virtually stopped passing through. Later, the chief secretary suggested, 'Come, let me accompany you on a visit to the Temple of Abalokiteswara.' And having escorted us there, left us to explore our surroundings.

The main temple was enormous and filled with innumerable statues and frescoes. The four-armed Bodhisattva Abalokiteswara drew our attention immediately and we prostrated ourselves and prayed with devotional fervour. This colossal image of the Buddha, covered in cloth, was surrounded by countless thangkas. Before it on an upraised dais were various objects necessary for the ritual worship of the Lord. Just in front of the lamp stood a number of small receptacles containing holy water and in a large vessel was an offering of rice grains. Of course, there were also a number of books. Once our prayers were over, we came out of the temple. Guruji had spent a year at the Drepung Gumpha and, therefore, began explaining its various aspects to us.

We would be staying at the monastery for three days. It had been apparent to us the moment we arrived in Tibet, that this was a country dominated by priests. An occupant of a government post or a senior official was, without exception, either a priest or a lama. And this point was driven home to us more forcefully once we reached Drepung.

As I had mentioned earlier, the gumphas in Tibet played the role of universities. There were three main gumphas in the north, south and west of the country. The largest was Drepung, followed by Sera to the south and Ganden to the north. Sera was situated one-and-a-half miles north of Lhasa, while Ganden lay thirty-seven miles to the north-east. The lamas and students of Drepung were divided into small groups and each was assigned separate houses, gardens and kitchens. Every morning and afternoon, they would congregate after meals and jointly thrash out the matter of handling the responsibilities entrusted to them. The food usually consisted of butter tea and a kind of gravy. In the evening, the students were given time to stroll around. Or else, they devoted it to the perusal of their religious texts. Not all of them were vegetarians. However, slaughter in any form was forbidden. So, the task of slaughtering animals for food was relegated to those living outside the monasteries and viharas and to Muslims, of whom there was also quite a large number.

There were no women students, but a great number of males swelled the student population. Most of them came from poor families. As a matter of fact, it could be said that all the trapas were imparted education free of cost. The others who were slightly better off occasionally brought offerings of butter, barley and similar foodstuffs. I had been under the impression that lamas only concentrated on meditation and prayers, but since my arrival here, I had had reason to change my mind.

The lamas were known as living Buddhas and watching them go about their duties, no one could have harboured doubts about that. The younger or ordinary trapas led a very tough life. Let us take, as an example, a typical young lama or trapa around twelve years old. He would not only be expected to rise at an ungodly hour in these cold climes, but would have to present himself for prayers almost immediately after rolling up and tidying away his bed. Most of the time, the rooms were bitterly cold. The trapas' garments were not particularly warm either and the woollen socks they wore had holes through which their toes wriggled out.

There was little respite for them, for studies would follow. Their studies would continue at a stretch from seven to ten in the morning, interspersed with meditation and prayers. The trapas' rooms were tiny and only a lucky few had windows. So, they would have to manage, somehow, and study by the light of lamps. It was only about a year since electricity had come to Drepung, but all the rooms were yet to be electrically wired. The average weight of the books these boys were required to study could go up to 3 kg! They had to climb up ladders to fetch the tomes; if they slipped somehow and fell, they would be crushed to death under the weight of those very books.

In the afternoon, there were chores to be completed like gardening, cleaning the temple and sweeping and swabbing the rooms before concentrating on studies again. Apart from the usual studies, the students were also taught certain handicrafts and mundane chores. They included embroidery on silk, weaving of textiles and churning milk into butter. The reward for any kind of inattentiveness on the part of these novices would be duly handed out by the lamas in the form of slaps and boxed ears. During the winter months, the life of the trapas became still more difficult.

Some lamas who wore red ribbons the way volunteers at functions did, were the terror of the gumpha. They were known as *dab-dab*. The slightest infringement of any regulation would invite a stinging blow from their wooden batons. Another distinguishing feature of the Drepung and the Sera Gumphas was their armed forces, known as the *dharma sena*. In fact, they were the only two gumphas in all of Tibet equipped with an armed contingent of lamas. All those who had joined the armed forces had started out as lamas. But the students who appeared robust and handsome, and were neither academically inclined nor particularly adept at scholarly pursuits, were sent to train in preparation for joining the armed forces. Annual competitions comprising events like tug of war, wrestling and digging holes in the sand with the feet were organized between the forces of the Drepung and the Sera Gumphas.

The three gumphas, regarded as the foundation stones of the country, exercised great influence on Tibetan politics. While Sera boasted a lama population of 5,000, Ganden housed 3,000 lamas. The Dalai Lama was the chief ruler of Tibet. Since he was still very young, the religious heads representing him acted on his behalf and decided on all matters. In the Revered Dalai Lama's court, there were eight ministers. The representatives of the three gumphas served in an advisory capacity. They were a part of the governing body which included the state secretary and some very senior lamas. If any decision needed to be taken by this body, all the three representatives of the gumphas would have to be consulted. Every year, the Dalai Lama had a conference of lamas organized in Tibet where discussions took place on matters related to Buddhism and innumerable debates were held as well. It was at this time that the Dalai Lama stayed in the Drepung Gumpha. It was also the time when the religious conclave took place.

The lamas here were very solemn indeed and it seemed impossible to visualize them laughing except at mealtimes. It did not seem as if the faith the students reposed in their mentors was an inborn conviction; there was an element of fear there too. Perhaps, the lives of the lamas were meant to be this way. Only by experiencing sorrow could joy be savoured. I might be sworn to silence as the Silent Monk, but with all my other senses alert, I began to absorb the mysteries of this world ruled by lamas and priests.

LAMAS AND LEARNING

IN TIBET, A country ruled by priests, Drepung, Sera and Ganden were the centres of learning, where every male citizen, starting from a ten-year-old daba or trapa to an eighty-year-old lama, could be imparted education. This was where a child gradually evolved into a full-fledged lama. A lama was an ascetic, a saintly person. Not every child or infant could be born as one; if the latter had enough good deeds to his credit later in his life, the title would be conferred on him. Moreover, the name of a lama who had been through several rebirths might be invoked and a new incarnation announced. Living examples of this practice were the Revered Dalai Lama and the Panchen Lama.

The moment a child was born, its parents had to decide whether they would send him to a monastery or not, for in Tibet, it was the only available educational institution and commonly believed to be the sole key to a bright future. When a child was around seven or eight years old, his parents approached the head of the local monastery to arrange for him to be interviewed by the authorities. It was then carefully ascertained as to whether the candidate was healthy enough for life at the monastery and if all went well, a day was decided on for his admission. If the head of the gumpha was already familiar with the child and his background, no further scrutiny was necessary. If not, the administrators made appropriate inquiries about him. Although the Buddhist faith, as practised in Tibet, made no caste distinctions, the progeny of blacksmiths and certain other specified sects were barred from admission to a monastery. The principle on which the gumpha's administration operated in this matter was the following: Buddhism did not legitimize killing in any form; therefore, selecting a candidate from a background where weapons were crafted for battle or execution would be in direct contravention of the faith's fundamental tenets.

Once the head of a gumpha issued the necessary authorization, the applicant was immediately granted admission. Those candidates who lived close by could become day scholars. If a guardian was reluctant to allow his son to go to the monastery at such a tender age, the child was advised to study under his tutelage for a few years more before joining the monastery. The guardian could either personally accept the responsibility of imparting instruction to the child or entrust it to a lama in the village.

The elementary stage of a student's life was known as Ge-Thruk. The village lamas who imparted instruction to young children belonging to this level were called Ge-Gan. No restrictions were imposed on Ge-Gan lamas as far as leading the life of a householder or even engaging in trade was concerned. After being educated under a Ge-Gan, a child had to undergo a fresh series of tests before he went to live in a gumpha. It was at this stage that the novice was given saffron robes to wear and his head was tonsured by the gumpha's barber. It was also at this point that his guardian was expected to make whatever payment he could afford. Much of the time, the amount he could afford determined his offspring's future.

The entire responsibility for a boy's upbringing lay with the head of the gumpha. The young trapa gradually acquired an awareness of his role in the scheme of things, a part of which was to serve his mentor. Years passed in this manner until he was around thirteen or fourteen, when he would have to sit for another examination. If he was successful, the boy was elevated from the level of Ge-Thruk to that of Ge-Niyen. It marked the beginning of his actual education when his habits and general character came under intense scrutiny. He was also under great pressure to learn to conform to the norms of behaviour expected of him. At the end of three to four years of study at this level, the novice would have to face another examination, comparable, to some extent, to the school final examinations that a student in the outside world sat for. His main subjects were religion, philosophy, history, mathematics and geography, with a special focus on religion and various religious rites and rituals.

If an acolyte intended to study beyond the Ge-Niyen level and go on to university, he would have to sit for a great many tests and enter into innumerable debates with scholars specializing in the subjects chosen for debate. If he managed to get through this stage of his education successfully, he was elevated to the position of a priest. But first, he would have to adhere to certain norms and go through specified rituals, known to lamas as Get-Sul or Get-Shul. These forbade a novice from drinking, killing and kidnapping, indulging in promiscuity and uttering falsehoods. In the gumpha or monastery, everyone had to lead a life of abstinence; in other words, eschew sensual pleasure in any form. It was also forbidden to eat at unscheduled times, indulge one's love for music and dance, use perfumes and fragrances, sleep in comfortable beds and, of course, to have anything at all to do with valuables like money, gold and precious jewellery. These were the basic principles of Buddhism. To reach the Get-Shul level, a student had to vow to follow thirty-six regimes which demanded rigorous control over his body and mind. Only when the body was free of all vice could the mind be unburdened enough to focus totally on the Enlightened One—the Buddha. Hostel life for the lamas was austere, their personal effects consisting of the typical garb of an ascetic, a pair of large bedspreads, a pair of blankets, a lamp, a bowl, a glass, a plate and some books.

At the Get-Shul level, all the lamas were entitled to state sponsorship and to the opportunities offered by the government. At this stage, a couple of years here or there did not really make much of a difference. What mattered more was mental discipline. It was from this level onwards, that students began to be recognized as lamas. But full recognition was still a long way off. Less than twenty years old, the students continued to be known as trapas. From now on, a trapa would be given the responsibility of looking after the temple.

It was also at this point that the lamas had to memorize Kangiour, the sacred religious text, and learn from their mentors how to analyse the various passages in it and explain them to others. There was much emphasis as well on copying the text and studying it in depth. Passionate debates were held on philosophy, where the mentors served exclusively as judges. The victors in the debate were honoured with the title of Gelong-Ma. From the age of twenty onwards, the lamas were trained in state administration and law and even in philosophy as part of the process of learning how to take over as chief of the gumpha. Serious meditation for attaining nirvana also began at this stage. Those who went in for state administration married and set up families of their own.

Those who opted for greater spiritual enlightenment and growth, on the other hand, accepted the harsh dictum of eternal celibacy.

The administrative heads of the gumphas in villages that were located far from Lhasa determined the future course of their students. But the chief political posts at the capital were allotted, invariably, to lamas from the Drepung, Sera and Ganden Gumphas.

A TIBETAN TALE:
HISTORY AND FAITH

THE BUDDHISM PRACTISED in Tibet was very different in form from that followed elsewhere in the world. On raised platforms in each temple were various images of the Buddha along with the idols of innumerable Hindu deities such as Kali, Tara, Durga, Bhairavi, Brahma and Saraswati, among others. What was worth noting, however, was the role of the occult in Buddhism. To understand the nature of this particular influence, one must delve deeper into Tibetan history and discover how the religion was introduced into the country.

Although accurate historical records of this period are yet to be established, Bon-Pa is believed to be the predominant religion of ancient Tibet. It embraced various occult practices that included casting of fatal spells, possession by evil spirits and invocation of demons to attain some objective or the other. The representatives of this sect would intimidate the average man in the name of religion and resort to extortionate tactics for personal gain. The Tibetans had always been a simple and devout people and failed to summon the courage to defy these false priests who reigned supreme. Every once in a while, an intrepid individual would take the initiative of trying to bring about a semblance of order and unity among the people, though, invariably, he would be forced to surrender to a superior power. And so, the story would be repeated. The Tibetan leaders or kings who came to power in this manner would, however, continue to tolerate the old custom of religious blackmail or 'sponsorship', whereby the self-appointed priests fed off the people. Propagating belief in the existence of dragons and evil spirits, the Bon-Pa faith strongly resembled some branches of the occult, though there were areas where it diverged from them dramatically.

Buddhism was introduced into Tibet in the seventh century, that is, almost 1,200 years after the birth of the Buddha, by the then king, Song-San Gampo. It is in his memory that Tibetan monasteries are called gompas or gumphas. Around AD 650, the redoubtable king invaded faraway China in a bid to extend his country's borders. Victorious in battle, he married the princess of China and brought her back to Tibet. At the time, India and China happened to be political allies and Buddhism was China's main religion. Inspired by his Chinese consort, the king of Tibet converted to her faith. On returning home, he attacked south Nepal. The vanquished king of Nepal, Anshu Verma, dealt with the crisis by signing a peace treaty with the Tibetan king. Its terms decreed that he surrender his daughter, Bhrikuti, to his Tibetan victor who married her and brought her back to his own country. During that era, Nepal was totally under the influence of Buddhism. Thus, through the Buddhist consorts of the Tibetan monarch, was the faith imported to Tibet from Nepal and China. It was under their abiding influence that King Song-San Gampo would accept Buddhism as the royal religion of Tibet. His second consort, the Nepalese princess, had brought, along with her Buddhist beliefs, a dowry of gold and silver and a retinue of Buddhist scholars. She had also been instrumental in having Lhasa's second Buddhist temple, the Ramose Temple, constructed. The Chinese princess, on the other hand, had brought in an exquisite statue of Shakyamuni, one of the many incarnations of the Buddha and the first such image of the Lord in Tibet, which would be set up and worshipped in the huge Jokhang Temple that the king would go on to construct in Lhasa.

That was the least of the king's contributions to the faith. Buddhism also completely changed his way of thinking. Eschewing warfare altogether, the monarch adopted the propagation of peace and joy as his mission in life. Filled with positive feelings, he initiated his own finance minister, Thon-Mi-Soboth, and the latter's family into the faith with the special incantation used by all Buddhists and instructed the man to visit India with an entourage of erudite and enlightened Tibetans. They would do well to absorb the tenets of true Buddhism from the Lord's very birthplace. Once that was accomplished, every Tibetan citizen would have to convert to Buddhism. It is quite likely that Emperor Ashoka of India was the only monarch before Song-San Gampo to have made such a concentrated effort to promote the Buddhist faith in his country.

The Tibetan finance minister, Thon-Mi-Soboth, came to India, appointed the highly knowledgeable Lipidutta as vice chancellor and personally undertook the responsibility of translating various texts in Pali and Sanskrit into Tibetan. It was around this time that the message of peace and the importance of meditation first began to be propagated in Tibet.

However, the country's predominant Bon-Pa religion was far from extinct. It had merely suffered a setback of sorts. For it was extremely difficult for the average Tibetan to tame his primitive fear of devils, demons and the supernatural. With the king's demise, the unscrupulous priests and occult practitioners moved back to centre stage and began preying on the people with renewed vigour. Since they had neither the authority nor the courage to flout Buddhism, which was the royally sanctioned religion after all, these exploiters chose to artfully manipulate and distort it by introducing elements borrowed from the occult and the various psychic sciences. Thus, the Buddhist faith, painstakingly established and encouraged to flourish by the late king, his consorts and his ministers, became the target, once again, of unscrupulous manipulators seeking to exploit it for their own ends. Under their influence, the people indulged in occult practices even as they followed the official religion. Largely because of this trend, the dragon was accepted as a symbol of Buddhism in Tibet, although the fact remains that it was also a dominant symbol of the faith as practised in China during that era. The battle for supremacy between Buddhism and the Bon-Pa religion would continue to rage for almost a century.

With the ascent of Thri-Sron-Ide-Tsan to the throne of Tibet, a sense of balance was swiftly restored to the country. The king gathered together his counsellors and announced, 'Though Bon-Pa is the ancient religion of Tibet, it is Buddhism that has brought peace and stability to our country. Moreover, it is only by following this faith that our ancestors have attained moksha and nirvana. To regard it as dispensable is, therefore, out of the question. A spiritual leader will have to be found who can explore the positive aspects of both Buddhism and Bon-Pa and come to some sort of decision whereby they can be judiciously combined for the greater good.'

Following an extensive search and a storm of controversy, an outstanding spiritual mentor was located in Kashmir. His name was Padma Sambhava. A scholar endowed with supreme knowledge, he was accepted as the spiritual mentor of Tibet and came to be known as Rimpoche or 'the Revered Mentor'. There are many who know him as the Urgiyan Lama, for he was born in the Urgiyan village of Kashmir. The legend surrounding his birth is also rather remarkable, for he was apparently not born of any human womb, but came into being inside a lotus blossom.

Having reached Tibet, Rimpoche immediately set about the task of reformation. He was well aware that if war were overtly declared against adherents of the Bon-Pa faith, it would merely provoke resistance against the propagation of Buddhism and end up undermining the latter's cause. So, exercising great discretion, he disseminated his own beliefs among the people and made progress. Inwardly, he was aware that all demons, ghosts, monsters and supernatural creatures would have to be vanquished from the minds of the people before the path to peace could be sought.

Rimpoche's message of unity disarmed all the sects. He brought the sceptics and unbelievers into his fold through a display of his occult and mystical powers. In no time at all, his fame had spread throughout Tibet. Even followers of the ancient cult began to seek him out as their mentor. At the same time, Buddhism became widely accepted as the royally sanctioned religion. Observing how effective Padma Sambhava's message could be and how potent his occult powers were, King Thri-Sron-Ide-Tsan threw open the doors of the treasury so that funds would be readily available for propagating the religion as far as possible. It was around this time that Tibetan scholars came to India for the purpose of enhancing their knowledge of religion, philosophy and Sanskrit. It was also around this time that Kamlasheel, an Indian scholar, won a marathon debate held in connection with Buddhism at the royal palace in Lhasa.

Guru Padma Sambhava was simultaneously a Buddhist monk, a practitioner of the occult arts and the Urgiyan Lama who disseminated knowledge among all communities without exception and accepted disciples into his fold. It was in this manner that he would gradually win the loyalty of even those who had been staunch worshippers of the ancient cult and his fame and glory would spread far and wide.

As the leading authority on the occult and mystical sciences and on virtually all branches of Buddhism, Guru Rimpoche set up a great many monasteries and viharas all over the country. He also established a number of temples dedicated to the practice of the occult sciences. His personal life was unusual to say the least. It is believed that he had four principal wives and countless mistresses. That in no way detracted from his fame and influence, however. Owing to the manner in which he had achieved a perfect fusion of the principles of Buddhism and the beliefs on which occult practices were based, Buddhism came to be firmly entrenched in Tibet. To spread the teachings of the Buddha, Guru Rimpoche sent lamas to distant villages as representatives of the faith and of the king.

In his old age, Guru Rimpoche wholeheartedly dedicated his life to disseminating Buddhism and enhancing its influence in areas where it was already established. With the passing years, he had distanced himself from the occult and moved closer to moksha and nirvana. This had so enraged one of his compatriots, an adherent of the ancient Bon-Pa cult, that he ended up murdering the sage. With Rimpoche dead, the brutal Bon-Pa priest destroyed priceless texts that had been translated into Tibetan from Sanskrit. He was later apprehended and beheaded for his crime.

Guru Rimpoche is worshipped in Tibet even today. He is probably the most powerful of the deities, rather like the Goddess Kali in Bengal, and the Ni-Ingma-Pa sect regard him as their most honoured mentor or god.

Despite great opposition from the ancients, the influx of scholars from India continued unabated. During the reign of King Ye-Ses-Od in the eleventh century, a group of young Tibetan scholars came to India to study Buddhism. At their invitation, a few Indian scholars also set off for Tibet to propagate Buddhism. The leader of that group, the great scholar, Atish Dipankar, set up the Kadam-Pa sect with the help of his able disciple, Brom-Ton.

This sect would subsequently gain renown as the Geluk-Pa sect of which the Dalai Lama is the head priest today.

In eleventh-century Tibet, the Geluk-Pa sect had flourished unrivalled, for the whole country had unanimously accepted the leadership of the Dalai Lama. In the fifteenth century, however, another sect, the Shakya, sprang into existence. It followed the middle path between the Ni-Ingma-Pa and Geluk-Pa sects and under the powerful patronage of Kublai Khan, swept aside several smaller sects to establish itself. The powerful Chinese emperor assured the members of the sect that, if required, he would extend all help to them, even if it involved sending in troops and arms. The Tashi or Panchen Lama is the head of this sect today. There are subtle differences in the practices of the two sects. Members of the sect that owes its allegiance to the Dalai Lama, for instance, are sworn to eternal celibacy. The adherents of the Shakya sect, on the other hand, who regard the Panchen Lama as their religious leader, are allowed to marry. Despite their apparent rivalry, both the Geluk-Pa and Shakya sects practise a form of Buddhism that is strongly influenced by the occult.

Thus did the two main branches of Buddhism come into existence in Tibet. At the outset, it was with the help of the Ni-Ingma-Pa sect—of which Padma Sambhava was the guru—that the Buddhist faith established itself in Tibet. The Kadam-Pa sect formed by Guru Atish would subsequently evolve into the Geluk-Pa sect with its stronghold in Lhasa and the Dalai Lama as its religious leader. It would be followed by the rise of the Shakya sect, headed by the Panchen Lama in Gyatse. As mentioned earlier, the Shakya sect had risen in the fifteenth century and all but wiped out the Geluk-Pa. At the time, a very powerful lama by the name of Song-Ka-Pa had appeared in Tibet. Playing the dual role of a social reformer and spiritual leader, he infused new life into the Geluk-Pa sect. And it was from around 1640 onwards, when Song-Ka-Pa made his appearance, that the whole of Tibet came under the rule of the Dalai Lama. Believed to be a previous incarnation of the Dalai Lama—he is, in fact, said to be repeatedly reincarnated in the form of the Dalai Lama—and, therefore, greatly revered, Song-Ka-Pa established the famous Ganden Gumpha.

From the fifteenth century onwards, Buddhism in Tibet has gone from strength to strength. Different sects have come up around monasteries and temples which serve as their nucleus. The Hinayana and Mahayana sects of Buddhism, once introduced to Tibet, came under the influence of the Chinese version of Buddhism along with that of the occult sciences and their adherents gradually converted to Bahuyana. To distinguish between them is a near impossible task for outsiders. What does stand out is the colour of the robes and caps their followers wear.

LHASA AND JOKHANG, THE CORE TEMPLE

WE STAYED AT the Drepung Gumpha for three days. Lhasa lay a mere four miles away. Having come so close to my goal, the prospect of waiting for three whole days before we could proceed further was sheer torment. But I had little choice in the matter. From this vantage point, the Dalai Lama's palace appeared as exquisite as a picture.

All the Nepalese students of the Drepung Monastery who had come from their country's three largest religious institutions, namely, Swayambhu, Mahabodhi and Naambuddha, were between twenty-five and thirty years old. After bidding farewell to all those we had come to be acquainted with during our stay here, we set out for Lhasa on the morning of the fourth day.

As we moved on, the Ki Chu river gave us company all the way. We passed horses and horse-drawn carriages on the road that was flanked by houses standing cheek by jowl. It was the first time after Gyatse, that we saw lorries plying. Often, we passed shops, restaurants and tents housing poor nomads. It seemed that even this road, paved with large slabs of stone, was under repair. The houses located in the heart of the city were visible in the distance. The path we were travelling along was no longer the lonely mountain track we were accustomed to; it had acquired a life of its own. By now, we were very close to the Potala; another couple of miles and we would be in the heart of the city. All of a sudden, we noticed rows of flags and chaityas of different sizes. The road ran up a gentle slope, leading us to the peak of a chaitya, shaped rather like the Swayambhunath Temple of Kathmandu. Ascending all the while, the road brought us at its highest point to a huge chaitya that looked as though it had been swathed in multicoloured prayer flags. From this point, the Potala, the holy palace of the Revered Dalai Lama, was still more clearly visible as a beautiful red house atop a hillock. A fourteen-storeyed structure towered near it. Guruji observed, 'That colossal building in front is called the Fargo-Kaling.' This gigantic chaitya on the banks of the river would have been clearly visible to every pilgrim who made his way here. We had finally reached Lhasa.

All of a sudden, we found ourselves surrounded by beggars. Guruji warned us not to give them alms. Then he began trying to convince them that we were not ordinary pilgrims, but poor mendicant lamas. It was, therefore, pointless to badger us. He was evidently successful in his endeavour, because they eventually let us off despite their initial scepticism about his claims. We moved on again. After going around the Fargo-Kaling seven times and offering our prayers, we stopped for a while in front of a tea stall to refresh ourselves.

It was from Fargo-Kaling that the city actually began. A flag welcomed all visitors to Lhasa, known as 'Hla-Sa', the 'abode of the gods'. According to many, it meant 'heaven' in Tibetan. The Mongols, in fact, had a similar meaning for Lhasa in their own language. A great many Indian ascetics believed that Kailasa, the heaven mentioned in the Hindu religious scriptures, was actually Lhasa. All the mysteries of the Himalayas lay buried here. At long last, our dreams had been fulfilled and we cried out in joy: 'Hail, Shakyamuni! Hail, Mahakali! Long live Chenreji, king of kings! Long live the Buddha, the faith and the sangha!'

Having offered our prayers to the different deities, we forged a path to the Potala through the crowd of city dwellers who had gathered around us. The royal palace was only half an hour away on foot. The houses we now passed evidently belonged to the Tibetan aristocracy and were constructed of wood. There were also several houses built of concrete with pagoda-shaped roofs, rather like those in Kathmandu. Ponds glimmered here and there and the city abounded in trees and shrubs. We also noticed a few parks. Had it not been for the Potala, it would not have struck us that we had just entered a nation's capital.

The narrow alleys of Lhasa were just like the ones that snaked through Varanasi. Having negotiated a few of them, we entered the premises of the core temple of both Lhasa and Tibet— the palatial Jokhang Temple, also known as the Shuk-La-Khang, which seemed to have somehow jostled itself into position between the crowded houses of the city, not unlike the way the Baba Viswanath Temple in Varanasi appeared to have carved a niche for itself. It would have been quite impossible to glimpse it from outside. Having entered the hallowed precincts, we prostrated ourselves before the Buddha.

This then was Lhasa, the city established by King Song-San Gampo almost four hundred years before Christ! The fort constructed on the summit of Potala Hill was now known as the Potala Palace, but a smaller version of it had existed in the remote past. Thousands of lamas and pilgrims arrived every day to offer their fervent prayers at the Jokhang Temple where the image of the Lord was supposed to be alive with his spirit and thereby exuded a powerful influence according to those practising the occult arts in conjunction with Tibetan Buddhism. Though I had been to a number of pilgrimage centres before, none of them had teemed with as many beggars as this one. But it was worth noting that none of these mendicants appeared to be the aggressive, grasping kind who would hound a pilgrim for alms. Despite their obvious need, there was a certain dignity about them. The core temple could only be accessed after passing through a huge courtyard. It was surrounded by innumerable smaller temples. The walls were carved with different versions of the Buddha. I gazed in wonder at them all.

The image that King Song-San Gampo's Chinese consort had brought from her country was nearly identical to the one at Sarnath, but for the features. They were unmistakably Chinese. What surprised me, however, was the kind of rituals followed here which bore a closer resemblance to Hindu rites than to Buddhist tradition. We bowed reverently before the image and paid obeisance by prostrating ourselves repeatedly during our circumambulation of the temple. Another round of Hindu rituals followed as we circled the temple again. It took us almost two hours to complete the entire sequence of rites and by this time, my fellow companions and lamas were awash with devotional fervour. The cries of the devotees rose in the air: 'Baba, rescue me! Dharmaraja … please save my son! Restore my husband's health … let something be done for my daughter…. Give us peace and prosperity and release us from this cycle of rebirth…'

The courtyard was so vast that instead of waiting in a queue and moving forward in single file, nearly sixty people flanking each other could enter the temple at a time. The pilgrims carried little pieces of yellow or white fabric as offerings to Shakyamuni, the main deity. Some devotees brought butter for lighting the lamps, while the affluent carried with them a variety of gifts and rice as offerings. All the members of our group had brought a shawl each to offer Shakyamuni. Darkness seemed to envelop us the moment we entered, but once our eyes had become used to the gloom, we noticed rows of lighted lamps lined up against the walls. A symbol of the immortal Shakyamuni, these lamps were never allowed to go out. As one moved further ahead, a pair of collapsible iron grilles were visible on either side of the raised dais. Though the iron doors were kept shut, the devotees could easily catch a glimpse of the Buddha.

Right before us was a colossal image of the Lord, its golden face serene and shining, its eyes painted and outlined, blue on white. The Buddha looked on affectionately, as though seeking to solve the problems of his devotees. Only the face of the image was visible; the body was completely swathed in shawls. In fact, it actually seemed to stoop somewhat under the weight of the shawls it supported! In front of the image, in a huge drum-like container that served as a lamp, a flame burned continuously. All the devotees poured the ghee they carried into it. Almost 4 kg of ghee was needed daily to keep all the lamps alight. In this container were thousands of smaller wicks from which bright flames glowed. It was a truly magnificent sight!

Flanking the door on either side was a pair of priest lamas. They arranged the items needed for the rituals of worship and accepted the shawls from the devotees before placing them in front of the Buddha, apart from taking care of every other ritual that was mandatory. In other words, they kept themselves very busy. Though the main entrance to the temple was never closed, the iron gates were thrown open only at nine in the morning and kept open till the evening. The rites of worship here were in keeping with occult rituals which had been incorporated into the Tibetan form of Buddhism. In the dim light cast by the lamps, I observed thousands of thangkas decorating the surrounding walls. They appeared to be as ancient as the temple itself.

The statue of Shakyamuni equalled the height of at least one-and-a-half adults and along with the platform it was kept on, rose to over thirteen feet. Shakyamuni was not merely Lhasa's most powerful deity; within that statue lay hidden the city's treasury. Apart from being plated in gold, the image was studded with the world's most precious stones. The crown was encrusted with innumerable jewels. The platform was fashioned from solid gold. Besides the spiritual wealth this image stood for, it would have been virtually impossible to evaluate the extent to which the treasures here enhanced the country's material assets. Rumour had it that the accumulated gold of the temple would have been enough to buy the entire world! Although this was mere hearsay, it could not be completely discounted either. All the objects used in the rituals of worship were made of pure gold. Except for the priest, there was no standing room for anybody. A steady stream of devotees and pilgrims passed through the temple all day. Consequently, for the purpose of meditation, devotees were expected to go to a special arena or *mandap*, where mattresses had been laid out. They had become nearly threadbare with use and devotees, therefore, carried their own blankets with them.

After crossing the courtyard to enter the Jokhang Temple, we had to move further on, passing through the mandap to reach the heart of the temple. All the rituals of prayers were offered here. On the opposite side of the mandap was a temple within a temple— the Temple of the Thousand Buddhas. This small place of worship could be described as a museum of sorts that contained a large collection of statues of different sizes. In fact, every imaginable idol of the Buddha had a place here. A careful examination revealed many of the Indian deities too, including Brahma–Vishnu–Shiva, Hara–Gouri and Saraswati, among others. The fusion of Chinese and Indian thoughts and trends was only too apparent here. Shiva's mascot, the serpent, for example, had been reinvented as a dragon here as was the lion, the mascot of the Goddess Durga.

After exploring everything here, we moved on to the second level, that is, to an area below the temple. I was absolutely stunned by the sight that confronted me. I had not thought to see it in the core temple dedicated to the Lord Buddha. For before me was a terrifying image of the Goddess Kali—the Protector of Lhasa. She was quite unlike the images to be found in Kolkata's Kalighat or Dakshineswar. Far more fearsome, Kali was depicted consuming the brains from a human skull! Although the Dalai Lama himself was a Buddhist, Kali was the goddess he prayed to. If hearing about it was a strange experience, it was far more amazing to behold. The image of the goddess, which was believed to be alive with her spirit and, therefore, emanated a tremendous power, was worshipped twice a day. The ceremony was conducted in accordance with the occult rites of Buddhism. Pilgrims usually paid their respects to Shakyamuni before visiting the Temple of Mahamaya. To the average man, Mahakali herself was responsible for creation and served as its protector.

I was enjoying the feel of my surroundings, when I came to my senses suddenly. I was sitting right in the centre, with the other lamas around me. How had I come out of the temple? Who had sat me down here? These questions began to surface now. A priest lama handed me a steaming cup of tea that refreshed me physically and mentally. Sadhu Baba was beside me. He caressed my head affectionately. 'This is nothing,' he said soothingly. 'Emotions often provoke similar reactions. This is merely the outcome of your having to remain silent all the time. Your pent-up feelings were denied an outlet and needed release.'

Be it mere emotion or an excess of it, logical explanations could, perhaps, be found for it, but the exhilaration and joyous sense of spiritual fulfilment that I experienced could not be expressed in words at all, whatever be the language of choice. It seems that I had lain unconscious near the doors of the temple for almost an hour. Needless to say, we had eaten almost nothing since the morning. The day was speeding by so fast. As evening drew near, we would begin exploring the remaining part of the temple.

We seated ourselves in an underground room. Darkness almost shrouded the entire temple. And down below, where we now found ourselves, it was darker still, for sunlight never penetrated this area. It was as if we were in the nether world and the tale we were told about this very room turned out to be very interesting indeed.

After the Jokhang Temple had been built, three of its rooms were dedicated to a trio of deities. The first room was intended for Shakyamuni, the second for other incarnations of the Buddha. The room above was reserved for the Goddess Kali. As in the other temples, this room too, had strong stone walls and was decorated all over with beautiful wood carvings. It was an architectural marvel of its time. The foundations of the temple had been laid according to certain occult specifications. Then, with due pomp and ceremony, the deities were installed in their respective places. A few days later, the priests and lamas observed a much diminished life force within the temple; lamps would be snuffed out, as if of their own accord, the ringing of bells would be muffled and it seemed as if the prayers of devotees and pilgrims were just not being heeded. Even the priests would forget their incantations during the ceremonies. It was as though an ice-cold demon had taken up residence in the temple. Had the results of spending so much money and conducting so many ceremonies to placate the gods come to nought? Even the king lost his peace of mind and ultimately sent for scholars, priests and practitioners of black magic. They carefully examined the temple and concluded that a wicked demon had made this temple his home. Those familiar with the occult sciences clearly stated that five demons had infested the place. At their words, everybody was overcome with grief—a place so sacred, home to the Buddha had been besmirched by the presence of evil spirits! Could there be greater cause for sorrow? The king sent a message across his kingdom: anyone who could exorcize the temple of these demons would be amply rewarded. Innumerable people turned up, but each one had to return home defeated. Finally, it was Padma Sambhava who came forward with the assurance that he would be able to do the needful. Thanks to his wondrous skills and mental power, all the demons surrendered and prostrated themselves before him. He captured them all and imprisoned them in this room.

It so happened that on a certain occasion, Padma Sambhava had to go out of Lhasa on some work. Before his departure, he repeatedly warned the lamas of the temple not to release the evil spirits under any circumstances. However, after he had left, a kind-hearted lama passing by this room heard the cries of the wicked spirits who appealed to him for mercy with the words, 'Rather than live in this prison, it is better that we cease to exist altogether!'

The priest felt very sorry for them and said, 'I do understand your predicament, but there is nothing I can do. Baba Padma Sambhava is not here at the moment. When he returns, I suggest you put your case before him.'

Noting that they had managed to attract the lama's attention and arouse his sympathy, the demons wept and pleaded, 'We have lost count of the days we have been without light; and there is no greater punishment than being cooped up in this darkness. Please permit us, even if it's only for a moment, to see some light. We will be content with that and you can lock us up again.'

Moved by these pleas, the priest unlocked the door with the intention of allowing the spirits out for sometime. No sooner had they emerged than they burst into mocking peals of laughter and began taunting the priest. 'You fool!' they exclaimed, 'we have never seen anyone quite as stupid as you! This is our temple and kingdom.' With that, they resorted again to the nefarious tricks they had played earlier. It was impossible to contain them and the poor priest greatly regretted his impulsive action.

In a short while, Padma Sambhava came to hear of what was going on in Lhasa. Though he was preoccupied with certain occult practices, he returned to the capital at once. Although the guru was very gentle and soft-spoken, he could, if required, assume the form of the vilest demon. As soon as he entered the place, he let out a thunderous roar of fury which made the demons quake. Picking up a massive boulder, Padma Sambhava hurled it in their direction. Noticing that boulder hurtling towards them, two of the evil spirits fled in terror, while three were imprisoned once again. Padma Sambhava observed the occult rites in such a way as to ensure that the demons would remain in bondage as long as the gods presided over the temple. They would be released only if alien invaders attacked it. That massive boulder now lay beside a pillar and merely touching it was believed to be highly auspicious for the person concerned.

Although we were blessed with a few more of the temple's bountiful sights, all too soon it was evening. We were circumambulating the temple—an integral part of our prayer rituals—when bugles and other musical instruments rang out and everybody rushed to the temple at once for evening prayers. Unfortunately, by the time we completed our circumambulation and our prayers, a process that could not be abandoned midway, the temple was so crowded that there was no room for us at all! We had to stand outdoors to participate in the first evening prayer session at Lhasa.

LHASA

OUTSIDERS WERE NOT permitted to stay within the Jokhang Temple. The house next to the temple that was allotted to the priests was used either by those lamas who conducted the religious services or by those responsible for the temple's security. There were no provisions at all for lamas visiting from beyond the border. Nearly a hundred lamas lived on the premises, but they were all paid wages. So, the possibility of our staying there was nil. Arrangements had been made for us to be put up in another old house and it would not be wrong to describe it as an ancient dharamsala. This was located in the direction of Fargo-Kaling, from where we had made our way here that morning. The house was certainly old, but the arrangements within were excellent; in other words, they met the pilgrims' every need. There was a kitchen stocked with wood for fuel. There was no toilet. For that purpose, one was expected to walk some distance in the direction of the river. But then, at no point of time had walking ever been a problem for us.

Not far from our dharamsala was the Kashak department, very similar to the Writer's Building in Kolkata. It was from this department that Lhasa and Tibet were administered. It was also the place to which the chief priest and ministers repaired for their daily accounts. There was electricity in Lhasa and the roads were certainly lit up, as were all the houses. But it wasn't an amenity everyone enjoyed. Only the wealthy were permitted to apply for electrical connections.

Although King Song-San Gampo undoubtedly did much for Lhasa, the city's actual evolution and progress had begun centuries earlier. Back in the fourth century, Lhasa had already been established as the heart of flourishing trade and commerce. Its first fort, built on a small scale, had risen on the summit of Potala Hill and would later be converted by the king into his palace. In order to help with the administration of Lhasa, lamas were recruited from gumphas across the country, the main ones being Drepung, Sera and Ganden. The head of administration—in other words, the Dalai Lama—would also be chosen from one of these three gumphas.

As the day dawned, I gazed through the window at the city. The sight that met my eyes was amazing indeed. Most of the houses were pagoda-shaped, rather like those in China and Japan. Between them, sprouted modern constructions that seemed totally out of sync with the spirit of the place. The heart of the city lay in the bazaar or marketplace. Here, all pilgrims were free to do what they pleased and come and go as they wished.

Our brother lamas rose at the crack of dawn and made their way to the temple, but Guruji and I remained behind. Though I had also come on a pilgrimage, my interest went a little further; I wished to explore as much of the city as possible. The market for textiles and woollens was particularly worth a mention. By the roadside, wool sheared from lambs was piled up like cotton wool in huge bags. Crowds thronged the shops selling woollen clothes of different kinds. There were also wholesale and retail markets. The retail shops were managed, for the most part, by neat, clean and well-dressed women. Lilting feminine laughter often rang out in the streets. There was scarcely anything on sale in the vegetable market; the crops had just begun to take root. The fields had been ploughed right after the freeze and thaw. It would take at least a month for the vegetables to sprout. Traders from Beijing (then Peking) had started visiting this place regularly and would probably be taking over very soon.

Though the Tibetan lamas were forbidden to kill living creatures, there were no restrictions imposed on their eating flesh.

The fish and mutton shops, therefore, enjoyed a brisk trade. Generally, the villagers carried baskets of dried and salted fish. The locals also brought fresh fish from the Ki Chu river. Meat and fish seemed to constitute the staple diet of the Tibetans. Due to lack of regular transport, there was an acute shortage of fresh foodstuff coming into the country from beyond its borders. One had to depend entirely on local crops. Moreover, it was only in this corner of the country, that is, in south-eastern Tibet, that a decent number of crops could be cultivated. The relatively lower altitude, the more moderate temperatures and the availability of level land made cultivation easier than elsewhere in the country. As a result, the region was densely populated. In fact, almost seventy per cent of Tibet's population was concentrated on either side of the Ki Chu river.

We entered the street of grocers where a wide variety of rice, lentils and other grains was on sale. We purchased some rice and lentils and received a huge bonus share in our privileged capacity as pilgrims. The *chura* or dried and processed milk of the Chamri cow was another very profitable business in these parts. The milk was processed and pressed into little slabs like chocolates and packaged in batches of a dozen or so. We noticed something else: at the other end of the market were beggars selling foreign currency. We discovered that a great number of Tibetan coins could be exchanged for Indian money. It was here that pilgrims bought loose change in local currency to give to beggars as alms. In the market, we noticed for the first time, tea stalls selling snacks rather similar to those available in India. Bread, biscuits, lentils and vegetables—everything was available along the road and the language barrier posed no problem at all for us. In Tibet, shops selling tea and liquor were plentiful. So far as fruits were concerned, oranges, apples and pears were grown in this region and did not, therefore, need to be imported. There were shops well-stocked with small thangkas, shawls and other material pilgrims might like to carry to the temple. There were also shops selling every other kind of fabric necessary for the rituals of worship and for the garments worn by the lamas and priests. Unlike in India, it was not the custom to take flowers to the temple as offerings.

The parade ground was located beside the bazaar. The police force of Lhasa gathered here and all important functions were held on these grounds. Most of the houses were painted in beautiful shades. Houses belonging to the aristocracy had pagoda-shaped terraces and near the point where their roofs ended were bright images of dragons that made them look like the city's living sentinels. There was no way the Chinese influence could go unnoticed; most restaurants offered a Chinese menu to customers and the manner in which the latter ate their food was also distinctively Chinese. Local people were more used to eating with chopsticks than with their fingers.

Lhasa was a compact city covering an area of no more than two square miles. In the north stood the Potala Palace. To the south flowed the river. The Drepung Gumpha rose in the west and Norbulingka—Chenreji's summer palace—lay in the east. On the second evening following our arrival, our whole group went to the temple once more to pray together and participate in the religious ceremonies reserved for that time of day. Here, the melodious hum of people praying in unison was different from what we had been accustomed to and we never tired of listening to it, though it carried on right through the night. Rising from the summit of Potala Hill, it was, perhaps, the most sacred prayer ever sent up by the human race.

POTALA, THE ROYAL PALACE

EVER SINCE WE arrived in Lhasa, the royal palace had appeared in the distance like a dream. The sight had made me restlessly impatient for a glimpse of the wondrous treasures inside. While the lamas fervently looked forward to visiting the Jokhang Temple, I yearned for the Potala Palace. I had confided my longings to Guruji often enough, but we had to be circumspect in all we did. Lhasa was thick with Chinese spies and if we so much as moved in the direction of the palace, we would be noticed right away. The Potala Palace was, undoubtedly, among the most coveted attractions in Lhasa and in all Tibet, but it was not crucial to the typical pilgrim's itinerary. His Mecca was, understandably, the Jokhang Temple.

On our third morning in Lhasa, Guruji suddenly appeared bearing joyful tidings. A lama he was closely acquainted with was working at the time in some department of the Potala. We decided to make our way there on the pretext of meeting him. The other lamas had already left for the temple early in the morning. We each had a cup of tea at one of the tea stalls lined up just below our dharamsala before setting off for the Potala.

From the northern section of Lhasa, it was a twenty-five-minute walk. If one were to try and describe the Potala, even the briefest summary would, perhaps, involve an allusion to its resemblance to a small hilltop, whose summit had been lopped off and replaced by a thirteen-storeyed house. In order to make that house accessible to those at street level, there were stairs of all kinds climbing up around it. Of all the palaces in the world, the Potala was believed to be the most beautiful. Behind it, against a striking backdrop of clouds, were mountain peaks lined up in rows. The palace could be divided into three distinct parts: the red central section with its golden dome-shaped roofs that resembled those of a temple, flanked by the two white houses on either side with sloping roofs, like the wings of a bird. The palace towered three hundred and seventy-five feet above Lhasa city. The Revered Dalai Lama's room was situated at an even greater height—over four hundred feet above ground level.

We arrived at a spot right at the foot of the hill and discovered that no matter how beautiful the Potala Palace might have been, the approach to it was filthy. The first eyesore that attracted our attention was a crowd of beggars, followed by the squalid hovels we passed. Piles of garbage from these dwellings littered the roads. It did not appear as if the city's municipal corporation took any interest at all in maintaining the roads and keeping them clean. Only showers or rainstorms could be credited with whatever cleanliness the area laid claim to. Stairs had been hewn out of the hillside and the palace was still quite a distance away. We continued to climb and having passed the shanties, entered a narrow alley. A few children were playing there and as we passed them, someone called out to us. We looked up to find an elderly lama hailing us from a window. Meeting our upturned gaze, he asked, 'Where are you headed?'

'We are looking for an old friend,' Guruji answered.

'It is obvious that you do not belong to Lhasa. What is your friend's name?'

'Yangche Lama,' Guruji replied. 'He is quite advanced in years.'

'Oh, I see! Take the alley to the left of the stairs. He is probably in the office right now.'

Thanking the man, we continued on our way. The roads to the Potala were actually flights of stairs and rather unusual ones at that; the main section was broad, whereas the steps close by it were exceedingly steep. If someone missed his footing at the top, there was no way he could stop himself from hurtling all the way down. We arrived at the address we sought and knocked on the lama's door. There was no response. Our loud raps resulted in a woman emerging from the neighbouring house. 'Yangche Lama left for Fadrong Marpo this morning,' she volunteered.

Thanking her, we began climbing the stairs again. In a short while, we had climbed to quite a height, but owing to the densely crowded houses lining the roads, it was almost impossible to catch a glimpse of what lay below. Fadrong Marpo was the local name for the red middle section of the Potala. The elevated portion of the hill was the point where the palace premises began. It had quite evidently been a fort at one time. The main road came to an end just below the red palace. On asking around a bit, we were able to locate Yangche quite easily.

We entered a room below the palace that lay in almost total darkness and asked an elderly gentleman about the lama we were looking for.

'Yangche Lama?' he inquired. 'What business do you have with him?'

'I am a friend of his,' Guruji replied, 'and have not met him for quite some time. So, I've come to look him up.'

'What is your name?'

No sooner had Guruji introduced himself than the lama almost jumped for joy. Even the near total gloom could not conceal the expression of delight on his face. Rising to his feet, he embraced Sadhu Baba. It was wonderful watching these two elderly men greet each other as though their youthful days had suddenly been restored to them. I prostrated myself before the lama and Guruji introduced me. Lamaji carefully studied my face in the dim light cast by the lamp. Then continuing to gaze at me, he asked, 'What is your name, young man?'

'Bimal.' The answer seemed to come spontaneously from within as I contemplated the radiant purity of his expression. Guruji was quick to add an explanation. 'That is, he is known to all as Mouni Baba, the Silent Monk,' he added, 'and he is my disciple.'

In the course of conversation, it became clear that the lama held India in very high regard. He had once visited Kolkata and had also been on a pilgrimage to Bodh Gaya. To the people of Tibet, Kolkata was a strangely fascinating place. The lama, it transpired, was an exceptionally talented individual. Not only was he a mentor, he was an artist and the examiner of accounts of a number of gumphas as well. At present, he was unable to work quite as hard as he used to once. He now kept track of all the clothing used by those living and working at the Potala. After discussing various subjects with him for almost an hour, we set out again. Lamaji accompanied us to the fourth floor, where half a dozen guards had been placed on duty. Unless one was known there, permission had to be sought from the guardhouse to explore the palace. This would have to be obtained from the State Police Guards or the Kashak department. Thanks to the lama interceding on our behalf and introducing us as his friends, we were not required to apply for permission and were allowed to pass through.

Years ago, when the Bon-Pa religion enjoyed a dominant position, the Potala had been the centre of meditation for ascetics. In the fifteenth century, the Fifth Dalai Lama had set about glorifying the Potala in earnest and it was during his regime that the Potala Palace, as it appears today, was built. There is a very interesting anecdote associated with its construction.

The Fifth Dalai Lama was renowned for his intelligence and formidable administrative abilities. It was during his time that the first geographical borders of the country were laid down. The revered leader had decided to build the most magnificent palace in Tibet on Potala Hill that, in beauty and structural design, would set its own unique example. All the experts from surrounding areas were summoned to Potala for the construction. According to the plan, the palace would rise thirteen floors high and contain nearly a thousand rooms. The work began with untold enthusiasm. Thanks to the fervour of the citizens and the largesse of the monarch, houses gradually started being hewn out of the hillside.

The second storey was almost complete when the revered leader fell ill. The ministers and courtiers were distraught. If at this juncture, he passed away, they surmised, the construction work would grind to a halt. Given the circumstances, this magnificent project was almost on the verge of foundering. The Fifth Dalai Lama was far-sighted, however. Even as he lay on his deathbed, he sent for all his men and told them, 'Do not let my condition dishearten you. Please do not stop the good work. Set your sights on fulfilling the tremendous responsibility you have voluntarily taken on. This work, once completed, will celebrate our glory and that of entire Tibet. This palace will be the pride of the Himalayas.' Then, he entered into more confidential discussions with his entourage.

The second floor of the palace was still under construction when the Fifth Dalai Lama breathed his last. His able ministers immediately hushed up the news of his death and kept it a well-guarded secret. They brought in an elderly lama who bore a faint resemblance to the deceased Dalai Lama and spread the rumour that the Dalai Lama was unwell. They claimed that whenever he recovered, he devoted himself exclusively to prayers and was, therefore, not available for an audience. Meanwhile, the mortal remains of the real Dalai Lama were interred in one of the rooms of the palace. Thus, no one ever came to suspect that the revered leader had passed away and the construction work continued smoothly for thirteen long years. The result was the Potala Palace as we know it today, resplendent in all its glory.

Then, with due pomp and ceremony, the mortal remains of the Fifth Dalai Lama were buried in the royal palace where they lie today. Owing to the good deeds of his past incarnations and the power of his spiritual calling, the Fifth Dalai Lama had been repeatedly reincarnated as Chenreji, a resident deity of his beloved Potala Palace. No other Dalai Lamas had preceded him. By virtue of his repeated reincarnations, the Fifth Dalai Lama was, in reality, the First Dalai Lama.

In the palace at Potala, there were seven huge temples, each containing an interred body. These interred remains were of seven bodies which had passed down the same soul, one to the other, over the generations.

The central edifice in the Potala Palace, flanked by the two white houses with gold trimmings, looked very colourful. As soon as we entered it, a lama took charge and accompanied us everywhere. He was probably the designated guide, because he would anticipate our questions and offer the required explanations.

At the heart of the main palace were thirty-five small temples of which the most remarkable was dedicated to Chenreji. It was actually a memorial, somewhat like the Taj Mahal in Agra, but with a difference. For while the grave and the memorial stone had been laid over Mumtaz Mahal's interred body at the Taj Mahal, here, an enormous gold statue of King Song-San Gampo had been constructed over the burial place. If the statue was really of pure gold, the Potala Palace was, indeed, the most magnificent, priceless and remarkable structure in the whole wide world. Beside the statues of Song-San Gampo and Chenreji stood the life-sized statues of the former's two consorts—the princesses from China and Nepal. From far away, it was apparent that the seven golden domes of the Potala Palace we had so admired were, in reality, chaityas. The chaitya of the Thirteenth Dalai Lama was the largest and bore a marked resemblance to the Jokhang Temple. It was visible only when one had climbed down a few steps. The memorial stone and statues were of solid gold. At least a tonne of gold had gone into the making of the dais on which the statue of the Thirteenth Dalai Lama had been placed. Of course, the statue itself was also of gold.

That no additional guards or soldiers had been deployed to protect the immeasurable wealth that lay scattered around the place was a tribute to the integrity of the Tibetan people, remarkable, indeed, in a world so riddled with greed and crass materialism. The walls were beautifully etched with decorative panels illustrating the life of the Buddha. These were also illuminating in the sense that they offered a vast fount of interesting facts. There were illustrations, moreover, from Chinese folklore and depictions of different beasts like the lion, dragon, horse and elephant, among others. On the veranda of the chaitya, paintings had been done on rows of expensive backdrops. Alongside, as if to preserve the harmony of the stone edifice, stood gigantic, beautifully engraved pillars. The Tibetans appeared to be very fond of the colours red, golden and yellow. Whatever be the choice of colour, a very bright shade of it was invariably used. The statue of Chenreji was over thirty feet tall and richly decorated with jewels and precious stones. Understandably, it was the main attraction of the seven chaityas. Neither the floors nor the verandas on the tenth floor were completely level. Even to go from one room to another involved either a descent or a climb. Truly specialized skills must have been called for to create this magical palace hewn out of the hillside. To satisfy my insatiable curiosity, I peeped out from one of the rear windows of the temple and was overwhelmed by the impression that the palace was floating in space. Before we could ask any questions, the lama approached us and began to explain every detail of our environs in a very soft voice.

We were now standing in Namgyetrachang, the gumpha of the Potala Palace which was inhabited by almost two hundred lamas. The monastery was completely independent in its function and belonged exclusively to the Potala. The resident lamas looked after all the chaityas of the Potala. The view from the window offered an entirely different picture of Lhasa, for it gave us a glimpse of the opposite side of the city. The huge gumpha in the distance was the renowned Chakpori Herbal Centre—the country's largest university for medical sciences and its most important treatment centre. It was, however, quite different from the hospitals in our own country. The treatment carried out there was in conformity with ayurvedic traditions and included local treatment methods prevalent among the hill people. Several renowned doctors and scholars from Tibet including Vairachara, Rinchen Jampo and Iang Lang had translated Indian medical texts into Tibetan. Many of the works by outstanding Indian scholars served as textbooks at this institute. The latter comprised around six large chaityas. From the point where we were standing, only the roof of the institute was visible. In the far distance, the Ki Chu flowed through a landscape that was striking in its beauty. We also caught a glimpse of Cho, the village that was situated just below the Potala.

The guide spewed out a rapid description of the surroundings in one breath, as it were, and almost before he was done, stretched out his hand for payment for services rendered. Then he disappeared, quite content with what we had given him. The man had insisted on being our loyal escort despite Guruji's familiarity with the Potala Palace!

The veranda was not only wide, but very long and just as dark. Almost nothing was visible in the dim light cast by the lamps. Some sections of the palace had no electricity; they only had lamps for illumination. The veranda was flanked on either side by rows of rooms and though we did meet lamas occasionally, as we passed those rooms, their age could not be discerned in the dim light. Guruji, however, felt that they were all quite old. All the water that was needed for the residents of the Potala had to be fetched from the Ki Chu river. This was done every morning through a kind of relay system, whereby buckets of water were passed from hand to hand, right from the river up to the palace! Of course, there was no dearth of manpower; any number of Tibetans were eager and waiting to serve their master.

The scarlet mid-section of the Potala with its abundance of chaityas and temples constituted its most sacred area. For the various administrators of this region, there was also a Department of Law and Regulations. In this very section was located the vast General Hall.

The Revered Dalai Lama's room too, was located in this part of the fourteenth floor. He only spent the winter months here; with the onset of summer, he took up residence at the Norbulingka Palace. Whenever he made the official move, all the citizens of Lhasa threw themselves into the attendant celebrations with unreserved enthusiasm, painting their houses in bright colours and decorating them with flags of different hues. The occasion marked the Spring Festival to celebrate the melting of the snows that would feed the rivers, a source of sustenance for so many lives.

In the Potala Palace were the living quarters of numerous highly placed lamas and government officials. Whenever any governor visited Lhasa, he stayed in the palace. The official guest house was always full. It was believed that the Dalai Lama's room was decorated with the most priceless artefacts in all Tibet. Among all the statues that we saw was a huge sandalwood idol of the Buddha made in Tibet. But it was scarcely visible in the dim light of the lamp. Some element of the occult had apparently been infused into the process when it was crafted, for whenever the statue was worshipped, the beautiful fragrance of sandalwood filled the mystical air permeating the Potala Palace.

Time passed all too swiftly and before we knew it, evening was upon us. Despite a thorough search, no tea stall could be sighted anywhere. Before losing all hope, we made inquiries of a young girl on the road. She led us to a house and knocked on the door. Immediately, a window was thrown open and the smell of buttered tea wafted out. Tea was already prepared. The moment we appeared, some salted butter was mixed into the brew and it was heated on a stove fuelled with wood. The teacups were quite presentable, but looked like they had never been washed. Completely disregarding this detail, we took a long sip. A little later, an elderly lama turned up and asked us without preamble, 'Where did you say you had your meal?'

'We have not eaten as yet,' we told him.

'What! You haven't eaten anything at all so far! Right! We will have our meal together.'

The lama instructed the woman in the shop to prepare a tsampa for the night, then set out with us to have a look at the terrace of the Potala. Unless one were a local and familiar with the roads and alleyways, finding one's way to the terrace was virtually impossible. On the thirteenth floor of each house was a large veranda and two or three floors above it was a vast terrace. Like the Mall in Darjeeling, the terrace here seemed to sprawl endlessly.

It afforded a complete view of picturesque Lhasa. From here, I could actually touch the peaks of the chaityas. Of the golden-hued domes, some were covered in sheets of real gold. Soon, a bell pealed, compelling us to descend, for no outsider was allowed to remain within the premises after the evening bell. The iron doors of the temple were closed. From that moment onwards, the guards took their duties very seriously. Every half an hour throughout the night, the sentries patrolled the roads and alleyways of the palace. While passing by the memorial stone in the red mid-section of the palace, the guards would call out loudly as part of their vigil.

The elderly lama revealed many other secrets of the Potala to us. The lower floors were equipped with an ample stock of guns, arms and ammunition. Although there was no official army as such, if Lhasa were ever attacked, the brave residents of the Potala would not hesitate to sacrifice their lives to defend their city.

As soon as evening had set in, we went down to the gates of the Potala. After passing the filthy alleys, we came to the old lama's tea stall. On catching sight of us, he gave us a toothless grin and said, 'I thought you had lost your way. You are lucky you did not go to the "Notun Kuthi"; then it would have been impossible for you to return today. The sentries on that side are extremely strict. The moment the bell rings, they close the doors and don't bother to check whether anyone has remained inside. Anyway, just see what I have cooked for you! It's so delicious that people get a whiff of the aroma wafting down the street and are seized with the longing to get a taste. There is cured lamb and eating it won't be a problem for you at all, because I have boiled and tenderized it. I have also thrown in a couple of small fish from the Ki Chu river. It is a bit expensive, but then, you are our honoured guests and we can hardly treat you to just anything at all. The elderly lama, in particular, has warned me. "Be sure to look after them well," he said, "they are close friends of mine".'

'Fine! Fine!' Guruji retorted. 'Now stop! Your culinary skills will be apparent once we actually taste the food.'

After the meal was over, we prepared to return to the city. In spite of our pleading with him a number of times, the old lama adamantly refused to accept any payment at all. He said by way of explanation, 'If I can use even a little of what I have in your service, it will enhance my share of accumulated good deeds. It is a source of joy to me that you have come here; don't deny me that pleasure by insisting on payment.'

We bade farewell to the elderly lama. He had only one request for me: when I next went to Bodh Gaya, could I please send him some soil from those holy grounds in an envelope? I gave him my word that I would. About an hour later, after lavishing praise on the quality of the cooking and prostrating ourselves before the lama in a gesture of respect, we set off down the dark road leading to the city.

LAMA LAMDUP

❧

EARLY THE NEXT morning, we were roused from slumber by someone calling out to us in a loud and persistent voice. Pulling the blanket over my ears to shut out the noise proved to be of little use and finally, I had no option but to get out of bed. Somehow managing to force my eyes open, I asked, 'Who is that?', then remembering my identity as the Silent Monk, quickly got a hold on myself. Guruji was snoring away to glory beside me and I was forced to wake him up. Whoever stood beside the door like an apparition, intent on waking us up, must have come bearing some important message. In the dim glow of the ebbing fire in the corner of the room, I saw a boy of around ten, wrapped in a shawl, shivering in the cold. I gestured for him to stand by the fire and he gratefully accepted. Just as offering a cup of tea to a visitor was the norm back home, in Tibet, inviting someone to warm himself by the fire was regarded as a gesture of courtesy and hospitality. Guruji had, in the meantime, awakened and was sitting up. The child looked at him and quickly repeated his message. He had a thick local accent and I could make out the name of Guru Lamdup, repeated a number of times. After warming himself by the fire for a while, the boy left.

Guruji explained that Lama Lamdup had come down from the Jokhang Temple. He was the chief priest of Tibet's renowned Kumbum Temple. Guruji had met him twice in the past. This lama had heard of Guruji's arrival in Lhasa and had, therefore, sent someone across to organize a private meeting. Another lama in our group had also woken up and was ready to accompany us. We knocked at the door of the house facing the chief priest's residence. The door was open and a woman came forward, illuminated by the dim light of the lamp. Since men and women dressed alike in Tibet, we initially mistook her for a man. Accompanied by her, we crossed a large veranda and entered a room. There was a fire in the centre. Seated in silence around it and deep in meditation were seven lamas. Some distance away, on a slightly raised dais, sat an elderly man, also lost in meditation. We joined them.

About an hour later, they emerged from their meditative state to the accompaniment of chanted incantations. The elderly man opened his eyes. His calm, serene expression inspired feelings of awe and reverence. Looking directly at Guruji, he smiled. It seemed as if he were showering Guruji with love and affection through that smile. A childlike innocence and exuberance emanated from him. He said, 'I had sent you a message yesterday, but as you were not available, I sent the boy across today again. We are meeting after a very long time, aren't we? I trust you are keeping well? I do hope you weren't inconvenienced in any way on your journey to Lhasa?'

Although he was meeting Guruji after so long an interval, in neither word nor manner did he betray an impulsive surge of feeling or a surfeit of emotion.

'Your blessings enabled us to make the journey without any difficulty at all,' Guruji replied. 'We had gone out yesterday and returned rather late. How long do you expect to be here?'

In response to Guruji's question, Lama Lamdup answered in his habitual mild tone, 'I had come here on some work and will be leaving today itself.'

There was no further conversation. Lama Lamdup closed his eyes again. Prayers began in a short while and everyone present entered a deep meditative state. When we came out of it, daylight had begun streaming in through the glass windows.

In appearance, Lama Lamdup closely resembled his fellow Tibetans. He was nearly six feet tall with a matching physique. Unlike the other lamas with their tonsured heads, he had a stubbly growth of hair on his scalp. His salt and pepper beard and moustache were sparse. Guruji had rightly remarked that determining his age was very difficult. He recalled that Lama Lamdup had looked almost the same even fifteen years ago. I had visited a great many pilgrimage centres and was, at the moment, in one of the most sacred places on earth. Yet, for the first time, it appeared as though the hallowed serenity of the Himalayas was shining forth from this one man. He seemed to be divinity personified and my heart overflowed with humility and gratitude at having been granted the privilege of being in his presence.

A couple of girls entered the room, carrying tea and sweets on a tray. They were very young, probably no more than fifteen. What was most striking about them was their elaborate coiffure, with the hair piled high on a kind of bamboo frame. On meeting my gaze, they smiled pleasantly and moved the plate in my direction to put it within my reach.

Then gradually, people began to gather in the room for a glimpse of the Revered Lama Lamdup. We remained seated there. Apart from Guruji, the lama addressed himself to no one. Sometimes, though, he would murmur softly, perhaps in communion with himself.

We spent the entire morning in the lama's presence before leaving with his blessings. After reaching the precincts of the Jokhang Temple, Guruji began reflecting on the advice given by Lama Lamdup. Anyone who gave it due regard would be sure to benefit from it: 'Lack of will is what plunges man into darkness,' Guruji said, explaining the lama's words of wisdom. 'It is the power of the will that leads to enlightenment. Unless the heart is replete with fulfilment, how will that state of mind be attained where one is free from all attachments? Understanding the mysteries of the universe by exercising logic and judgement is to know Mahayana. Our wanderings are motivated by the need to seek reprieve from sorrow. According to the Buddha, no matter how far man might travel to elude the pain of sorrow, he can never escape it. In order to safeguard himself against it, he must first delve deep into the root cause of sorrow. Only when it has been determined, can he try to find a means of escaping it.'

I grasped a part of Guruji's explanations. But to actually feel their truth within my heart remained an experience beyond my ken.

NORBULINGKA, THE DALAI LAMA'S SUMMER PALACE

MOST PILGRIMS TO Lhasa restricted themselves these days to the Jokhang Temple and the marketplace, but it was not so in the past. No sooner would a pilgrim reach the temple than there would be hordes of locals surrounding him, clamouring to take him on a tour of the Potala Palace and other important sites in Lhasa. Guruji told us that the guides of Lhasa charged a mere pittance and it hardly cost anything at all to hire a pony for a full-day tour of the city.

While wandering about, I rediscovered the child in me. For the past few days, I had been contemplating the possibility of meeting the Dalai Lama and ultimately confided in Guruji about my desire. He acquiesced at once to my request, explaining, however, that meeting the Dalai Lama would be difficult and might give rise to all sorts of complications. Though he was the chief lama of Tibet, the Dalai Lama was, to all intents and purposes, the country's ruler. In order to meet him, an application would have to be sent through a number of departments. Besides, it greatly displeased the Chinese if the Dalai Lama met any foreigners. Permission would have to be sought from the Chinese authorities before any meeting with him could be arranged. The fact that I was an Indian was simply going to complicate matters further. However, Guruji was not one to be disheartened. 'We'll see,' he said, 'something or the other can surely be worked out.'

He pointed out some houses in the distance and revealed that they were the personal property of the Dalai Lama. We came to a halt outside a massive boundary wall and bowed in greeting to the two sentries posted there. Hidden behind these walls was the beautiful Norbulingka Palace. Guruji knew an employee there and taking the permission of the guards, we entered the offices located inside. Signing our names there, we made inquiries and were told that Kha-Ongche, the man we were looking for, lived in a particular house and we could try our luck there.

He was a gardener and lived in a small house on the premises. A woman answered our summons when we knocked on the door and appeared startled to see us. Then, pulling herself together, she asked, 'What can I do for you?'

'Is Kha-Ongche at home?' we inquired.

'No, but his son is home. Let me call him.'

A well-built young man emerged from the room wearing a Western-style hat. Tibetans were generally very fond of this kind of headgear. Guruji introduced us right away and said, 'I am an old friend of your father's and would like to meet him. Where is he?'

'Oh, you are looking for Father, are you?' the young man answered. 'He is by the lake. Let me take you to him.'

As Bhaban, Kha-Ongche's son, led the way, I took the opportunity of looking around the palace. It would have been more appropriate to call it a country house, rather than a palace. In a short while, we reached the lake where I noticed the profusion of ferns that grew all around us. The surface of the lake was covered thickly with lotus leaves; within a month or so, the flowers would begin to bloom. For the first time in Tibet, I had come across a flower that bloomed in the water! Of course, it was difficult for such blossoms to survive the severe cold. What amazed me, especially, was the sight of the stately swans that glided around the lake. When we had gone some of the way, we noticed some men working in the garden. At the sight of strangers, they stopped what they were doing and stared at us.

One of them, an elderly man, began walking towards us. Then suddenly, he recognized Guruji and rushed to embrace him, the way one would a long-lost friend. The man was Kha-Ongche and I was introduced to him. Pointing to me, Guruji explained, 'This is my disciple and he has taken a vow of silence.'

The man addressed me affectionately. 'You have chosen the right path,' he said.

Guruji told him that I loved gardens and if, by chance, we could catch a glimpse of the Dalai Lama, he would be gratified. Kha-Ongche was reassuring and enthusiastic as he said, 'Come, first of all, let me take you around the garden.' Then washing his hands and feet in the cold waters of the lake, he got ready to do so.

I remained silent as Guruji interpreted his friend's words for me. 'The garden of the Norbulingka Palace is truly a marvel,' he said. 'Known as the Jewel Garden, it is rare among its kind, not just in Tibet, but in the entire world. Though situated practically on the roof of the world with its harsh climate, myriads of flowers bloom here, as if through some mysterious process.'

Kha-Ongche was one of the garden's supervisors and extremely proud of the fact. At one time, he had travelled to Kalimpong and Darjeeling and taken special courses in horticulture. The garden was vast and sprawling and practically every variety of flower that bloomed in the world could be found here.

As we were passing through, Kha-Ongche said in reverent tones, 'Among the people practising archery here is the present Dalai Lama's brother-in-law. The other members of his family all live here. Separate living arrangements have been made for them. When the Dalai Lama is in the Potala Palace, his duties afford him no respite at all. When he comes here, however, he breathes a sigh of relief. This garden is a truly enchanted one and contains not just flowers, but a great variety of fruit-bearing trees as well. The "Dog Garden" is also located here and houses the specially trained imported dogs that belong to the Dalai Lama. He owns two cars as well—gifts of the British government.'

We were strolling through the Norbulingka Garden in this manner when Kha-Ongche abruptly stopped in his tracks and alerted us to someone's presence. 'You are very lucky indeed,' he remarked. 'Chenreji is pleased with you.' With that, he prostrated himself at once and we followed suit. On rising to his feet, he pointed out the Dalai Lama who was slowly passing by.

It was the custom in Tibet that when the Dalai Lama passed by, everyone should stand back with palms joined together, in readiness to greet him with due respect. Before us, a small procession of ten people began to move forward. There could be no question of failing to recognize the Dalai Lama. A pair of immensely tall and hefty guards preceded him. Bringing up the rear were eight people. At the centre of them all was the young Dalai Lama in bright saffron robes. Silently, the procession went by before I was fully aware of what was happening. It all seemed like a dream. The Dalai Lama saw us, but seemed not to register our presence. His tonsured head and serene expression were strongly reminiscent of the Buddha. It was as though he had conquered all the travails and sorrows in life. Yet, he looked very, very young. I would discover later that he was born in 1935 and, therefore, hardly five years older than I was.

We came out of the garden and on to the road again. In reply to our expressions of gratitude for giving us this wonderful opportunity of seeing the Dalai Lama, Kha-Ongche made light of his own contribution to the experience by remarking, 'This really isn't anything special. We see him all the time. Pilgrims come here regularly and take a tour of the palace, but fail to catch even a glimpse of him. Your good fortune is simply the outcome of your worthy deeds and His divine mercy.'

I had seen the Revered Leader for no more than a few minutes, but far from calming me, the experience fuelled in me a desire to know a lot more about him than I did at present. Our group spent almost the entire day wandering around the Norbulingka Palace with Kha-Ongche Lama and in the evening, we took our leave. In the Potala, I had discovered outstanding examples of art and great material wealth. The soul of the Potala seemed enchained by all that gold and jewellery. At the Norbulingka Palace, though, the ambience was quite the reverse; one could bask in the freedom the soul enjoyed, untrammelled by worldly riches, compulsions or concerns.

THE DALAI LAMA

THE BAZAAR OR marketplace in Lhasa constituted its life force. The main road here branched off in six different directions and was flanked on either side by palatial mansions. But some of them were quite old. This was the city's only thoroughfare and could be compared to the streets of Kolkata. It was on this very road that the annual fair of the Tibetans took place. Every morning, I would accompany the other lamas to the first prayer session at the Jokhang Temple. Then I would quietly slip out in the direction of the city.

On one such occasion, while walking down the road, I was amazed to see the following at the entrance to a huge house: 'Trade Agent, Mr Chimi Tshewang, I.Sc., Calcutta', written in Tibetan and English. Quite unconsciously, memories of Kolkata must have been stirred within me and without quite realizing what I was doing, I must have paused there. At that very moment, the door opened and a young man with a fair complexion and dressed in a traditional Nepalese outfit stepped out. His bearing was patrician and his clothes expensive. On his head was a Nepalese cap. The man must have been somewhat surprised to see a foreign lama standing in front of the door and asked me in Tibetan, 'Is there something you want?'

I did not answer. He too, was silent for a while. Then he asked in Nepalese, 'Have you come on a pilgrimage?'

This time, instead of remaining silent, I replied, 'Yes, indeed I have.'

He seemed to be about my age. Having met someone of my own generation after such a long interval, I could not resist engaging him in conversation. We began chatting there and then by the roadside. The young fellow appeared trustworthy and I told him about myself. I told him how I had come along on the pilgrimage in the guise of the Silent Monk and that this was probably the only opportunity I would ever get to visit Lhasa. So, I occasionally preferred to wander around on my own. The young boy seemed to be thrilled at my words; it was as though he had made a new discovery. He immediately ushered me into a beautifully furnished room. And when I told him that I came from Kolkata, he all but embraced me! It took no more than half an hour for a deep bond to grow between us. Chimi Tshewang, the name indicated on the nameplate at the entrance, was the boy's father. He was a trader and had business ties with Kalimpong, Siliguri and Kolkata. The boy's name was Yeshi Tshewang. He was a student and came home on vacation for two months every year. I was eventually introduced to his mother, his three younger brothers and his two sisters. His mother stroked my hair fondly and suggested, 'Why don't you stay back and have a meal with us this afternoon?'

I had no reason to object. On the contrary, it was an honour for a stranger like me to be so warmly welcomed into the fold by this respectable Tibetan family. Yeshi's two uncles worked at the ministry. His paternal grandfather was a famous lama, while his maternal grandfather was a renowned artist. It was from this family that I would come to know of the Dalai Lama's history and it was only to Guruji that I would confide that I had met them.

In Tibet and, particularly, in Lhasa, the Dalai Lama was known by a number of different names. The Tibetans pronounced it as 'Ta-Le-Lama', in imitation of the Mongols who first honoured the Dalai Lama by addressing him thus. He was also known to the Tibetans as Rimpoche, meaning 'The Lord', and was addressed by a variety of other names as well. As an incarnation of the Buddha, he was the Living God of Tibet and blessed with eternal life. He was the country's ruler, chief priest and divine spirit all at once. His rebirth in different manifestations was preordained, so that he could rule over his people. The Dalai Lama discharged all responsibilities that fell to him, but he did so without allowing himself to become involved in worldly matters. It was from 1641, that is, the era of the Fifth Dalai Lama, that this history had been on record.

Once the Dalai Lama died, he was reborn into an aristocratic family. Just before his demise, he would sometimes indicate to his close associates, often indirectly, where he would be reborn. This made the search for the new Dalai Lama a little easier. The process still remained fraught with complications, however. No one, for instance, had the audacity to ask the presiding Dalai Lama about where he would be reborn in the future. Many felt that it risked giving the impression to the Dalai Lama that his time was over and he was no longer cherished. If, for whatever reason, he died without giving specific instructions or directions as to his future birth, the responsibility of choosing the next incarnation from among the children living throughout Tibet fell to the most erudite and clairvoyant lamas. Of course, in Tibet, it was not merely the Dalai Lama who was reincarnated. Lamas at the highest levels of the religious order were also reborn.

After the death of the Dalai Lama, the onus of finding the newborn child lay mainly with the ministers of the land and the head priests of the three principal gumphas at Drepung, Sera and

Ganden. These men held consultations with clairvoyant lamas from other monasteries. Deciding upon an appropriate time that was tied up with the death of the Dalai Lama and considered auspicious as well, elaborate arrangements for collective prayers were made, after which the concerned lamas sat in meditation. The whereabouts of the new Dalai Lama subsequently emerged, either through the meditative process or through dreams. Sometimes, they were conveyed through a divine message. The kingdom's chief clairvoyant communicated this highly confidential piece of information to the minister and the chief priests. Subsequently, an investigative committee was set up, its members being elected from among the most learned lamas of the land. This committee broke up into separate groups and, in keeping with the counsel of the chief clairvoyant, dispersed in different directions across Tibet in quest of the new Dalai Lama. Even after the child was found, he had to prove in a number of ways that he was, indeed, the true incarnation of the Dalai Lama.

Meanwhile, the council of ministers continued to rule the kingdom on behalf of the Dalai Lama. The clairvoyants and astrologers of the Samiye Gumpha were regarded as the best of the breed and could describe in detail the sign that would prove without a shadow of doubt whether a newborn child was actually the reincarnation of the Dalai Lama. The chief clairvoyant of Lhasa was Nechung. Even if all the physical signs stipulated by the clairvoyants were not always visible when identifying the new Dalai Lama, most of them were, in fact, present in the chosen boy.

When his identity had finally been determined through the physical characteristics indicated by the clairvoyants, a combination of objects that had been used by the deceased Dalai Lama and other more commonly available items were presented before the child. If the latter were, indeed, the chosen one, he would unerringly pick out the objects that had once belonged to the former Dalai Lama and show no interest in the other articles. As an infant, the Thirteenth Dalai Lama had, for example, chosen the symbolic *Vajra*—lightning. When he was brought to the palace, he was able to point out what, in effect, were his own possessions from his previous incarnation! Sometimes, even an incarnation who was no more than five years old could be uncannily accurate in choosing his favourite religious text and reading aloud from it too! With extensive evidence to support the selection, there was no longer any doubt that the spirit of the Dalai Lama had, indeed, been reborn in his new incarnation. The Fourteenth and present Dalai Lama too, had a very interesting history. All this was likely to seem illogical and unsubstantiated to scientists and academicians who had nothing to fall back on but theory and dry facts. It would be quite impossible for them to appreciate anything with the remotest connection to the mystic, the occult and the pre-ordained.

The Thirteenth Dalai Lama, Thupten Gyatso, was a much loved and respected man. During his long reign, he was responsible for introducing social and political reforms in Tibet. His memorial stone in the Potala Palace was the most opulent of them all and served as the focal point of fervent prayers by devotees. Right after his death in 1933, a special committee was formed to administer Tibet till the next Dalai Lama could be chosen.

The concerned authorities were summoned to the palace and entrusted with the responsibility of finding the deceased Dalai Lama's true successor. Unfortunately, the Thirteenth Dalai Lama whose mortal remains had been carried to the Norbulingka Palace had left no instructions whatsoever about his next incarnation. This posed a major problem. In order to resolve the issue, all the lamas meditated and tried, thereby, to communicate with his departed soul. At that very moment, a fleecy cloud like the ones that float across the sky in spring appeared in the north-eastern corner of Lhasa. After the usual deliberations, the astrologers and clairvoyants announced that the region over which this cloud had appeared was the very same where the Honourable Chenreji had been reborn. Amazingly, the body of the deceased Dalai Lama, which had apparently been in a different position, was discovered to have turned to face this region.

This was taken as an auspicious sign. However, the astrologers continued to wait for more conclusive proof. Another two years went by in this manner before the astrologers decreed that the moment was at hand for the rebirth of the Dalai Lama, for after two long years of celestial bliss, it was time for him to be reincarnated.

In 1935, all the leading astrologers, along with those directly involved in the process of selection, travelled to Lamoy-Latso, one of Tibet's most sacred lakes. For Tibetans, this was among the holiest of pilgrimage sites. Since ancient times, sages had been coming here for meditation. According to many, deities dwelled in the lake's waters, but only the truly devout and deserving were able to sight them. Astrologers could apparently discern in its clear waters a reflection of the past, present and future. Once again, the lamas in search of the new Dalai Lama prepared for a round of meditation.

After prayers, meditation and all appropriate ceremonies were over, an unexpected mystical phenomenon manifested itself. From the centre of the lake, three glowing letters of the alphabet floated up suddenly and were just as abruptly extinguished, vanishing into the darkness. The initial response was to regard it as part of some incantation, but within minutes, another clear picture floated up from the depths of the lake to the surface, depicting quite distinctly a gumpha with a bright, glowing dome in gold and green. Almost right next to it stood a farmer's hut with a green-tiled roof. The erudite scholars gazed in wonder at the picture that had appeared before their very eyes on the surface of the water and had almost as mysteriously disappeared into the unknown depths. After returning to the gumpha, all the astrologers and clairvoyants sat in consultation and took nearly a year more to come to some sort of decision. An investigative cell was also set up and consisted of the most senior lamas in the hierarchy. This main cell was further divided into numerous smaller groups which set out in search of the Dalai Lama. The occult experience at Lamoy-Latso Lake remained a closely guarded secret.

One of these groups reached Takstar village, situated in Dokham, Lhasa's north-eastern district. The lama in charge was awestruck at the sight of the famous Kumbum Gumpha. Not only was it exactly like the gumpha which had appeared in the picture floating on the surface of Lamoy-Latso Lake, but the rustic dwelling beside it was also identical to the one that had appeared along with it.

All the experts present were thrilled at the discovery and a young lama from the group was sent to investigate. He returned with the information that there were a great many children in that farmer's house and the youngest was about a year old. The leader of the group made his calculations and, without frittering away time in idle conversation, put up for the night at the gumpha there. Not only was the Kumbum Gumpha of particular importance to the tantrik sect of Buddhism for the spiritual and religious values it propagated, but the lamas living there had also reached the highest levels of spirituality and succeeded in attaining nirvana. Besides, the education imparted by it was of a very high standard. The Kumbum Gumpha was also famous for the monks who had taken the vow of silence. Its lamas welcomed the investigators. The eldest son of the family that lived in the rustic dwelling was also found at the gumpha. His youngest brother was about two years old. Other than that, there was no further conversation with him.

The next morning, the leader of the lamas who comprised the investigative team dressed himself in the shabby garments of a menial. He instructed his colleagues to wear expensive clothes and called on the owner of the rustic dwelling. The latter was a man of modest means who earned his living by tending yaks and hens and farming in whatever little plot of land he owned. He was quite taken aback at this early-morning visit from so many lamas, but also very happy at the prospect of being allowed to serve them. Among the visiting lamas, a servant had been outfitted in the garb usually worn by the group leader. All the lamas were shown due respect and all courtesies were observed as they were invited to take a seat. After some idle conversation, the lamas expressed a desire to have a look at the farmer's youngest offspring. The man's heart swelled with pride at the thought of his son being the recipient of special blessings and he called in his wife who entered the room with their two-year-old.

In keeping with his role as a servant, the actual leader of the group stood back humbly. The child, however, went straight up to him and, tugging at his hands, asked to be picked up in his arms. Greatly embarrassed, the father begged for forgiveness and asked the person he assumed to be the group's leader not to take umbrage and bless the child. At his words, everybody fell silent, but the child approached his father and announced confidently, 'No, Father, I am right. I want to stay in his arms. He is the senior lama in the most important gumpha in Tibet.'

Everyone was stunned at the words the child had lisped out. Then the actual leader came forward. The moment he saw him, the child voiced yet another demand. 'Give me that necklace you're wearing,' he commanded.

'Why, what will you do with it?' the senior lama asked him. 'I will wear it,' he replied, 'it belongs to me.'

The senior lama disguised as a servant could no longer contain his joy and embraced the child. Then he disclosed the truth that he had kept to himself all this while. The child was right, he admitted; he was, indeed, O Keot-Sang Rimpoche, the head lama of the gumpha. The necklace he was wearing had been given to him a very long time ago by the Dalai Lama himself. His drab attire hadn't for a moment deceived the child, because he was the Dalai Lama incarnate. And that was how Tenzing Gyatso, the Fourteenth Dalai Lama, was discovered.

After returning to the Potala, the rest of the lamas were informed and arrangements were made to bring the Dalai Lama to Lhasa. However, due to various political and financial constraints imposed by the Chinese, his arrival was delayed for another three years. The Dalai Lama's entire family accompanied him to the capital and was treated with great honour. There were festivities throughout Tibet in joyful celebration at his coming.

As soon as the five-year-old Dalai Lama reached the Potala, he recognized the lamas who had been close to him in his previous incarnation. He even knew their names! Then the child pointed out in great detail all the changes that had been made since he had last been there. He had no problem recognizing the baton he had once used and which had been kept along with those of the other lamas. Every Tibetan was familiar with the Dalai Lama's background and considered it auspicious to talk about it to one another.

I had visited the Tshewangs only thrice, but refrained from dropping in of my own accord when I learnt from them just how vicious the Chinese traitors who now occupied the country could be.

LHASA: THE LAST DAYS

WE WERE BEGINNING to plan our departure from Lhasa, when a message arrived from the ministry at Kashak, granting us permission to visit the Potala. These were joyful tidings indeed! True, I had already been to the palace with Guruji. But the fun of going there in a group with the other lamas was something I had missed out on. Along with this joyous missive came news that stunned us. The local Han or Chinese authorities had decreed that we were to leave this place as soon as possible. Furthermore, they strictly forbade us from travelling together. We would have to split up into small groups. The last directive had the effect of a thunderbolt.

Potala: Apart from the main thoroughfare, there were many smaller paths leading to the Potala. The route that lay to the south, known as the Pilgrim Route, was broad and easy to navigate, familiar to most foreigners and generally used by tourists. Another equally accessible route used by the Revered Chenreji was known, for obvious reasons, as the Dalai Lama Route. There were innumerable other less-travelled paths which were impossible for anyone to use, other than a local. But all routes involved climbing long flights of stone stairs.

Our tour was a very short one. Our itinerary included only a few selected places, to which we were taken around by Ogeyan Dorje, an employee of the Potala who served as our guide. We were led to the room where the formal investiture ceremonies for the Dalai Lama were conducted. From here, various sections of the Potala, including the living quarters of the Revered Leader, were clearly visible. In this very room had been signed the contract between the Dalai Lama and Francis Younghusband, the British traveller and representative who had come to Lhasa in 1904. The ties that had been forged at the time between Tibet and British India had remained intact. We reached the roof by turning past the side of the dome. From that vantage point, the view of a ring of mountains encircling the level land of Lhasa was stunning in its beauty. It was as though Nature herself had constructed a barricade around Lhasa and lent it a unique character all its own.

Ogeyan Dorje showed us around the upper section of the Potala in an hour, then took his leave. Thanks to his rapid-fire commentary in Tibetan and poor visibility in the dimly lit interior, we remained almost as much in the dark as we had originally been without the benefit of his services. He somehow completed the task assigned to him and Guruji interpreted as much as he could of what the man had offered by way of information and explanation. It left us in little doubt that Ogeyan Dorje did not much care for the task he had been assigned as our guide.

It took us almost an hour and a half to reach the Potala from the dharamsala where we had put up. The way back involved a smooth descent and, therefore, posed no problem at all. The elderly members of our group seemed a little worse for wear as we finished our afternoon meal of boiled vegetables and flour. We were deciding on our future plans when Ogeyan Dorje suddenly appeared. Not bothering with preliminaries, he said, 'If you have finished your meal, we will leave right away for the Norbulingka Palace. Tomorrow, I won't be able to spare the time. I will also arrange for you to have a glimpse of Chenreji. He makes a brief appearance every evening.'

The Dalai Lama at the Norbulingka Palace: Each member of our group bought a special kind of white material from a shop near the Jokhang Temple. It was the custom here to offer it to the Dalai Lama, the way we offered flowers to dignitaries back home in India. We reached the Norbulingka Palace shortly before the onset of evening. It looked rather like the kind of residence an affluent family would live in. A great many Tibetans waited by its white boundary wall. The Dalai Lama did not make an appearance for the poor and needy of Tibet; the latter contented themselves with touching the boundary wall and going around it. Only during special festivals, when the Honourable Chenreji went by, did the common man feel blessed and honoured by a glimpse of him.

As pilgrims coming all the way from faraway Nepal, we were, however, a tad more privileged. Arriving at the main palace door with Ogeyan, we prostrated ourselves and paid our respects. Then, instead of entering by that door, we went around to the rear and found another entrance that had been cut into the wall. A guard had been posted there, but as Ogeyan was acquainted with him, we encountered no resistance. We were permitted to enter, one at a time. The moment we were all inside, the door was locked behind us. We were then led to a small bungalow. Three Tibetans approached us at a run and came to a halt only when they caught sight of Ogeyan. After they had exchanged a few words with him, they asked us to wait there and went off to the bungalow which was actually the Dalai Lama's private temple in the Norbulingka. At the Potala too, the Dalai Lama had a private temple reserved exclusively for his own prayers. As we reached the veranda, one of the Dalai Lama's aides approached and greeted us with a smile. Guruji and I refrained from disclosing to the others that we had already met this gentleman in the garden.

As we entered the room, we came face to face with a gigantic statue of the Buddha. We prostrated ourselves and paid our respects to him. Rising to our feet, we noticed someone sitting in a chair. None of us were left in any doubt that this was, in fact, the Dalai Lama. There were four other people around him. Guruji offered the Revered Leader a shawl and we followed suit before taking our seats. Smiling, he looked at each one of us and extended a warm welcome. Once we were all seated, the Dalai Lama led the prayers and we joined him. After they were over, he bestowed his blessings on us. He spoke to us for a couple of minutes, showering us with fulsome praise for our enthusiasm and devotion. The tall aide at his side then gestured at us to withdraw and we respectfully took our leave. We had spent all of five minutes in the Dalai Lama's presence.

Having reached Lhasa, we had managed to realize our long-cherished dreams. We had circumambulated the Jokhang Temple and prayed inside. We had toured the Potala Palace. And being granted the privilege of spending some time in the Dalai Lama's company was blessing indeed! Could a pilgrim have desired more? Now all that remained to be done was to spend two days at the Drepung Monastery before returning to India. The following dawn, we prayed to Goddess Mahakali at the Jokhang Temple before our departure from Lhasa.

Drepung Gumpha: We reached the Drepung Gumpha that very night. Since we had been there before, on our way out from Gangtok, we encountered no problems whatsoever. We were even allotted the room we had occupied earlier. In keeping with the directives issued by the Chinese authorities, from this point onwards, we would have to split up into smaller groups. After spending a number of days in Lhasa and at the Drepung Gumpha, certain facts had come to light: It transpired that we were quite mistaken in our assumption that the Dalai Lama was the supreme authority of the entire legal machinery of Tibet. The Chinese influence, even over the country's internal affairs, was becoming more noticeably pervasive. A huge Chinese military camp had been set up a short distance from the Drepung Gumpha. There had always been an abundant supply of Chinese goods in the markets of Lhasa; this had now significantly increased. On the pretext of protecting the Tibetans from invasion, the China Peoples' Liberation Army (PLA) was hemming the country in like an octopus with its multiple tentacles. The Chinese had even made inroads into Tibetan politics—all in the name of furthering education and fostering friendship.

The number of students at the Drepung, Sera and Ganden Gumphas had declined to less than half of what it used to be once. Of the few students from Bhutan and Sikkim and who had come to study at the Drepung Gumpha, most had already left. The Nepalese students who remained would be returning home by the end of the year. That night, I discussed various issues with Guruji. He firmly believed that to have come so far and return without visiting Kailash and Mansarovar would be nothing but a waste of a perfect opportunity. The very sound of these two names on Guruji's lips sent a tremor of anticipation down my spine. The thought of going to Kailash seemed to move me to the core. Guruji's replies to the few more questions I asked revealed the following. The route was arduous enough to be virtually inaccessible, but very precise directions were available to guide the pilgrim. The Brahmaputra was right before us. To reach Mansarovar, all one had to do was follow the watercourse back to its source. And right next to it was Kailash Mountain, the site of the holy pilgrimage to Kailashnath for Hindus.

GEARING UP FOR KAILASHNATH

༈

THE PILGRIMS GRADUALLY began leaving the Drepung Monastery in batches, with Guruji and his entourage of three monks taking the lead. It was a decidedly tough trek, especially, the onward journey which was almost entirely uphill till Gyatse. Right from the start, when we had set out from Gangtok, and up to this point, I had been carrying Guruji's thick blanket on my back. Now, I handed it back to him with extreme reluctance. Guruji was a man free from bonds of any kind. His actions were motivated by his strong sense of duty. To bid farewell to him tore me apart and it took a great deal of effort on my part to keep my feelings from surfacing.

Another four days passed and finally, all the pilgrims had left in twos and threes. I was supposed to be part of the last group, but ever since I had talked to Guruji, thoughts of Kailashnath—the most sacred of pilgrimage centres—possessed me and would keep swirling around in my head. I urged my fellow pilgrims to go ahead, with the promise that I would join them later.

Meanwhile, I had almost completely mastered the Tibetan alphabet of which Sanskrit was the root language. Tibetan, however, was comparatively much easier to learn. I was no longer under any compulsion to play the role of the Silent Monk; that guise had been necessary only until we offered our prayers at the Jokhang Temple. I had also made friends with some Nepalese trapas and gleaned a handful of hitherto unknown facts from them. All the students of the gumpha apparently had to be thoroughly familiar with the mystery of what they called the *Mandala*. An in-depth knowledge of that, it was believed, would empower one to solve all the mysteries of creation. There was also a branch of mathematics they were required to study at length for years. It was, apparently, capable of enhancing the power of human judgement.

System of administration: The Dalai Lama and the Panchen Lama constituted the two life forces of Tibet. The Panchen Lama lived in

Shigatse. He had established his position almost independently, as it were. Apart from matters that had a direct bearing on Shigatse, he kept himself aloof from every other concern pertaining to Tibet. To all intents and purposes, it was the Dalai Lama who ruled the country. It was a fact, of course, that on the pretext of strengthening Tibet's political and military position, the Chinese authorities were now making persistent efforts to undermine the religious leader's influence on his people.

The administrative system headed by the Dalai Lama was divided into two sections. The upper division, consisting of the *Iksang*—a group of high-ranking lamas—was primarily in charge of the administration of all the gumphas as well as the religious ceremonies carried out there. Members of the second division, known as the *Kashak*, were responsible for maintaining law and order in the state. In Tibet, the nobility, generally known as the Giyerpa, enjoyed a rank secondary only to that of the lamas. Young men from aristocratic families were eligible, on completion of the appropriate course, to be directly recruited into the country's administrative services. The prime minister or Chikap was, as a general rule, designated head of the Kashak. Although Tibet's five provinces—U-Sang, Gartok, Kham, Chang and Loka—were likely to have undergone some changes under political pressure from the Chinese who may well have taken some of them over almost completely, as much administrative power as could be retained in the circumstances was still in the hands of the Chikap.

Warfare: Though its history is not on record in its entirety, like every other country in the world, Tibet too, has had to defend its borders against perpetual enemy attacks. It was only from the time of King Song-San Gampo's reign, that the history of the country began to be chronicled in a somewhat organized manner. It has been established that despite his kingdom being virtually tucked away in a remote corner of the Himalayas and, ostensibly, protected from military aggression, this seventeenth-century monarch was often compelled to lead his men into battle to defend his territory. The first war between Tibet and China broke out, because the emperor of China refused to give his daughter's hand in marriage to the Tibetan king. The latter emerged victorious in battle and wrested as compensation from the Chinese emperor a vast expanse of Chinese territory and—his daughter's hand in marriage.

During the era of Kublai Khan, Tibet was forced to sign a peace treaty with China. As a result, its position was relegated to that of a Chinese province. Henceforth, the effects of Chinese domination would begin to weigh heavily on the Tibetans. Being a deeply religious people, however, with a greater focus on spiritual concerns than on the material, they continued to enjoy a virtually independent existence in spite of China's hegemony. More significantly, the impact of Tibet's religious influence was deeply felt, as Buddhism rapidly spread across the length and breadth of China. A case in point was the Chinese province of Manchuria, where the branch of Buddhism practised by the Dalai Lama's Geluk-Pa sect was accepted in the fifteenth century as the royally sanctioned religion. For Tibet, it was a great honour indeed.

It was around this time that the tradition involving the Dalai Lama's reincarnation came into being. The first Dalai Lama of Tibet, Gen-Tung-Dri-Pa, belonged to the Geluk-Pa sect and established his first religious circle at the Tashi Lumpo Gumpha in Shigatse. But gradually, Buddhism split up into divisions and, subsequently, into still smaller subdivisions. In 1587, the Mughal Emperor Aldan formally chose the leader of the Geluk-Pa sect as the Vajradhara Dalai Lama.

In the meantime, the Fifth Dalai Lama had visited Beijing in 1562 and further strengthened the bonds between the two countries. In the nineteenth century, however, a rift developed in the relationship. It was around this time that China's attention was diverted to her own internal affairs and Tibet found the opportunity to slip out of her grasp. India being under British rule at the time, Tibet was forced to establish an amicable relationship with Britain.

During this period, Tibet became embroiled in a number of wars. In 1788, Gurkha soldiers invaded Tibet, but were repelled with the help of Chinese soldiers. In 1856, Nepal wielded great influence on Tibet and in 1857, Nepalese soldiers entered into a pact with their Chinese counterparts so that they could travel to Tibet.

In 1904, Francis Younghusband embarked on his famous expedition to Lhasa. Mistaking it for a foreign invasion, the Dalai Lama fled to China. The Tibetans evidently found it difficult to countenance the fact that the benevolent, all-powerful Dalai Lama could desert his country and his people to seek shelter beyond its borders. Not a word of reproach escaped anyone's lips, however, for it would have been unseemly for the common man to discuss the Revered Dalai Lama's actions. The situation, however, served the Panchen Lama's interests to perfection.

From that moment onwards, Tashi Lumpo, the Panchen Lama, would become an abiding source of reassurance for his beloved subjects and take on the onerous responsibility of safeguarding the interests of his country and its citizens. They in turn, conferred on him the reverence and love due to the land's most important religious leader and he came to be popularly known as Tashi Lama. It was in 1911 that the Chinese Revolution broke out. Considering this a golden opportunity to release Tibet from Chinese clutches—Beijing was too engrossed in its internal problems at the time to pay heed to what was happening in its protectorates on foreign soil—the Thirteenth Dalai Lama pronounced his country to be 'a free and independent kingdom'. The outcome of this declaration was unexpected, to say the least. A number of lamas who belonged to his sect and were in favour of forging bonds with China, began to vehemently oppose their religious leader. In the ensuing chaos, the Dalai Lama's life came under threat and he was forced to flee the country. Arriving in Darjeeling, he sought refuge with the British and urged them to intervene in his favour. Having enlisted their help in 1912, he declared Tibet an independent nation.

Instead of attempting to take on the all-powerful British, Beijing accepted the terms of the Shimla Conference in 1913. Though the Chinese did, indeed, sign the treaty, they had always believed Tibet to be an integral part of China and found it impossible to countenance its existence as an independent country. The period between 1911 and 1949 marked Tibet's golden era during which it flourished in every respect.

That the Fifth and Thirteenth Dalai Lamas were luminous landmarks in the history of Tibet was only too apparent from the memorial temples dedicated to them in their country. Many Tibetans could not, however, accept the Dalai Lama's assertion of Tibet's independence. Under the leadership of the Ninth Panchen Lama, certain lamas who were pro-Chinese, along with some members of the nobility, began to agitate against Lhasa in 1924. The canny Thirteenth Dalai Lama took immediate steps to quell the unrest, forcing the Panchen Lama to flee to China where he breathed his last in 1937.

According to reports, the Panchen Lama had always been in favour of China. The Chinese authorities subsequently played a major role in the official investiture of the Tenth Panchen Lama, where the rituals performed were in keeping with the Shigatse tradition. They promoted his cause and continued to support him in other ways. As the years passed, the beliefs and customs followed by the Panchen Lama and the Dalai Lama grew increasingly divergent. After the death of the Thirteenth Dalai Lama in 1934, the Chinese regime under Chiang Kai-shek concentrated its efforts on reincorporating Tibet into China.

Around this time, a government mission was sent from Beijing to Lhasa bearing a message of condolence. Now, if custom were scrupulously adhered to, nearly three years had to elapse before the Dalai Lama could be reincarnated. The quest to pick him out from among all the children in the country took about another year or so. In the case of the Fourteenth Dalai Lama, it was in 1940, almost six years after the demise of his predecessor, that his official investiture could take place. At the time, he was only five years old and the administrative council ruled the country on his behalf till he came of age.

By 1956, large areas of Tibet had come under Chinese rule. This included Chamda, the Fourteenth Dalai Lama's birthplace. On the pretext of providing aid, Chinese soldiers had infiltrated into virtually every village in Tibet. The red banner of the Peoples' Liberation Army was visible throughout the country, fluttering defiantly from every flagpole.

IN SEARCH OF THE ROUTE
TO KAILASH

THE DREPUNG GUMPHA had an extensive library that housed at least thirty-six thousand volumes. There were, moreover, innumerable other religious tomes in the temple. Despite so many texts being at my disposal, I could not find a single map in any of them marking out the route from Lhasa to Kailash. To disclose to the others my intention of embarking on such a journey was unthinkable. Yet, I was impelled by the desire to know more about this great pilgrimage centre.

As the last of the departing pilgrims in our group, I asked my brethren to go ahead without waiting for me to catch up. Furthermore, I told them not to worry if they did not see me again, claiming that it was all the will of the Lord. His plans for us would always emerge triumphant. That was the last time I would see my fellow pilgrims. During the second week of May 1956, I left the Drepung Monastery at dawn.

My plan was to reach Sangpo village. I anticipated no problems in finding the right direction to my destination, as there was but one main route. Following that very same route, we had entered Lhasa about a week earlier. I was carrying a blanket and a few provisions given to me by the residents of the gumpha. Two days before my departure, the barber had tonsured us all, but by then, I had almost become seasoned to the climate. Guruji had taught me well the art of imbibing Nyasa and it was probably due to its benefits that coughs and colds failed to trouble me seriously. By afternoon, I had passed Sangpo.

At this point, a new path ran ahead, leading to Gangtok via Gyatse. It was the main route for those covering the distance on horseback or on the backs of mules. Instead of taking it, I chose the less-frequented one close to the river that turned west right away without any detours. The risk of losing one's way along this path was remote. The icy waters of the Brahmaputra flowed towards Assam. I set out in the opposite direction. Surely, at the end of the journey, I would reach its source in the glaciers of Tibet.

It was only because of Sadhu Baba, my mentor, that I had reached Lhasa from Gangtok. Now that I was off to Kailash, I mentally geared myself to go it alone. I would be my own solitary companion and would have to exercise great caution to circumvent problems and avert danger.

THE EXORCIST OF SANGPO

PASSING THROUGH SANGPO and Chusul two days earlier, I had come across no more than a couple of small villages. I had sustained myself on bread prepared with water from the Sangpo and toasted over a fire fuelled by dry grass. It tasted like manna from heaven. I spent my first night alone in an abandoned hut. If my progress continued at this speed, who could stop me! The road was uneven and strewn with boulders. But what made my journey worth the effort was the fascinating diversity of the landscape that prevented monotony from setting in.

On the second evening, I unexpectedly found shelter in what looked like a small hut. There were remnants of burnt firewood inside. If I added it to the dry grass, lighting a fire would be no problem at all. The sky gradually assumed a rosy hue and while there was still light, I completed my prayers and meditation on the bank of the Sangpo. I was making my way back to the hut nearly an hour later, when I was stopped short by the sight of a man—a Tibetan from the look of him. Smiling, bowing and greeting him in the traditional way, I tried to avoid conversation, but that was not to be. He stood in my way, preventing me from moving on, and asked me something in Tibetan. Unfortunately, his accent made his words quite incomprehensible to me.

I examined the man carefully. He was wearing the red garment of an ascetic, but from the dark, grimy tinge it had acquired, it seemed likely that it had not been washed for a very long time. Moreover, it was patched all over. The man had long hair, coiled up on top of his head, and hardly any beard or moustache to speak of. Going by appearances, he seemed a bona fide Tibetan, probably from the north. On his feet were thick woollen socks and an ancient pair of military boots. His entire appearance seemed to shriek out his vocation—that of a mendicant.

In my hand was the mug I was carrying to the banks of the Sangpo to fetch water for preparing the bread that would constitute my meal. Finding nothing else to talk about, I gestured to say that I was going to prepare some food and he was welcome to join me. My message probably got across and smiling, he accompanied me. Back in the hut, I found another blanket laid out beside mine. On top of it sat a bundle, all tied up. Quickly taking out some matches, my companion built a fire. Not a word was exchanged between us. Then he pointed out some utensils and the ownership of the hut was established in no uncertain terms.

As the night lengthened, we continued to sit in silence by the fire. There was no window as such and I gazed through the door across the Sangpo at the spectacularly beautiful sight of the majestic mountains that lay beyond. I was spending time with a perfect stranger in completely unfamiliar surroundings. At first, I had taken him to be a local tramp. Then I reasoned he might be a hapless beggar. However, looking at him for a while, I realized that his face had a strangely compelling beauty.

We had been enjoying the warmth of the fire when, suddenly, a man's shadow fell across the door. The newcomer was somewhat taken aback at my presence and I blurted out an introduction of sorts in a hotchpotch of fractured Tibetan and Hindi. The man I had taken to be a tramp then took over and the newcomer and I gradually came to be acquainted with one another.

My elderly friend's attention was now riveted on the newcomer. What followed quite amazed me. The man took a human bone out of his bag. It was, unmistakably, a thigh bone. Then out came a human skull and, subsequently, a shrivelled piece of goatskin. Their owner put the objects aside and an intense conversation ensued between my two companions. From his manner of speech and the items that had emerged from his bag, I gauged that the newcomer—and the owner of the hut—could be none other than a local exorcist.

Having slept quite soundly all night, I woke up very early. When I emerged from the depths of slumber that winter's morning, I found that the fire had gone out. My blanket was a tangled heap. As I quickly prepared for morning prayers, my eyes fell on the bag belonging to the hut's other occupant. Wanting to inform him of my imminent departure, I looked for him and found him outside, deep in meditation. On the ground in front of him was a sketch of a square-shaped box. An aura of such peace and serenity emanated from him that I could not help bowing my head in respect. It was as though inside those tattered clothes was the Buddha himself. Silence cast a spell on our beautiful surroundings. Sunrise was still some way off.

Following the man's example, I too, sat down to meditate. By the time I emerged from the session, rays of light were peeping in from between the trees. Looking at me with great fondness, the man asked, 'Trapa?'

I nodded in agreement. Making an effort to explain myself, I said to him, 'I am a pilgrim from Gangtok. I have been to Lhasa and am now on my way to Kailashnath. That is why I am trying to reach the source of the river.'

My gestures and the repeated mention of Sikkim and Darjeeling probably had some effect. As I was about to leave, he gestured at me to wait. Or, at least, that's what I thought he was trying to do. I had no second thoughts about agreeing to do so. After all, I had plenty of time on my hands. Moreover, my curiosity about this exorcist was insatiable.

Later in the day, the two of us went down to the river and caught some fish by trapping them with a length of cloth. I was very keen on finding out how he planned to cook the fish, but I was to be disappointed. For he began eating them raw! Quite certain that following his example at that time of the day would turn my stomach, I invited him to have the whole lot. Without batting an eyelid, he polished them off, not even bothering to add some salt to improve the flavour.

The position of the sun apparently determined his movements. For no sooner had it started getting warmer than Mr Exorcist picked up his bag and virtually dragged me along to wherever he was headed. My own views about the matter were not sought.

We moved southwards, in other words, towards the point from which the Himalayas actually began. If one continued to move south and crossed the Himalayas, one could reach India. The sun overhead felt comfortably warm and walking was no strain at all. The trees were bright with touches of emerald here and there and even the sere grass was flecked, every now and then, with random streaks of green.

By the time we reached the village my companion had been making for and halted in its midst, word had spread like wildfire and everyone knew about our arrival. My friend took the bone out of his bag and drew an enormous circle. Then we seated ourselves right in the centre. Gradually, people began to gather around us. The children arrived first, followed by the elderly. Then came the young men, few though they were in number, accompanied by their wives. The latter turned out to be the real owners of every house and the reigning authority of their household.

I had imagined that some magic tricks would be on show. But no, my companion turned out to be far more talented than I had given him credit for. A great number of patients seeking treatment began to cluster around us. Most of them suffered from coughs and colds. The exorcist examined the colour of their eyes and seemed to arrive at a diagnosis right away. His treatment simply involved ringing his bell thrice and muttering aloud some mantras as he circled the concerned patient. A little later, he would ask the person concerned a few questions. Within a short time, the patient would start drooping, as though on the verge of dozing off. That, apparently, was the sign that a cure had been effected. This trend continued for a while until a rather different kind of patient turned up.

Some of the village women dragged in a young girl and placed her in front of my companion. Although the girl was shrieking, her ailment was not apparent. As soon he saw her, the exorcist placed the skull on the ground so that it faced west. Drawing a circle on the ground, he stood me within it. He whispered the '*Om Mani Padme Hum*' incantation into my ears and I poured all my powers of concentration into it. In the courtyard, he planted three sticks, each nearly three feet long, in three different directions, tying their top sections together. Then he crowned the sticks with the skull. Having bound the young girl by her hands and feet, he drew another circle and stood her inside it. The girl continued to rant and it was clear that she was insane.

The crowd and I stared in wonder at the man's antics. The final tool, the human thigh bone, was then extracted from his bag. I had observed that this was his most precious and powerful weapon. Next, he shouted out some spells which I utterly failed to make sense of. Then handing me the bell, he asked me to ring it.

A woman stepped forward from the crowd and placed a bowl containing a drink of some kind in front of the Great Exorcist. Stopping in his tracks, he took some sips from the bowl and passed it on to me. As I drank out of it myself, I realized that it was a form of locally made beer. It was the first item of food or drink that would be passing my lips that day. A separate bowl was brought for the girl and she was fed from it. Though the day was beginning to wane, Mr Exorcist did not pause in his dancing. His quick, energetic steps had slowed down a great deal. Remarkable, though, was the fact that none of the spectators had drifted away. They continued to take a lively interest in the proceedings.

As soon as evening began to descend, it became really chilly. The people around us started bringing out blankets. They seemed on the verge of leaving; yet, nobody actually did. It was not yet dark. My poor hands were numb from ringing the bell without a break. All of a sudden, the onlookers were stunned by what they witnessed: The skull was rattling violently. It seemed as though it were being vigorously shaken. At this sight, my hands stopped ringing the bell, as if of their own volition. With a harsh reprimand, Mr Exorcist commanded me to continue. A great many people in the audience had started fleeing in terror. Quite a distance lay between the skull and the exorcist and there was no breeze at all; yet, that skull shook violently from time to time. I began to chant the incantation aloud, putting my heart and soul into it.

It could be surmised from the air of expectation around us that this was precisely the moment the people had been waiting for all afternoon. Ever since the skull began shaking, they had clutched each other and squatted on the ground in groups. Fear and anxiety were writ large on their faces. At one point, the skull shook so violently that it fell to the ground. Almost simultaneously, the demented girl howled in terror and fainted. The exorcist then approached her and breathing into her nose, ears and mouth, continued to chant his spell aloud. He then proceeded to untie the ropes that bound her. The girl rose to her feet. Suddenly conscious of her surroundings, she covered her face in embarrassment.

Had I not witnessed this scene first-hand, I would have found it impossible to believe. There were innumerable questions surfacing in my mind. I could not decide whether what I had seen had been treatment for a lunatic or a method for exorcizing an evil spirit. Admittedly, the powers of the exorcist had greatly impressed me. The girl's guardians were delighted and invited us for a meal. At their home, wooden planks had been laid out on the cold floor to reduce the chill factor and covered with straw which served as a kind of perfunctory mattress. This was clearly the living room of the dwelling. The girl's mother brought in two steaming bowls of barley soup and the girl herself carried in some cured meat. We relished the meal. Though I had also joined my exorcist friend for some beer, I hadn't guzzled all that much.

Once the meal was over, the women carried away the dishes along with the lamp, leaving us in darkness once more. Suddenly, I was startled by a noise coming from very close quarters. On looking around, I realized that it emanated from none other than the Great Exorcist who was snoring away to glory! I followed his example by groping around for a bundle of straw beneath which I crawled, snuggling into its warm depths.

The next day, my exorcist friend woke me up. Observing that he was up and ready to leave, his bag slung over his shoulder, I clambered out of bed at once. It had grown still colder at night, but ensconced as I had been under the bundle of straw, I had not felt the chill. As we walked along, I fell to shivering violently. The exorcist laughed at my plight and handed me some dry leaves to chew on. In no time at all, my body had warmed up again. We began to climb. From a height, the Sangpo Plateau appeared as beautiful as a painting. That would be the exorcist's chosen halting point. Although no burnt embers or wooden logs lay scattered around, it was obvious that the place was a cemetery. The ground was strewn with human bones and various body parts. In this particular region of Tibet, the customs relating to the disposal of corpses had evolved to suit the circumstances—an acute shortage of firewood. The local funeral rites were, understandably, somewhat different from those observed in other parts of the country. Here, the deceased were laid to rest at a spot high up in the mountains. Left to the elements, they remained at the mercy of vultures, dogs and other scavengers. A certain Tibetan sect even dismembered the bodies of the deceased in keeping with the common belief that a man's body, left intact, was prey to evil spirits. A dismembered corpse, on the other hand, was safe from such dangers.

In spite of searching long and hard, the exorcist failed to find a single bone that was suitable for his purpose and looked a little disheartened. We moved on. From the moment I set eyes on him, the Great Exorcist had fascinated me. He was filthy. His teeth had a yellow cast. His hair was matted and a deep cut ran across his forehead. And yet, despite it all, his was an overpowering personality. I felt no great urge to find out whether he was an impostor, a charlatan or someone of that ilk. His greatness shone out of his face. That was enough for me.

As we crossed another village, the inhabitants came rushing out, the way people do when they are eager for public entertainment. Like the other villages we had passed through, this one too, was small. But it had a tea shop in the centre and the roads were broader. We settled down in our places at the tea shop. The customers exchanged news and views. Right near the village, a herd of sheep browsed in the freshly sprouted grass. Patients began to trickle in. The exorcist examined them and prescribed appropriate treatment. Only in one instance did he use the skull, coins and bell again—in the case of a child suffering from fever. It was evident from the cases we came across that the villagers here suffered from no serious ailments.

After drinking two bowls of chang, we were off again. Payment was unnecessary—the shopkeeper was quite happy with the Great Exorcist's blessings.

Henceforth, we would follow the river. Its direction would lead us to our next shelter, where a villager was already waiting for us. The reason became clear as soon as the man took off his shawl. On his back was an old sore which had turned septic. From what I could gather, my friend, the exorcist, was reassuring his patient after a careful examination of the sore. He knew the exact procedure to follow. He made a fire and burnt some chunks of coal till they glowed red-hot. The patient was asked to lie on his stomach and, without warning, the burning hot embers were applied on his wound and covered with some mud. The man rested for about half an hour, then prepared to leave. Primitive rustic treatment, but what wonders it seemed to work! The man returned home contented.

At dawn, the following day, I bade my friend farewell. I asked him for details of the route I should follow, but he could not come up with any clear answers. In this region, the river flowed silent and deep. Even while walking along its banks, one could hardly hear it. The silence seemed to suggest the presence of a tremendous force lying leashed beneath the surface of the water. I could see signs of grass and a few small trees. They were somewhat like guava trees and some had sprouted new leaves. The view from the south was blocked by mountains. From the north, it was stunning.

It remained very cold all morning. As the sun moved overhead, the atmosphere grew warmer. When afternoon was approaching, I heard sudden peals of laughter; village girls at play, I surmised. Moving further ahead, I found that my hunch had been right: Around a dozen people were bathing together in the river. Some of them were young girls. It might be just about possible to take a quick dip in such icy waters, I mused. But swimming and frolicking in them didn't bear thinking about.

Suddenly, my gaze was drawn to a narrow path. It was the one I would have to follow, because from this point onwards, the river had taken a bend. From the river itself rose the massive barricade of mountains. Had I even wanted to, I would have found no way of progressing in that direction. So, following the narrow trail I had chanced upon, I started descending. This was not a proper road at all, but a path that had been naturally forged by the footsteps of people walking this way for years. Owing to the wall of mountains on the right, this area lay in shadow, blocked off from the rays of the sun. As soon as I had crossed the barricade of mountains, I noticed some houses on a little plot of agricultural land. A pair of donkeys stood about. Some hens too were visible. The people there looked startled to see me.

I moved on, keeping the river in my sights. After crossing the mountain, I would have to turn back to the watercourse which lay to my right, for the Sangpo was my only guide on this solitary journey. As I put my bundles down on the ground, the crowd that had been gathering around me began to swell rapidly. Ignoring the children, I tried to light a fire by gathering the dry leaves and twigs lying around me. A man approached and forbade me from starting a fire there. Smiling, he gestured at me to follow him, which I did unquestioningly. As we reached the house he had led me to, people clustered around me in the courtyard. The man went in and emerged a little later with some sweets which he offered me. I accepted them gratefully. The people around seemed to enjoy the sight of me eating. When I was done, the man forced some more sweets on me to tide me over the next couple of days, so that I need not bother about provisions for the journey.

Rising to my feet, I blessed them all in the name of God, then set off again. What I found really convenient about travelling through Tibet was the route itself, usually just a solitary road leading out, with neither crossroads nor junctions to complicate matters and cause confusion. Keeping the mountain to my right, I reached the Sangpo Valley late in the evening.

A NIGHT OF TERROR

IT TOOK ME about an hour more to reach the river. By that time, darkness had set in and the sky was bright with stars. Apart from those stars, I had no other light to guide me and I had to stumble and grope my way through. Loneliness was not my sole problem. The cold proved to be the greatest trial of all. I had kept my head well covered and the blanket wrapped snugly around myself. But it afforded me no relief at all.

Having walked for hours without a break, I was exhausted. The sweets I had been given were long over. And the moment arrived when I had no strength left to carry on. Dispirited and unable to cope with the bitter chill, I collapsed by the wayside. Wrapping the blanket still more tightly around myself, I curled up, the way a dog does when it is preparing for a nap, and went to sleep.

I dreamt that I was in a strange kingdom. It had neither king nor subjects. Its only reality was the snowflakes that were drifting down from the sky every now and then. The situation was nightmarish and I woke up to find my heart thudding and my entire body trembling with cold and terror like that of a sacrificial goat during its final moments. The cold seemed to knife through my blanket and clothes and penetrate my very bones. Although I was inclined to keep lying there languidly, the cold forced me to get up. I was in lamentable condition. I feared that all the heat had seeped out of my body. I remembered certain yogic exercises that stimulated body heat and restored my body to some semblance of normalcy. My mind was in a quandary over what I should do next. Ultimately, I decided to set out again.

Starlight was the only available illumination to guide me on my way. I chose one particular star to focus on and began walking. The cold grew in intensity. Somehow, I found it impossible to get back into stride. I started chanting aloud the Mani incantation and kept in step with its rhythm, breathing in and out as I went. I was wondering what hour of the night it was, when I suddenly noticed a thin sliver of a moon barely making its presence felt. In the silence that enveloped my surroundings, I felt I must be the only person alive in the embrace of a night without end.

Suddenly, my eyes were drawn to a sight in front of me that sent a shiver down my spine and made my hair stand on end: Someone was walking just ahead of me. I tried to get a clear view of him, but in the dim light, all I could make out was that he might be a practitioner of the occult. There was little I could do but follow him. He was the only ray of light in that relentless gloom. Having followed in his wake for a very long while, I was forced to come to an abrupt halt, for I was now positioned to the right of this mysterious entity.

I looked at him closely, but could discern little in the dim light. Ever since I had entered Tibet, lamas were almost the only type of people we had seen. Practitioners of the occult or of witchcraft had not come to our notice so far. Although I stared at the stranger, I failed to grasp what sort of person he might be. Nor was I familiar with the language which might have permitted me to communicate with him. I also noticed to my utter amazement that he was stark naked. His hair was coiled and knotted and fell down his back. He carried nothing in his hands.

Ahead of me, the path petered out. It was here that the river flowed into a waterfall. Pausing there for a while, the ascetic started moving towards the river. As though in a trance, I followed him. The watercourse had narrowed down at a certain point and seemed no wider than a stream. Stepping gingerly on the large boulders scattered around, we made our way across. After reaching the other side, the man did not wait for me, but moved off in a southerly direction. Though I was eager to do so, I could not follow him.

Then the cold hit me again in waves, starting all the way down in my toes and rising up through my body. I was forced to sit down by the river and take off my shoes. I discovered that they were soaked through. While crossing the river, I had not even noticed when they had got drenched. I rubbed my bare feet with the blanket and, within a short while, was able to get the blood circulating and work up some heat. There could be no question of putting on those shoes again. Yet, walking barefoot did not bear thinking about. By then, the ascetic had vanished without a trace. Why he had served as my guide throughout this segment of my journey and helped me cross the river and, above all, who he might be were questions that would remain unresolved and contribute to the eternal mystery of this experience.

The solution to my current problems was offered right away by the loud crowing of a cock. A glimmer of hope, at long last! Picking up my shoes, I started walking barefoot in the direction of the call. Surely, there was bound to be some villages nearby? Within minutes, I came across some arable land. As was the usual trend in this country, a pack of dogs greeted me with a volley of barking and kept circling me till a man came forward with a lamp. When he drew close, all I could manage was a request to be led to a lighted fire. Observing a trapa in such a sorry state, the man led me to his house right away. He asked for no explanations; my condition said it all. Taking me to a room, he pointed at the bed and urged me to go off to sleep.

STRANGERS BECOME FRIENDS

I AWOKE TO sunlight streaming in through the window and sat up in bed with a yawn. Memories of the previous night flooded back at once. It all seemed like a dream. Right away, I started jotting down all that had transpired before any of the details could elude me. The uncanniest experience of all was, of course, what had occurred just before dawn. I had been on the verge of dying from exposure when this naked ascetic had turned up from nowhere and guided me across the river to this house, where I had been granted refuge.

The moment I stepped into the courtyard, sunlight washed over me. Some children lay on a mat in the courtyard. An old woman was spinning on a local loom. The dogs slept peacefully and the puppies gambolled around the place. At the four corners of the courtyard stood four houses. They were strong, durable structures made of stone chips set in hardened soil. They had tin roofs and doors and windows made of wood. A man approached and it was apparent from his demeanour that he was the one who had rescued me, led me solicitously to his house and invited me to sleep in his room. He asked me to follow him. I obeyed and the children and even the dogs brought up the rear.

A short while later, we reached a chaitya. In no time at all, a crowd from the village had also gathered there. As far as I could read the situation, I would have to officiate as priest. By now, I was certain that there were no other lamas in the gumpha. Everybody sat around us. Though the chaitya was a small one, it had all the essential requirements to make it self-sufficient. A seat had been laid out beside the chaitya along with all other items necessary for the rituals of worship. The villagers—a total of forty-one people—waited expectantly.

My host humbly asked me to lead the prayers. I hesitated, because I hadn't a clue as to what I was expected to do. I had no idea of what rites I should perform nor even the incantations I was meant to chant. I sat down, however, without betraying my inner turmoil. Never before had I faced a similar situation. Closing my eyes, I summoned up all the self-control I could muster. Suddenly, the solution presented itself. The visage of my nocturnal saviour swam up before my eyes. He was the true God, Lord and Mentor of the entire region. My heart surged with joy and with the sincerest devotion, I expressed my gratitude and offered up my prayers to Him.

After observing a prolonged period of silence, I rose to my feet. It was now time to submit to the outpourings of love and respect from the villagers who began showering me with gifts and offerings. A woman presented me with a white shawl, a sign of the highest regard. Touched by these gestures, I found my eyes brimming with tears. Somehow, I remembered the Almighty and pulled myself together. After circumambulating the chaitya with the villagers, my host and I began making our way through the village once more.

'Are you an ascetic from India?' asked my host.

The question was an unexpected one and I refrained from answering it. After a pause, he began again, 'We are very happy to have a Hindu ascetic in our village.'

There is no denying the truth that when swayed by powerful feelings, one finds it impossible to express oneself except in one's mother tongue. The simplicity of the villagers and the spontaneous way they had accepted me into the fold, as it were, triggered a response in me that swept away all the constraints I had been labouring under. Oblivious to the situation and my surroundings, I allowed my native Bengali to take over and began reciting from my favourite scriptures in Sanskrit.

Addressing my host, I spoke from the heart, keeping nothing from him. In bits of fractured Tibetan that I somehow put together, I admitted, 'Yes, you are right. I am an Indian and I travelled with pilgrims to Tibet. They were all Nepalese lamas. After I was ordained, I had accompanied them to Lhasa. They have returned home now. I am the only one travelling along this route so that I can reach Kailashnath.'

The man jumped for joy, as though he had discovered a rare treasure. Refusing to heed my pleas, he told everyone present what he had learnt about me. I discovered gradually that this was Dingbo village and my host's name was Eegi. He and his brother,

Gibit, were married to the same woman. In other words, the lady, who looked about fifty years old—a random guess on my part— had two husbands. All the little girls I had seen were Gibit's children. I thought it a very creditable feat on the lady's part to be able to make both men happy. It was Eegi who volunteered these details. This kind of marriage was the norm in Tibet and widely accepted. There were, perhaps, few families in the whole wide world as happy and cheerful as this one.

After resting for two whole days in Dingbo, I set out for Shigatse. I moved west, with the Sangpo keeping me company. The route from this point was quite simple to follow and used by the villagers to travel to Shigatse. One would have to move further south following the course of the Sangpo and continue walking for a few days until another river, the Niyang, came into view. There were ferries available to cross it and on the opposite bank lay Shigatse. This meant that henceforth, I would not be required to cross any river other than the Niyang. The discovery was a source of great relief to me.

SHIGATSE

EVER SINCE WE had set out from Gangtok for Lhasa, we had come across a village every night. A village indicated the inevitable presence of a gumpha close by. The latter was a resting place for lamas. So, as far as accommodation for the night was concerned, we had faced no problems whatsoever. But a traveller going to Shigatse from Chusul via Sangpo would have no such luck. There was virtually no habitation on the way and apart from the tiny village of Dingbo with its population of forty-one, I had, in the past five days, come across no more than half a dozen houses belonging to desperately poor farmers. Their intense devotion to their faith, intrinsic to their nature, touched me to the core.

Almost a hundred and thirty miles separated Shigatse from

Lhasa. Had I travelled by the main road, it would have taken me around eleven days to reach my destination. Following the Sangpo was the easier option for me. Of course, the route I was following defied description, for it was hardly a road at all. Merely avoiding the boulders in my path was an arduous job and it took me nearly thirteen days to reach the banks of the Niyang river.

On the afternoon of the thirteenth day, while walking along the Sangpo Valley, another valley suddenly came into view on my left. I had, so far, been skirting the massive rockface that was the Himalayan range and it seemed to have abruptly fallen away. Before me stretched a vast tract of level land. A village stood in its midst. It dawned on me then, that I had reached Shigatse. I came upon a prosperous village by the banks of the Sangpo and started walking through it till I had reached its outskirts and discovered that it was the very point where two rivers had met. Here, then, was the Niyang river.

In the course of conversation with the people I met there, I came to know that there were designated places along the riverbank from which the ferry left—one to cross the Niyang river and the other to go across the Sangpo, known elsewhere as the Brahmaputra. To avail of the latter, one would have to cross the Niyang. The ferry service was available once or, perhaps, twice a day. Passengers intending to go across had to stand on the banks and shout out for the boatman. The ferry would come from across the river to fetch passengers, that too, not more than twice a day. The boatman was usually reluctant to go to the effort for merely one passenger.

On reaching the riverbank, I could not find a likely landing place from which I could board the ferry. Nor could I sight a boat. The Niyang was not very wide. But since this place was located near its source, a wide, sandy bank flanked the river on either side. It was close to Gyatse that the Niyang was joined by a tributary and became a mighty force.

Unable to find a way of getting across the river, I was forced to return to the tea shop. When I asked the young boy there about it, he rushed to the bank and looked across the water before returning with a glum expression. It would not be possible to go across that day, he announced. The boatmen had already dropped anchor. Noticing my crestfallen expression, he consoled me with the reassurance, 'There is no need for you to worry. You can spend the night in my shop. A fire burns here and you will be quite comfortable.'

There could be no better arrangement and I acquiesced quite happily to his suggestion.

As evening drew near and there was still some daylight, all the shops downed their shutters. I paid the boy a token sum of money as advance for allowing me to stay overnight at his shop. The expression of joy that lit up his face is impossible to describe. In terms of the local currency and its value, I had probably paid him almost four times as much as he would normally have received from a local and he was thrilled to bits about it. In an impulsive outpouring of gratitude, he even invited me to share a meal with him and I lost no time in accepting his offer.

We woke up very early the following morning; that is, we were jolted into wakefulness by the young girl calling us. Tea had been prepared without my even asking for it. I quickly paid and rushed to board the ferry. Accompanied by two others who also wanted to cross the river, I reached the point from where the boats collected passengers.

The boat was an amazing sight indeed. I had never seen anything quite like it before. It resembled an enormous leather bucket. Somehow, we all managed to squeeze in and take seats. Had we remained standing, the contraption would probably have capsized. Two planks of wood were used as oars and there seemed to be no way of steering the vessel. One had to depend entirely on the direction of the current. From what I could see, the boat was, somehow, managing to make its way to the opposite bank. On reaching its destination, it was carried to the landing stage. Otherwise, there were strong chances of it being swept away by the Sangpo. Finally, we had reached Shigatse.

It was one of the largest towns in Tibet, second only to Lhasa. The third largest was Gyatse, followed by Yatung, the last having developed at the confluence of the Niyang and the Sangpo. This was the domain of the Revered Panchen Lama, known locally as Tashi Lama or Panchen Rimpoche. He was believed to be related by religious ties to the Dalai Lama and recognized as the latter's spiritual brother. The Panchen Lama was deemed the reigning authority on religious functions and public relations in all of Tibet, while the Dalai Lama was in charge of political and administrative affairs. In actual fact, the Dalai Lama himself was the spiritual leader of Tibet, while the Panchen Lama was a kind of state administrator and the ruling authority of Shigatse, Gyatse and Phari. Like the lama of Shigatse, the Panchen Lama was one of the country's most illustrious personalities.

Shigatse itself could be split up into three distinct parts. The first of these was a fort, the principal military base for the Chinese invasion many years back. Even today, this served as their headquarters and was used as a base for the protection of the Tashi Lama and the maintenance of law and order. Right below it lay the city, the main business centre and marketplace. Not far away stood the Tashi Lumpo, the region's main gumpha. As the Panchen Lama's residence, it was comparable to the Potala of Lhasa. Like the Dalai Lama, the Panchen Lama too, had a summer palace—the Kun-Kiyapling—located almost twelve miles away. Sadhu Baba had already told me a great deal about Shigatse.

No sooner had I climbed further up from the sandy banks of the Niyang river than my eyes fell on a large town. The houses there seemed thickly crowded together and I made my way towards them. The town itself stood on a vast stretch of level land sprawling across the Sangpo Valley. All the roads converged at a point somewhere near the market and it was in that direction that I gradually headed. The place seemed rather similar to Gyatse, the roads being almost entirely given over to a plethora of donkeys, yaks, sheep, hens and dogs. As in the market in Kalimpong, the roads were flanked on either side by a crowd of shops and Sherpas milled around the place.

I stopped in my tracks abruptly. Right in front of me was a sign that said 'Hotel' in Hindi and English. Hoping that a notice posted in Hindi implied that someone or the other would know the language, I approached the building. A man there stared at me in amazement. Smiling at him, I asked in Hindi, 'The message on the signboard outside your house is in Hindi—do you understand the language?'

He listened to me attentively. Then, instead of offering an answer right away, he twirled a finger around his fancy, though rather sparse moustache, giving the matter serious thought. Suddenly, he rose to his feet, stepped out and gestured for me to follow him. Crossing the road, we paused before a beautiful pagoda-shaped house. He asked me to wait outside and went in. A little later, he emerged with another elderly man in tow and smilingly welcomed me. As soon as I laid eyes on the second man, I was filled with respect. His voice was tender with affection as he asked, 'Have you come from Gangtok?'

I was amazed to hear him speak such fluent Hindi. 'Yes,' I replied, ' Yes, indeed, I have.'

It was impossible to lie outright to so upright and honest a man. Giving a brief potted history of the past couple of months, I said to him earnestly, 'I am longing to go to Mansarovar so that I can take a dip in the holy waters. Please help me with advice on which route I should take and how I should follow it. If you can see your way to doing so, I will be eternally indebted to you.'

My words seemed to place the man in a real quandary. He merely emitted a grunt of acknowledgement and absent-mindedly threaded his fingers through his sparse beard. Asking the person who had brought me there to leave us, the man took me inside the house and sat me down in a room. In the course of conversation, certain crucial facts came to light. I immediately requested my grandfatherly saviour to repeat what he had just said. He smiled and observed, 'Though Indians are inclined to call it Mansarovar, none of the locals will understand what you are talking about. They know it by an altogether different name—Mapham Tso or, perhaps, Mavang Tso. "Tso" means "sarovar" or lake. Right next to it lies the Langak Tso, which you Indians know as Rakshas Taal. These two lakes are inextricably linked. Tibetans, however, consider the gumpha there of far greater importance than the lakes. For them, Kailashnath is not that important a pilgrimage centre. Ask people the way to the Diraphuk Gumpha and they will give you directions right away.'

The man wrote out the names in Tibetan on a sheet of paper. The moment they had been written down, I memorized them—Mapham Tso, Mavang Tso, Langak Tso, Diraphuk Gumpha. Even if I should misplace my diary or the bit of paper on which the names had been noted, the directions to Kailashnath would be intact in my memory.

That afternoon, my surrogate grandfather invited me over for lunch. On any other day, this would have been more than welcome, but at present, my mind could focus on nothing beyond the dream of reaching my utopia—Kailash. An immediate departure in quest of my goal seemed imperative. My heart thrilled to the thought that I had, at last, managed to obtain the directions to Kailashnath.

Grandfather or Dadu, the secret nickname I had chosen for him, insisted on my eating a proper lunch and it was after a very long time that I enjoyed a meal of rice and vegetables, with mutton to top it all. Lunch over, I was about to leave after thanking my host, when Dadu leapt to his feet and grasped my hand. 'Where do you think you are off to now!' he exclaimed. 'Sit down and relax for a while.'

I could not bring myself to ignore his gently fond reproach, and meekly went along with his wishes.

THE PANCHEN LAMA

SOMETIME BEFORE EVENING set in, Dadu asked me suddenly, 'Have you seen the Dalai Lama?'

'Yes, I have,' I replied, 'but I did not have the good fortune of talking to him.'

'There is no sense in conversing with him at present,' the man retorted. 'He is still a child and, besides, he is surrounded by people all the time. The Panchen Lama, on the other hand, is different. He knows well enough how he should handle things.'

I stared at Dadu in amazement. It was quite obvious from his tone of voice that his respect for the Panchen Lama far exceeded that for the Dalai Lama. For him, the latter was a mere child. As I talked to my host, I came to know much more about these two religious leaders. 'At one time,' said Dadu, 'the Panchen Lama himself was the supreme religious authority of Tibet. He had, in fact, explored and comprehended in its totality the mystery that was the religion of the lamas followed in Tibet. But the Dalai Lama's entourage upset the existing balance of power through their political machinations and the position gradually came to be usurped by the Dalai Lama, though, in all fairness, the latter could not really be held responsible for what had transpired. Holding the religious leader up as a front for their political manoeuvrings, members of the Dalai Lama's close circle took over all the important official posts in Tibet. There was even a time when the child Dalai Lama died before he could officially assume power. The ministers and their devious strategies were entirely to blame for this state of affairs.

'Come, come to this room and have a look at this photograph. Do you know who this is? This is the Panchen Lama, the predecessor of the present one whose official investiture took place in 1923. Instead of making a deal with the British, he fled for his life to Chinghai where he eventually passed away. In 1952, he was born once again in that province. Enlisting the help of the British, that Panchen Lama returned to Tibet when he was still a child. If the Chinese had not come to his aid, he would never have regained his influence in Shigatse. This Panchen Lama later came to be known as the Panchen Erdeny. Besides, don't you see our marked resemblance to the Chinese, both in appearance and temperament?'

It was quite apparent from Dadu's observations that he was a staunch supporter of the Chinese or Han. He divulged further information. The Han, it seemed, were now an indomitable presence in Tibet, having proliferated throughout the country. It was only in Lhasa, apparently, that they were still unable to exercise complete control, because the Tibetan capital had retained its importance as a Buddhist stronghold and the influence of the gumphas along with that of the lamas running them was still a formidable one. Moreover, members of the Kaloon sect of the aristocracy who constituted the Kashak division of the Dalai Lama's ministry brooked no interference in any quarter from the Chinese. The latter had, in fact, thrown their doors wide open to the Tibetans. There was no longer an official border between China and Tibet and Tibetans were now travelling to China quite frequently.

The Panchen Lama was, according to Dadu, the most far-sighted of all the lamas and with very good reason too. After all, he was the spiritual mentor of all the lamas in Tibet including the Dalai Lama. He had honoured to the last the treaty signed between the Dalai Lama and the Han. As a result, the latter were now willing to make all necessary contributions for the welfare and development of the Shigatse region. In the past, there had been no motorable roads for traffic in Tibet, but the Chinese had subsequently constructed five roads. Now, one could reach Shigatse by jeep directly from Kathmandu. The Chinese were going out of their way to do all they could for the upliftment of the Tibetan people. An airport was under construction not far from Shigatse. Groups of young Tibetans, men and women, were going to Beijing in pursuit of higher education. Starving beggars who would once spend all their time wandering the streets now had an opportunity for employment with the Chinese army. There were plenty of jobs available in the military barracks scattered around the country.

Shigatse was a beautiful city located in the Sangpo Valley. Its pagoda-shaped houses had a unique appeal. Inevitably, Chinese slogans marched across their walls. On the mountain, at some distance from the city, stood the palace of the Panchen Lama. Pointing out five huge memorial stones, Dadu informed me that they were dedicated to the Panchen Lamas of the past. The palace and gumpha of the Panchen Erdeny were housed in one building and known as the Tashi Lumpo. One of the largest gumphas in Tibet and deemed especially sacred by all lamas, it could accommodate almost four thousand monks. Its walls were beautifully decorated and its library enjoyed international renown. Every article of worship used in the temple was made of pure gold.

Though Dadu had made no comments about them, the Chinese soldiers moving along the streets did not escape my notice. I learned in the course of conversation that the forts at Shigatse and Gyatse were manned and patrolled by Chinese soldiers to ensure improved vigilance and security along the border.

Coming to a crossroad, Dadu pointed out a paved road and said, 'That leads directly to Kathmandu. What is the sense of travelling alone to Kailash? It is an extremely tough route and you will not be able to make it.' With tender concern, he warned me of the hazards of undertaking such a journey.

For the first time in a very long while, I would be sleeping in a real bed, not a makeshift one, and the dream of snuggling under a real quilt in this bitterly cold climate had finally come true. I had planned to get up very early, but by the time I surfaced, it was around 8.30 a.m.! Out on the road and heading towards my destination, it suddenly occurred to me that in spite of spending almost a whole day with Dadu, I had forgotten to ask him his name. We had grown so close, it had quite slipped my mind that he was not related to me.

Since I had already covered some distance, it did not make sense to turn back for the sole purpose of finding out Dadu's real name. I reasoned with myself that it hardly mattered. I would always regard him as a fond grandfather. What struck me as really strange, though, was that despite my having kept nothing from him, he had completely misunderstood my words. He had taken me for a Nepalese lama from Kathmandu who had played truant by parting from the group of pilgrims he was travelling with, because he wanted to go to Kailashnath on his own. It had completely escaped him that I was a native of India. This was yet another indication of his simplicity and his natural inclination to take people at face value. It was probably why he had repeatedly pointed out the way to Kathmandu for my benefit.

ON THE WAY TO KAILASH

AFTER SPENDING A night in Shigatse, I had set out on my journey again equipped with directions, provisions, recharged batteries and fresh will power. The dream of going to Kailashnath now seemed a real possibility. I prayed to the Almighty and asked for guidance to do His will.

The road at this point was ideal for traffic and I kept to the edges as I walked. The surroundings were very pleasant and the warmth of the sun enhanced my sense of well-being. Keeping to the left of the unconquerable Himalayas, I followed the directions I had been given and moved on. As evening approached, I reached the fork in the road I had been looking for. Both the roads here were well constructed. The one on my left, that is, to the south, ran on towards Kathmandu. The other one moved further ahead of the Sangpo and bifurcated, the two paths heading north and west respectively.

Swimming across the Sangpo in this severe chill was out of the question. Besides, the river was very wide at this point. There was a small tea shop near the ferry-landing stage. Without a moment's hesitation, I made my way there. A huge boat was anchored at the landing stage. Some Chinese soldiers squatted nearby, chatting over their cups of tea. I did not have to ask for a cup; tea was handed to me in a large bamboo container. This was my first direct encounter with Chinese soldiers. I followed their example and squatted there, savouring the hot tea.

We waited there endlessly, without a clue as to how long we would have to do so. Then suddenly, with the evening almost upon us, the Chinese soldiers rose to their feet, as if coming to life after sitting for an hour. Their skill and ability to work hard impressed me greatly. Within minutes, they had reached the boat, using a kind of aluminium plank to serve as a makeshift ramp, so that cars could drive up it and into the boat. Within half an hour, everything had been organized and three lorries and a couple of jeeps loaded on to the boat. There was another surprise awaiting me. Quivering violently, the boat's engine was revved up. I had not even noticed that the boat was motorized! Observing me staring at the vessel in amazement, a couple of soldiers beckoned to me and asked me to board. Since I had been waiting for the crossing, I complied right away.

We had crossed the Sangpo and it was from this point in my journey that the actual route to Kailash began. I had no further need for directions. If I followed the road all the way west, it would take me to my dream destination. I spent the night in an abandoned house. I was moving in a direction that went against the current of the river. In other words, I was travelling towards its source. The road was much smoother than the one to Gyatse. In fact, it was almost monotonous. A dry, nippy cold pervaded the area. The chill that settled in at night was vanquished by the harsh heat that scorched the region during the day. Had there been clouds in the sky, the extreme cold would, perhaps, have impeded my progress. But the sky over Tibet was clear and sparkling with hardly a cloud in sight. The brilliant sunlight during the day and the twinkling stars at night inspired me to maintain a steady pace and move on.

On the third day after crossing the Sangpo, I reached Laka, a small village. As soon as I entered it, I noticed a crowd of villagers gathered there. It transpired that I was the first lama who had visited the place in a long while. After I had sat down and rested for a while, an elderly woman approached carrying an infant in her arms. She prostrated herself before me with due respect and addressed some remarks to me through toothless gums. I did not make any kind of response, because there was nothing for me to say in the circumstances. Though I did understand a little Tibetan, the woman's dialect defeated me completely. She wasn't, however, one to give up so easily. Ultimately, I ended up blessing her and the baby, a gesture that satisfied her no end.

There was no escape from the attentions of the villagers. They were all around me. In the afternoon, one of them honoured their guest by bringing along some tsampa. After the meal was over, I stretched out for a rest while they looked on. As evening approached, the young people started returning home from their work in the fields and the entire village seemed to come to life.

That evening, I shared a communal meal with the villagers. Afterwards, everyone seated themselves on straw mats and a huge pan filled with some brew was placed in the centre. Then the crowd began a round of choral singing with everybody joining in. They all sang beautifully, with a fine sense of rhythm and harmony. As the night advanced, it grew colder still and people began huddling together for warmth. In a while, the singing came to a halt. Two of the women rose to their feet and poured out some of the liquid from the pan into small bowls which they served to everyone present. One of the girls handed me a bowl as well. Eagerly, I drained the cold contents to the last drop. I gathered it was some kind of Tibetan beer and it seemed to add an extra zest to the singing, for the latter was resumed with increasing gusto, followed by a form of dancing that was powerfully reminiscent of the tribal rhythms and steps of Bengal.

The stage on which the performance was taking place had a wooden frame with a tin roof. There were no walls to speak of and the cold was now intense. But there was no way I could leave until the dancing had come to an end. Finally, everyone drifted home. All that remained was the empty stage and myself—a pilgrim destined for a long journey. I crawled beneath some straw for warmth; after all, I would have to spend the night there. The night passed like a dream. Early the next morning, before the village was awake, I took my leave. The only witnesses to my departure were a few stray dogs.

I could not help admitting that the road cutting through this valley was very well maintained. The wall formed by the Himalayas ran parallel to the Sangpo. That posed no problem at all. What was hard to bear was the monotony of the journey, in no way helped by the sameness of the landscape. Even if one walked for hours on end, the topography hardly changed. The mountain to the north of the river had fallen back a mile or so. Trees were scarce. The river, hugged by its sandy banks, stretched endlessly and, in the daytime, the rays of the sun glancing off the water were blinding. There was hardly any habitation at all in this area, quite unlike our experience along the route from Gangtok to Lhasa when we had often crossed a series of villages. That part of Tibet was evidently much more densely populated than the area I was now passing through. The houses I came across after leaving Gyatse behind me were few and far between. Occasionally, I would notice the tents of Tibetan gypsies or military camps manned by Chinese soldiers. On the fourth day of my journey down the Sangpo route, I came across lorries for the first time. At first, I could not believe my eyes. But then they drew close, raising a cloud of dust.

While I had been part of a group, I had encountered no problems whatsoever. Guruji, my guide and mentor, had been there to take care of everything. My current situation presented a stark contrast to what had gone before. Now, there was no certainty at all about where and how I would spend the night. I walked on, completely dependent on the Almighty. As soon as I saw the sun on the verge of setting, I would begin looking for somewhere to lay my head for the night. On two occasions, it had taken me almost till dawn to find a shelter of sorts. I was grateful for any sort of roof over my head.

These experiences would afford me the chance of enjoying a sense of untrammelled freedom from the bondage of the corporeal body. While walking along, I would experience the feeling that my body and my soul were two separate entities. In reality, we were all travellers on a journey that led us from our worldly lives defined by narrow, finite boundaries towards the eternal and the infinite, much in the same manner in which my spirit drove me along my present path in its quest to pay homage at Kailashnath.

And so my journey continued. I rested for two days at the gumpha in the small village of Gebuk. Praying helped lessen my sense of ennui to some extent. The Gebuk Monastery had nearly become defunct and was, inevitably, overrun by rats which did not even spare the shawl draped around the image of the Buddha that presided over its temple. However, the decorations on the walls remained intact and the thangkas and heavy tomes had not moved an inch from their usual place. Neither had the light wooden mask atop the door.

On the second day of my sojourn there, a group of thirteen villagers gathered together and asked me to go through the rituals of prayer using the traditional instruments of worship that had lain untouched for months. They informed me that it had been nearly a year since the presiding lama had gone to Shigatse and not returned. The Tashi Lumpo had not sent any replacement for his post. The villagers had left to work in the Chinese camps and returned to Gebuk from time to time. The occasional visit was good enough for them and kept them happy.

Three days after leaving Gebuk, I arrived at Saka, yet another village. Then it was back again along the same monotonous road. From this point onwards, the road appeared to be slowly gaining height. Looking at the Sangpo, I realized that I wasn't mistaken in my assumption. The river seemed to flow with greater force than it had earlier and the currents were much more powerful. Four days after I had passed through Saka, I reached Pasaguk, the next village on the route and the largest I had come across since Latse Jong. It was afternoon when I arrived and judging by the crowd, I surmised that the village boasted at least a thousand inhabitants.

THE SAGE OF PASAGUK

PASAGUK, A TRANQUIL village on the banks of the Sangpo, had a leisurely, unhurried air about it. As soon as I entered it, I noticed a herd of yaks peacefully chewing the cud. Evidently used to the comings and goings of pilgrims like me, they ignored me completely. A few young children stopped in their tracks when they saw me and stuck their tongues out in a gesture of respect. At the centre of the village, my gaze was drawn to a pillar from which fluttered row upon row of white flags. Right afterwards, I noticed a gumpha and my heart surged with joy. After circumambulating the temple as was customary, I touched the Mani Chakra and entered the place of worship.

At first, it seemed pitch dark inside in contrast to the glare of sunlight outdoors. In a short while, however, I was able to make out the colossal image of Abalokiteswara. On a dais below him were arranged rows of bowls containing water. Rice grains and a huge lighted lamp fuelled with ghee and serving as the life force of the temple paid homage to the Buddha. I took my seat and tried to meditate in an effort to calm my body and mind. Having found a shelter of sorts after such a long while, I wished to offer my humble thanks to the Lord.

Somehow, I managed to alleviate my hunger pangs by chewing on the dry rice grains. When the heart was full and content, the consumption of food ought not to have been more than a minor concern. I had, however, observed that at mealtimes, it was virtually impossible for me to quell the craving for food. According to ascetics, the mind moved on an elevated plane, unperturbed by physical urges. But the rationality of that argument eluded me. If one were to apply plain and simple logic, how did one explain the fact that the mind, if it were indeed travelling on such a high plane, could actually descend again to the level of the body? I pondered on these matters. These days, I found it quite easy to become deeply engrossed in my own thoughts and while away the hours in this manner.

I decided to spend the night in the gumpha, for there could have been no place more appropriate in the given circumstances. As evening approached, I wandered around the village. This part of Tibet closely resembled a desert. After sundown, the village began to reveal signs of life. It was likely that the villagers worked elsewhere and returned home at the end of day. After wandering about here and there, I returned to the gumpha. It was a relief that none of the villagers asked me any questions.

No boundary wall surrounded the gumpha. It consisted of nothing more than a small house, a chaitya and the open field. The house was probably intended for the lama who conducted prayers and I found out where the kitchen lay. Everybody here had free access to the gumpha's kitchen. In Tibet, the gumphas were generally left unlocked, unless a particular reason dictated that they should be under lock and key. Of course, the majority of the villagers had never even seen a lock and key in all their lives. Such an instance of innocence and honesty would have been rare indeed in any other part of the world.

Very early in the morning, a voice roused me from deep slumber. I somehow managed to surface from the fog of sleep that enshrouded me. Looking around, I found a lama with a tranquil expression standing right in front of me. Greeting him, I rose to my feet.

'Where have you come from?' he asked.

'I am Indian,' I replied. 'I had gone to Lhasa and Drepung with a group of Nepalese lamas. I have now left them and am on my way to Kailash.' In the early hours of dawn, I bared my soul to this near divine presence.

Geshe Reptin—for that was the visitor's name—smiled faintly, then suggested, 'Come, let's go to my room; we can talk there.'

I followed him into the next room. Pristine in its cleanliness, it contained a made-up bed in one corner and a desk beside it. On the latter were notebooks, pens and a great many tomes. Several thangkas adorned the walls. There was also a small wooden image of the Buddha. Ignoring all else, he led me towards it and remarked, 'Isn't it beautiful? The Mahabodhi Society of Calcutta gave it to me as gift.'

I looked at him and asked, 'You have been to Kolkata, have you?'

'No, I haven't actually. I lived in Darjeeling and Kalimpong for a number of years.' He asked me to sit beside him on the bed and inquired, 'Do the people of Shigatse and Lhasa know that you are from Kolkata?'

'No, they don't,' I answered, 'I told them I was the Silent Monk from Nepal.'

He burst out laughing and declared, 'If you have managed to come so far, I do not think there is any further cause for worry. The Almighty Himself has probably taken you under His wing.'

The lama explained that the gumphas were the life force of Tibet and constituted the basic foundation for all academic and religious activity. Unfortunately, political intrigue had vitiated the country's spiritual climate. Provisions from the Tashi Lumpo had almost dried up. For their survival, the lamas had to sell the assets of the gumphas to which they were assigned and depend entirely on the villagers. The government continued to amend its laws on an almost daily basis and the Chinese authorities were doing their best to bring about an improvement in the country.

Finally, the lama remarked with a sigh, 'Perhaps, this is what Lord Tathagata wants? To ensure that the wheels of the world are turning and the sanctity of religion is preserved, he continues to be reborn on earth. Perhaps, change is what he is looking for. All that happens is his will.' Looking at me, he asked, 'When you are back home, will you still remain true to your vows as a trapa?'

'B-back home?' I stammered. Somehow, I managed a response of sorts. 'Once I go back,' I said, 'I will probably try and complete my schooling like any good Bengali lad. After all, I must get my school leaving certificate.'

'No, that is not my question,' he interrupted. 'What I want to know is the following: You have now been ordained as a Buddhist. Will you continue to respect the principles of your new faith, once you return?'

Having heard him out, I was silent for a while. 'Yes,' I finally answered.

'What do you know about Hinduism?' he asked.

I was at a loss for words.

'Do you know any incantations?' he asked me then.

'Yes, I do. I have memorized a number of verses from the holy scriptures.'

'Just a superficial knowledge of the verses is not good enough. You have to understand their meaning in depth and feel it from within. The very fact that you were born a human being is the reason you have been given this chance. You must put it to good use.'

After a session of prayer at the temple, we came back to Geshe Reptin's room. The two people who prepared his meals and did his grocery shopping were waiting in front of the house. After issuing instructions to them, he led me to a secret chamber in the room.

It had no doors. He lit a lamp and asked me to look at the pictures there, promising to return in a while. We could converse later. Handing me the lamp, he shut the door. Had I not trusted him implicitly, I would certainly have felt trapped and overwhelmed by claustrophobia. To be honest, the suspicion that I was, indeed, trapped had surfaced for a fleeting moment, but I had banished it from my mind.

The room was strange; not even a pinprick of sunlight penetrated it. The first object my eyes fell on was an enormous and fearsome idol, looking as though it were ready to pounce on me. This was an image of Jamantak, a nine-headed god with thirty-four arms and sixteen legs, its central head shaped rather like a buffalo's. This deity, who had defeated his rival in battle, was regarded as the King of Death. The image was painted in aggressively loud hues of red, blue and white. The sight was terrifying enough to make anyone scream out loud. Behind the statue and painted in a circular pattern were fifty human skulls. Brightly painted flames spewed out from around them. Calm and gentle in comparison was the Goddess Kali worshipped in the cemetery.

My journey alone from Lhasa had strengthened my mental resilience to a great extent. The darkness of the night no longer intimidated me. Lifting the lamp and moving it down the chamber, I looked around at all the different pictures—both tranquil and terrifying—that surrounded me. Suddenly, I felt someone tap me on the shoulder. My heartbeats lurched into a swifter rhythm. The flame of the lamp also began to flicker suddenly. Despite my best attempts to get a hold on myself, I realized that fear was getting the better of me. Striving to regain my composure, I seated myself on the ground and attempted to focus my mind in meditation on the benign and protective aspect of the Goddess Kali.

Having recited the mantras aloud, I found myself retreating deep into myself. Instead of the swish of air, what reverberated in my heart were the sounds of the mantras. Then a moment arrived when all consciousness seeped away and I was left in an inert heap in a corner of the room.

I awoke as if from a long, refreshing sleep. The thangka in front of me was clearly visible now. The room seemed bright with light. When I turned, however, I found that the lamp had gone out. It was my turn to be amazed yet again and with good reason too. For through the gap under the door, I could see the last rays of the ebbing sun. How had time flown so fast? I was used to meditating for an hour or so. But this time, I had meditated for more than six hours without a break.

When evening approached, I went to the lama's room and sat down. His gentle smile was like a shower of blessings bestowed on me. After a prolonged silence, I observed, 'It is a matter of great surprise to me that I have been meditating over such a long period of time. Is it because this place is especially sacred?'

'An especially sacred place!' he repeated after me. Then, following a pause, he continued, 'This comes about through practice and with the blessings of the spiritual mentor.' He fell silent for a while before carrying on. 'You were afraid, were you not? Why you alone? Jamantak is greatly feared by the entire world. He dominates it and it is only by the grace of the Buddha that mankind can even nurture hopes of being rescued from his clutches. What saved you was the fact that you surrendered yourself totally to Mahamaya instead of allowing fear to get the better of you. She protected you. You have been ordained and have a spiritual mentor to guide you. You have been blessed with a glimpse of Chenreji and have offered prayers at the Jokhang Temple. All this contributes to your identity as a true Buddhist ascetic.'

'But believe me, the truth is that I know absolutely nothing about being a lama. It was because I wanted to come on this pilgrimage that such measures were initiated. I underwent no preparation at all for my present state of being.'

'Those who study Buddhism or the religion of the lamas take a long, long time to understand its fundamental tenets. It takes another few years to absorb and appreciate its nuances. Unless one is especially blessed by one's spiritual mentor or happens to be the beneficiary of accumulated blessings acquired through meditation during one's previous incarnations, it is impossible to understand the Buddhist faith and the occult sciences. Take an aspect of Hinduism, for instance—devotion. If one is able to bring oneself to submit totally to the Supreme Power, attaining the Absolute lies within the realms of possibility. But that concept has little credence as far as we Buddhists are concerned. We believe, on the other hand, that everything is attained through the power of meditation.'

I pondered over the difficult path I had chosen for myself.

There was the lama, talking about the intricacies of the metaphysical; and here was I, worrying about the cold and rocky path that led to Kailash!

'The fundamentals of the faith adopted by the lamas,' my companion continued, 'have come from India. The great Yogi Guru Padma Sambhava and the renowned philosopher, Shanta Rakshit, were our mentors. It was they who laid the foundations.'

I wasted no time in asking him a question that had been lurking in my mind for quite sometime: 'What exactly is the mandala? It is everywhere in Tibet, but what exactly is its function?'

Nodding vigorously, the lama continued, 'If one's insights into the significance of the mandala are not far-reaching, it will seem no more than a projection of different geometric patterns and diagrams. But exploring its depths will reveal the truth that lies at its core. The mandala is a miniature of the whole universe. It is the first expression of man's thoughts. That is the form serving as the base on which commitment to meditation and devotion to the faith grows and evolves.'

Rising from the bed, the lama approached the window and gestured at me to join him. Pointing to a mountain in the distance, he asked, 'What do you see before you?'

In the waning light of the setting sun, I saw the blurred contours of a mountain. I gathered he was drawing my attention to it. Looking at him, I answered, 'A mountain.'

'You are right. It is, indeed, a mountain. If a house has to be constructed, its foundation must be firm. It is only a strong base that ensures a beautiful and stable house. That foundation is the mandala of the house. At the base of the mountain is another colossal foundation that lies beyond the scope of our imagination. It supports this extensive area that has risen from it. The stabler the mandala, the stronger the structure of what is built on it. It symbolizes yet another form of will power. If a course of action is not planned out properly, it will not lead to anything of consequence in the future.'

I do not remember exactly when I dozed off listening to his words. When I woke up very early the next morning, I found that I was sprawled across more than half the lama's bed, while he lay curled up in the little space that remained. The lama himself must have covered me with the blanket at some point during the night.

Silently, I got out of bed and completed the rituals of prayer. I noticed, then, that the villagers were going somewhere in a group. It reminded me of the tribals back in India who set out to look for work in some prosperous village or the other.

A little later, the lama woke up and with all due respect, I took his leave. He embraced me affectionately and murmured, 'God bless you. Take care.'

In the meantime, Mumbu, one of the men who looked after the lama's daily needs, had brought in tea and some boiled potatoes for me to carry as provisions for the journey. As I ate my snack, the lama wrote out a letter for me to carry. To the north of Mapham Tso, there were two gumphas—Langbona and Diraphuk. The lama had written to the head of each, requesting him to ensure that all necessary help was extended to me. A letter of this kind was as valuable as a treasure in this country and I accepted it with gratitude, though that could never measure up to all that the lama had done for me, including the constructive suggestions and practical help he had provided me with.

Then I was on the road once more.

TRADUM

WITH PASAGUK BEHIND me, the route suddenly seemed to turn hostile. About an hour or so after my departure, I found huge crowds on the banks of the Sangpo. A great number of khaki tents had sprung up as well. There was no doubt in my mind that this was a military camp and, therefore, to be avoided as far as possible.

Stepping off the main road, I took the uneven, rocky path to the right. Keeping the river behind me, I veered northwards with the intention of moving at an angle of thirty-five to forty degrees around the river and turning back again to the main route further down. Negotiating that rocky path was sheer torture, but I persisted nonetheless. Not long afterwards, I was brought up short by an aggressive mountain stream whose turbulence spilled forth in gurgling sounds that resembled a young girl's incessant giggles.

At first, I could only think of this as yet another obstacle thrown my way. Down below were the Chinese and the path around the river appeared to peter out at this point. Once I had pulled myself together, however, the situation seemed to acquire a different dimension altogether. The Sangpo, a symbol of eternal life, had been born and nourished by many such mountain streams. On entering India, the river assumed its other name—Brahmaputra. It was this very stream, a miniature version of the river, that metamorphosed into a raging force of water in Assam.

What I had initially perceived as an insurmountable barrier was increasingly taking on the aspect of a dear friend who promised to solve the mystery of life for me. It was as though while moving further north, I had unexpectedly come across a companion to converse with on the way. After I had walked for nearly an hour, the rushing waters of the stream gentled to a steady flow and fortune seemed to smile on me once more. Tucking up my clothes so that they stayed clear of the water and holding my shoes high above my head, I prepared to cross the river. The sight of the crystal clear water had led me to mistakenly assume that it could not be all that cold to the touch. But when I stepped in, my body seemed to go numb in a matter of seconds. Then I remembered the invaluable advice Sadhu Baba had given me. He had warned that the rivers of Tibet were freezing cold and one should never make the mistake of simply wading into the water. Just as oil was massaged into the body and absorbed by the skin, river water should also be rubbed over the body to get it acclimatized to the cold. Had this fact remained unknown to native Tibetans, crossing the river anywhere in the country would have been an impossibility.

The path to the ultimate pilgrimage site was certainly arduous, but hope flowered within me that my dream would come true. At the source of the Sangpo lay Kailashnath, my dream, the culmination of my fervent prayers. Since there were no shelters on the way where one could halt overnight, I had to keep walking. The following dawn, I arrived at a small village. Moved by the sight of a young ascetic at their doorstep, the villagers accorded me a devout and respectful welcome and offered me shelter. A woman served me a bowl of hot yak's milk. It tasted like nectar. Her impoverished family led me to a room in their house so that I could stretch out and rest my weary body. Repose, at long last! I had been walking for two consecutive days and could not resist the sight of that bed, lined with straw. After spending a day and a night in that devout woman's house, I set out again after offering my prayers and bestowing my blessings on the household.

Within twenty-four hours or so, I had come across yet another couple of streams that also flowed into the Sangpo. The bridges spanning the river were positively ancient and put up in a manner that could at best be described as rough and ready. Boulders had been placed in the water at intervals and ropes strung up. One had to somehow pull oneself along these to the other side. About an hour after crossing the second river, I came to a house and was, as usual, greeted by dogs. A couple of young boys approached me and asked, 'Where do you intend to go?'

Tibetan children are quite shy and usually not given to friendly overtures. I was, therefore, delighted to find that these boys were different and answered, 'Tso Mapham.' This had the effect of magic and as I passed through the entrance, they accompanied me.

Observing the rapidly growing crowd, I reverted once more to my role as the Silent Monk. They urged me to follow them and I could do little but agree. They must be from some neighbouring village, I thought, and had probably come here for a picnic. After having tea with them, I remained silent for a while more. Then I beckoned to them. I chanted the Mani prayers aloud before retreating into silence again. A hot meal was served to me, the kind that is just perfect for a picnic lunch, and as the evening drew near, I set off with them. There was a hot-water stream nearby. Local people sometimes came here for a bath or simply for an enjoyable interlude. If I had known about this stream earlier, I too, could have bathed in it. But there was no sense in harbouring regrets. The villagers also gave me the welcome news that the next big village, an hour away on foot, was Tradum. Having absorbed this bit of information, my heart began to pound with joyful anticipation.

We set out for our next destination. The sun had set and darkness enveloped us. An hour later, the first lights of the village came into view. It was impossible to make out in the dark how large the village was, where exactly its boundaries began or even what kind of a place it might be. I came to know from my companions that this was Tradum. As we began walking through it, the shape of the monastery loomed up. My new-found friends accompanied me to the entrance and went their way. Asking me to wait in front of the door, one of the boys who had served as my escort remarked, 'It is beautiful inside and visiting lamas stay here.'

At a mere touch, the heavy doors opened and I stepped inside. There was a lamp burning in a corner. Closing the doors behind me, I moved towards it. As I made to pick it up, I realized that years of use had almost permanently sealed its base to the ground.

The extreme cold in this room of the monastery was something I could simply not reconcile myself to. I got up a number of times to warm my hands in the faint heat thrown off by the lamp. In spite of trying different positions, I found it quite impossible to fall asleep and minutes later, was shivering violently. When I found no way of warming myself, I decided it was pointless to try and sat up. Instead of whiling away the hours in this manner, I might as well start walking towards Kailash, I thought. At least, I would be nearer my goal by that many miles. I remembered quite well that the lamp had been to my right as I entered the room. It followed quite naturally, then, that it would now be to the left as I made my way to the door. So, if I kept the lamp to my left, the door should be straight ahead. All these calculations came to nought, however, for I just could not locate the door! There was no way I could pick up the lamp and search for the exit, because there was a good chance of the flame going out in the attempt. Having no other options to turn to, I lay down again. In order to generate body heat, I set about doing some yogic exercises and that helped.

As the shivering subsided a little, it seemed to me that the room was growing warmer. Usually, the cold intensified with the approach of dawn and I began to prepare myself in anticipation. My sense of direction was gone and there was no hope of finding the door before it was light. But amazingly, the cold had suddenly subsided noticeably. Was daybreak imminent and the sun's rays about to enter the room? As a general rule, the most uncomfortable nights were the ones that never seemed to end. It appeared incredible that such a bitterly cold night could be over so soon. The sight that met my eyes when I opened them left me speechless! Beside me on the mattress lay a sage and in front of him was a receptacle containing the red-hot embers of a coal fire. I rose to my feet at once and prostrated myself before him. Even as I sat there, I began to doze off and observing my state, the man gestured at me to lie down. It was the first time I had seen a long-haired sage since I had entered Tibet. I was keen on talking to him, but found it impossible to keep awake.

The boys from the village who had accompanied me to the monastery the day before were the ones to wake me up in the morning. They were joined by a couple of girls. After they had greeted me respectfully, I blessed them and led the prayers. The girls had brought some food for me: a kind of hard butter, handmade bread and jaggery.

My companion for the night was nowhere in sight. I assumed he had left at the crack of dawn. The morning light streamed in through the open door. The latter had been so close by. Yet, I had found it impossible to locate at night. To resolve the mystery, I walked towards the spot where I had seen the lamp and was brought up short. There was no sign of it! Nor was there even a trace of a shelf of any kind on the wall. A mystery indeed! As the children were standing by the door, I had to put the matter aside for the time being.

I followed the children to a middle-class home. There were yaks and ponies tethered in the courtyard and moving past them, I went up to a wooden veranda. The house was made of timber with beautifully intricate work all over. Soon, all the members of the household emerged, put out their tongues in greeting, as was the custom, and stood back in silence. Finally, it was the turn of an elderly lady, whose wrinkled face seemed to radiate with the beauty of her simple and devout soul. She welcomed me with a new shawl, in keeping with Tibetan tradition. After some time had elapsed, an old man approached, leaning heavily on a stick and barely managing to cover the distance that separated us. I was about to bend over and touch his feet respectfully, when I stopped myself in time. In Tibet, such a gesture would have provoked outrage. A lama did not greet an ordinary householder in this manner.

Someone emerged from within the house, carrying a large receptacle containing burning coal. The girls standing around me wore garments of brilliant hues and beautiful necklaces made from semi-precious stones. Almost every woman there wore an exquisitely worked waistband.

Following an afternoon meal of tsampa and a round of prayers and blessings showered on all present, I set off once more. If this kind of routine continued, I feared I would become downright lazy. Besides, Kailash was beckoning to me and simply whiling away time on the way seemed to make little sense. Tradum was quite amazing, rather similar, in fact, to Yatung, at least in size. The open market was very like the ones you would come across while travelling to Bhutan via Hashimara. Most of the area was taken over by yaks, ponies and sheep. Just across the Sangpo, rows of Chinese military camps were clearly visible. A pair of boats ferried people across the river.

A huge gumpha came into view after I had walked on for a few minutes. Since the road turned in that direction and went past it, there was no way of avoiding the monastery. I had, at the moment, no desire to stop by. Just as I was pondering on my course of action, a group of young lamas (trapas) came up to me from the market. There was no way of escaping them. It was customary for every pilgrim to stop by a gumpha that was on his route and pay his respects to the head lama. His failure to do so would be deemed a slight. Since the trapas had seen me, I had little choice but to accompany them to the gumpha. Flanking the road on either side were rows of houses, all attached to the monastery. Among them was the main temple. The dome was golden, probably to ensure that it was visible from a long way off. Since I had reached Tradum at night, it had escaped my notice earlier.

After touching the chaitya of the core temple and spinning the prayer wheel, I circumambulated the temple, then entered it. Facing me directly was a colossal image of Manjushree. I noticed some lamas busy studying their texts. Ignoring them, I began to examine the decorations on the walls. A lama came up and stood beside me. 'Where have you come from?' he asked me affectionately. I indicated by a gesture that I was sworn to silence and could not, therefore, answer his question. He whispered, 'Our Geshe is here. Go and pay your respects to him. He will bless you.'

I sent up a brief prayer. Though I was supposed to have taken a vow of silence, speaking in the presence of a Geshe or the head of a gumpha was not frowned on. On the contrary, it was considered a way of accumulating good deeds. The moment I entered the room, there rose a murmur of prayers being recited aloud. In the corner of the room, a lama sat by a tiny window. He gestured to me to take a seat. From what I could gather, the Geshe was probably engaged in the act of teaching. Occasionally, he would read from a text before explaining some point to those around him. The oft-repeated words, *Kaal Chakra* (Circle of Time), were beyond my comprehension. After quite some time had elapsed, all the lamas left. Only the Geshe remained. 'Who are you?' he asked me. 'Where are you from?'

In such sanctified surroundings and, moreover, in the presence of so pure and pristine a person, uttering a falsehood would have been an unpardonable sin. If I did indulge in it, it might drag me back to the base world, even after I had succeeded in reaching the threshold of Kailash. Instead of answering his query, I prostrated myself before him, then sat up. The benign and tranquil Geshe blessed me before repeating his question.

I answered humbly, 'I am a pilgrim. I accompanied a group of Nepalese lamas from Gangtok to Lhasa. I parted from them at that point and am keen to make my way to Diraphuk Gumpha.'

He was silent for a while. Then he asked, 'Where is your hometown?'

This was precisely the question that made me uncomfortable. Simply being an Indian was good enough reason for being denied entry into Tibet straight away. Ever since I had passed the Chinese military camp at Tradum, I had had a premonition of disaster. I remained silent for a while, but the Geshe was waiting for a reply. Another stretch of silence ensued before I said, 'My Guruji is also Nepalese and the leader of this group. I came all the way so that I could carry his luggage for him.'

Denied a direct answer, the Geshe asked, 'You are Indian, are you not?'

My heart sank. I feared the worst, but replied calmly, 'Yes, I am.'

'That was apparent the moment I laid eyes on you. I visit India fairly often, but recently, it has not been possible for a number of reasons.'

The Revered Geshe then began conversing with me in fractured Hindi. His friendly attitude was a source of great relief to me. This grave, autocratic personality suddenly seemed to become positively garrulous. In the course of conversation, he asked, 'Do you have the authorization you need to enter the Diraphuk Gumpha?'

'I'm afraid not. I am not familiar with the language spoken in this country. Besides, I would prefer to speak as little as possible. That is why I have no papers with me.' Then I asked him, 'How long will it take me to reach Mansarovar and Kailash from here?'

'From eight to ten days.'

'Is the route a very arduous one?

'It certainly is!'

'May I request you for some advice about it?'

Geshe paused for a while before saying, 'Tradum is the biggest city on the route to Kailash. After setting out, you will reach Giyabunak in a day or two. Next on the route lies Samsang. These are common villages. Then you will come to Thokchen, the trading centre for gypsies. It is from here that they leave for India every year to sell precious stones. There is a gumpha there and staying there overnight will not be a problem. Mention my name if you need to. Woollen garments are on sale there for very reasonable prices.' The Geshe came to an abrupt halt. He left the room without a word and returned carrying some coins. He handed them to me with the words, 'Keep these. They will come in handy.'

I accepted the gift without a murmur. There was another piece of advice he gave me that seemed invaluable. It included his observation about there being no Chinese military camps along the route from Tradum to Mansarovar and Kailash. I had imagined these to be my biggest obstacle. Before taking leave of Geshe Lama, I had one more request for him. 'I spent last night in the temple that is located at the entrance to Tradum,' I told him. 'I can find no explanation for certain incidents that occurred while I was there. Would you please hear what I have to say?'

He was stunned by my words and exclaimed, 'What! You spent the night there?'

'That's right.'

'There is no point in my listening to the details of what transpired last night. I know a great deal about that gumpha. It has been abandoned and infested with many accursed souls.'

Accompanied by two young lamas, I left Geshe's room.

Arrangements were made for me to stay with two other lamas in a room on the first floor that was very nearly pitch dark. It contained nothing but a couple of boxes, a pair of small beds made up on the floor with blankets, four huge wooden books to write in, some garments belonging to the ascetics, a couple of aluminium plates and a tumbler. Even in this bitterly cold weather, the lamas were not given anything more to make their living quarters more comfortable. Theirs was a truly tough life. They had chosen to embark on a spiritual journey. By ensuring that the body just about survived, they were compelled to progress along the path designated for them by sheer force of will. Only those who were able to proceed without being deflected from their goal would succeed in attaining nirvana.

AT THE END OF MY TETHER

THE CHINESE MILITARY camp now lay on the other side; in other words, to the south of the river. That was the point from which the Himalayan range began. So, there was no need to fear the presence of Chinese soldiers. In no way, however, did this indicate that the path that lay before me would be an easy one. From the time we had set out from Gangtok, we had crossed unforgiving terrain and faced innumerable difficulties, but my strength of mind had been unwavering. Even now, my resolve was firm. My physical strength, though, seemed to be ebbing rapidly.

Eighty per cent of the Tibetan population lived in Gyatse, Shigatse and Lhasa. This part of the country was truly a desert and almost totally devoid of a human presence. It was supposed to be summer, but who could have guessed that from the dry, bitterly cold weather? Thanks to snowfall, the temperature here remained below zero most of the time. The landscape comprised mostly level terrain. No large mountains could be seen to relieve the monotony. On one side flowed the Sangpo, flanked by its sandy banks; on the other stretched a flat expanse of land strewn with rocks. Needless to say, the road I was travelling by was not a permanent one; it was subject to the vagaries of nature. To the south of the river rose the towering Himalayan range; to the north lay the stark Kunlun Mountains. I walked through the bare, rough terrain of Changtang. Some gypsies had set up camps, but I had no desire at all to go there and visit them. Whenever the gypsies saw me, they rushed forward and pestered me for alms. It wasn't easy getting away from their clutches.

During the short span of life I had gone through, I had navigated miles of exceptionally arduous terrain and endured many hardships. I had climbed steep mountains, crossed forests teeming with ferocious beasts and withstood the fury of thunderstorms that prevented me from moving in any direction while they lasted. True, there were no wild animals to be found here, but the cold was so intense that the body seemed to be caught in a paroxysm of shivering all day. There was no sign of a tea shop on the way. When the sun rose during the day, I would spread my blanket out by the road and sleep. At night, I tried to cover as much of the distance as possible. I hadn't had a hot meal for two successive days and somehow appeased my hunger with the meagre provisions I carried. In order to break the spell of overpowering silence around me, I recited aloud my prayers and all that I had learnt and even talked to myself. The only thought my mind focused on was the following: I have to carry on.

My physical exhaustion and weakening resolve were steadily eroding my faith in my ability to carry on. In my current condition, Sadhu Baba's advice, the enthusiasm I had witnessed in the lamas and even my own initiative in undertaking this journey seemed rather pointless. What purpose would be served by accumulating good deeds? Perhaps, the life of the ascetic I had chosen, the donning of this special garb, the stockpiling of good deeds, the afterlife and nirvana were a mere fallacy, nothing more than a lie, pure and simple. Everything ultimately boiled down to a quest for survival. Was there truly any difference between one man and another? Was there any standard by which the learned could be distinguished from the ignorant? People earned their living by various means. All pursuits were merely a way of sustaining oneself. So, what sense did it make to pursue the path I had chosen simply on the basis of some religious principles?

Despite my mental turmoil, I was still moving on. But I could see myself suddenly questioning everything that had motivated me and enabled me to come this far. My mind was increasingly at odds with my soul, hostile to the spiritual urge that drove me on towards my destination. From the time I had left Lhasa, I had developed a stubborn cough that showed no signs of subsiding as I travelled towards my goal. The thought had even started recurring that if the Chinese authorities apprehended me now, it would probably be for the best; at least, I would have a chance to rest my weary body. I found it terribly painful to bear the impact of the wind slicing through me. Fresh green grass had just begun to sprout; there was nowhere I could even have looked for and found a few blades of dry grass that might have served as fuel for a fire.

In no time, evening was upon me. Gazing at the distant Himalayas, I began to dream of my own country, the one I had known and left behind. Spirals of smoke rose from the banks of the river. I rubbed my eyes in disbelief and looked again. Smoke continued to uncoil heavenwards. I gave myself no more time to ruminate. The smoke might be rising from fires burning at Chinese camps, but the Chinese were human, after all, I reasoned. Soon, I had drawn close and found some Tibetans warming themselves by a fire. The sight of the fire renewed my flagging life force. Seeing me approach, the men put some water on to boil in an ancient kettle. A conversation with them was all it took for the Silent Monk to be restored to life. I paid them enough money to take care of tea for us all. To find such a generous lama at the end of the day made the owner of the ferry boats who was among the men burst into peals of joyful laughter and I joined him. There was no doubt at all in my mind that I owed my rebirth that day to the boat owner-cum-tea stall owner and to the hospitality this group of Tibetans would extend to me that night.

I came to know from these men that Thokchen was just a day's journey away. I was now at Samsang village. Giyabunak had probably been lost somewhere in the darkness of the night.

A FEW STEPS MORE TO HEAVEN

I WAS NOW on the verge of reaching Kailash, my goal, my dream. Thokchen, a city in the Chang Lang Desert, was a rather remarkable place. On a particular day every year, all the gypsies in Tibet would come down and congregate here. They would spread out their wares of woollens, precious stones, thangkas, statuettes and other artefacts for prospective buyers. The wealthy gypsies and other traders bought these items from them at very low prices only to resell them in the markets of Nepal, India, Sikkim and Bhutan.

From this point, the mountain trail showed up again, hugging the Himalayas and moving north-west. The Sangpo, a continuation of the main stream that originated in Mansarovar and was known as the Samo-Sangpo, had joined a small mountain stream at this point, but its turbulence had not abated and it raged on in a tangle of currents. Meeting with resistance at every step in the form of small stones and pebbles, the river spewed out a perennial spray of swirling white foam. Crossing the river at this point posed no problem at all. By wading into the water and stepping carefully on the large stones, one could easily reach the other bank. I had observed that the Sangpo ran in two separate streams from a point not far from Samsang village. One carried ice-cold water from the Himalayas. Since I now stood on the other side, I did not spare it much thought. On the other side of the Sangpo, lay the Tibet– Nepal border. What with the military presence along it, there was no question at all of my heading in that direction. I would come to know later, that in that direction lay the historical origins and geographical source of the Brahmaputra river. For Tibetan pilgrims, Samsang Prayag was a site of great religious significance. Without proper directions to guide me, I had failed to recognize this sacred spot. What I had assumed to be the northern tributary of the Sangpo was, in reality, the Mariam river or the Mariam Chu as the Tibetans knew it.

From Thokchen, I would be moving along the Samo which had flowed down directly from Mansarovar. In other words, I would cross the Mariam Chu. Thokchen, locally known as Tasam, was located at a height of almost 15,700 feet. Nature here was magnificently alive in its beauty, with the mountains and rippling waters of the river affording a vista that was balm for the eyes and the soul. Rising from the midst of the innumerable snowy peaks to the right was Nanda Devi. Far to the left was the Annapurna range.

This village was typical of the ones located high up in the mountains. Its wooden huts were occupied by people who looked far from prosperous. For very little money, I was able to make arrangements for a fire, hot water and a reasonably comfortable place to stay for the night. From my room, I could gaze upon the wondrous beauty of the mountains. If the Himalayas viewed from Tiger Hill in Darjeeling had impressed me with their splendour, they now left me speechless with awe. Every single peak appeared to be the manifestation of a divine spirit. I almost had the feeling that with a little concentrated effort and meditation, centred on their incomparable beauty, one could commune with their very soul.

All morning, the subject was discussed and analysed for my benefit by Dongaldada, the owner of the house where I had put up. Tibetans were generally tall and well built, but this man was tough and stocky like the Sherpas. His two front teeth were missing and he smiled all the time, given as he was to laughter, rather than to speech. The very picture of happiness, neither trial nor tribulation appeared to have touched him so far.

The small open market at Thokchen held a powerful appeal for me. It was like a common selling arena where everybody knew every other person. The sessions of idle chatter and laughter that ensued here seemed never-ending. During the summer, Dongaldada's ancient house was converted into a dharamsala, a kind of hostel. From the plains of Tibet, devotees would take this route to the most sacred of pilgrimage spots and the residents of Thokchen went out of their way to see to their needs. All the horses and yaks available were laden with goods for the pilgrims and the locals were only too eager to provide for them in any way possible. It is difficult to determine how much profit they made from the pilgrims' arrival, but the inhabitants of Thokchen were certainly much more preoccupied during this season than they were at other times of the year. For those pilgrims who were unable to perform all the rituals themselves, Tibetans were engaged to act on their behalf. They were quite content with very little money and some food. This being the last village on the way to Kailash and Mansarovar, pilgrims who arrived here were quite busy with last-minute purchases.

One of the major attractions of the market at Thokchen was the herbal medicine sellers and their wares. All that a man might need to preserve his health and protect it from ailments was available in a dark and dingy room. Those selling the potions looked like the filthiest beggars in the world. The appearance of each could well have been described in terms of a human skull placed atop a bundle of rags. A corner of the room where they had set up shop had been converted into an open toilet; the other served as a kitchen where arrangements for cooking were in place. The salesmen spat with gusto on the wooden walls. One could never have imagined a shop selling medicine to be in such an appallingly unhygienic state. This sect of Tibetans was held in high esteem by their countrymen, second only to the lamas. The volume of their business increased proportionately as the weather grew warmer. About a dozen shops here remained open throughout the year. The open-air shops by the wayside were set up only during the summer. The main attraction of the market at Thokchen was, however, wool, evident in the extensive display of garments fashioned from it, including everything from sweaters and shawls to caps and socks.

Earlier, I had invariably been wary of marketplaces and regarded them as areas where I should tread with caution. The market at Thokchen, however, offered me a glimpse of a different world altogether. The lama had given me money to buy something warm for myself and I rummaged through a pile of cardigans and caps. This, then, was what pure wool was like! The thick strands were interwoven into beautiful patterns and were available in a wide range of colours. The more expensive variety had stones and beads worked into them. The salespeople could not be bothered with a cash-strapped buyer like me who was young to boot, and ignored me completely. A long and thorough search later, I chose a sweater and a pair of gloves. There were other articles available too, like leather coats and jackets and something the Tibetans called the *chutki*, a cross between a cover sheet to be used in bed at night and a shawl that would come in handy in winter. Also on offer were light woollen shawls that were comparatively less expensive and Chinese goods like cups and saucers. Much of the fabric available in the shops bore watermarks of the Buddha in various incarnations and forms as well as of several other Tibetan pictures. Foodstuff like barley, cured meat, rice and lentils among others, was also readily available.

I noticed for the first time that in this market, bargaining was frowned on. For each item, the salespersons quoted a price they remained firm on. Haggling over an article was deemed an insult to the seller. I could not be certain as to whether the same business practice prevailed in the rest of Tibet.

The main place to hang out for a bit of idle gossip and relaxation was the tea shop. Just outside it, a couple of girls mixed butter into the tea in large bamboo containers. The moment they saw me, they paused in their work and stuck their tongues out in a gesture of respect.

After I had had my tea, I made for the Mariam Chu. An entire lifetime would not have been enough to enjoy the pristine beauty of the stream's crystal-clear waters and the snow-clad peaks of the distant mountains. I remembered the Almighty and thanked Him with all my heart for the kindness He had shown me. As I stood there, my thoughts suddenly winged their way home to that little village in Ichhapur with its sultry climate. Just to contemplate where I had ultimately landed up seemed to be no less than a dream. After I had lingered for a while, the intense chill caught up with me and forced me to start walking again.

On the way back, I caught sight of Dongaldada. The moment he saw me, he smiled and asked, 'Did you buy that sweater?'

'Yes, I did,' was my reply. 'Nice and warm, isn't it?'

'Oh, yes! It most certainly is.' Then came the announcement I had been looking forward to. We would be setting off the very next day.

I could hardly contain my joy. I struggled for composure and told myself, 'Be calm and patient and you will surely reach your ultimate goal.'

The following day, Dongaldada's mother woke me up at the crack of dawn. A short while later, Dongaldada himself emerged from the next room and greeting me with due respect, invited me to go in. There I discovered three more Tibetans, none of whom I was acquainted with, warming themselves by the fire. Right beside it was a huge bowl containing a hot, soup-like broth called *thukpa*. Everybody took sips from it and so did I. Thukpa turned out to be a kind of barley and mutton gravy. It was still pitch dark and the stars glittered brightly in a sky that seemed so close overhead that I felt I could, with a little effort, have reached out and touched them. Ignoring both the freezing cold and the dark road, we set out.

Initially, I had thought to myself that if this was, indeed, the road that led directly to Kailash, what was the point in Dongaldada accompanying me? But shortly after setting out, I realized how necessary his presence was. The first obstacle we encountered appeared in the shape of fast-flowing mountain streams. There was no easy way of crossing them. Most of the bridges in this part of the country were makeshift structures consisting of stones and ropes placed at strategic points. Merely *placed*, let me add, not held together by a cement binding or anything of the kind. Many of the bridges were on their last legs and Dongaldada had to carefully test each one before stepping on to it. There were several occasions when, instead of using the bridge, we were forced to wade through the water.

Moreover, the cold that swamped us along this route was almost impossible to withstand. The atmosphere was dry, the sky cloudless. The faraway mountains seemed very near. If one absent-mindedly stepped out of rhythm while walking, breathing difficulties surfaced almost right away. Who could have imagined that this was one of Tibet's main thoroughfares? Not a soul was in sight. And the silence around us was only broken by the sound of our breathing, of our footsteps as we progressed and the occasional clatter of a loose pebble as it rolled down the mountainside. There was virtually no conversation between us. The blanket on my shoulders and the small bundle I carried grew heavier with time. My feet seemed to be frozen numb and the tip of my nose felt as though a thousand pins were pricking it constantly. Despite all these inconveniences, we carried on, buoyed by the hope of fulfilling our one dream—to reach that most sacred of pilgrimage sites.

Dongaldada probably appreciated my plight. He stopped and

now, even the smile on his face seemed to fade. Somehow managing to retain his gap-toothed smile, he asked, 'Are you all right?'

'No, I'm afraid not. Because of the cold, my ears and nose are all pins and needles.' In that moment of crisis, the little Tibetan I had learnt failed me entirely. I kept exclaiming in Bengali, my mother tongue, 'By God, it's cold! I'm freezing to death! It's bloody cold!'

As an experienced guide who was used to leading pilgrims to the holy site, Dongaldada appreciated what I was going through. He stopped at once to take out from his bag some bits of wood and a matchstick. He proceeded to light them and held them up in my direction. I warmed my hands and ears and nose. He also handed me something that looked like a small pebble and told me to put it in my mouth and keep chewing. The body would apparently warm up slowly and maintain that temperature.

'Is it medicine of some kind?'

'This is *thuma* and no better medicine can be found in all Tibet,' Dongaldada replied with pride. He broke off some portions and handed them to the three of us.

After recovering somewhat, we set out again. As evening approached, we chose a small, abandoned gumpha for our overnight halt. Dongaldada announced, 'We have come a long way. If we can keep up the pace, by tomorrow afternoon, we should be reaching Tso Mapham.'

Joyful news indeed! But what I needed right then, more than anything else, was to lie down and seek oblivion in sleep.

HEAVEN, AT LAST!

I HAD ALWAYS assumed that Mansarovar was the true source of the Brahmaputra. From Thokchen onwards, I began to be assailed by doubt. I had noticed that the river was suddenly flowing in the opposite direction. Had I lost my sense of direction, then?

Early the next morning, after prayers at the gumpha, I put the question to Dongaldada. Smiling, he proffered a simple explanation. The Sangpo was the main river of Tibet. It was from this particular region that the river had sprung and was known in India as the Brahmaputra. As the snows melted, they gave birth to innumerable small streams. Some of them met and merged at Samsang and took on the name, Sangpo. All the smaller streams we had crossed until we reached Samsang had been independent watercourses, having no connection at all with the Sangpo, though several of them bore the name as an appendage to their original names. We continued to follow the Sangpo's course. This river along with the Samo-Sangpo both flowed into Tso Mapham or Mansarovar, as we Indians knew it. This was the reason I had mistakenly assumed that the Sangpo had reversed the direction of its flow. We were now following its course in our bid to reach Mansarovar. All around lay snow and yet more snow. The trickling noise it made as it melted resounded in the silence. The source of the Sangpo or the Brahmaputra lay in the southern Himalayas, almost seventy miles away. We had set out very early in the morning, moving towards that source, and the route had been fairly easy to negotiate. From Thokchen, situated at nearly 15,700 feet above sea level, we had been steadily descending towards Mansarovar, located at about 14,900 feet. To reach our destination, we would, therefore, have to go almost 750 feet down. We had been walking for almost an hour, flanked by mountains. Gradually, they fell away and the landscape too underwent a noticeable change.

Then came that auspicious moment. As soon as we rounded a small hill, heaven lay before us. It was, indeed, heaven, and we stood there motionless, our senses sharply attuned to what lay before us, drinking in the ethereal vision of its glory. Not a word was uttered, as all sensation and experience associated with the everyday world remained suspended. Here, nature transcended the dictates of the rational mind and paved the way for a true communion with the soul. In this extraordinary place, nature defied description and even an attempt at defining it in words would have been inappropriate, a mockery of its real essence.

The feelings that coursed through us were those of a traveller who had stumbled upon freedom after groping for directions and losing his way. Except for Dongaldada, we were all first-time visitors to this heaven on earth. Before us lay a vast tract of level land and a small hillock rising from it. The focal point of that expanse of land was a pair of lakes: Mansarovar, followed by Rakshas Taal. In the far distance, rising like sentinels, were the mountains. To the south was the Gurla Mandhata range; further north, from behind a pair of mountains, a snow-capped white triangle of a peak rose towards the sky. It was the magnificent Kailash.

It was a sight, an experience one could never have enough of. After saying our prayers, we lingered there for a while before moving on. Before us, a huge flag hung from a pole; below it stood a small chorten in the form of a heap of stones. We went around it and, in keeping with custom, picked up a few pebbles lying nearby and added them to the heap.

From this point of the Samo-Sangpo, Mansarovar was clearly visible. Several mountain streams fed by the melting snows flowed into the lake. Dongaldada advised us against going around Mansarovar, because there were no bridges that would enable us to cross over. Tibetans attempted it only when the surface of the lake froze and served as a natural bridge. Dongaldada and the three Tibetans would be going on to Purang. He turned to ask me, 'Is it from here that we go our separate ways? What are your plans?'

What did I want to do? It was a question I had to ask myself. My goal had been to reach this point. I hadn't really thought beyond that.

'What do the other pilgrims do after arriving here?' I asked Dongaldada.

He burst out laughing. 'You have reached Tso Mapham,' he observed, 'and yet you do not know what to do next! Everybody offers prayers here and there are priests who do the needful. They pray for you and for your forefathers. Apart from being a sacred ritual, a dip in Mansarovar will bring peace and redemption for the souls of your ancestors. You can accompany me if you so desire. I know people who will be able to guide you.'

Dongaldada knew everything there was to know about Mansarovar, Rakshas Taal and Kailashnath. When I asked him whether there were any Hindu temples in the vicinity, he answered in the negative, but added that every year, a great many Hindu and Nepalese ascetics came here on pilgrimage. They stayed in the gumphas and chaityas situated around Mansarovar. Dongaldada believed that there was no difference at all between Hinduism, Shakya and Chenreji. At Mansarovar, the most sacred pilgrimage site in the world, everyone was equal; only the language of communication varied from person to person.

In the course of our conversation, I informed him that I was carrying a letter addressed to the heads of the Diraphuk and Langbona Gumphas. I would, therefore, have to make my way there.

Dongaldada sprang up enthusiastically. 'That's marvellous!' he exclaimed. 'I have always believed you were extremely lucky.' He gave me the directions to my destination and informed me that just ahead was Ding Tso, a small lake. From there, the Langbona Gumpha was only a day's journey away. When I arrived there, the lamas at the monastery would be able to advise me on the best course of action to follow. Dongaldada thought it inadvisable for me to proceed directly to Tso Mapham, because the possibility of getting swallowed up in a veritable maze of small rivers and streams was very real. The route to Kailash was quite simple. Keeping Tso Mapham to the left, I would have to walk straight ahead in the direction of Kailashnath.

Handing him two rupees, I expressed my gratitude for all he had done. He was just as happy to receive Indian coins and took his leave after offering some useful tips.

Having bade each other farewell, I set out for my destination. The hazy view from the other side of Mansarovar beckoned from afar; the snowy peaks looked unimaginably beautiful. As afternoon drew near, I was struck by the sight of an entire herd of yaks. What could they possibly survive on in these cold climes, I wondered. Were these beasts wandering wild in the area? Perhaps, it was quite natural for them to do so in this region? Drawing still closer, I noticed the rows of tents put up by gypsies.

Having come all the way down to level land, I began walking through the gypsy camp. The tents were deserted. Not a soul was in sight. The yaks looked up at me, but remained silent. Blades of grass had just begun to sprout and the beasts wandered about happily, searching them out and browsing peacefully. Slowly, the sun came up. As its rays spread far and wide, the landscape around Kailash took on a new appearance. The ensuing warmth was most welcome and made walking immensely enjoyable.

Most of the gypsies were children. Angelic in their innocence, with the freshness of roses in full bloom, they were the most beautiful individuals in the entire group and quite untroubled by the bitterly cold climate. The middle-aged among them sat around basking in the sunlight. To be able to live in the proximity of such sacred environs was reason enough to be considered blessed. These people seemed to radiate purity, so unsullied were they by worldly concerns. Through what kind of prayers could I possibly confer blessings on them? It was for me to seek blessings from them, on the contrary.

Blessing them all, I set off once more, trailed by the entire group of thirty-four. Not a word had been exchanged with them and yet they felt impelled to follow me. It seemed as though the thought of bidding me farewell was painful for them. Finally, a river forced us all to a halt. It was narrow and not very deep either, but crossing it would have been difficult. Observing my consternation, the gypsies asked me to go further ahead. I followed their advice and discovered that some boulders had been arranged to form a makeshift bridge. From this point, getting across to the other bank would be no problem at all. I had imagined that the gypsies and I would now be going our separate ways. I realized I was mistaken, however, when they all crossed the river with me. Suddenly, I found that we had reached the shores of Mansarovar. There it lay, to my left. To my right was another small lake. From the clear blue waters of Mansarovar, tiny waves undulated and gently lapped against its shores. I rushed to the water's edge and cupping some water in my hands, sprinkled it over my head.

Judging by the position of the sun, it was probably midday. Looking back, I found the group of children still in pursuit. Meeting my glance, they gestured at me to follow them. I had probably gone wrong somewhere. Or why else would they have taken the trouble to follow me all the way? Pondering over the matter as I followed the children to the shores of the lake, I was unprepared for the wondrous sight that met my eyes: a pair of beautiful swans gliding about in the water. In these frozen wastes, their very presence seemed unbelievable. But it was certainly real! As pure as the pristine white peaks in the distance were the swans in the crystal-clear waters of the lake and the sight of one against the backdrop of the other was no less celestial than an actual glimpse of heaven—or so I felt. Then it gradually dawned on me that it wasn't just a single pair of swans that swam before me; an entire bevy of swans was joyfully gliding over the waters.

Soon, we were joined on the shore by another group of Tibetans. They were in the process of drying fish and I assumed, at first, that they were locals. I realized, subsequently, that they belonged to the group of friendly gypsies I had met earlier. Handing me a special kind of fish, they urged me to try it. I was hungry by then and knew that lamas were not required by their faith to be vegetarians, although they themselves were not allowed to kill a living creature. So, I readily agreed to a meal with them. Served along with the fish was a thick piece of handmade unleavened bread. I was beginning to understand now why the gypsies had been following me. It was close to their mealtime and by offering me food, they hoped to shore up their stock of good deeds.

It was the gypsies who would give me precise directions to the Langbona Gumpha. They told me that come what may, I would have to move north, skirting the shores of the lake, and carry on in this manner for quite a distance until I came to a river. Further up, I would see a bridge. As soon as I crossed it, I would arrive at the Langbona Gumpha. Whenever Tibetans gave directions, they used terms like 'some time', 'a long time', 'half a day', 'the entire day' and 'a couple of days'. The concept of an hour was, quite possibly, beyond their sphere of experience and meant little to them. Of course, this would apply not to the learned lamas, but to the average Tibetan.

MY FIRST NIGHT AT MANSAROVAR

MY ENCOUNTER WITH the gypsies must have been ordained by the Lord. How else could I have explained the swiftness with which I managed to reach the Langbona Gumpha? As evening approached and the sun dipped towards the horizon, setting the sky, the mountains and the surrounding lakes ablaze with a fresh palette of colours, the world seemed to acquire a new dimension altogether. Nothing, however, could surpass the beauty of the peaks along the Gurla Mandhata range on Tibet's border with India. The rays of the sun seemed to light up the peaks in a flare of gold and silver. The Kailash summit looked just like the Kanchendzonga as it had seemed to me when I saw it from the gumpha in Gangtok. According to the religious texts, I would learn later, a glimpse of Kailashnath cleansed a human being of sins accumulated through seven successive incarnations, while a dip in the holy water of Mansarovar purified him and rewarded him with true freedom. Gazing at the vista before me, it was not difficult to believe it.

As darkness descended abruptly, I accelerated my pace, deciding to keep the sights for later. I had some difficulty locating the river and there was no way I could cross it. I turned and started moving north. There was no road to speak of; I was merely making my way by stepping from one boulder to the next. In spite of my wondrous delight at the ethereal beauty of the place, a feeling of regret kept gnawing at me. I had imagined that having reached this most sacred of pilgrimage spots, I would come across none other than the holiest of ascetics, deep in meditation by the shores of the lake. But where were they?

Darkness had just about set in and my eyes had not yet become used to its pitch-black shroud. It was through sheer luck that I had managed to reach this far without a major mishap. The cold had started setting in with a vengeance. I wrapped the blanket around me like a shawl and used it to cover my head. I was wearing gloves, socks and specially made Tibetan shoes. Nothing, however, seemed to ward off the chill. By then, my eyes had got used to the darkness and I began my frantic search for the monastery. Just like a dharamsala, the Langbona Gumpha had a series of doors, one after the other. It was difficult to determine which of them was the main entrance. Not a sound escaped from behind any of those doors. Not a chink of light showed anywhere. It seemed that after extinguishing all the lamps, everybody had gone off to sleep. Without an alternative, I began knocking on all the doors, one after the other, but in vain. There was no response.

I engaged in another round of knocking, rapping loudly on

the doors this time, hoping that perhaps, there would be someone inside. I wasn't far wrong. Before I could knock on the door of the room at the end of the corridor, someone seemed to be stirring, roused by the din. I thought to myself: whoever it may be, I need a refuge for the night. I can always offer my abject apologies for having caused a disturbance at night. If need be, I will throw myself at his mercy. To keep warm, a shelter for the night was indispensable. Throwing caution to the winds, I was about to thump on the door, when it was suddenly thrown open. Before my very eyes appeared the vision of a great soul. My hair seemed to stand on end. I was struck speechless and in a flash, all my strength seeped out of me. Inside the room, a fire lit especially for prayers burned brightly. In the starlight and the dim glow of the fire, I caught a clear glimpse of his face. It was that extraordinary individual, the ascetic who had rescued me one freezing night from certain death and used his mysterious occult powers to help me cross the river. A luminous glow seemed to emanate from his person. He had been my saviour in the past and had come to rescue me again. Who dared claim that God didn't exist? It was the Almighty Himself who had appeared before me. His head was a tangle of matted hair piled up in coils. All that he wore was a small loincloth and his magnificent physique was truly a sight to behold.

That wondrous man said, almost to himself, 'There is no lamp in this room. So, go to sleep. I will talk to you in the morning. You are exhausted. Now lie down.' Having said that, he stretched out in front of the fire. Its dim glow was more than enough for me to study him by. While I shivered in spite of being covered with blankets piled one on top of the other, he lay comfortably on a blanket, naked but for his loincloth. Instead of sleeping, I drank my fill of the sight of this visionary. It was an unexpected glimpse I had been offered of the Lord Himself. That I was actually sitting at the foothill of the Himalayas seemed quite incredible to me. Doubts assailed my mind. Absorbed in such thoughts, I have no idea when I fell asleep. I woke up very early in the morning and looked around me at once. He had vanished. I could not contain my grief at having lost him again.

Suddenly, a gentle voice reciting verses reached me from the next room. The verses appeared to be in Sanskrit. Hearing a familiar language spoken after ages, I could not resist the temptation of peeping through the door into the next room. My heart surged with joy, just the way it had when I had caught sight of Sadhu Baba in the market at Gangtok. My ascetic from the night before was sitting facing an image of the Buddha and reciting aloud from the holy book, the Gita. I entered without any hesitation whatsoever and surrendered myself totally to his will.

He paused in his recitation and blessed me before we began our long conversation. From his Spartan lifestyle and the minimal garb which seemed to afford him sufficient protection from the cold in this freezing climate, it was only too apparent that he was a great yogi indeed. From his distinct articulation of Hindi words, it appeared very likely that he was originally from India. When I mentioned the first occasion on which I had seen him on that lonely road and the way he had vanished later, he replied that he was meeting me for the first time right here. I had probably seen someone very like him on that earlier occasion, he contended. He was unwilling to entertain further discussion on the matter. When he asked me my name, I told him everything in great detail. I mentioned having run away from home to Gaya. There had been no plans at all about coming to Tibet, I confessed. It was only for Sadhu Baba and the way I felt irresistibly drawn to him that I had embarked on the pilgrimage that had brought me here.

He heard me out carefully, then gazed at me unblinkingly. Before that piercing stare, I was forced to avert my own gaze. Right in front of us was a huge image of Abalokiteswara. The sage began reciting verses from the holy scriptures. As he read on, he explained to me that all gods were one and the same. No matter which manifestation of the Almighty we addressed, our prayers always reached that one Ultimate Power. I listened to him mesmerized. More than the contents of the religious text he was reading aloud, what I thirsted for and could not get enough of was his sheer presence.

A moment came when we ventured outside. The Langbona Gumpha was not very large, but about the size of an average monastery. Apart from us, there was not a living soul there. We circumambulated the gumpha seven times. Then turning towards the Kailash Mountain, we offered our prayers to the Sun God.

In a bag hanging from a corner of the room, was some wheat and flour. The ascetic's sole worldly possession was a cracked aluminium bowl. All the food he consumed consisted of wheat boiled in water drawn from the river. Having achieved some semblance of familiarity, I asked him, 'You are almost naked and yet able to withstand the severe cold. Is it merely the outcome of so many years of yogic practice?'

Smiling, he answered, 'No, not quite. Ashes constitute the ultimate secret of keeping warm. In our life on earth, everything is maya or illusion. In this life, everything can be burned to cinders. What remains is nothing but ashes. That is Truth in its essence. If you burn to cinders all desires and impulses—rage, greed, intoxication, lust—nothing remains but ashes. Be in no doubt whatsoever that this is the true nectar of the gods. Even the mighty Shiva who asks nothing of us, is seated on a bed of ashes. If we too can transcend to that level and do the same, no earthly sin can ever lay hands on us.'

Having offered his advice, the great man added, 'My dear boy, that you have been able to make your way here is the outcome of the many good deeds you must have carried out in the past. Pilgrims from India on their way to Mansarovar almost always opt for the route via Almora. It is easy, direct and takes no more than two to three weeks. But you have come here via Lhasa, which is the route chosen by Tibetans. You are indeed blessed. Tell me about the purpose of your pilgrimage and I will try and help you.'

I was amazed by his words and asked him what they meant in this particular context.

'I refer to the primary intention with which each pilgrim undertakes the journey,' he replied. 'When an individual visits a pilgrimage spot, he must offer prayers hoping for the fulfilment of the wish or desire that has motivated him to embark on the pilgrimage in the first place. At the end of an arduous journey paved with obstacles, the pilgrim prays to God for His divine mercy. As a result, he is blessed by the Almighty who then proceeds to grant him his wishes.'

I assured Baba that I entertained no such expectations. Even at the Jokhang Temple in Lhasa, I had not asked for a thing. Nor had I come all the way here with the purpose of asking for something specific. In fact, I hadn't known about this custom at all. It was the first time I was hearing about it. I begged Baba's forgiveness for this lapse on my part.

'Nothing in this world happens without a reason,' Kailash Baba consoled me. 'We are reborn because of the deeds we were responsible for in our previous lives. Depending on the nature of those deeds, we are granted either happiness or suffering in this incarnation. If you have come here of your own accord, without being motivated by the need to have a wish or desire fulfilled, you are truly a great and enlightened soul. Yogis claim that if you come to Kailashnath free of desires or longings, you attain true freedom.'

I explained to Baba that I was actually a sinner. To avoid being parted from Sadhu Baba, I had allowed myself to be initiated by him into the Buddhist faith and had become a lama. To dupe the Chinese who might have apprehended me otherwise, I had played the role of the Silent Monk.

'And despite it all, you have still reached this great pilgrimage site, have you not?' was Baba's response to my words. 'If your goals are righteous, nothing more is required. If nobody is harmed by your actions, your chosen path is the right one.'

As I conversed with him, I remembered the letter I was carrying and handed it to him. Taking it from my hands and examining it from every angle, Baba confessed that while he could speak and understand Tibetan, he could not read the language. I came to know from him that he spent the better part of the year in his native Almora. He had no ashram or refuge of his own. This was his seventh journey to Mansarovar. Every time he came here, he stayed for about a month. Although he looked no more than sixty, he was actually a great deal older. Thanks to yoga and other exercises to tone the body, his physique was still remarkably muscular and supple for his age.

It was from Kailash Baba that I would learn about Mansarovar and Langbona Gumpha in great detail. I had known that many people referred to Thokchen as 'tasam', but presumed it was the local name for the trading centre. What the word actually meant was something close to 'police station'. In this region, towns that had a police station or government department were called *tasam*s and it was there that the best market of the area was set up. Pilgrims to Kailashnath and Mansarovar had to go to a tasam for stocking up on provisions and there were many such tasams all around the lake. Pilgrims who approached the lake from the south did all their shopping in Taklakot. The many gumphas around Mansarovar looked like ordinary homes and were used as dharamsalas by Tibetans during the summer, after the snows had melted. Although most of the pilgrims were Buddhist occult practitioners, both Hindus and Buddhists regarded Mansarovar as the most sacred pilgrimage site in the world. In fact, a good number of Hindu pilgrims made their way here either to have certain religious rituals performed or to seek solace following a bereavement. Priests and those responsible for organizing religious ceremonies were available locally. No Hindu places of worship nor even their relics were to be found here, however. And no one could say for certain whether such temples had once existed in this area.

Though some of the most sacred sites in the world were concentrated in this region, the flow of pilgrims had all but petered out. Even four years before my arrival, the place would have been crowded at this time of the year. Now, not a soul was in sight. The gumphas that served as dharamsalas around the place had almost taken on the appearance of graveyards. The routes from Kashmir and Almora to this area had virtually been sealed. I had seen for myself what the route from Sikkim had been like. All the affluent pilgrims had been from India. It was the reason why the gypsies flocked to Kailash and Mansarovar in summer. Selling woollens and precious stones to pilgrims had constituted the backbone of their trade.

Apart from the gumphas, there were the black tents of the nomads. There could have been no stronger race than theirs nor people quite as gentle. Though Kailash was politically a part of Tibet, the influence of Bhutan on this area was decidedly marked. The Government of Bhutan owned the main market or *mandi*. Owing to political problems, however, tradesmen from Bhutan had virtually put a halt to their visits to this area. A number of lamas had given up their religious activities in the region and moved to either Kashmir or Bhutan. Due to a number of reasons, the Langbona Gumpha had been abandoned. Kailash Baba had been here for almost two weeks. He had completed all the religious rituals and gone around Kailashnath in silence. He would be leaving the place after a short rest.

Baba indicated the room where he had gone to complete his *Cham* ceremony. Cham was a Tibetan word, he explained. It meant solitude. Going through the ceremony involved bringing one's concentration to bear on the divine. And this had to be achieved in complete silence and solitude. It was a ritual integral to the practice of the occult sciences. Having committed himself to a specified period that could range from anywhere between three days to a couple of years, depending on his mental powers, the person going through the ritual would enter a pitch-dark windowless room through a narrow winding passage where not a chink of light penetrated. All the man was allowed to have with him inside this confined space was a pair of blankets and his prayer beads. During this period, the man's hunger was appeased through meals left outside by a lama who indicated his presence by clapping his hands once. Once the meal was over, the empty plate would be left outside to be collected. There would be no conversation at all, no other form of contact with the world outside. This was apparently the best possible way to commune with one's soul.

All the yogis who practised this ritual, year after year, ultimately attained mastery over the occult sciences. This was not the path to freedom, but a means of acquiring extraordinary powers. Kailash Baba had been in confinement for three months. His eyesight had greatly deteriorated as a result. However, owing to the benefits of special yogic exercises, he had succeeded in regaining what he had initially lost. While I shivered in the cold, all wrapped up though I was against it, Kailash Baba was always barefoot, his only concession to the climate being a blanket he threw around himself at the approach of dusk. He went about his business serenely with no apparent signs of discomfort.

As he contemplated the beauty of Mansarovar that had acquired an indescribable quality in the waning light of the setting sun, its blue-green waters turning a pristine blue, Baba was moved to declare that it evoked a response in men that was quite different from the ordinary. While beauty as we knew it in the material world aroused in men a desire to share it with others, the celestial quality of Mansarovar belonged to a different plane altogether. It embraced the divine and to feel and sense it from within, I would soon have to brave the chill and take a dip in the lake's holy waters. It was for man to absorb that ethereal beauty as far as possible so that he could truly appreciate its essence. It was for him to use it as his inspiration to evolve and transcend his limitations as a human being.

Our holy scriptures, he informed me, were replete with stories surrounding Mansarovar which, apparently, none but the truly pious could cross. It was supposed to be the abode of a large number of deities. Historians contended that it was through the Aryans who were awestruck by the sheer beauty of this place when they arrived in India, that the world came to know of its existence. Local lamas and Tibetans in general believed that the Buddha presided over the centre of the lake. He was said to sit in the shade of a tree that bore fruit filled with nectar, promising immortality and deliverance from all forms of earthly grief and from the travails of maladies and aging. Going around Mansarovar in winter according to prescribed norms was certain to bring nirvana to the person who attempted it.

When we returned to our room in the evening, it was quite another Kailash Baba who surfaced. The man who was forever smiling grew grave all of a sudden. I lit a fire and turned to him sitting on his blanket, lost in a meditative trance. In silence, I spread my blanket as well and seated myself on it, firmly gripping the prayer beads in my hands.

KAILASHNATH

THE NEXT MORNING, Baba woke me up very early. I was amazed to see that he had already prepared a hot broth, for he ate only once a day. As soon as I was up, I started reciting my prayers, as had been my habit for the past one month. Even after I had finished observing all the rituals, dawn was yet to break over the horizon.

After ensuring that I had eaten, Baba said to me, 'I will give you the directions. I would suggest you set off right away for a view of Kailashnath. Show this letter to the lamas at the Diraphuk Gumpha and you will have no problems at all. Stay at the gumpha for three days. Then come down. You will see me again in Parkha.' He then gave me instructions on how to go around the Kailash Peak.

Kailashnath seemed altogether different at this hour, on the verge of unveiling its mystery, yet elusive and half-shrouded in shadow. There wasn't enough light to see it as it should be seen—the light of true knowledge to dispel the darkness of ignorance. And so, I began my prayers to the Sun God.

I had been on the road for quite a while when I came to a crossroad where two paths met. It was time to leave Mansarovar. I sprinkled water from the lake over my head and prayed to the Lord. Then I set off north. Appeased, Kailashnath drew closer and this time, the journey was smooth, untroubled by fatigue or discomfort of any kind.

Then came that momentous hour. The sun came up; light danced on the pristine snow-capped peaks around me. Apparently, the sole witness to this splendour, I could only gaze on in speechless wonder. In spontaneous acknowledgement of His greatness, my head bowed to the Almighty. It was now clear to me why Baba had woken me up so early and sent me here.

There was a range of two mountains to the north of Mansarovar and Rakshas Taal: La and Jhong. The peak that rose the highest amongst them was Kailash. That was where I would have to head. Kailash Peak crowned the mountain like a temple. Since climbing the eternally snow-clad peaks was out of the question, I would have to pay my respects the way it was usually done—by scaling either La or Jhong. Around sixteen to twenty miles lay between the Langbona and Diraphuk Gumphas. I had probably already covered around six miles. The sun was high in the sky. Walking was a joy. And I no longer felt the least bit tired.

Fairly high up on the mountain, I came to a village which was similar to Thokchen. Situated at nearly 15,000 feet, Parkha had eleven one-storeyed houses along the road. Nearly all were vacant. The road I was travelling by now and which I had left behind after Thokchen to come to Mansarovar was the same one that led to Gangtok, Ladakh and Kashmir. Some donkeys, yaks and dogs were peacefully dozing behind a house. I came across a tea stall—the first of its kind I had seen in Kailash. It was propped up anyhow with stones, clay, bits of wood and rope. Muffled in blankets, the two men inside stared out at me. 'Is this the way to Tarchen?' I went out of my way to ask them.

Silently, they pointed ahead. I too, wasted no more words on them and carried on walking. As I was on my way out of Parkha village, I suddenly chanced upon a bazaar. All the villagers were gathered there. This was probably the only village in the entire Kailash region. Ignoring them totally, I carried on in a northerly direction. About an hour after leaving Parkha, I came to Tarchen, another village. On an ancient wooden placard were written the words 'Kailash Nath' in barely decipherable Hindi letters. This was the first time I had come across any kind of road direction in Tibet. In all likelihood, some Indian pilgrim like me had left it by the wayside. A short distance from it was a stone with 'Kang-Ripoche' written on it in Tibetan. This was the point from which one actually began to go around Kailashnath.

Tarchen was located at a point from which the pilgrims began and ended their journey. The last leg of the journey covered a distance of between thirty and thirty-two miles and could generally be completed in just a day. Another more arduous religious ritual took longer—almost sixteen to twenty days. Of the five monasteries in the area affording pilgrims the opportunity of resting or praying during this process, the Diraphuk Gumpha was the largest. There was only one house in Tarchen and it had no doors at all, though at one point of time, they must have existed. Life in this area was centred around a number of gypsy camps inhabited by eleven-odd people. Pilgrims could not only buy frozen milk, butter and provisions for the journey from them, but could also pay them to complete the pilgrimage on their behalf. The gypsies also hired themselves out as guides for the journey for a negligible sum of money.

There was nothing I could possibly buy from them. Nor was there any question of my hiring a guide. From Tarchen, a road led directly north, while another initially ran north-west before turning to go further north. Baba had advised taking this second route. At 15,100 feet, Tarchen stood almost 200 feet above Mansarovar. The lake, along with Rakshas Taal and the vast expanse of level land in between, was clearly visible from the village. While Rakshas Taal was shaped like a kind of jagged triangle, Mansarovar was distinctly circular. Some distance ahead flowed the La Chu, a mountain stream along whose banks the snow was yet to melt. Crossing the makeshift bridge at Pema Phuk, I arrived at a gumpha. It was the first of the five I would come across during my peregrinations around Kailash. As soon as I reached it, a pair of lamas emerged to greet me. Encouraged by my response, they approached and informed me that this was the Niyaring Gumpha.

Keeping the La Chu to my left, I moved on. The route grew steadily steeper. The warmth of the sun overhead afforded welcome relief, however. I was now at the foothills of Mount Kailash. From a distance, this mountain looked mysteriously alluring and exuded a powerful appeal. Up close, however, it lost its claim to uniqueness and seemed no more than a colossal mass of rock which grew alarmingly larger with every step as I approached it and seemed to swallow up petty humans like me. So, having merely reached the foothills of Kailash was enough for me to lose myself in a myriad thoughts and feelings. From where I stood, the peak was invisible. The surrounding landscape was stunningly beautiful. To my left ran rows of mountains, their peaks cloaked in snow that had only just begun to melt. Numerous small streams merged together to form a kind of rivulet. They bubbled with life as though only too glad to lend a word of encouragement to the lonely pilgrim.

After some time had elapsed and I had crossed a bridge made from tree stumps laid out one after the other, my eyes fell on a house. I surmised that it might be the Diraphuk Gumpha, that is, the second gumpha on the route, and I was right. Further on, I came across a chorten and a prayer flag. From this vantage point of around 16,200 feet, the silvery pinnacle of Kailashnath was clearly visible. At long last, I had reached my destination and was free to surrender myself, body and soul, to the Almighty. I knelt in reverence before Him:

'*Om Namah Shivaya … Om Namah Shivaya…*'

I found the main temple of the Diraphuk Gumpha quite easily. I entered it and began praying before the image of Lord Buddha right away. Beside it were idols of Demchig and Bhagavati Dorje Phagma. It was clear from the form and structure of the statues around me that it was only in terms of divine intervention that the mysteries of creation could be understood.

After prayers were over, I settled down to meditate. In the dim light cast by the lamp, it was Manjushree's image that slowly took over my thoughts and filled my mind completely. By the time I emerged from the session and came outside, the day was nearly spent. Not noticing anyone around, I surveyed my surroundings. The gumpha was like a huge double-storeyed house. I could hear sounds coming from the rear and made my way there. I paused in front of a room and peeping inside, found some lamas deep in conversation. They seemed to be gearing up for some sort of argument.

I did not have to utter a word to announce my presence. Seeing a stranger in their midst, they came up, one by one. Greeting them respectfully, I handed over the letter. It passed through many hands before reaching an elderly lama. From the cap he wore, it seemed likely that he was the head lama of the Diraphuk Gumpha. He appeared quite well fed, his weight bearing down heavily on the seat beneath him. He read the letter through a number of times and carefully examined it from every angle. I was unaware of its contents, but it seemed to me as if the lama accepted what was written in the letter without being able to bring himself to believe in it wholeheartedly. I stood there, the Silent Monk, hoping that a poor pilgrim from a faraway land would be welcomed, fed and given shelter for the night. The head lama completely ignored my presence, however. His attitude was discouraging in the extreme and plunged me into a state of despondency. The flood of sheer joy at sighting Kailashnath died away abruptly.

There were twenty-one young lamas around me. Having evoked no response of any kind from them, I took the initiative and announced, 'I am very hungry. Could I hope for some alms? I am also badly in need of rest.'

I thought the import of my words would be easy enough to grasp, but for some reason that eluded my comprehension, the entire group seemed frozen into immobility. It was difficult to gauge their attitude. I seemed to have committed a sin by intruding on them at that precise moment. Not being left with an option, I went back to the temple again. I would, at least, get a semblance of rest there. Perhaps, fasting was de rigueur for a pilgrim before he reached Kailashnath. Perhaps, it was the reason why the lamas at the gumpha had refrained from offering me a meal and, thereby, placing an obstacle in my path to spiritual fulfilment.

The temple belonging to the Diraphuk Gumpha could be best

described as a library and printing press rather than as a place of worship. On one side were the necessary arrangements for prayers and the daily ritual of worship. The other side was given over to thousands of books and the paraphernalia required for hand-printing manuscripts such as wood, ink and paper. The walls too, were fitted with shelves that were crowded to the rafters with books. A piece of cloth displayed in front of each tome clearly indicated its title.

As I was wandering around, looking at it all, some lamas entered the temple and gathered around me. I found their silent approach a bit unnerving, until I realized that their intentions were honest. They all wanted to get to know me. Without exchanging words, we conversed with each other through speaking glances. Then following their gestures, I accompanied them to the kitchen. There, two more lamas waited in front of the stove. Acknowledging my presence with a smile, they offered me food—rice with a curry of cured meat which I was tasting after aeons. I ate my fill. Long before dusk set in, the lamas finished reciting their prayers and sat down for their evening meal. Since the kitchen was warm and cosy, I spread out my blanket in a corner and settled down on it. Except for the temple where lamps burned, there was no illumination here at night. Apart from saving fuel, it was also beneficial for the health. Having had a meal not long before, I did not eat again. Comfortable in my corner, I fell asleep almost immediately.

The next morning I woke up very early, just around the time the lamas were beginning to stir and were seized by fits of coughing. I hastened to get myself ready and swiftly completed my ritual of prayer so as to make an early start for my journey around Kailashnath. Since Baba had already given me directions to my destination, I anticipated no problems at all in getting there. A road led in a northerly direction from the Diraphuk Gumpha along the banks of the La Chu towards the source of the Sindhu River. Another route crossing the river went right around Kailashnath and came back to Tarchen. With only these two roads available, the risk of losing my way did not arise.

Crossing the river, I began to move east. It is quite impossible to convey to someone unfamiliar with the region the searing impact of that dry cold. Snow swathed almost everything around me in a blanket, looking either like patches of cotton wool or mountains of salt. Even the roads were thick with snow that had not yet melted completely. One of the two paths climbed steadily upwards. It was the first time I would be negotiating a snowbound road in Tibet. Light and fluffy in appearance, the snow had turned into a hard crust below my feet. It formed at zero degrees before it fell, but well below freezing point, it became rock-hard and layered the ground, making it dangerously slippery. Had the Tibetans not given me a pair of their special shoes to wear and I had not been careful, it would have been the end of me. Exercising extreme caution, I somehow managed to make my way through.

Though I was proceeding slowly enough because of the steep incline in the road, I had started panting. Soldiering on for almost an hour, I finally reached the highest point and heaved a sigh of relief. Before me was a vista of consummate beauty. To my left rose the Kailash Peak. Facing me was Mansarovar and Rakshas Taal. Between the Kailash Peak and Mansarovar was the smaller Neten Peak, known to Tibetans as Yelak Jung. According to devotees of Shiva, this was his mount, the sacred bull. Others believed that it represented Nandi. Dolma La, the highest point of the area around Kailash was situated at a height of 18,600 feet. To the right of Dolma La, I could see Gouri Kund, a small lake. Though it seemed not far from this point, it was actually almost a mile away. The snow that had come down from the mountains in avalanches had accumulated there. No river flowed into Gouri Kund nor traced its source to it.

Stepping off the road, I moved carefully in the direction of this lake. When I tried dipping my hand in the water, however, I made contact with solid ice. This was an entirely new experience for me, a phenomenon I had only read about in books so far. But the reality was novel and thrilling. Touching the surface of the lake, I found it hard and firm. Then I threw some stones at it, but the ice refused to crack under the impact and the stones merely collected on the surface. I stepped on it very cautiously to test whether it could take my weight. Gradually, as I started walking across, a rare feeling of joy overwhelmed me. It seemed incredible that I should be walking across a lake!

The thrill of the experience was touched, however, by a shade of anxiety. If the miracle that enabled me to walk across a frozen lake suddenly transformed the latter back into its natural state, my plight would be a sorry one indeed! The centre of Gouri Kund would witness the end of my life span. But if that did happen, would it really matter very much? Embracing death in these sacred environs surely ensured eternal life for the person concerned. I tried to rationalize my fears. From the centre of the lake where I now stood, I looked down into its depths below the icy surface. I could see some mossy growth and a bed of stones at the bottom. Once in a while, trapped air bubbles would rise up, glistening like diamonds, and appear to float in the water. As I walked across the lake, I slipped and took a couple of tosses. Fortunately, I had my blanket and shawl to cushion the impact of my fall or I could well have had broken limbs to contend with as well. Walking across the slippery ice, I noticed, was something like trying to climb the steps of a village pond overgrown with moss. Thankfully, this lake was not as large as Mansarovar and I was able to reach the opposite shore in half an hour.

Once I had crossed Gouri Kund, I came across several mountain streams. I had descended quite a long way below and here, the snows had begun to melt. I could hear sounds nearby and shortly came upon the Jhong River. This was a narrow watercourse and crossing it would not be difficult. It was here that I caught sight of a camp of gypsies. To be more precise, it was they who saw me. Three children—a couple of boys and a girl—caught sight of me and sticking their tongues out in greeting, practically dragged me to their camp. The boys were about ten years old and the girl even younger. As we approached their camp, the adults emerged and prostrated themselves before me.

The gypsies wanted to sell me some of their wares at really low prices, but I fell back on gestures to indicate that I did not need anything. Unable to sell me woollens, the gypsies opened a few tins and showed me some precious stones from the area. Unfortunately, no matter how cheap they were, I had no money to spare for anything at all. That did not deter them, however. They then produced some herbal medicines which were ostensibly guaranteed to cure the ailments for which they were intended.

I finally managed to persuade them that I would be far better pleased if they gave me a bowl of warm milk, hot tea or something to eat, instead. I offered some coins as payment to the woman I was interacting with. She immediately brought out some frozen milk from the corner of her tent. Breaking off a few pieces, she handed them to me, confessing that they had nothing more to offer. But it was enough for a hungry man.

From this place, Rakshas Taal and Mansarovar appeared very close by. I began to move on, hugging the banks of the Jhong Chu. The sun was directly overhead when I reached the Juthulphuk Gumpha.

After completing the formalities, I was about to knock on the door of the room assigned to me, when the door to a room nearby opened and a lama emerged and welcomed me with a smile. He was an older man, over fifty, at least. He had a scholarly air and commanded respect. I was led to his prayer room right away. Once our prayer session was over, we entered the kitchen where a couple of Tibetans were warming themselves by the fire. The moment they saw me, they rose to their feet. From my stance, it was obvious to them that I was a monk sworn to silence. There were no lengthy introductions. Two bowls of hot tsampa were placed before me. Expressing my gratitude with a gesture, I took a sip.

From Juthulphuk, pilgrims moved on to the dharamsala at Tarchen. That was the point at which the end of the Kailash pilgrimage was formally declared through ritualistic prayers and ceremonies. Baba had advised me to move straight on to Parkha where I was to meet him. So I started following the route to Parkha or the nearest tasam and reached the Parkha crossroads before nightfall. From there, I looked across at the Kailash Peak. Going down on my knees in reverence, I sprinkled some water from the river on my head and declared the end of my Kailash pilgrimage.

KAILASH BABA

NO SOONER HAD I crossed the tea stall at the crossroads than I noticed some men approaching me at a run. I stared at them in amazement when they informed me that Guruji was waiting for me. Guru? I repeated the word under my breath and wondered who it could possibly be. In Tibet, any lama was a guru, a mentor. The man I regarded as God Himself was Kailash Baba. Had he then travelled all the way from Langbona Gumpha just for me? Keeping such questions to myself, I followed the men. I found Kailash Baba in a house next to the tea shop. The moment he saw me, he said, 'Come. I knew you would not stay in the Diraphuk Gumpha for more than a day.'

I touched his feet respectfully and thought to myself, 'You can read my thoughts or else how would I have met you again so soon?'

Baba declared that the administrator of the region was a deeply pious man himself and that Parkha was one of the notable villages in the region. The tasam here was better known than that of Thokchen. All pilgrims to Kailash and Mansarovar came here to stock up on provisions. Right beside Parkha village lay Rakshas Taal or Langak Tso. It was Baba himself who told me about the unique nature of the place. Rakshas Taal and Mansarovar were twin lakes separated by a mile or so and one was indistinguishable from the other. Ravana is believed to have worshipped Sridevi on the shores of Rakshas Taal, from which the famous Sutlej River had also originated. During the winter months, devout Tibetans embarked on a journey that took them around both the lakes together. According to many, the hidden treasures of the gods lay buried in the strip of land separating the lakes. Gold was to be found in the sands there, but merely touching it was considered a grievous sin and no Tibetan ever stooped to it. On one occasion, the locals had apparently presented the Revered Dalai Lama with a huge gold nugget gathered from this area. But he had declined to accept it with the explanation that no human being had any claim to what rightfully belonged to the Lord.

Early the next morning, we saw the swans again, swimming regally around the lake. The distant mountain peak had just acquired the rosy glow of dawn. Some boys were collecting dead fish that had come floating in on the waves. There was no perceptible difference between the two lakes. The ambience around them was exactly the same. The Lang Chu and the Jhong Chu that went nearly all the way around Kailash, merged together before flowing into Rakshas Taal.

Right next to the point of confluence was a small one-roomed wooden hut. Beside it was a chorten constructed by heaping together pebbles and stones gathered from the ground around it. The door of the room was ajar. We entered the hut to find five men already assembled there around a large container with a fire burning inside it. I went up to join them. Baba commanded, 'Prepare two bowls of chang for us.'

One of the men got up at once and fetched water from the lake. He told me that a certain type of grass grew beside the lake, from which a delicious variety of bread could be made. The men now seated in the room came here every morning to gather it and sold it in the market. The tea warmed us and we settled down comfortably. Since I always carried my blanket with me, I laid it out on the floor and Baba and I seated ourselves on it, facing each other. All of a sudden, Baba asked: 'You had mentioned that your parents were no longer alive. Do you remember their names?'

'Certainly!' I replied.

'Do you recall your paternal grandfather's name?'

'I do.'

'That will do.' Baba arranged himself in a yogic posture and asked me to concentrate on my remembered image of the Kailash Peak.

A few minutes later, he proceeded to recite verses from the scriptures and asked me to repeat them after him. I obeyed him without understanding the meaning of the words and without even knowing why I was uttering them at all. The heat emanating from the burning firewood along with Baba's booming voice lent the room an atmosphere of sanctity. When we emerged an hour later, the sun had risen. Walking along the lake's pebbled shores, Baba explained, 'The faith followed by the lamas embraces the worship of the Buddha and the practice of the occult arts.'

The rivers originating in this region flowed down through many lands, bringing a taste of nectar to all creatures on earth. There were four main rivers flanking the four faces of Kailashnath: to its north lay the Ashwamukh or Tamchog Khambab from which the Brahmaputra sprang; to its west flowed the Hastimukh or Langchen Khambab from which originated the Sutlej; to its east ran the Singhamukh or Senge Khambab—the source of the Sindhu; and to its south lay the Mayurmukh or Magcha Khambab from which sprang the Karnali. Considered to be among the most sacred watercourses in the world, these four rivers, believed to support the Buddha, were supposed to cleanse a man of all sins if he bathed in them.

We walked on and came to a halt at the confluence of a river known as the Ganga Chu. Baba looked at me and said, 'Strip off your clothes and step into the water.'

I thought to myself, 'A dip in these icy waters might just ensure that I never come up again,' then rebuked myself at once. What had I to fear in the near divine presence of this man? I did as I was told and began taking off my clothes. To my great astonishment, Baba plunged into the water himself! From the ease with which he swam in the river, one might have imagined that far from being freezing cold, the water was actually warm. Somewhat reassured by the sight of him in the water, I tentatively dipped my toes in the river. Another surprise! Far from being chilly, the water was warm! Snow lay all around us; yet warm water flowed into the Ganga Chu. Having spent a long time in the water, we finally surfaced on the other bank of the river, that is, further south. Baba continued wearing his wet loincloth. Taking out some of the ashes he had kept wrapped in a twist of paper in my bag, he carefully rubbed them over his entire body.

From this point which was equidistant from Mansarovar and Rakshas Taal, we began descending in a southerly direction. As we walked, I suddenly confessed to Baba, 'I recited the prayers and incantations as you had advised, without understanding a word of them.'

'I have given you new life,' was his response. 'Beginning with repentance, followed by prayers and, last of all, offerings to the Almighty. Your journey to Kailash has been worth it.'

As we continued on our way, Baba pointed out some mountains and indicated their names. 'The road that runs past that mountain is directly bound for India. One of its many names is the Gurla La. The route from India right up to this point comes from there; in fact, you followed a route no Indian ever chooses. Don't worry, the way back is far smoother.' Suddenly, he came to an abrupt halt and asked me to memorize some names that he repeated for my benefit.

As I attempted to jot them down, he forbade me from doing

so, declaring that memory was a far more reliable guide. I repeated after Baba: 'Taklakot ... Lipulek....'

Having reached the foot of a mountain, we kept it to our right as we moved along the shores of Mansarovar. We arrived at the Gosul Gumpha on the shores of the lake just as the sun moved overhead. As we entered the gumpha, Baba said to me, 'You will stay here tonight. Tomorrow, you will return via Gurla La.'

His words struck me with devastating impact, as though he had just conveyed some tragic news.

The Return: As soon as Baba entered the gumpha, he seemed to stir its inmates into a fury of activity. Someone held out a huge robe fashioned from blanket material for Baba to wear. Another person made special arrangements for him to be seated. Through the sheer good fortune of being Baba's companion, I too received a fair share of attention. Baba took his seat and immediately started reciting prayers. Then everybody present seemed to become deeply absorbed in meditation. When we had emerged from that state, we accompanied Baba to the lakeside in silence and spent some time there pacing up and down. It was quite a while before we returned to the gumpha and sat down to our meal of boiled potatoes and boiled cauliflower over which flour had been sprinkled as though it were salt. Neither Baba nor any of the lamas there ate salt. The meal was followed by another prolonged period of silence.

A marked change had come over Baba from the moment of our arrival at Gosul. That cheerful and jovial man I had known seemed to have vanished. Soon after dusk had fallen, we all retired for the night, focusing our minds on our prayer beads. Ever since I had met Baba, I had preferred the invocation to Lord Shiva instead of the Mani incantation. While I had put in effort to master the latter, it did not come to me naturally. The former, on the other hand, seemed instinctive and dear to my heart. Sitting cross-legged on the bed, I remembered Kailash Baba and focused on the prayers I had been taught.

Of all the lamas at the gumpha, Ridang Lama was the most revered. It was he who oversaw the efficient administration of the gumpha. The lamas of this monastery were not always in residence. During the winter, they left for the large gumpha to the south. It was about a month since they had returned for prayers and to enhance their store of good deeds. Moreover, it was usually ascetics from India who stayed at this gumpha on the way to Kailashnath, beginning their special prayers from this point. Even those pilgrims who chose to travel to Mansarovar, despite all possible hurdles, began their journey from this monastery, for the distance from Gosul to Rakshas Taal and Mansarovar was the shortest possible one.

I slept soundly, but woke up before daybreak. Everybody appeared to have caught a cold and it was impossible to sleep with all the coughing around me. The fire in the huge container had almost died out. I went to the kitchen quickly and fetched some wood to stoke it back to life. Then snug in pullover and blanket wrap, I went out. There was no more than a faint touch of colour in the sky and the stars still gleamed brightly. Slowly, I made my way to the southern side of the lake. A pair of swans swam in the waters and my eyes were drawn to a fire by the shore. As I drew closer, I found three men sitting and warming themselves by it and I joined them.

Stretching before me were the sacred waters of the lake. Was this, perhaps, what true fulfilment was all about? Across the lake, the sun was about to rise. From where we sat, it seemed as though the sun were emerging from the lake itself. And then, that enchanting vision appeared again with the silver peaks of the Gurla Mountains beginning to awaken. To the north, the Kailash Peak raised its head, followed by the play of light and the magical transformations it wrought to the surrounding landscape.

When I returned to the gumpha, everyone was praying alongside Baba. I joined them. When the prayer session drew to a close, I found Baba's gaze fixed unblinkingly on me. Unable to bear the intensity of that piercing gaze, I averted my eyes. Baba nodded in the direction of a lama and announced, 'Dukhang Lama will be going to Taklakot today. I would like you to accompany him. You will have no problems in seeking out the right path.'

Baba's words were a blessing in itself, but my heart was heavy at the thought of being cast out of paradise.

Dukhang Lama called me outside. He was about forty and aristocratic in his bearing. In fractured Hindi, he told me gently, 'I know how despondent you are feeling at the thought of leaving

Guru, but do not despair. He has thoroughly assessed the matter and weighed its every aspect. Accept his words as your guideline.'

I nodded and asked, 'When will you be setting out?'

'Right now,' he replied. 'If we leave at once, we will be able to reach the Simbiling Gumpha by tomorrow. Some food is being prepared for us before our departure. As soon as we have taken the tsampa, we will set off.'

Within an hour of coming to know that I would have to leave Kailashkhand, all arrangements were made for our departure and soon, we were ready to set out. When I approached Baba to take his leave and touched his feet in respect, he placed his hands on my head and blessed me. But he did not utter a word.

Having walked for nearly an hour along the shores of Mansarovar, we came to a stone-bedecked chorten. We rested there for a while and I cupped some water from the lake into my palms and sprinkled it over my head. Touching some of the water to my lips, I murmured aloud some prayers. Then we carried on. Soon, we came across another small lake not far from Mansarovar. It bore a striking resemblance to Gouri Kund and was roughly the same size, but its waters were much colder than that of Mansarovar. I came to know that it was called Sushupto.

As Dukhang Lama explained it to me, Mansarovar was supposed to be imbued with a special significance. When our mind was steeped in darkness, he went on, we were incapable of experiencing happiness. With the blessings of Lord Demchek, however, the unenlightened mind awakened to knowledge and was transformed into Mansarovar. The latter symbolized the awakened, enlightened state of mind that paved the way to true freedom.

Then the moment arrived for us to begin negotiating the ascent, a sheer climb of at least 1,200 feet. We began moving up very slowly, the way we had in Yatung. Kailashnath was now directly behind us. We had to pause for breath frequently, because the path ran at a steep incline. No prayers were uttered nor incantations chanted along this route. What sustained us was solely the image of Kailashnath. It was an arduous route and even in this chill, I found myself bathed in sweat. The question of comparing my plight to the way Dukhang Lama was bearing up to the ordeal did not arise at all. He was, after all, a native of this region.

We reached the summit of the mountain we had been scaling. From this vantage point, I had a clear view of Kailashkhand, the most sacred of pilgrimage sites and—of India, my motherland. It was here that we would be bidding farewell to the celestial Kailash. The way back was easy and involved a descent all the way through. This area of the Gurla Mountains was still almost entirely covered in snow which would take about a month to melt. On our way down, Dukhang Lama observed, 'You are truly blessed. There have been ascetics in the past who have failed, despite every effort on their part, to even speak to Baba. You, on the other hand, actually stayed with him!'

Instead of offering a response to that remark, I asked him, 'Where does he live?'

'He has no fixed abode,' the lama answered. 'Whenever he arrives here, he moves about everywhere. Everybody respects him and longs for his company. Baba worships the sun and people say he is gifted with occult powers.'

'Does he come here every summer?'

'He is a yogi. For him, the question of seasons is irrelevant. He comes whenever he wishes to. Ponder on the following: For the past year or so, the flow of pilgrims from India has virtually come to a standstill because of the political situation. But none have been able to prevent Baba from coming here.'

'Why should anyone prevent him from coming?'

'Lhasa is beset by a great many problems these days. Owing to strained relations between China and India, the Chinese have closed down all routes used by Indian pilgrims. You are not familiar with the paths we Tibetans use. Besides, being apprehended by Chinese soldiers could cause you endless worries. That is why Baba asked you to accompany me. I will explain the entire route to you.'

Dukhang Lama parted with many more facts about the region. The expanse of level land was Purang. Lying beyond it at the point where it ended, stood the Simbiling Gumpha, the largest in the region. The name 'Simbiling' had been derived from Shivaling, worshipped as Lord Shiva. Perhaps, a temple dedicated to this deity had existed here in the remote past. The cluster of dwellings closest to the gumpha belonged to Taklakot, the most prosperous village in the locality. Every three months, an open-air bazaar was organized here for three days. A number of other big shops also dotted the place. In the past, Hindu pilgrims would stay in this village, hire donkeys and yaks for their pilgrimage and begin the journey to Kailash. All that was required for the pilgrimage would have been available here once, but that business had come to an end. The place had also become infested with thieves and robbers who would prey on unwary pilgrims arriving from elsewhere.

Evening was about to descend when we reached Kardung. This was no village at all, but an extended slum. A roof had, somehow, been fixed atop some walls made of clay and stone. Taking the owner's permission, we sought shelter for the night in a small tea shop. The man was satisfied with the meagre sum we offered him as payment and early the following morning, we set out again after consuming bowls of hot tea. The path swooped down dangerously. Beside us, the river rushed along a deep ravine and forged a path through the mountains. At every moment, it seemed as if we would slip on the stones and plunge to our death.

That evening, we reached the beautiful Simbiling Gumpha. From a distance, it looked like a small village. Drawing close, I realized that it was actually a huge house cut out of the mountainside and resembled the Udaygiri Mountains of Orissa. Just below it, like a dream flowed the Karnali River. Dukhang Lama belonged to this gumpha and we went to his room right away. I told him that I would not be needing a meal. Just arrangements for me to sleep somewhere would suffice.

He looked at me and said with a smile, 'Stretch out here, will you? I will arrange for us to be provided with an extra couple of blankets. There is an acute shortage of fuel in these parts.' With that, he left the room.

A long time later, Dukhang Lama returned and asked, 'You did not eat anything yesterday, did you? You must be terribly hungry!'

He then took me across a hall into a pigeon-hole of a room and asked me to look through the window. I was amazed by what I saw. The village of Taklakot was only a short distance away and it evidently enjoyed a high degree of prosperity. We crossed the terrace and entered a room made of timber: the kitchen. The lama there along with three trapas greeted me with a smile. I was handed a large bowl of butter tea and some ordinary tea and asked to enjoy a light meal.

We came out of the kitchen and stood in the sun. I found the Simbiling Gumpha striking in its architectural beauty that recalled the Drepung Gumpha in Lhasa. And no wonder! This was the main branch of the Drepung Gumpha and owned by it. An organization had been set up to run the Simbiling Gumpha's administration efficiently. Four senior lamas and thirty-three trapas or dabas lived here. All the expenses incurred for the purchase of blankets, ghee and food were borne by the Drepung Gumpha. There was a man especially appointed to take charge of the purchases. The latter, along with the Revered Khengpo—the head of the Simbiling Gumpha—was entrusted with the responsibility of running it. The Revered Khengpo was directly appointed by the Drepung Gumpha and served as their representative. There were half a dozen more gumphas, both big and small, under the aegis of this one.

After I had finished my meal and thanked the lamas who had served it to me, Dukhang Lama led me in to meet the Revered Khengpo. The room we entered was located within another and beautifully decorated. It had two windows and the light streaming through them made everything sparkle. The walls, like those of the Potala, were beautifully designed. Even the ceiling bore an enormous golden painting of the Buddha. Attached to each of the pillars in the room was a huge thangka, depicting various aspects of Buddhism. The revered head of the gumpha was seated on a bed near one of the windows. He wore a loose robe with long sleeves and a triangular cap. An embroidered shawl covered his knees. Completely ignoring me, the two lamas engaged in a detailed discussion of various matters. I could follow bits and pieces of the conversation, but most of it eluded me completely. It was certainly clear that I was the main topic of their dialogue. After this had continued at length, we bowed low and touching the Revered Khengpo's feet as a mark of respect, came outside.

Passing through vast halls, we reached the main temple of the gumpha. As soon as we entered it, we noticed a bright golden image of the Buddha. Beside it were two smaller statues of Tathagata. Facing the large idol was a smaller statue of the Buddha in a meditative posture. The larger image must have been at least six feet tall and was flanked on either side by a pillar. A dragon symbolizing, in all likelihood, the devil himself, embraced each pillar. The heads of the two dragons leaned in to the Buddha. I noticed the lighted lamp. We took our seats on the dais.

A Buddhist temple in Tibet was actually a small museum of sorts containing artefacts and objects of immense value. Particularly worth a mention was the huge array of thangkas that adorned its walls. In small alcoves built into the walls were ranged innumerable books, each beautifully preserved by hanging curtains. Observing my expression of awe, Dukhang Lama remarked, 'This is nothing at all. Our actual library will stun you. In this region, it is our gumpha alone that houses the entire version of Tangiour and Kangiour.'

Then he sat up straight and continued, 'Now let us come to the matter that concerns you. A slight problem has cropped up. I had wanted to take you around our village. There are plenty of people here who are reasonably fluent in Hindi. I had wanted to introduce you to them. But, the head lama objects to it. First of all, this is a prohibited area for Hindus [what he meant, in this instance, was 'Indians']. So your sudden appearance might give rise to a lot of awkward questions. Secondly, for any kind of contact with Indians, permission has to be sought from the authorities in Lhasa. As in other regions of Tibet, here too, the People's Army keeps a strict vigil. The local authorities of Purang district are just a name. They have no real authority. The head lama feels that it is best if you do not go out of the monastery. If "they" catch sight of you, there might be problems you could well avoid.'

I needed no further explanations from Dukhang Lama. This was no novel experience for me. I knew my plight only too well. I would have to leave the gumpha at the first opportunity to evade 'them'.

Dukhang Lama assured me that this was the main route to India. So far, soldiers had not patrolled the road chosen by people seeking asylum in India. As evening approached, he set out with me again. Crossing the river and keeping Taklakot to our left, we descended still further. Looking at the distant mountains, my companion said, 'The road to the left is the one that goes to India. Lipu Lek is the last border village of Tibet, Nepal and India. It is thick with Chinese soldiers. So, avoid it. Lipu Lek lies at a height of almost 16,700 feet. If you remember, we crossed Gurla La at

16,200 feet. So, you realize it will be a bit of an arduous journey for you. You are fortunate that the moon will be rising tonight. Undertaking a nocturnal journey will, therefore, not be a problem for you. Just below that mountain is a narrow path. If you take that path and reach its highest point, you will notice that it slopes down to the plains on the other side. You can then assume that you are in Indian territory and need harbour no fears of being apprehended by the Chinese. If you start out now, you will be able to cross the mountain before daybreak. Be careful, though. There will be ice on the paths.'

Not only did Dukhang Lama give me all the useful tips I needed for crossing the border without a hitch, he also handed me a small bundle and said, 'This contains provisions for two days and you will be able to manage. But a word of warning: even if your throat is parched, do not under any circumstances drink melted snow.'

And so my journey began once more. Keeping the Karnali river to the left, I began moving in the direction of Lipu Lek. Within half an hour, I was in the mountains again. Keeping my sights trained on the summit of the mountain, I continued walking. All too soon, it was night. I knew that I would have to carry on without a break, because I could not afford to linger in the area at daytime when the risk of being spotted by Chinese soldiers was phenomenal. Not only would I be in serious trouble then, but Dukhang Lama and all those at the gumpha would also be deeply concerned over my fate. So I really had no choice but to continue on my way. Had I not faced a similar experience while crossing the Gurla La, I might have been sorely tempted to halt for the night. Dukhang Lama had been right. In the bright moonlight, the snowy white peak of the Lipu Lek was clearly visible.

Plodding along steadily, my attention was drawn to some lights to my right. I stopped in my tracks, deciding that they probably came from tents occupied by Chinese soldiers. Swiftly, I stepped off the path I had been on and veered off to the path on the right. It was a narrow escape all right and it was my silence that had saved me. For the only sound to be heard was that of my laboured breathing. I put to good use the trick that Sadhu Baba had taught me—of walking in rhythm to my breathing. And once more, the Mani incantation came to mind.

And so, I walked through the night as though in a trance. I realized suddenly that the peak I had been keeping in my sights had vanished. Far off to the right was another peak. It was now becoming clear to me that I was nearing the summit. Because of the great physical exertion I had to put myself through during the journey, I had been stopping frequently to catch my breath. I now felt that this was no longer necessary. I had already climbed my way to the summit. In the far distance, the Kailash Peak had once again unveiled itself. I had no problems at all in recognizing the roof of the 'temple'. I paused to pay my respects to the sacred sight and sent up my prayers to the Lord.

The morning stars had begun to fade when I found myself quite close to the border. I had no more than an hour or so in hand. Within that time, I would have to reach the mountain slopes. All this while, my feet had been crunching over stones and the dust from crushed pebbles. Then suddenly, I felt the sensation of grass underfoot. But that was impossible! I looked down and saw that though it wasn't grass, it was some kind of thick moss or lichen. I felt as though a carpet had been laid out for me. I reached the slope at dawn and could barely contain my joy. I had returned from Kailash and actually touched my motherland once again. I had managed to escape 'their' attentions at the border and crossed over into my own country.

It was almost noon and I was about to cross the first row of pines, when there were harsh cries of 'Halt! Halt!' In minutes, I had been surrounded by soldiers. To my enormous relief, they were all wearing Indian Army uniforms. Quite naturally, they asked me a great many questions and led me to a camp nearby. I explained that I had gone to Kailash with Guruji. He would be rejoining me later at his own convenience. Fortunately, there was a Bengali at the camp and it was he who began interrogating me. The truth of my statements was proved beyond a doubt. The soldiers showered me with praise and treated me to buns and hot tea before releasing me. It was from them that I came to know I was now completely safe and had reached Nandankanan—the Valley of Flowers.

This was a whole new world and there was no yardstick by which I could have compared it to Purang Valley in any way. On the other side of Lipu Lek stretched a kingdom of ice and rocks and boulders, for no vegetation could possibly have survived the intense cold. Out here, as far as the eye could see, there was only lush green grass and an endless sea of colourful flowers and foliage.

This was truly heaven on earth. I had come from an eternally beautiful world—the heaven of the gods. The hostile climate and shockingly low temperatures were natural impediments to any man intending to trespass into such terrain. Human beings could only visit it as pilgrims, as devotees offering prayers and respectful salutations. But this breathtakingly beautiful place was accessible to all. True fulfilment lay here. I felt that all the flowers here had bloomed for me alone and were happily welcoming me back into their fold.

I had avoided certain villages along this route. Before me was the Dhabali Ganga. Ahead lay Dharchula and Berinag followed by Almora. From Almora, I would go on to Nainital and Kathgodam, where I would have to board a train. There were no further impediments in my path—no mountains, streams or snow to present an obstacle to my progress. After a glimpse of Kailash that promised eternal freedom, I was on my way home. What awaited me there, I wondered—freedom or bondage?

TIBET'S ETERNAL FLAME: MILAREPA

WHILE WRITING THIS book on my experiences in Tibet, I had felt a strong urge to add a few words about Milarepa. At that point of time, however, I knew precious little about him. After all, I was simply a boy who had run away from home and had been blessed enough to travel to the most sacred pilgrimage site in the world in the guise of a lama.

For Tibetans, a reference to the Buddha automatically involves a discussion about Milarepa. Tibet has always been a country shrouded in mystery, a part of the latter having to do with its preoccupation with the little-known art of the occult. Born in

AD 1052 in the Gun Thank Province of Tibet to Serab Giyaltsen and Karmo Kiyen, Milarepa was regarded as a master of this branch of the psychic sciences. He had a younger sister, Peta. Even before he was born, his father, Serab, had promised Milarepa's hand in marriage to his friend's daughter, Jese. When his son grew up to be a young man, he accepted Jese as his spouse, but the couple neither shared a physical relationship nor ever lived together.

When Milarepa was only seven, his father fell prey to an incurable disease. Even the best physician in Tibet found it impossible to effect a cure. Serab Giyaltsen then called his family and close friends to his deathbed and told them, 'You are all my loved ones and very dear to me. I have this last request and I appeal to you to ensure that my wishes are honoured. I am leaving all my property, my wealth and assets, for the upkeep and welfare of my wife and children. My wife is not a worldly woman and does not understand such matters. Please look after them all. Accept the guardianship of my minor son and explain his responsibilities to him when he attains adulthood.'

He died soon after.

Not long after his death, Serab's brother wrested the property out of his sister-in-law's hands and even turned the family out of their palatial home. Mourning her late husband, the widow Karmo Kiyen had to endure this act of cruelty as well. But what could a woman who had not learnt to fend for herself possibly do? On the streets now with her young children, she received no help at all from the so-called friends and well-wishers who had surrounded her husband when he was alive. They feigned ignorance of all that had transpired, for none dared to raise his voice against Serab's nefarious brother.

Karmo Kiyen managed to find a shelter of sorts for herself and for her offspring and started living there, helped by a few of her husband's sincere friends. The widow continued to be harassed by her brother-in-law, however, and matters ultimately came to such a pass, that Karmo Kiyen was forced to take to the streets again. She tearfully told her son, Mila, that his uncle was responsible for all the tribulations they were having to endure and begged him to avenge such injustice on her behalf. Or else, she would have no other option but to commit suicide then and there.

Though still a child, Milarepa had gleaned wisdom from his

past incarnations. He listened to his mother's words in silence, then promised her that he would avenge the cruelties his family had borne. Bidding farewell to his beloved mother and sister, Milarepa left home to master the art of the occult.

Eleventh-century Tibet abounded in a whole host of practitioners specializing in the occult sciences. A wise and worthy mentor in the field could only by found through a stroke of great good fortune and the accumulated good deeds of this life and past ones. It did not take Milarepa long to become a part of this sect and master the art.

Meanwhile, casting off all semblance of decency, Milarepa's uncle had turned into a money-hungry monster, his greed further inflamed by the pleasurable experience of feasting on his ill-gotten gains. Milarepa's mother and sister were, at the time, somehow managing to eke out a living that barely fetched them a meal on most days. It was around this time, that the entire village, particularly the uncle's friends and relations, was invited to attend a wedding in the family. To the amazement of all present, just when the festivities were at their peak, the house in which the ceremony was taking place suddenly collapsed with a thunderous roar, burying the bride, the groom and all the guests under the rubble. Hearing the commotion outside, Milarepa's mother clung to her daughter and quivered in fright. Then she emerged to see what the matter was. When she realized what had happened, she burst into transports of joy and exclaimed at the top of her voice, 'My Milarepa has brought this about! He has, on behalf of his parents, avenged the injustice done to his family! It was he who sent the thunderbolt that destroyed the house!'

Though the house had been completely demolished, Milarepa's uncle and aunt had managed to save their lives by hiding in a corner of a room. But they would still have to pay for their sins. At first, they found it impossible to believe that their nephew could have wreaked such havoc through some kind of magic, but gradually came to accept it as the truth. Their hatred for his family grew, however. A time arrived when Milarepa's uncle and aunt went to such extremes in their harassment of the family that Karmo Kiyen found it almost impossible even to beg on the streets.

Unable to tolerate such cruelty any longer, she sent a letter to her son through an emissary. Not long afterwards, Nature wreaked vengeance again. It was the time of year when new crops were just ready to sprout. Despite a clear blue sky, there was an unexpected hailstorm and all the crops were destroyed. Once more, Karmo Kiyen rejoiced.

Despite his mother's delight at the misfortune suffered by the villagers, Milarepa deeply regretted the devastation wrought by his secret powers. He had tried to conquer hatred through hatred, he mused. Was this the true path to spiritual progress and enlightenment? Mastering the occult arts, he realized, had not led him to the path of freedom. He had, on the contrary, become further enmeshed in the dark web of black magic. In the process of contemplation, Milarepa was beginning to discover himself anew.

He began wandering through the mountains, exploring their every nook and corner in his search of a true mentor. And ultimately, he was successful in his quest. It was in Guru Marpa, a disciple of Guru Naropa, that he would find his mentor. Guru Naropa himself had been among those who propagated the teachings of Atish Dipankar, the guide and mentor of the learned Vikramsila. Guru Marpa, on the other hand, had brought back from India all the knowledge he could glean, along with precious books and tomes. As Milarepa's mentor, he would put his disciple to the test in countless ways to prepare him for his true destiny. Thus began Milarepa's quest for ultimate freedom, taking on the form of a desperate struggle for survival.

Among the trials Guru Marpa put his disciple through, the first involved the construction of a ten-storeyed house. 'I wish to build a ten-storeyed house here,' the guru began. 'There are a great many stones and boulders lying around; they must all be arranged, one by one. The house should be circular in shape and aesthetically pleasing. You will have to accomplish the task on your own. Let us see the strength of your powers as a magician! After you have completed this task, I will initiate you.'

The very reference to initiation flooded Milarepa's entire being with joy and he put his mind to the Herculean task he had been set. The foundation of the house had to be laid. The stones had to be cut to size and arranged individually. It was a difficult task for any human being and for Milarepa too, because he had to carry it out without resorting to his magical powers. Soon, the stress of hard labour scraped off his skin. The flesh on his back broke out in sores from carrying heavy boulders. Milarepa carried on with a smile, nonetheless. The only thought that kept him focused was the key he would ultimately obtain to eternal freedom.

The first floor of the house had just been completed, when Guru Marpa paid him a visit. Without preamble, he raged, 'Who asked you to build the house in this manner? Demolish it at once!'

Without a word of protest, Milarepa obeyed his mentor's command and dismantled the structure he had so painstakingly erected by the sweat of his brow. Despite the hardships of working in a harsh climate like that of Tibet and with rough stones for raw material, the young man resumed his construction and had almost completed the second storey, when Guru Marpa visited him again. He was severely admonished for his pains and not only ordered to start from the very beginning, but to do so in another location.

This process of demolishing what he had built and reconstructing it again continued for sometime. But finally, Milarepa could take it no more and broke down. His mentor's wife, Damema, who sometimes brought him food to eat at the worksite, shed silent tears at his plight. It was she who assumed the role of his mother and stood by him in his darkest hour. In spite of all he had been put through, Milarepa did not utter a word of reproach against his mentor.

Then came a day when it became impossible for him to continue working, because of the state to which he had been reduced. The tender-hearted Damema described to her husband how Milarepa now lay on his deathbed and pleaded with him to show his disciple some mercy. Guru Marpa, who in no way shared his wife's feelings, admonished her roundly for pleading his disciple's case. He declared that he refused to be taken in by play-acting. He also reminded his wife that only after the ten-storeyed house had been constructed would he initiate his disciple as promised. Milarepa's condition deteriorated still further. Yet, the hard-hearted Guru Marpa showed no signs whatsoever of relenting. Finally, when Milarepa had even lost the strength to get out of bed, he asked for his guru's permission to leave, as it would now be impossible for him to satisfy the conditions that had been laid down for him. But he was severely castigated again and told, 'What right do you have to go anywhere at all? You have surrendered everything of yours to me. I own your body and your soul. Walking away from it all is no longer an option you can choose to exercise.'

Milarepa accepted his mentor's argument without demur. He realized that he could not possibly withdraw what he had already surrendered to his mentor, whatever might have been the reason motivating him to do so. Damema eavesdropped on their conversation and then, without a word to her husband, went off to nurse Milarepa.

When she went to call him in the morning, however, Damema discovered that Milarepa had left, carrying only some books that belonged to him. Her mother's heart could no longer fight back the tears that rose to her eyes. Even her harsh disciplinarian of a husband was moved to tears.

Milarepa returned to his mentor after he had recovered completely. He had, after all, surrendered, body and soul, to him. Damema embraced him joyfully. Guru Marpa too, was glad to see him, but refrained from expressing his feelings.

When the question of Milarepa's initiation came up, Guru Marpa made it clear that there could be no question of initiation unless his disciple fulfilled the conditions laid down by him. His mentor began testing him all over again. Damema tried to help in her own way by offering Milarepa one of her costly jewels to give to his mentor. However, Damema was Guru Marpa's wife and what belonged to her also belonged to him. Therefore, in the strictest sense of the term, the jewel could not be considered a gift from his disciple.

This situation persisted for a while. As a mother, Damema found it intolerable and thought it was akin to chasing an illusion. So, taking matters into her own hands, she wrote to Nongdun, Guru Marpa's chief disciple and an exponent of philosophy, asking him to send Milarepa some rare ingredients, essential for the rituals of worship and prayer. These could then be given as an offering to Guru Marpa. Considering the opportunity of serving his mentor's wife a rare privilege, Nongdun did the needful without delay. Thus did Milarepa move a step forward in his quest for freedom. It was followed by the phase of intense meditation he would embark on. Finally came the moment Milarepa had been looking forward to with such intense longing and had prepared himself for, both mentally and physically.

With full ceremonial rites, Guru Marpa initiated the young man as his disciple, paving the way for the realization of all he had sought. That very day, Guru Marpa embraced him and declared, 'You have fulfilled the task you had set yourself. Through intense and painful labour as well as emotional trauma, you have burned to a cinder the results of your past deeds. It was only with the intention of releasing you from the consequences of your knowledge of the occult arts that I inflicted such pain on you, knowing fully well, of course, that you would be able to bear it. If your mother, my wife, had not burdened you with her affection, you would have reached your goal even sooner than you did.'

However, before his prayers could attain their ultimate fulfilment, Milarepa had to go in search of his hapless mother and younger sister. Aware of the havoc his past actions had wrought on his village, he did not enter it, but began making inquiries from its outskirts. He was told about the outcome of his own exploits and the repercussions they had had on the people concerned. He learnt that his uncle and aunt were still alive. So was his fiancée, a woman in her prime, who continually prayed for and looked forward to his return. His mother, Karmo Kiyen, had passed away and his sister was a mendicant, begging for alms at every door.

Milarepa's heart cried out in anguish at all he had heard and as evening approached, he silently entered the village. Thanks to his yogic powers, the night was no longer dark to him and the stars were like guiding lamps. He saw the ruins of his uncle's house and their own abandoned hut. It was in shambles and all that remained of it were its four walls. From amid the debris of rags and broken furniture and household articles, Milarepa managed to rescue his mother's mortal remains. Nothing remained of it apart from a few bones. The following day, he buried her remains in a spot close to the village and built a beautiful memorial stone above it. Sitting beside it, he prayed for eternal freedom.

Then began Milarepa's meditation in a cave close to the village. A few days later, he came down to the village once again to ask for alms. In all innocence, he had presumed that people would have forgotten the past. But, perhaps, there was more he had to atone for. The first house he visited turned out to belong to his uncle. Like a wounded tiger, the latter leaped on him and, rounding up the villagers, had him soundly thrashed. He also set ferocious dogs on him. Saving himself somehow by diving into the pond, Milarepa emerged once again and burst into song. He sang of the revenge he had sought and the repercussions it had had on the people of his village. However, he also sang of the developments that had led up to these tragic events and the role his uncle had played in them. Milarepa added that his path was no longer that of rancour and vengeance, but of peace, forgiveness and freedom. He concluded that he had forgiven his uncle and would pray to the Lord to pardon him. Even his hard-hearted aunt was moved by these emotionally charged verses. Henceforth, wherever Milarepa's uncle went, he was harshly rebuked for what he had done.

Then, it was the turn of his fiancée, Jese. In the full bloom of youth, she had eagerly awaited his arrival. Milarepa explained to her that his life would, henceforth, be a harsh one, defined by abstinence and sacrifice, for nothing of worth could ever be obtained without sacrifice. That was why he had chosen this particular path to freedom. He did not feel it was fair of him to bind anyone to its rigorous discipline. However, there were no obstacles to Jese meeting him occasionally. Milarepa then offered his former fiancée advice on how she should spend the rest of her life. And she accepted it graciously.

With Jese's help, Milarepa also managed to meet his sister, Peta. She was now a beggar on the streets and had no idea of the rigours he had gone through nor of the reason that had motivated him to do so. To her, he was no different from her—a mere beggar. If occult powers could not bring forth riches, she reasoned, what was the use of having such powers at all? Peta was also given permission to visit him in his cave and undertook the responsibility of bringing his meals to him.

Milarepa fulfilled his social duties and obligations and turned to meditation. The lonely cave was his sole habitation. His study of the scriptures and religious texts began in earnest as he perused the books that his gurus, Marpa and Naropa, had brought back from India. Naropa had, by then, attained salvation, but continued to live on in certain individuals even after his demise. He would appear in a dream and declare to Marpa that Milarepa was, in fact, his chief disciple.

Guru Marpa was pleased with Milarepa's devotion and steadfastness and permitted him to move a step further in his chosen path. He imparted all his knowledge to him and acknowledged him as his most able successor. In fact, years later, Milarepa would be appointed the head guru of Marpa's ashram. He preached to people through his songs that spoke of ultimate freedom and the means of attaining it by spurning all worldly desires.

Milarepa did not meditate in any one cave for long. If anything about it disturbed or bothered him, he simply moved elsewhere. Through the years, he would, therefore, move around the different caves in the Himalayas, spending his hours in meditation. For him, the mountains posed no barriers, for he believed that the body was but a slave to the mind. Where the mind went, the body would be compelled to follow. Gradually, people came to know of his songs and his powers and would gather around his cave. In time, Milarepa's fame spread throughout the country and he came to be regarded as the greatest sage in all Tibet.

The great ascetic recalls the wandering monks or minstrels of Bengal. Music and the arts seemed to find a home in him. The death of this great man also occurred in a strange and painful way. Milarepa was a true friend of the poor and a sort of father figure to them. The faith he preached was very simple and direct. The manner in which he simplified religion for the masses was looked on with disfavour by the lamas of his day, because they themselves continued to exploit religion, turning it into a kind of business to serve their own ends. This particular sect of lamas consisted of adherents who were extremely wealthy and influential in society. Lama Saphua was one of them and very envious of Milarepa's rapidly spreading popularity. Moreover, he deeply resented the fact that some of his own followers had gone over to him. He invited Milarepa to a debate, but lost to him. Saphua then left no stone unturned in his efforts to instigate him in one way or another, but failed miserably. Desperate, he decided that Milarepa would have to be done away with, whatever be the means employed to do so. Or else, the very existence of lamas like himself would be at stake.

After much reflection, Lama Saphua hatched a terrible conspiracy. He asked one of his many mistresses to take on the responsibility of killing Milarepa. He wore down her initial reluctance by convincing her that the sage was actually a fraud and devoid of true knowledge. Surely, it was no sin to dispose of such a man. Rather than being a sin against humanity, his death would greatly benefit all mankind. Handing her some curd, he told her that should she feed it to Milarepa, he was certain to die. No human being could possibly survive the effects of such a potent poison. Moreover, the sage never disappointed his devotees. He would be sure to accept the food and their objective would be achieved.

Since there was always a steady stream of people meeting Milarepa with some sort of food as offering, none suspected Lama Saphua's mistress as she made her way to the cave. Smiling, the sage greeted her and said, 'I know why you have come. But please go back today and return tomorrow.'

The young woman's heart quaked in fear and touching his feet respectfully, she somehow made good her escape. Observing his plans come to nought, Lama Saphua now became desperate. He assured his mistress that Milarepa could not possibly guess what the curd contained. However, having seen the sage's calm and serene visage, the young woman refused to cause him any harm. Not in the least put off by her reluctance to follow through with his plans, Lama Saphua convinced his mistress to do his bidding by promising her marriage and the gift of a rare and valuable jewel.

When the young woman next visited Milarepa, he welcomed her warmly and said, 'I know what is motivating you to do this. But if I accept your food today and breathe my last, you will not get the jewel you were promised. It would be better if you obtained your gift from him before coming here and doing what you need to do.'

Once again the woman was petrified at the way he had read her mind and fled from him. But she was unable to resist the temptation of the reward she had been promised. Meanwhile, Lama Saphua was more than eager to give the young woman anything she desired to achieve his goal. Handing her an extremely valuable jewel, he said, 'Now go and do the job. I will entertain no further excuses.'

When she went back to see Milarepa, he told her, 'A man is born to die. My time is approaching. Lama Saphua and you are merely the means to the end. The main standby of my life is forgiveness and I forgive you both. I discarded anger and envy long ago. That I have accepted poison from you is a fact I will keep a closely guarded secret for your own safety. Not a soul will get to know about it.'

Then the great man ate the poisoned food. Realizing that Milarepa was indeed the true devotee of Lord Buddha, while Lama Saphua was not, the young woman cried out loud and fell at the sage's feet.

While an ordinary man would have succumbed to the effects of the poison at once, Milarepa staved off death for a few days more to prepare his disciples and well-wishers mentally for his eventual demise. Though he bore the physical effects of the poison, the sage completely disassociated his mind from the pain his body was enduring.

Soon, people came to know that Milarepa was ill, but none knew the reason. It was Lama Saphua, however, who was most disconcerted at seeing him alive even after consuming the poisoned curd. In an agony of doubt and unable to restrain himself any longer, he made his way to Milarepa. To create the impression, particularly in the presence of an audience, that he was overflowing with compassion, Lama Saphua asked, 'Who is responsible for your state? You are a great man, invested with much learning and occult powers. Transfer your ailment to me and let me die in your place.'

Milarepa remained calm, even in the face of such shameless hypocrisy. His voice tinged with great affection, he observed, 'Someone who had been visited by the demon carried out this act. The pain of this poison is terrible indeed. I cannot transfer it to you. Physically, you will not be able to bear it.'

The sinner was now in turmoil. He was desperate to find out how much Milarepa knew. At the same time, this was the most opportune moment to test the strength of Milarepa's occult powers. So, in an outward display of empathy, he began to beg and plead that he might shoulder Milarepa's pain. Ultimately, the sage was forced to reply, 'You will never be able to bear this searing pain. I have projected it on the door outside the cave—take a look.'

Everyone gazed in that direction. In a short while, the hard wood seemed to shrivel in a fiery heat. The people there could only shudder in horror as it became clear to them what kind of agony Milarepa was going through. However, Lama Saphua still persisted, 'That is only wood, and these kind of occult tricks can be easily demonstrated. I, however, am of human flesh and blood—the strong and robust Lama Saphua. I beg of you, please transfer your disease to me.'

Now, Milarepa relented and said, 'All right. I am transferring a minute part of my agony to you. See if it is bearable. If not, let me know at once.'

Within seconds, Lama Saphua had fallen to the ground and was writhing in agony. In the throes of acute pain, he came to realize that Milarepa was truly a great ascetic and an incarnation of the divine. Enduring even that minuscule portion of pain, Lama Saphua felt he was on the brink of death and would surely breathe his last in no time without Milarepa's intervention. As he bruised himself rolling around on the floor in pain, Lama Saphua acknowledged to himself the great disaster he had invited on himself. Somehow casting himself at Milarepa's feet, he said, 'Please save me! I have been given my just dues!'

The moment he uttered those words, all traces of the disease vanished. Given a fresh lease of life and moved to atone for his sins, Lama Saphua asked the benign and forgiving Milarepa to accept him as a disciple. The sage's aunt too, atoned for the wrong she had done his family and accepted him as her spiritual mentor.

After ingesting the poison, Milarepa continued to live for a few more days, during which he gave his disciples his final words of advice on earth. Then, at an auspicious moment, he transcended this earthly world and passed into the other. He continues to live on, however, in the hearts of Tibetans as the revered ascetic, the beloved Maha Guru of all time.

AFTERWORD

LHASA ONCE MORE IN
THE NEW MILLENNIUM

LIFE MOVED ON at its own pace. The boy who had run away
from home in 1956 crossed the threshold of 2004. Blessed by the
Almighty Kailaseshwar and fortified by an inner strength, the
young lad nurtured the secret words that had become a part of
him and explored the wondrous, many-splendoured world around
him. Not content merely to absorb the sights he came across, he
threw himself, body and soul, into the experience of savouring the
audible, tactile and visual beauty that the earth abounded in. The
journey from Kolkata to Kailash had marked his period of initiation.
It was now the turn of the Silent Monk to become an explorer of
the world. He owed this transition from a mere boy to an evolved
human being to the blessings he had been destined to receive in
abundance, blessings that uplift a man and elevate his soul to a
sublime level.

Fate, the consequences of past deeds and the blessings of a
spiritual mentor depend on the will power exercised by an
individual. Like the three stages of spiritual progress, Satya, Rajas
and Tamas, man has, over the ages, been led in the direction of

ultimate enlightenment by a combination of will power and the strength that comes from knowledge and action. This, in fact, is the source of the occult or mystical wealth derived from the waves of blessings that flow through our daily lives. Life as it exists in the frail human body depends on mundane physical processes. Keeping us alive is this life source, our direct link to the Almighty, like the umbilical cord binding the infant to its mother. Whether or not we believe in God makes little difference to Him. On the contrary, it is we who must deal with the consequences of our belief or lack thereof. Air, light, fire, water, earth and sky are the blessings He showers on us. How we receive them is our choice. The blessings from the Divine Being continue to flow in abundance whether we seek them or not.

Possessed of a mind and body that are gifts from Him, I wander all over the world and marvel at His creation. Sunrise and sunset, oceans and lake and mountains, cities and human beings, animals and insects—all are but an expression of His creativity. In some parts of the world, the wonders are impermanent, joyous or horrific. Joy and sorrow, hope and despair, everything that finds expression, is but a minuscule facet of the inexpressible. All I do is contemplate, contemplate to my heart's content; that is what brings me true realization.

Having completed my journey to Lhasa, Kailashnath and Mansarovar, I had repeatedly asked myself, 'How did it all come about?'

The answer remained elusive.

'What did I achieve from it?' I had asked myself next.

And the answer was instantaneous: 'You have achieved far more than you needed to.' The abundance of divine blessings that was my gift, proved to be my asset for the future. Even today, when I set off on my travels—and I have been visiting the various pilgrimage centres across India right from 1956 onwards—it is that very asset I find myself depending on blindly. That capital is nothing but a vast store of divine blessings and experience that will always stand by me.

When the Revered Dalai Lama arrived in India as a refugee in 1959, I was not particularly concerned about the political situation in Tibet. To my way of thinking, even if a king were dethroned, he still remained a king. Matters relating to Tibet or the Dalai Lama were, therefore, not really of the utmost importance to me. However, for reasons unknown even to myself, I went to Dharamsala via Delhi in 1963. Unfortunately, the Dalai Lama was not in town at the time and I failed to meet him. In 1967, I set off on my travels once again. In the course of conversation with people I met during the journey, the subject of the Dalai Lama came up a number of times. But the main concern at the time was to find a way of ensuring that the Dalai Lama, the most important person in Tibet, and his millions of refugee followers could return to Lhasa. A lot of thought was given to ways in which the support of international law at The Hague could be availed of and the Dalai Lama reinstated in the royal palace at Potala through a peaceful dialogue with the Chinese authorities. The Dalai Lama had met all the world leaders and sought their help in the matter, but to no avail. The world was still facing the threat of a third World War. While China, Russia, America and France were all obsessed with Vietnam, the two great powers, America and Russia, were bracing themselves for the Cold War. The exiled Dalai Lama had no recourse, therefore, other than religion. Eschewing attachment in any form and committed to the principle of remaining uninvolved in the political drama that was building up, the Dalai Lama serenely embraced the path of non-violence, bore his refugee status with a smile and chose our country as his own.

In 1972, the bicycle tour I had embarked on came to an end. A bike knows neither how to swim nor how to fly! As a result, I could not visit all the countries I wanted to in a single trip and was compelled to begin all over again. I would earn some money and resume where I had left off. As my financial situation had somewhat improved, however, I would be able to afford whatever transport I could get hold of instead of always travelling on foot. In the course of my travels, I visited the North Pole and the South Pole along with a number of islands and gazed upon peaks that were eternally covered in snow.

Innumerable requests began pouring in. 'Describe to us all you have seen, all that you have experienced,' they urged. That is when I began writing travelogues. I was no professional writer, but I found myself putting down my thoughts, my views and my experiences simply to express myself. I drew inspiration from the indications I received from everywhere that the untold tales of my childhood and youth would now have to be given concrete form. It was as though someone had handed me a pen and commanded, 'Now write!' Accordingly, I put down my experiences—all that had happened to me—in my book, *Mahatirther Shesh Jatri*. This particular title had been settled on, because ours was the last group of pilgrims from India to travel to Lhasa before the Chinese government imposed a ban on Indian visitors to Tibet. While recounting all that had transpired during our pilgrimage, I began delving into my store of memories and ended up reviving them again. Something within me was awakened and seemed to incite me to rebellion by clamouring, 'Come on. Let's go to Tibet once more!'

I tried to quell that inner turmoil by persuading myself that I should wait a while; the right moment and opportunity would surely present themselves.

I have often found myself lapsing into a reflective mood while writing the book. On a number of occasions, I have found myself musing that a day would certainly come when the doors of pilgrimage centres like Jokhang, Mansarovar and Kailashnath would be thrown open to the world. No political situation in any country could ever be deemed permanent and all we needed to do was hold on to our patience. Many a time had tears smudged the ink in the manuscript of my book while it was being written. Perhaps, that was my offering to the Almighty? Then, all of a sudden, came the answer to my prayers—an opportunity thrown my way.... I managed to meet the Dalai Lama thrice in three consecutive years—in San Francisco, Geneva and Lausanne. I asked him about his plans of returning to Tibet. 'There is no cooperation whatsoever from the Chinese government,' he replied. 'There are no security arrangements in place and the political situation remains unchanged.'

His response had caused me much anguish. Was it possible for the whims of the Chinese government to rule the life of a man who had the Buddha as his mentor and was divinely blessed with his guidance, a man whose guardian was Time itself? Of course, I am no scholar, which was probably why I failed to understand the import of his words that day. Later, it dawned on me that though the scholar, the sage and the spokesman were one and the same person, the Dalai Lama had to present a different persona to various people on individual occasions. Perhaps, a similar situation had arisen during the sacred battle at Kurukshetra, when Sri Krishna had formulated a policy spanning all barriers of time, locale and situation.

Claude Levenson, a journalist friend of mine had put the following question to the Fourteenth Dalai Lama, Tenzing Gyatso: 'A few years ago, you were living in the world-famous Potala Royal Palace in Lhasa. You are now wandering around the world and visiting various countries. Would you say a few lines about your experiences and what has appealed to you most about them?'

The Dalai Lama had said in reply, 'Of course I will. The experience of living at the Potala is quite distinct from that of travelling around the world. The two belong to entirely different realms. At the Potala Palace, I lived a sheltered life, completely oblivious to the world outside its walls. I was also a great deal younger than I am today. I was expected to be circumspect and careful in the extreme about every step I took. After my status was reduced to that of a refugee, all these restraints and restrictions were flung aside. I have been able to look at the world, not at one remove, but directly, through my own eyes. I have come to be acquainted with many people and have forged close relationships with several of them. I may have lost my kingdom, but I have gained innumerable friends and continue to do so. It is they who surround and protect me. I live in a whole new world now. I have travelled through a great many countries—Europe, America and Russia. Initially, I would be quite nervous at the prospect of having to answer all the questions I anticipated being asked. But that is no longer the case.'

I discovered through many such interviews that the guiding spirit of the Potala Palace was an ordinary human being. I also realized that though the Dalai Lama was only five years my senior, in every other way, he was a great deal older. After three consecutive interviews, I was aware of the extent to which he inspired affection in me and of how close I had grown to him. And there were many questions that he anticipated and answered of his own volition.

Meanwhile, Tibet had been in turmoil and it would not be out of place to run through some landmarks in its history before moving on with my story. In 1959, His Holiness, the Dalai Lama, had undergone great risks to make his way from Lhasa to Siliguri via Assam, accompanied by over a million devotees and aides. The Government of India, with Nehru at the forefront, had extended a warm welcome to him and a satellite town was set up for him in Dharamsala. Then while feigning friendship with India by spouting the popular slogan about India and China being brothers, China had attacked our country. Soldiers from both sides of the border were observed in Nepal, Sikkim, Bhutan and Assam. Thousands of Tibetans became martyrs to the cause of defending their country from Chinese domination.

In 1965, the Chinese government declared an autonomous Tibet. About a year later, that is in 1966, the Cultural Revolution served as the pretext for carrying out a vicious campaign of persecution during which unspeakable atrocities were perpetrated on the gentle Tibetans. A shameful chapter in the history of Tibet was written in blood. Aware of what was happening in the country, the superpowers chose, nevertheless, to remain deliberately non-committal. Every city and town of Tibet grew bloody with the massacre of innocent men, women and children. In the name of the Cultural Revolution, every priest belonging to a gumpha or temple was murdered in cold blood. This rampage in the guise of propagating 'culture' continued for nearly a decade. The might of Chinese cannons destroyed almost five thousand chaityas, viharas and temples. Over fifteen lakh people out of a population of approximately sixty lakhs were killed. Word of the purge, carried out on such a massive scale, spread across the world.

Tibetans having gained the sympathy and support of the international community in 1978, the Chinese government went ahead and declared that Tibetans were free to practise their faith once again. It was around this time that young Tibetan men and women chose to voice their protest against Chinese atrocities.

In 1979, nearly twenty years after the Dalai Lama had escaped from Lhasa, his representatives met with the Chinese government to discuss matters pertaining to the reality of an independent Tibet. Although three discussions took place in quick succession, they turned out to be little more than an exchange of words and the issue remained unresolved. To put it briefly, Tibet was to remain a part of China.

In 1987, young Tibetan men and women threw caution to the winds and started breaching the barricades set up by the Chinese soldiers, so that they could approach American and European tourists visiting the country and tell them of their plight. They were desperate to let the world know how they were being deprived not only of their rights as Tibetan citizens by the Chinese regime, but also of basic human rights. Outraged by what they regarded as the audacity of the Tibetans, the Chinese authorities issued orders to shoot them at sight. Those who failed to fall victim to the soldiers' bullets were rounded up and thrown into prison. Though the authorities made every effort to hush up the incident, the tourists' cameras had captured images of the terrible brutalities that had become a part of life in Tibet. And for the first time since Tibet had been taken over by China, American and European newspapers carried detailed reports of Chinese atrocities. The deceitful mask the Chinese had been sheltering behind to dupe the world was ripped off and destroyed forever.

When the Tibetan New Year came around, sometime between 1987 and 1989, the Tibetans revolted again. The Chinese moved swiftly against them, killing the rebels and having the survivors incarcerated. It was around this time that the Panchen Lama breathed his last. The residents of his town, Shigatse, turned their grief towards organizing a movement to oust the Chinese and succeeded in mobilizing mass support. Realizing that matters were getting out of hand, the authorities issued a decree prohibiting Tibetans from congregating in a public place. Complete curfew was clamped down on the country.

Meanwhile, in the capital, Beijing, the Chinese army was using tanks to quell a student rebellion. Thousands of innocent young Chinese who had merely demanded their rights as citizens, were crushed to death in the process. This time however, the authorities had distinguished themselves by using brute force against their own people. The Tiananmen Square massacre would mark an unspeakably heinous moment in a bloody chapter of world history, provide gruesome evidence of how a totalitarian regime could reign supreme simply on the basis of the power it wielded and illustrate the true meaning of the expression, 'Chinese torture'.

Europe registered its protest against the draconian measures adopted by the Chinese government by conferring the Nobel Peace Prize on China's hated opponent, the Dalai Lama. The Chinese government, in turn, was strident in its protest against the decision and expressed its grievances in very strong terms to the Nobel Peace Committee. Its efforts in that direction proved to be ineffectual, however, and it was reduced to merely wallowing in envy.

These developments had troubled me deeply from the time of my first visit to Tibet. Initially, I had, like everyone else, decided to boycott China, determined that I would not visit Tibet again until the tyrannical Chinese regime had been ousted. I had also felt that it would be a sacrilege to witness the consequences of what the Chinese authorities had done to the country they had forcibly occupied, a country which rightfully belonged to the Dalai Lama and the Panchen Lama. I did not feel at the time that I could bring myself to look upon the ruins of the innumerable historically priceless chaityas and temples they had destroyed in the name of the Cultural Revolution nor to gaze at the sacred waters of the Brahmaputra, now sullied with the blood of thousands of innocent Tibetans. And so, I had kept putting off my visit to Tibet. So long as that regime was in power, I had told myself, I would not step into that country again.

Despite all the reasoning I subjected myself to, my inner voice was insistent. 'Don't try to appease your mental turmoil through reasoning,' it urged. 'Go where your heart leads. It is not logic that prevails on the path to freedom. The basic tenet or religion of a wanderer is to travel. Do not allow yourself to be trapped within the narrow confines of logic and reasoning and thereby lose your way.'

Listening to that voice carefully, I realized that I would have to visit Tibet again. Awareness dawned that the land of the Dalai Lama was not a product of the Chinese government, but a creation of God. We were social animals and if we were to survive in society, political and social storms would have to be weathered. The promise a wanderer made to himself was to move ahead— whatever be the situation—without any ties to hold him back or prejudices to obstruct his path. That, in fact, was what experience was all about. It would be foolish to shy away from passing through a forest simply because thorns might prick one's skin and potential hazards lurk within. Man had not, after all, avoided crossing the seas merely because it had been difficult to do so, had he?

No matter what injustice the Chinese regime might be perpetrating on its citizens, how could I possibly neglect the innocent, suffering Tibetans? Ignoring Tibet meant consigning a large segment of the innocent children of the Himalayas to oblivion. I had, therefore, little choice but to heed the dictates of my conscience. Whatever the risks, I would visit Tibet again. I would enjoy its natural beauty once more and savour the essence of its spirituality. I would experience the warmth of its people and absorb its unique ambience. And as I had done during my first visit, I would go around Kailash and Mansarovar.

Perhaps, the urge to defy all odds has something to do with the mystery associated with the forbidden. A locked room always holds a certain fascination for those prohibited from entering it. And so it was with my desire to go back to Tibet, a country now caught in a tussle between the Chinese attempt to destroy all traces of its indigenous culture and demands from the international community that Tibetan citizens be granted their legitimate rights. Prospective visitors from the West began to hound the Chinese government for permission to enter Tibet. It was becoming increasingly clear to the authorities that unless they threw open their doors to the world, there was every likelihood of those doors being broken down eventually. Moreover, the Chinese were keen on entering the arena of international trade and realized that it would be foolish to ignore the commercial possibilities offered by Europe and the United States of America.

So, exercising great circumspection, they began issuing visas to foreigners. The People's Republic of China had also taken note of India's growing stature among Third World countries. And it was not merely in the field of commerce that India excelled. It was also well on its way to becoming a nuclear power. In 1959, the Chinese had been able to ignore India's military capability, but now the situation had changed, with our country playing a rather different role in world politics. India was no longer a weak nation, reined in by the British. In its new incarnation, with a strong army at its disposal, it was a power to contend with. The Indian armed forces were keeping a vigilant eye on the Himalayas. The sort of injustice that had been inflicted on Tibet all these years would no longer be tolerated. With these various factors in mind, the Chinese government began its peace initiative. A new door to the Himalayas was opened. Once more, Indian pilgrims were granted permission to travel to the sacred sites of Kailashnath and Mansarovar.

We had been the last group of pilgrims to enter Tibet before the Dalai Lama fled to India and the Cultural Revolution took the country by storm. However, the wanderer in me did not have to wait for long. Before 1990 came around, I had been to Kailashnath twice by treading new paths. The purpose of my visit was to pay homage at Kailashnath and take a dip in the holy water of Mansarovar. I had flown from Nepalgunj to Simikot in a small plane. From there, I had no option but to cover the distance on foot, at least up to Nara. Five days later, I passed the highest point, the Nara La, situated at a height of 4,620 metres. Taking the only officially sanctioned route that existed between Nepal and Tibet and following the course of the Karnali river, I passed through the dangerous mountainous area where Nepal's timeless Hamla district was located, and arrived at the first Tibetan village across the border. Sher stood at 3,560 metres above sea level. Jeeps, mini buses and trekkers now plied frequently between Sher and Darchen. Jeeps passing through Sher-Purang and Gurla La, flanked by Rakshas Taal on the left and Mansarovar on the right, brought passengers directly to Darchen. It was from this city, dotted with a number of dharamsalas, big and small, that the journey to Kailashnath began.

As far as roads and transport were concerned, extensive development had certainly taken place in this remote region. The local gypsies now had a permanent place of their own. What really attracted the eye was, of course, the military trucks and all the paraphernalia that went with them.

All that pilgrims ever looked forward to, however, was visiting Kailashnath and Mansarovar. They would gaze at Kailashnath from a distance, as though in a trance. Pilgrims heading for Benares, Haridwar or Kailashnath invariably conducted themselves in the age-old manner of Hindu devotees. Having reached their goal following an arduous journey—one undertaken over the ages by generations of pilgrims—they would observe ancient traditions with all the fervour and enthusiasm one reserved for the new. All faiths apparently followed the same basic norms.

Visiting Kailashnath twice in rapid succession, I realized that the door that had been opened for pilgrims was, in reality, intended for trekkers to pass through. Men and women in quest of adventure made their way to this forbidden country nestled in the Himalayas to test in its unforgiving climes their physical prowess and mental strength. How far I travelled in the least possible time, what heights I ascended to, at what spots I set up camp—I jotted down all the facts in my diary in minute detail. The sacred mountains, however, remained inaccessible, oblivious to everything. Indian pilgrims travelling to this country via Almora faced all problems that came their way with a smile in the hope of accumulating good deeds and absolving themselves of their sins. Of course, as with humanity in general, even the pilgrims varied in their attitude and mentality. All men were individuals, after all.

In order to visit Kailashnath and Mansarovar, pilgrims were required to travel in a group from Delhi and have their permits procured from the Chinese authorities with the Indian government acting as an intermediary. Every step of the process had to be routed through the Chinese authorities. Tibet had only one airport—Gangar, at Lhasa. The city was a two-hour drive away from the airport by jeep or mini bus. Chengdu and Kathmandu served as links with other countries.

Since 1990, I had been making repeated attempts to secure permission to travel independently across Tibet and had written as much in my visa application. If one's application was turned down once by the authorities, waiting out a period of two years before submitting a second application was mandatory. My patience was infinite, however, and instead of allowing myself to become disheartened, I applied for a visa yet again. According to the reply sent by the authorities, travelling in a group across Tibet was permissible. Moving around independently was restricted to Lhasa. Of course, they had valid reasons for prohibiting individuals from travelling alone beyond the capital. The linguistic barrier might prove to be a serious hindrance for individuals like me who were not conversant with the language spoken in these parts.

Shortly afterwards, I became involved in preparations for the expeditions to the North and South Poles as a member of the team comprising men who were eminent explorers in their own right. Its success naturally gladdened our hearts and gave us a sense of achievement. Having taken some time off to recover from its rigours, I applied for a visa again to travel across Tibet on my own.

This time, my visa application was backed by concrete evidence of my experience and skills as a veteran traveller. Interestingly enough, I was summoned, the very next day, by the ambassador, Mr Ling, who greeted me with a smile and explained, 'You are conversant with neither Tibetan nor Chinese, the official language. So, for your own convenience, I would recommend that you take a Tibetan interpreter along with you wherever you go. We will then have no objections to your going wherever you want to, barring the restricted areas, of course.'

'Thank you so much!' I replied, pleased. A few weeks later, the year 2000 would be upon us. This was surely the best gift the millennium could have given me.

We set off on the scheduled date from Geneva, passing through Delhi and Kathmandu before arriving in Lhasa. I would be in the Tibetan capital after a long interval spanning four decades. The moment our flight touched down at Lhasa, I prayed to Kailashnath. Elation coursed through me as did a myriad emotions that filled my very being with a rare joie de vivre. I recalled the young boy I used to be once, a fugitive from home who had travelled from Gangtok to Lhasa with a group of ascetics so many years ago.

Someone at Customs welcomed me with the words, 'Mr De?'

'That's right,' I answered.

'I am Srongsheeshi, your interpreter. Welcome to Lhasa.'

As I entered the capital, I looked around me. What had happened, I asked myself. Where had I landed? Where was the Lhasa I had dreamed of? Just as Sadhu Baba's earthenware pot had smashed to smithereens in Gaya, my dreams shattered into tiny fragments. I stared at my surroundings in bewilderment. Srongsheeshi welcomed me once again as the car reached the hotel.

After checking in at the reception, I handed over my passport. The girl at the desk greeted me in English. 'Welcome to Lhasa!' she said. 'Your room is on the first floor. Number 108. Do go and relax while I have tea sent up.'

I thanked her for my room which, I thought, had an auspicious number. I carried no extra luggage. Everything I needed was in my backpack. As I entered the room, I was in for another surprise. It was done up with understated French elegance. Putting the bag down, I looked out of the window. The view was quite different from what I had expected. The revolution had wrought a massive change in Lhasa. Everything had been aggressively modernized. I had heard about it, but now I was seized by feelings I had never experienced before. I discovered for myself that the Lhasa of my adolescence was lost forever. I found myself breaking down in despair. Was this what I had returned for? It was a real shock for me, a terrible culture shock.

Tea accompanied by biscuits was sent up from Reception. It was quite cold, but I was well equipped for the climate. Quickly gulping down the tea, I set out, barely able to contain myself any longer. Srongsheeshi came up, rubbing his hands together, as soon as I emerged from the hotel.

'Sir, our boss wants to have a word with you regarding the places on your itinerary, your accommodation and your transportation charges. He will advise you on all such matters.'

I realized that there was no way I could avoid the man. Nor would it be prudent of me to do so. So I replied, 'All right, then. Come along.'

I was led to an office on the ground floor of a newly constructed house not far away. It looked somewhat like a police station. The moment I entered the room, the officer there invited me to take a seat. Then nudging the heater towards me with his foot, he continued in English, 'You must have noticed that we have electricity and even the telephones are working. Have a look at our computer. You can book hotel rooms in Beijing, Shanghai, Chengdu, Kunming, Nanjing and Xian directly from here. They are all decent five-star hotels. Each hotel has a restaurant, a coffee shop, a piano bar, a dance floor, a tennis court and a gym. You can avail of whatever you want, change in local currency, a guide, a private car—everything! Look, you can even find out what the temperature is.' The gentleman was evidently more than eager to show me all his gadgets.

I was forced to cry a halt to the proceedings. 'I'm sorry, but I'm awfully tired today,' I told him. 'I'll come back again tomorrow.'

'All right, that's fine with me,' he replied. 'You have seen that every sort of information is available from here. Please pay Srongsheeshi five dollars—his fee for today.'

I agreed to do so quite willingly and left his office with a sigh of relief. 'I'd like to explore the city on my own today,' I told

Srongsheeshi. 'Here's your five dollars. I'll meet you at the hotel tomorrow.'

But whatever I said made little difference. There was obviously going to be no respite for me.

'I owe you a lot of work for the five dollars you've paid me. I have done nothing for you today. All right, then. I will remain by your side. Or else, the boss will think that I am playing truant.'

'All right,' I agreed resignedly, 'but please remain silent unless you are asked a question.'

Srongsheeshi acquiesced to my request.

The hotel bore the same name as the city in which it was located—Lhasa. And it probably revived my memories of the city from my previous visit and created an aura of mystery. Pausing at a point between two roads, I caught a glimpse of the Potala Palace. Look, it seemed to call out to me, I am still here! In the new Lhasa, I was suddenly confronted by a fleeting image of the old. My heart surged with joy and I turned to Srongsheeshi and suggested, 'Let's go to the Potala.'

He looked at his watch and said, 'There are no restaurants there. Let us eat here first before making our way there.'

'Fine,' I agreed, 'let's go to a good Tibetan restaurant.'

'Why not leave that for another day?' he suggested. 'Let's go, instead, to a good Chinese joint today. A Tibetan restaurant offers no variety, sir.'

Having come all the way to Tibet, I would have to eat in a Chinese restaurant. Well, all right, I told myself, I was willing to go along even with that. Tibet was now a part of China. So how could I refuse? Starting from Kolkata and going on to Delhi, Geneva, Paris, London and New York, there were Chinese restaurants galore. If I did not venture to turn down an invitation to eat at a Chinese restaurant anywhere else in the world, why should I make it a point to do so here, I thought.

It was not really to appease my hunger that I sat down to the meal. It was to acquaint myself with the way food was served here that I ordered spring rolls and chop suey. Srongsheeshi asked for beer and roast duck. It had struck me as rather odd that the roads of the capital seemed swept clean of all its natives. Some distance away from the restaurants, however, people wearing heavy leather jackets and headgear like Amerindians could be seen clustered around billiard or table tennis games on the roadside. We were served Chinese black tea. When we asked for chang, the owner explained, 'It is usually not available, but I will prepare it for you by blending butter with the tea you have been served.'

The owner's suggestion left me in no doubt whatsoever that he was Chinese. I did gain something, though, by coming to this restaurant with my guide: A growing rapport with the man. 'Do you know how to play billiards?' I asked Srongsheeshi.

'Of course I do!' he replied, 'I play a good game. And what about you?'

'I'm afraid I don't,' I answered 'But isn't a billiard set very expensive?'

'Not at all,' he answered. 'On the contrary, it is quite affordable. Besides, one can play for free in any tea shop or club. The people running clubs, schools and other establishments have become quite shrewd these days. The village yokels turn the wheels and the youth play games. After all, one needs some means or the other to while away time!' Srongsheeshi burst into loud peals of laughter.

'Perhaps, you're right,' I said. 'In that case, the prayer beads are also a way of passing time. Right?'

'You've hit the nail on the head! These are nothing but old habits! If we have to improve our lifestyle, we must catch up with the times.'

The words and the convictions that prompted them were clearly the result of forced indoctrination. The dishes we had ordered were brought in.

'Tell me,' I said to my companion, 'this road is Barkhar, isn't it?'

'Are you familiar with it?' he asked in turn. 'Have you been here before?'

'I have read magazines and seen several documentaries on the place,' I replied promptly.

'Oh, that explains it! We will take this route to the Potala Palace. It's the easiest one to follow.'

I was circumspect in my conversation with Srongsheeshi and paid the bill at the end of our meal. In American dollars, it was next to nothing.

Emerging from the restaurant, I had walked some distance when, suddenly, my heart started beating wildly. 'I've found it! I've found it!' an inner voice seemed to exclaim, 'I have finally rediscovered the long-lost Jokhang Temple of my youth!' I rushed forward, propelled by a surge of elation and prostrated myself at the doors of the temple along with the other pilgrims who had come to offer their prayers. My presence there was a token of my love and respect for God. It was not motivated by some urgent prayer I wanted answered. And so, I surrendered my entire being, my heart and soul, to the deity of Jor Rimpoche. Having paid obeisance in Tibetan fashion, I rose to my feet and looked around me.

I noticed that the Jokhang Temple had remained quite unchanged over the years. With the crowd of new houses and buildings that had come up around it, however, it seemed a little hedged in. That was all. I found my joy resurfacing and my fortitude resurrected at the very thought of my being back here again. The pillar decorations at the entrance of Jokhang, the innumerable prayers offered there, awaiting fulfilment, the fragrance of incense sticks and the burning lamps—all created an aura that took me back four decades in a matter of moments. In no time at all, I was in communion with the Silent Monk who lingered somewhere within me.

The path circling right around the Jokhang Temple was known as Barkhar. The shops and markets clustered around the area were mostly full of antiques, prayers beads, bells, old coins and many such artefacts. Some sections of the Jokhang were completely modern. Yet, the parts adjoining the temple remained unchanged. The walls of the temple had darkened with the soot deposited by smoke from lamps and incense sticks kept burning continuously over the years. Unable to contain my exhilaration at being here again, I told Srongsheeshi, 'I'll be calling it a day now. Early tomorrow morning, much before breakfast, I will be coming down again. You need not accompany me here. I will find my way. Meet me here around nine and we will go to the Potala. Now, I will return to the Jokhang Temple. I loved its ambience.'

'Fine,' he replied, 'would you like to buy joss sticks? There's a certain shop I know of where you can.'

'Let's go there then,' I suggested. 'It will be cheaper there, I hope?' I added, in the manner of Americans.

After pointing me in the right direction, Srongsheeshi left.

Having completed my purchase, I returned to the temple. All around me were simple and devout Tibetans. The ambience of long ago was revived in my mind again. In the courtyard, I prayed in the traditional manner, prostrating myself, straightening up and beginning all over again. All the pilgrims there seemed to have found their own way of combating the pain involved in executing these movements

The next morning, at five-thirty, I set off for the morning prayers after completing my ablutions. It was bitterly cold outside and a dense fog had settled in. As luck would have it, however, on reaching the main temple premises, I found everyone snoring way blissfully! I presumed that they had, perhaps, fallen asleep after the early morning prayers. Some of them had developed hacking coughs that could be heard all over the place. Unfortunately, my unfamiliarity with the local language proved to be a barrier to communication. I just could not make myself understood. I waited it out till almost seven o' clock, the sole devotee, before returning to the hotel.

The receptionist entered my room with breakfast at eight and said, 'Good morning, sir. I believe you had gone jogging very early in the morning? It's very chilly out there. Do be careful that you don't catch cold.'

I was quite amazed at the way elements of the American lifestyle had caught up even with this remote Himalayan kingdom! 'Yes, I had, in fact, gone out,' I told her. 'Are there no programmes on at Jokhang?'

'Jokhang opens at eight in the morning with prayers and readings from the holy scriptures,' she replied.

'I noticed a lot of people sleeping out there.'

'They have certain pledges to honour,' she explained. 'Once all commitments are honoured, they will be leaving. Natives of Lhasa are not permitted to stay there.'

It was apparent that the norms of worship had changed. Everybody had to follow government directives.

Srongsheeshi was punctual and we made our way to the Jokhang Temple. Prayers had already started and offerings were being made to the deity. The head priest and other ascetics had started chanting in deep bass voices. The presiding deity of Jokhang had awakened with a lot of pomp and ceremony. Observing those swaying saffron robes, I seemed to find in them the rhythm of the Himalayas. When I rose to leave after an hour, Srongsheeshi said, 'Here, you only see saffron caps. In other monasteries, you will find red caps. They represent the two main streams of faith in Tibet.'

I concurred and added, 'The colour of their caps might be different, but both branches look up to the same Buddha for their spiritual guidance and growth. No matter what transport is availed of, reaching your destination is what matters, doesn't it?'

'Yes, you're right,' Srongsheeshi replied, 'that's what my father says too.'

It was the first time my guide had referred to anything personal.

Minutes after we had left Barkhar Bazaar, the shining beacon of Lhasa, the wondrous and holy Potala Palace came clearly into view.

It looked exactly like it had appeared to me in the past. My heart began thumping in excitement. Suddenly, my eyes were drawn to a couple of ladies who were mixing tea and butter in those huge traditional containers I had mentioned. Their hair was immaculately dressed and they wore brightly coloured outfits. Around their necks were strings of colourful beads. As soon as our glances met, they put out their tongues and greeted me with deep respect. One of them was young; the other had wrinkles drawing deep furrows down her face. We paused before their stall and that greatly pleased them. We went to the adjacent shop and asked for chang. My memories of the journey to Kailashnath were still vivid, but I was yet to recapture in its fullest sense the time I had spent in Lhasa so many years ago. Salted tea, prepared the traditional way, was still available in Lhasa, but the ambience I remembered was missing.

Atop the Marpori Mountains stood the thirteen-storeyed palace of the Dalai Lama. My heart bled at the thought of the palace being without its monarch since 1959 when Chinese soldiers had taken over and occupied the heartland of the Geluk-Pa sect.

Like any museum, the Potala Palace was open to members of the general public, but certain sections of it were out of bounds for tourists. Having climbed the wide staircase and passed through the verandas that lay in semi-darkness, visitors were left to their own devices. After negotiating the clammy darkness and dank rooms, we were only too relieved to come out onto the terrace bathed in bright sunlight. At first, I had presumed that Srongsheeshi and I were to be the only tourists. As it turned out, however, there were eight of us in a group. One had to purchase tickets, as in a museum, to visit the Potala and usually it was either the hotel where one put up or the tourist agency that saw to the arrangements. I observed that the Jokhang Temple and its courtyard were clearly visible from this section of the Potala Palace and the entire city of Lhasa, a heart-warming sight indeed, stretched out before us.

As I had mentioned earlier, the Potala Palace was divided into two sections comprising the White Palace and the Red Palace. It was in the white section that all the Dalai Lamas had lived and been reincarnated after their deaths. It was from here that they ruled the whole of Tibet. In the adjoining Red Palace grounds were all the royal temples. After the death of the Dalai Lama, the memorial stone set up in honour of his various incarnations along with their jewel-adorned, richly bedecked gold-plated statues made the place a storehouse of fabulous wealth and splendour. The guide whispered to me and the words sounded harsh: '…The Fourteenth Dalai Lama, Tenzing Gyatso, spent his childhood in this palace. In 1959, his aides and followers escaped to India with him.'

I ignored all such remarks.

The golden lions and dragons atop the pagodas, visible all the way from the terrace of the White Palace to the highest point of the red one, dazzled our eyes. Here, one could only gaze in wonder, but not in silence! The constant click of cameras, the steady drone of conversation and the glare of flashlights would not allow the mind to wander in the realm of dreams. Descending from the terrace, we entered the Red Palace. The beautifully intricate decoration on the walls could not be clearly discerned in the gloom. Furthermore, staining the walls and pillars of every temple was a layer of black oil. The guide declared with great pride, 'These beautiful decorations have been utterly ruined by smoke from burning candles and incense sticks and through the excessive use of wood coal. The Cultural Revolution has put a halt to such rituals that are little more than an expression of blind faith, unsubstantiated by science. We are now committed to conserving this treasure of the Chinese government. We are trying to have these thangkas and wall paintings cleaned and plastic-coated so that they can be preserved for many more years.'

After wandering about the mysterious rooms of the Potala for nearly an hour and a half, we came out. It was such a beautifully decorated edifice, I thought, and a well-maintained one, but for some mysterious reason, it was little more than a haunted house in my eyes. The rebellious spirits of those long dead seemed to crowd around me in their efforts to enlist my sympathy and I imagined them clamouring, 'Free us ... free us ... free us...'

It seemed to me that I would have to choose between being sensitive and sensible. It would quite simply have to be one or the other. We started moving towards the Jokhang Temple once more. Unlike the temples in India, where certain restrictions were imposed on devotees who sought to enter the premises, in Tibet, any pilgrim was free to enter a temple and pay his respects to the presiding deity by touching its feet. Owing to the extreme cold, no devotee was expected to have freshly bathed before entering the temple premises. Nor was he required to take off his footwear. I suddenly remembered having noticed, during my earlier visit to the temple, a precious metal alloy image of the deity Mahakaal to the right as soon as one entered. Beside it had been the image of a female deity, probably that of Mahakali. Encountering no resistance to my entry, I found the same image of Mahakaal, now grimy and neglected, standing beside the incense sticks and the piles of rice grain. Then I asked myself where Mahakali could possibly have hidden herself. I found myself steeped in a kind of ethereal joy and the whole day passed in a trance.

Observing my apparent lack of interest in Tibet and Lhasa, Srongsheeshi now found himself in a rather awkward position. He feared he might be losing a client. So, taking the initiative, he asked, 'Would you like to eat at a Tibetan restaurant today?'

'Of course I would!' I answered with a smile, adding in a very friendly manner, 'Srongsheeshi, I am going to ask you a couple of very personal questions. You are free to decide whether you want to answer them or·not. I will not take offence if you choose not to.'

A little hesitantly, the young man replied, 'Fine, go ahead...'

'Are you a Tibetan?' I asked him. 'Do you belong to Lhasa?'

'Yes, we are all Tibetans,' was his answer. 'We come from the village near the Kichu river. It takes nearly an hour to get there, that too, by jeep.'

'Then let me be honest with you. I have come to Tibet to explore the country and to get to know its people. I have been to China and have visited Shanghai, Beijing, Hong Kong, Jiang and Chengdu. But I have come here specifically to see Tibet. It is my request that you show me the original Tibet as far as possible. Of course, if this is at all feasible.'

Srongsheeshi pondered for a long while before replying, 'Give me some time, will you? I'll be back in half an hour. Go to that shop there with the gas cylinders outside the entrance. I have informed them in advance that you'll be having your meal there. There's rice, lentils, fish and vegetables and tea afterwards.'

I agreed right away and on going there, discovered that the owner of the restaurant was a Tibetan born and bred.

However, it was almost an hour later that Srongsheeshi returned, accompanied by an elderly man. The young man introduced the stranger to me with the following words: 'This is my father, sir, a very amiable and friendly man! Since I am a guide, I have to go along with whatever the boss decides. As a government guide, I am expected to abide by certain regulations and cannot answer all questions. But my father isn't bound by them and is at liberty to answer any queries put to him. We can take tourists anywhere in Lhasa. As a matter of fact, we can even invite them home for tea. But if the visitor is anyone associated with the Dalai Lama or a member of the press, we have special officers escorting us. You will appreciate that we too, are human and have to earn a living to survive. We have to secure our children's future. Our interests will be harmed if we do not toe the line.

'Ever since the Dalai Lama left this country, we have been living in hope every day of our lives and dreaming of an independent Tibet. Forty, no, forty-five years have gone by. We get to hear that the Dalai Lama is visiting places like Paris, London and New York. People are extending their support to him and bringing pressure to bear on China so that it is forced to grant Tibet its autonomy. The Dalai Lama will return to Lhasa once more and the flags of an independent Tibet will surround the Potala. I am now thirty. How long can I keep waiting? My parents belong to the era that has gone by. They have infinite patience. Our generation does not.

Those of us who talk of the Dalai Lama are issued warnings by the authorities. Those of us who aim for high posts are immediately transferred elsewhere. There are even people who have disappeared without a trace.

'Do you know that we constitute less than half the population of Lhasa? To avail of new business opportunities here, hordes of people from China are coming down to settle in our midst. On the pretext of trade with China, increasingly larger numbers of Chinese are being brought in. We, on the contrary, are not given similar opportunities. On some flimsy pretext or the other, we are ignored.

'Sir, believe me, we are also human and we want to survive. We are, somehow, clinging on and trying to survive. We are Tibetans and if we have to die, we would prefer to do so in our own country. We do not want to die as refugees. The only means of survival is through education. At least, the Chinese are providing us with that one facility. Let us see what happens in the future.'

Srongsheeshi paused as the food was brought in and served, a kind of light casserole containing mixed vegetables. It was cooked in our presence while separate bowls of rich pork were placed before us. The guide served as interpreter for his father who did not know English.

'This is my treat,' I told Srongsheeshi. 'Please don't hesitate to order whatever you want.'

Reassured, Srongsheeshi ordered a beer right away. During the meal, his father, whose name I did not know, began to speak: 'You cannot imagine the feeling of joy that swept through me when Shee spoke of you last night. It is only because of India that religion hasn't become extinct in Tibet today. For us out here, the language of religion is being eclipsed a little every day. In India, on the other hand, both the Tibetan language and religion are fiercely alive and growing. It is not merely the Revered Dalai Lama who is in India; a great many of our well-known and respected scholars as well as devout people live there today. Please feel free to ask me whatever you want to know. I will tell you all I can. My four elder brothers are in India and the youngest lives in Kathmandu. I have been there thrice.'

While his father was talking to me, Srongsheeshi interrupted with something urgent that he had to communicate. 'Before I forget,' he began, 'in case my boss or anybody else asks, you are here to find out about the Tibetan language and about the health and hygiene of this country's citizens. Be very careful. The government disapproves of all questions relating to religion, society and the Dalai Lama.'

Although Srongsheeshi's nickname was Shee, he did not want me to address him thus; we shared an official relationship, after all.

Thus began another story about Lhasa, one I had heard innumerable times, but was now witnessing for myself. Tourists had no problems eating in restaurants, particularly in Tibetan ones. Whatever be the hour, whenever a tourist entered and asked for a meal, it was happily prepared and served. Meat was readily available these days. The Chinese loved pork, and vegetables were being brought in from China at the time. We left after finishing our meal.

Srongsheeshi's father thanked me warmly for the meal and pointing to some shops in the distance, told his son, 'Introduce this nice gentleman to Lobsang Tashi,' before leaving us.

Deep within me, the young lad disguised as the Silent Monk gazed in speechless wonder at his dream world of Lhasa. I decided not to go out anywhere that day. Evening had descended on the city and I needed to absorb all that I had been taking in since the morning. It would be wiser to take it easy. I returned to the hotel. My room was quite plush and the heating worked well. Hot water too, was easily available. The establishment did not suffer by comparison with any standard Indian hotel.

Sitting on the sofa by the window, I gazed out at the view. I pondered on what my plight had been at the time of my first visit to this city and what it was now. On the previous occasion, physical discomforts had been of little consequence. It was the mysteriously alluring world of the mind and the soul that had preoccupied us all. Now, however, while the body was shielded from the harsh cold outside and there were arrangements for every sort of comfort, the Lhasa I had come in quest of still eluded me.

The following day, I set off with Srongsheeshi once more. Taking the Barkhar route, we reached the Jokhang Temple. The daily prayers and rituals had begun. I was fortunate, however. The moment we arrived there, a priest led me to the burning fire. Pointing to a spot near it, he suggested that I sit there and meditate. I followed his advice, and with Srongsheeshi joining me, soon became caught up in the ambience of prayer and meditation around me.

I left a little later, after acknowledging with a gesture the priest who had helped me to find a place for myself. Once outside, I bought candles of butter and incense sticks and made an offering to the Almighty.

Meanwhile, the shops around Lhasa had opened and the atmosphere of a fair ground prevailed. All kinds of wares, both old and new, were on offer. Old coins and articles used by lamas in the past made up a major portion of the goods on display. Taking the path that led to the north of the Jokhang Temple, we walked along the pavement and entered a charming boutique where we came face to face with Lobsang Tashi. He showed us around his establishment with great enthusiasm and we took in the display of thangka-beads, bags and dresses, particularly a special garment worn by lamas.

'I am not a lama,' I told him, 'so, will I be allowed to wear a garment of this kind?'

In response, Tashi smiled and answered, 'These are all clothes worn by Tibetans—both lamas and the ordinary citizen. A great many tourists buy them and even take them overseas.'

'They take them overseas as well?!' I was amazed.

'Of course! A number of organizations have trade links with the Chinese government. It is they who make all the arrangements. And why not? All our goods are handcrafted in Tibet. Are you interested in a potted history of our shop?'

'I most certainly am,' I replied.

Observing my enthusiasm, the gentleman asked us to be seated. Then having ordered tea from next door, he began giving us the background details of his shop. 'We have a total of five establishments,' he said, 'and we offer a hundred per cent guarantee that all the goods sold by us are handcrafted in our monastery by lamas. In the past, they had concentrated solely on prayers and meditation, but times have changed. In the past, we had the Dalai Lama and the Panchen Lama who constituted both the country's leader and government. They would allocate government funds to meet the expenses of the monastery. The government today does undertake the repair of certain monasteries, but it is the devotees who bear the expenses for the food consumed there. We are somehow managing to eke out a living. God only knows how long we will be able to carry on in this manner. It is fortunate that the Dalai Lama lives in India. The Panchen Lama passed away after spending twelve years in the Chinese dungeons.'

What Tashi had to say quite amazed me. How, I wondered, could he voice such thoughts, when he was living in Lhasa with all its restrictions imposed by the People's Republic of China! I could not contain my anxiety any longer and burst forth with, 'I am a tourist. Are you sure you won't be harassed for talking so freely to me?'

Srongsheeshi appeared to be interpreting my words quite well. For Tashi burst out laughing and replied, 'Shee has probably not told you about me. I am Lobsang Tashi, a disciple of the Panchen Lama. I am a lama and was in gaol for twenty long years. It was only recently, in 1997, that I was released from captivity. After the Revered Panchen Lama left for his heavenly abode, the Chinese government handed over a lump sum of money as compensation to all the monks of Tashi Lumpo, the core monastery, so that they could pay for their meals and meet their living expenses. I was on the committee. With the money we received, we opened these five boutiques. The income we earn from them provides us with the funds to run the monastery.'

'You have mentioned the committee. Will you please explain what it is all about?'

Chang—authentic Tibetan tea—was served in old bamboo containers, each of which could hold enough to fill at least three or four regular cups! The magic of the salty buttered beverage lay not in its flavour. But merely sipping it made one feel as though one were absorbing the very essence of Tibet. Sipping his tea, Tashiji continued.

'By the committee, we mean those of us who have been working in the administrative section of the various temples and gumphas in the past. Many of us have been released from prison by the government because of our rectitude and exemplary conduct. The new government has set up a committee comprising such men. Among us are government representatives who hold the actual reins of power; we merely provide a front for them. However, we are educated and knowledgeable in certain ways and we have experience in some matters. So, the government cannot disregard us entirely. Those of us who are ascetics work without pay of any kind. The expenses for our meals, clothes and transport are all borne by that government grant. While I run these boutiques, there are others like me who teach languages, take on responsibilities involving the daily rituals of worship or the celebration of various festivals. People of a certain age like us are called upon to maintain the standards of education and keep our heritage alive.'

'Do we take it then that everything is just as it used to be in the past?'

'Tibet had two great seers—the Panchen Lama and the Dalai Lama. One has gone to his eternal abode and the other is a homeless refugee in India. Our country has been without a spiritual leader for some years now. So, how can I claim everything is just the way it used to be? But I'm afraid I can't divulge more than I already have. Have a look around you and judge for yourself.'

Thanking him warmly, we purchased some souvenirs from his shop and left. Tashi had one stamped with my name and presented it to me as a gift.

I accepted his suggestion and started looking around the place myself. There was no question of being judgemental. I was simply an observer. A new clinic had been set up at some distance from the hotel. Srongsheeshi hoped we would pay a visit to the place as his uncle worked there. Besides, permission to visit the clinic had already been granted by the authorities, in case tourists were interested in health and educational issues.

The next day, we went to the Jokhang Temple again to pray. As usual, the priest asked me to take a seat. Sadly, I was unfamiliar with the Tibetan language and could not join the others in prayer. Once the prayers were over, we had another cup of tea before making our way to a new locality known as New Lhasa. And it was new indeed and glaringly different from the old Lhasa! The houses and shops selling different wares were as busy as the roads. The area resounded with the blare of radios and microphones. Arriving in this new section of the Tibetan capital which seemed to have developed in a rather haphazard and unwieldy manner, we felt as though we had suddenly entered some town in China. The clothes worn by the people here were all modern and the Tibetans on the streets seemed to be greatly outnumbered by the Chinese. At the hospital, we made our way through the crowded outpatient department and entered an office.

The medical officer in charge welcomed me. Since he was conversant with English, we could communicate with each other without the services of an interpreter. 'I'm afraid we're terribly busy today,' he explained in a tone of regret, 'and I cannot escort you around. I have heard that you are Indian and live abroad. You've learnt a great deal about us, I'm sure, most of it from articles written by journalists which play up everything that is negative. A lot of good work has also been done and is still being done. You should know about it too. Tourists, that is, foreign journalists do not understand our language. They therefore pick up isolated bits and pieces of information from non-government people and publish articles based on them. I don't have much spare time today. Or else, I would have shown you around myself. Allow me, however, to offer you a few pertinent facts. Our government is striving hard to improve the country's educational facilities and the economic condition of the people. A large number of new schools and hospitals have been set up all over the country, but nobody here wants to go to school. China is a vast country and in order to preserve national unity, a common language is required. The Tibetans do not want to learn Chinese. Unless they are educated, how will they be eligible for government jobs? We had helped start the Barefoot Doctor Programme in connection with a government project to teach villagers about the methods of acupuncture treatment. But nobody turned up! Tell me, what can we do?

'We want to revamp Lhasa completely. The government has no other objective but to make Tibet evolve and prosper like other Chinese provinces. We urge people with appropriate degrees and qualifications to apply for government posts. Besides, do you know something? You must have seen Lobsang Tashi's boutiques? That gentleman is on the Chotsok Committee, the government's religious programme. Its members oversee all temples, monasteries and religious institutions in Tibet and are empowered to decide how much money is to be allocated to or spent by any organization. Foreigners assume that we have scant respect for religion because we are communists. That is patently untrue. We are, in fact, helping to keep the country's heritage alive through this committee. I can go on at about the greatness of Tibet's present and future. But unfortunately, I am very busy today and cannot spare the time for it. Do get in touch with our Third Officer. He will show you around the hospital.'

The officer excused himself and left on his rounds. I merely listened to all that was being said. The Third Officer was Srongsheeshi's uncle. Here, the practice of addressing a man by his name or by prefixing his name with a 'Mr' was not prevalent. The form of address to be used in each case was determined by the official post a man held. I had been somewhat taken aback by the thorough briefing on Tibet I had been given by the medical officer the moment we entered the clinic. Srongsheeshi explained, 'It's the new government policy. It is impossible to know who is working for what purpose and where!'

I took an instant liking to Srongsheeshi's uncle. 'Ask me your questions and I will answer them,' he suggested with a smile.

'I believe all the viharas and other such holy places in Tibet are run by elderly lamas like Lobsang Tashi, aren't they?' I asked.

'Yes, they are,' he replied, 'but these lamas have no power at all. These days, all such institutions are being repaired and renovated. They are Tibet's chief tourist attraction.'

'The other officer claimed that despite the number of primary and secondary schools that had come up, there were virtually no students. Is that true?' I asked him.

'Yes, it is,' he confirmed, 'and the main reason is the language problem. Chinese is a complex language and Tibetans believe that in attempting to learn it, their children will forget their own language and culture and go over to China.'

'Why are the village hospitals empty?' I inquired.

'People suffering from minor ailments in this country do not go to hospital for treatment,' he explained. 'It is only when something is seriously wrong with them that they turn up. The tragedy is that the barefoot doctors are incapable of curing such ailments, because their medical education amounts to no more than a three-month course in Beijing. I too, was in Beijing for seven years during which I studied anatomy and physiology. I subsequently went in for the course in acupuncture. There is another problem: Tibetans have lost faith in the Chinese.'

'Why don't they trust them any longer?' I asked.

'For two reasons: firstly, the Chinese had created havoc in this country in 1959 on the pretext of propagating education and culture and secondly, Tibetans have still not been able to forget the inhuman torture to which they were subjected between 1987 and 1988.'

The gentleman spoke of these matters with such casual ease. And the import of what he said completely refuted his officer's claims. Unable to keep my curiosity in check, I asked, 'Tell me, isn't it dangerous for you to speak as frankly as you are doing now?'

The gentleman smiled a little and answered, 'Danger lurks at every step, but that doesn't stop us from talking the way we do. Of course, it also depends on what kind of tourist we are speaking to. From 1959 onwards, Tibet's religion and heritage have been brutally suppressed by the authorities on the pretext of taking China's Cultural Revolution to new heights. They tortured elderly religious leaders and forced them to submit to Chinese state policies. Many thousands of Tibetans have gone to India or Nepal. These days, the wise old Tibetan, the original citizen of this country, is rarely to be found within it. These men have all left Tibet.

'The new generation of Tibetans began its agitation in October 1987. In their bid for a free Tibet, many young men and women laid down their lives. Those who joined the movement were thrown into prison. This persecution continued till March 1988. There is no new leader in the country today. Those who remained were sent abroad on the excuse that they needed to further their career or improve their standard of living.

'You will come across many Tibetans around the Jokhang Temple and Potala Palace. None of them are locals. They all hail from the surrounding hilly areas. The new Lhasa overflows with Chinese from Sichuan, Kinghai and Yunnan. Of those who administer and coordinate this influx, starting from the army to even the hospital staff, almost everybody comes from Beijing. They know only too well that our spine has been broken and what we reveal to tourists will hardly make a difference to the state of affairs in this country. Rather, they flaunt themselves and proclaim to the world, "Look, here it is—an independent Tibet under Chinese occupation!" Tourists are free to go where they please and even to take photographs. The Tibetans are quite well off. The new generation of Tibetans has accepted the dictates of the Chinese government.

'Yes, it must be admitted that every word uttered comes to the notice of the authorities. Unless we provoke them by organizing public gatherings, openly opposing the government in Beijing or giving the Dalai Lama or anyone associated with him more importance than they deem fit, they will not harass us in any way.

'I have talked to you so freely, because you are from India, the country of Gandhi. In the past, our sages, beginning with the Buddha himself and going on to Narupa, Marpa, Milarepa and Padma Sambhava, all studied Indian philosophy and gained their wisdom from it. Even being in your presence is a way of accumulating good deeds. But it's time to take you on a proper round of our hospital.'

With that, Srongsheeshi's uncle showed us around the place. 'This long queue,' he explained, 'consists entirely of outdoor patients who were issued tickets in the morning and asked to wait their turn. Most of them suffer from stomach ailments, headaches or pain in the hip joints. There is a separate department for women. Our instruments for accident surgery are all new. We will be getting a scanner very soon. Have a look at the children's' department. We keep a vigilant watch on their vaccinations and nutrition. The building for infectious diseases is in that direction. We won't be visiting it. No harm in taking precautions. Birth control and family planning are two of our very successful projects. This is the first hospital of its kind in Lhasa, full of experienced doctors trained in modern methods of treatment. Our modern gadgets often frighten our patients into running away from the hospital!'

And, indeed the hospital's clean premises and modern ambience were praiseworthy. It was clear from all that I observed there that good work was also being done. Finally, came my last question: 'How many of those patients are Tibetans?'

The gentleman scratched his cheek thoughtfully and answered, 'Very few. Very few indeed. But Tibetans are forced to come here when they meet with accidents. There are also plenty of delivery cases. But the fact remains that we have gained immensely from this modernization.'

We left after thanking him warmly for the trouble he had taken to show us around.

Having reached the road, I turned to Srongsheeshi and

observed, 'Isn't it strange? I have heard both versions now—the Chinese and the Tibetan.'

Srongsheeshi sighed deeply and answered, 'I am an interpreter and, therefore, familiar with both languages.'

I let him off for the day.

The next day, I went on a survey of the Potala Palace. The path that allowed a round of the palace was known as the Linkhor. It was the time of the full moon and an auspicious moment for undertaking such a journey. Pilgrims who had travelled great distances to come here would frequent the temple and pray fervently, each in his own fashion. It was almost nine o'clock by the time we left the hotel and reached the temple. When our prayers were finally over and we set off, we found that many of the pilgrims were already ahead of us. It was a colourful sight and a beautiful one. It was the first time since I had arrived here that I saw nothing but Tibetans and my heart felt relieved of its burden.

Srongsheeshi said, 'All of them have travelled long distances and most are illiterate. Perhaps, they aren't even aware that there is no king anymore in the Potala Palace! So for whom is this tour intended?'

Placing a hand on Srongsheeshi's shoulder, I told him in a friendly manner, 'Rather than describing them as illiterate, it would, perhaps, be fairer to refer to them as simple believers. They are rural folk and though the Fourteenth Dalai Lama is no longer in the palace, the memorials of all the past Dalai Lamas are preserved there. Besides, within the palace is the temple. The devotion of these people is directed entirely towards them. Is it a sin to believe in your grandfather just because he is no longer alive?'

Glancing at me, Srongsheeshi smiled and remarked, 'You are truly wise. I cannot help but accept the logic of your argument. Is this what Indian philosophy is all about?'

'Yes,' was my firm answer. I prostrated myself on the ground and thus began my homage.

'None of those around us are natives of Lhasa,' Srongsheeshi explained. 'It is obvious the moment you set eyes on them. Most of the Chinese in Lhasa are Han. They do not come here on pilgrimage. After the agitation in which Tibetans took part and the persecution they have been subjected to, they are afraid to practise their religion openly. However, some religious institutions are reopening and thanks to government initiative, efforts are under way to revive the past once more. That young couple in front of us, with hair tied back in ponytails, hails from the Chang Tang region in the north; it is much colder there than it is in Lhasa. The inhabitants of that area always have woollens on. The two women just ahead of them come from the Tsang region. Farming is their livelihood. Look over there, at those people dressed in black trousers and jackets rather like cowboys in western movies. They are in the business of trading in yaks. Having made a good profit, they have come down from Lithang, east of Kham. You will notice something quite amusing now. Let us quickly move ahead of them.'

As we overtook them, the words, 'Kuchi kuchi' came to our ears. Glancing at me, Srongsheeshi laughed. 'Do you know what that means?'

'No,' I replied.

'It means "give". In other words, they're begging for alms. While on a tour of this sacred place, no pilgrim ever overtakes another. Those who do so are obviously tourists. Begging from tourists is not prohibited. You must have noticed that the number of beggars in Lhasa has gone down appreciably and we owe it entirely to the efforts of the Chinese government. Look at this handsome group of people to my right, so simple and straightforward! Do you know who they are? The brave Khampa warriors from the Kham region! In fact, these heroic and God-fearing gypsies are so courageous, that even the Chinese authorities are in awe of them. In 1959, when the Fourteenth Dalai Lama escaped to India, it was these intrepid warriors who prevented the Chinese soldiers from pursuing him. Every Tibetan will acknowledge without any hesitation whatsoever that it is these Khampas who still preserve the ancient traditions of the country.'

I forbade Srongsheeshi to move ahead of the other Tibetan pilgrims. Tradition, I felt, deserved respect.

It took us two-and-a-half hours to complete the tour, after which we made our way to the crowded area of Barkhar and drank the salted tea available at the fair. Then we returned to the hotel. Drawing closer, Srongsheeshi said shamefacedly, 'Beautiful young Chinese girls are available in Lhasa these days. Since the army headquarters are located here and plenty of businessmen frequent this city, a whole new locality has come up. We are guides and provide all kinds of information. So...'

I smiled and said, 'Thank you. We'll meet again tomorrow.'

A couple of days went by in this manner. The more I observed of what was going on around me, the more I had to pause and take stock. There was change everywhere, change on a massive scale! Everything I observed around me offered clear indications that in the political, commercial, religious and cultural arena, Lhasa was truly overrun by the government of the People's Republic. For a country's capital offers, oftener than not, insights into its true identity. For a couple of days, I thoroughly explored the old and new Lhasa before travelling beyond the city's perimeter with Srongsheeshi.

Not far from the city stood two Buddhist viharas: Sera and Drepung. Almost fifty kilometres away was Ganden, the third monastery. When the Dalai Lamas were in power, these three institutions had been the strongholds of Tibetan religion and philosophy. The Panchen Lama had reigned over Shigatse.

Sera, according to many, was, by far, the best Buddhist vihara and centre of learning for the lamas. It had carved its niche in the Buddhist world by offering its students access to different aspects of knowledge and by maintaining exceptionally high scholastic standards. It stretched over a sprawling expanse of land and was the principal seat of the Geluk-Pa sect. In local parlance, it was known as Dop Dop and consisted of five universities.

In 1959, when the Dalai Lama became a fugitive, almost nine thousand monks were living in the Sera Monastery, excluding the soldier inmates. For Sera was also the principal centre of training for the Tibetan armed forces. The Dalai Lama's bodyguards, in particular, were recruited from this monastery. As a result, his departure from Tibet had provoked the Chinese government into bringing great pressure to bear on the Sera Monastery and eventually led them to mount an attack on it. The People's Liberation Army of China had assumed that this religious institution housed all the soldiers. Therefore, along with their own troops, they had brought along special cannons with which to attack the monastery. The onslaught caused the death of innumerable resident scholar monks and patriots. Those who survived fled with the wounded. The scars of that heinous military attack on Sera are still visible today.

Owing to the deplorable Chinese attack on the monastery, all its programmes ground to a halt. The laws subsequently enforced in the name of the Cultural Revolution were calculated to eradicate all intellectual debate and traces of a progressive culture. But who could destroy what was destined to survive? While the Chinese authorities were introducing legislation to curb the activities that contributed to the pride and renown of Tibet's Sera Monastery, Indian lamas, Tibetan expatriates in India and the Dalai Lama's supporters went on to establish the New Sera Buddhist Vihara on Indian soil. I consider myself blessed in being able to participate in the magnificent and moving occasion that marked the inauguration of this religious institution by His Holiness the Fourteenth Dalai Lama in December 1997. The latter had repeatedly expressed his gratitude to the locals as well as to the Tibetan refugees of Karnataka's Bylakuppe for their efforts in making this possible.

But in 2000, at a convention organized in Geneva to honour him, the Dalai Lama had admitted to me, 'India's Bylakuppe has captured the essence of the religious education imparted at the Buddhist viharas, particularly in the area of debate. This is mainly due to the fact that most of the teachers and mentors of the Sera Vihara have come away to India. But sadly, nearly all the learned teachers have passed away. Perhaps, they have been reborn on Indian soil and are toiling for the preservation of Buddhist religion and culture?'

Not all is lost, however. The Chinese authorities are, at present, organizing the repair and renovation of the Sera Vihara. Devotee artisans are engaged in repairing the thangkas, the artwork on the walls and the neglected statues. People are arriving in droves from the rural areas to help in the repair work on the walls. The tourists who visit the country are also exerting pressure on the authorities to restore the vihara to its original condition when it was a religious institution of some consequence.

What was most heartening, however, was my discovery that the main body of the temple had been left intact. Hygriba was just as it had been—undisturbed. The basic chambers had been rearranged. But even by lightly scratching on the walls, one could revive the fragrance and feel of what it had been in the past.

Srongsheeshi introduced me to the chief priest. The moment he heard I was from Bengal, he said, 'Milarepa … Arpa … Larpa

... all imbibed knowledge from their mentor and guide, Atish. There must be a huge temple dedicated to him in Kolkata?'

'I'm afraid not,' I replied in a tone of regret, 'there is no monument commemorating him either in Kolkata or in its immediate vicinity. It is you and your brethren who have kept him alive in your memories. I have recently written a play in Bengali dedicated to the Tibetan mentor and guide, Milarepa. It is being staged across Kolkata. Through the message it communicates, we are trying to propagate Milarepa's philosophy.'

Overjoyed at my words, he said reverentially, 'Please come and have a meal with me this evening. While we eat together, I will have the pleasure of listening to all you have to say.'

It was my misfortune that though I was ready and willing, Srongsheeshi informed me, 'Transport has been arranged for two o' clock and there will be problems if we do not return by nightfall from our tour of Drepung. If you wish to come here, however, a programme can be set up for later.'

I had the distinct feeling that the ascetic had wanted to say something important to me. Unfortunately, the moment passed and whatever it was remained unuttered.

The area covered an extensive expanse of land dotted with temples, monasteries and chorten. But instead of the original nine thousand inmates, there were only two hundred today. Occasionally, when students had enrolled for various courses, the number swelled to almost four hundred. Students came here for higher education and stayed for periods varying from three to twelve months, whereas in the past, students were known to stay for ten years, a period that might easily stretch to twice that length of time. I reflected that many years had passed and these changes were, perhaps, natural and inevitable.

Having spent nearly two hours at the Sera Monastery, we were on our way again. The driver of our jeep was Chinese, a cheerful, agile know-all. The fact that he did not understand English was, however, a blessing. In the course of conversation, he remarked, 'I believe that before the Chinese occupation, thousands of students would come to study at this huge university. But today, they have nothing to do. How do the people here while away the hours?'

As soon as Srongsheeshi had interpreted his words, I answered, 'I have been to your capital, Beijing. There was an emperor there in the past. Now the emperor is no longer there, but the palace remains. From the historical point of view, the place has tremendous importance and value. Thousands of government employees have been recruited to maintain the royal palace and all it contains. Their duties also involve keeping the interiors of the palace clean and dust-free for visiting tourists. Here, the Sera Monastery and the Potala Palace are also serving to keep alive the ancient memories of Tibet. The lamas have a slightly more important role than the government employees in Beijing in that they are trying to keep alive the ancient knowledge that used to be imparted in the temples and monasteries of this country. That is also the objective of the Chinese government. Time moves on. You drive a car, Srongsheeshi acts as an interpreter and the lamas carry on being lamas.'

The driver conceded the point. The car stopped for petrol. Nearby was a restaurant, whose owner, obviously a Nepalese, had inexpensive and excellent Nepalese food on offer. I understood the scenario. Stopping for petrol was merely a pretext. A couple had emerged from within the instant our car pulled up. Their appearance indicated that they were from Nepal. They greeted us cordially, palms joined together. Srongsheeshi placed our order—rice, lentils, chicken and fried potatoes.

As soon as he saw me, the gentleman remarked, 'Sometimes, there are customers from Nepal. But there are hardly ever any Indians. I will serve you food of such quality that you will always remember this meal.'

With an hour in hand, I set off with Srongsheeshi to visit a neighbouring village that was made up of around fifty to sixty dwellings. All the houses were constructed from old stones layered with clay and were topped with thatched roofs. There were children playing outside. It was a pleasure gazing upon this old and familiar sight. The villagers greeted us by putting out their tongues in the usual manner.

'This is actually a Nepalese village,' Srongsheeshi explained. 'You must have noticed in Lhasa that two communities are doing quite well in business. They travel to Beijing as well as to Kathmandu. It is also a fact that they engage in a bit of smuggling on the side. However, there is no doubt that they are extremely hardworking and persevering.'

'Which are the two communities?' I inquired.

'The Nepalese and the Tibetan Muslims,' he told me. 'They are not particularly concerned about the turmoil that afflicts this country. Their primary concern is trade. They were there during the time of the Dalai Lama and they are still around.'

Going around the place, I found that despite being Nepalese, these people had adapted themselves quite well to the Tibetan way of life. It was time for our meal and we returned to the restaurant. And true to his word, the owner proved to be quite a chef.

'I have very good flour in stock and have made some hand-rolled bread for you,' he informed me.

'Thank you so much,' I replied.

After the meal was over, it was back to the jeep. We set off again and in a short while, the Drepung Vihara, a beautifully carved fort nestling against the mountainside, came into view. As the vehicle pulled up, raising a cloud of dust, groups of lamas came running out. On catching sight of us, they lined up alongside the jeep, palms joined in greeting, as though we were celebrities! They seemed to be familiar with Srongsheeshi, the driver and the official jeep.

An elderly lama came forward and greeted us. 'Should we organize a meal for you?' he asked.

'No, thank you,' we replied. 'We have just had our meal.'

'Then you must have tea with us before you leave. I believe you are from Bengal. That is wonderful! You must be familiar with Pali? I had studied the language for a year. But these days, there is no teacher available for it.'

The gentleman was obviously delighted by our arrival. He had been instructed over the telephone to talk to me about the new system of education and so launched into his lecture.

I stopped him midway by reminding him, 'I don't think we've been introduced.'

'I am the deputy chief here. Our chief lives in Lhasa. Look, this is the famous Drepung Buddhist Vihara. It is the largest and holiest institution of its kind in all Tibet. The Second, Third and Fourth Dalai Lamas lived here. They reigned over this great country much before the Potala Palace was built. Construction on the Potala Palace was begun in the era of His Holiness the Fifth Dalai Lama. It was from here that the Dalai Lama conceived the idea of the Potala and oversaw its construction. His memorial stone lies in the Potala Palace whereas here lie the memorial stones of the Second, Third and Fourth Dalai Lamas. Actually, till the era of the Fourth Dalai Lama, Drepung was regarded as the capital of Tibet. The core temple palace and Buddhist vihara were constructed in 1416. This place housed four great universities and a palatial chamber for the congregation of people coming from as far away as India's Ladakh region. The representatives of the Dalai Lama here would travel as far as Kham, Amdo and Ladakh.'

He continued to talk as I gazed in mesmerized wonder at this unique marvel nestled in the mountains. The paintings on the walls were as beautiful as the images on the thangkas and the innumerable shelves accommodating books. There were plenty of temples and stupas around and flags fluttered in the breeze. My wonderstruck gaze fell on a pair of dilapidated temples.

Drawing my attention away from them, the deputy continued to spout all that he had been trained to say. 'The government quarters were located here in the past,' he went on. 'Around them were the living quarters of the zamindar and the ruling authorities. Almost eight thousand people used to live here on a permanent basis. But at the time, no adequate arrangements were in place for health care. There was only one treatment centre for distinguished lamas and the extremely wealthy. No one spared a thought for the poor. Now, a Barefoot Centre has been opened for the purpose of teaching acupuncture. The government is keeping a stern eye on education. All citizens have to be educated and there will be no beggars in the country. Earlier, by focussing on religion, the feudal government of the time would safeguard its own interests and ignore the needs of the poor. All that has changed. Since 1959, the great cultural and economic revolution has seen to it that cultivable land is granted to farmers free of cost. Tibet can no longer be described as a barren, desert-like region. Its fields are now full of crops and vegetables.'

'You did not say much about that huge dilapidated building there, did you?'

At my question, he swallowed before answering, 'When the Chinese soldiers were engaged in a heroic struggle to rescue the poor and contribute to the welfare of Tibet, a few selfish individuals and wealthy persons tried, in their own interest, to prevent them from doing so. Chinese cannons put paid to their nefarious plans and this building merely bears witness to that conflict. It must be obvious to you that a war can never be one-sided.'

As soon as the man paused, I asked him, 'The inhabitants of this place were unarmed, peace-loving Buddhist lamas and monks. Why did cannons have to be used against them?'

'The lamas were peace-loving,' he countered, 'but they were puppets in the hands of the feudal government.'

I put forth my next question: 'Where were you trained and educated in order to run this monastery?'

'I was in Beijing for three years and my first posting was in Chengdu. After spending a year there, I was promoted and posted here. My mother tongue is Tibetan and the official language is Chinese. In future, instead of two languages, we will have only one. All the old religious texts and scriptures are being translated into Chinese. That will simplify matters for the average citizen.'

After finishing our tour, we had a cup of tea together before our departure. Needless to say, after our visit to Sera and Drepung, I was in no frame of mind to see anything else. To witness the damage that had been done by cannons to the Buddhist viharas pained me greatly. In place of the picturesque houses and stupas that stood in front of us, a scene of mass destruction with gentle and peace-loving ascetics being slaughtered in cold blood rose up before me. I was in no mood to enjoy the mountainous beauty of Drepung and preferred to turn back to Lhasa. On the way back, we stopped at the Ramche Temple for fifteen minutes and had a cup of tea at a nearby stall.

Back in Lhasa, I let Srongsheeshi and the driver off for the day. It was only 4 p.m. I went up to my room and lay down on the bed. There had been much worth seeing in the Buddhist viharas and we had also managed to cover a great deal. But try as I might, I could not shake off the memory of the damage done by the Chinese cannons and all the wanton destruction it bore testimony to. The image continued to float before my eyes. Unable to relax or rest, I went out again.

Amazingly enough, there wasn't a single Tibetan to be seen anywhere. Milling around were Chinese soldiers and yet more Chinese soldiers. All the street names and shop hoardings were in Chinese. In certain places, the street names were in English for the exclusive benefit of visiting tourists. There was nothing in Tibetan and I had been given clever answers to my queries about it. 'The Tibetans are quite familiar with their own roads and do not need directions,' I was informed smartly. Srongsheeshi told me that the signboards in Chinese were intended for Chinese army personnel, Chinese businessmen and Chinese government workers. A Chinese song in a shrill female voice blared out of a transistor. Was I really in Tibet or in Chengdu, I wondered.

We spent two more days in Lhasa where the two main attractions were the Jokhang Temple and the Barkhar Market. The rest was 'made in China', so to speak. The Potala Palace was little better than a museum now. My experience here was no different from that of travelling to either Athens, Rome, Paris or Prague and visiting the museums there, looking at the artefacts in any European city or going through the palaces of Delhi, Jaipur and Hyderabad. The guides directed us through all the narrow alleys and talked of art and culture, but no one mentioned the country's religion and philosophy. No sooner was the present Dalai Lama mentioned than they referred to the 'Dalai Seventh' or the 'Dalai Eighth'.

It was time I left Lhasa, I thought. I had been to Mansarovar and Kailashnath a number of times, but had not come this way since 1956. I visited the tourist office to plan a trip outside Lhasa. Srongsheeshi's boss showed me every possible courtesy and I broached the subject of my tour and the car I would need to hire for the purpose. I needn't have worried about these details, for I discovered that all the arrangements were in place. I chose an itinerary from the available ones. A group of tourists who had come in from their native Germany would be going trekking north of Lhasa. I chose to join them. I proposed going up to Naam Sarovar. Everyone was happy, the tourist officials even more so. They were going to make a substantial profit on the cars, drivers and guide we hired as well as on the restaurants we would visit. In short, everything. But the greatest benefit of all was that such tourists would ask no questions either about the Dalai Lama or about the country's religion and politics.

The total expenses for the entire trip—US$20 a day— that would last three nights and four days, would be shared between five of us. We would be spending the first night in a rest house. On the second and third nights, we would camp out. The tourist officer informed us that we had benefited from the arrangement, because the trip was now costing us only half the regular price. For a similar proposal coming in from abroad, there would have been an additional charge of US$410, with another ten dollars levied as a fee towards the government fund allocated for conservations. It was only because we were making the booking from Lhasa that we were saving ourselves twenty dollars.

'I really appreciate that,' I said in reply. 'Thank you so much!'

No sooner had we left the tourist office than Srongsheeshi remarked, 'You really are very lucky. They weren't keen on granting you permission to go alone to the Ganden Buddhist Vihara. The advantage in having German and American tourists visit is that they don't ask too many probing questions.'

We set off early next morning, leaving our luggage behind in the hotel, because we would be coming right back here four days later. The jeep, a four-wheel drive, was quite a spacious vehicle and could have comfortably accommodated eight passengers. There were only seven of us, including the driver. Three of us sat up in front with him, while the rest sat at the back. The driver claimed such a journey was possible even with a passenger load of a dozen tourists. Two of the Germans had actually brought their girlfriends along for what they regarded as an adventure trip. The group was a cheerful and friendly one and I soon came to know Mark and Judith, Hans and Eliza. They had put up at another hotel and the jeep arrived after picking them up. Having exchanged introductions and greetings, we got in and were on our way.

The first destination on our itinerary was Lhasa's Norbulingka Palace, followed by a tour of the modern township. From there, it was all the way to Ganden where we would be having lunch. Before we reached Norbulingka, however, Srongsheeshi launched into his commentary. When he realized that his voice was being drowned out by the noise emitted by the jeep's engine, the guide picked up the mike.

'Look this way,' he began, 'this very modern Internet site building is the first of its kind in Tibet. Look at the avenue—so broad and clean. All along it are several representative offices with headquarters in Beijing. The old Lhasa and the new are as different as night and day. All the Chinese national festivals are celebrated here, not forgetting the annual procession of the armed forces. It is truly a sight to behold! The Tibetan New Year, the Festival of Shakyamuni and other such traditional festivals are held in the Jokhang Temple and in Old Lhasa. All such customs and traditions have been preserved.'

The guide's words implied that had it not been for the intervention of the Chinese government, Tibet would have remained more or less the way it used to be four hundred years ago. The car stopped at a Chinese restaurant so that we could have tea and take some pictures of the new Lhasa. As I had noticed earlier, the indecipherable signboards in this area of the city were mostly in Chinese. Then we started out on the route to Norbulingka. I observed, when we reached it, that it was exactly as I remembered it, except that it looked, at first glance, as though it had acquired a fresh coat of paint.

'Now, take a look at the Norbulingka, the Dalai Lama's summer palace,' Srongsheeshi began. 'It is hardly comparable to the Potala, but the architectural structure and the designing of the doors are similar.'

At the very sight of the Norbulingka Palace, my mind seemed to retreat into the past, seeking a comparison of the edifice as it now appeared with the way it had been. Some of my past impressions matched those of the present. But an unbreachable divide separated the perspective of the Silent Monk I had been so many years ago from the views I now held as an adult. Dismissing the inevitable urge to fall back on comparisons, I concentrated on Srongsheeshi's words.

'This place,' he went on, 'located to the west of Lhasa, had originally been a wasteland, overgrown with trees and weeds. But it had an underground spring. The temperature of the water there was just perfect for bathing. The Seventh Dalai Lama had been greatly troubled by an aching foot and he found great relief after bathing in the spring water a couple of times. Since then, he would come every summer to bathe there. Coming to know of this, the resident commissioner from the Qing Dynasty built a small house here and named it Wunaopozhang. Locals had their own name for it, of course, but the main objective was to ensure that the Dalai Lama's visit was as comfortable as possible whenever he came down.

'Then the Dalai Lama himself had a palatial edifice built here and named it Gesangpozhang. Construction began on the interiors and on accommodation for visitors. The garden was also laid out. The old place was properly paved in concrete and transformed into a sacred bathing area. Once the construction work was over, the Dalais spent the summer months here, absorbed in study, till they reached the age of eighteen. In the summer, the ambience here is worth experiencing.'

Listening to him revived the past for me. An image flashed in my mind of the Fourteenth Dalai Lama, Tenzing Gyatso, that strapping young ascetic I had seen in this very place years ago. My first glimpse of him had remained firmly embedded in my memory. His appearance had seemed strangely mesmerizing to me at the time. I now found myself travelling back to that moment in the past when the charismatic personality of the Dalai Lama, an emblem of Tibet itself, had overwhelmed a sixteen-year-old fugitive from India. I found myself having to drag my mind back to the present with considerable difficulty. Where was the similarity, I wondered, between my memory of the man I had seen then and the person I met in Lausanne last year? Of course, there was a link between the latter and the princely figure I had stolen a glimpse of in the garden at Norbulingka. Some unnamed persons had so firmly bound that young ascetic in the fetters of religion and meditation that he had had no freedom at all to gaze at the world. It was the same individual I would set eyes on in Dharamsala, Gaya, France and America. And I would discover to my surprise that beyond the confines of the Potala and the Norbulingka, he was a different man altogether, a free man.

Did the two not share the same mind, the same soul, I wondered. I could not have presumed, as an adolescent, to be familiar with the glorious story of this great Tibetan personality and so, a boy with a different mindset altogether had gazed in wonder at the monarch of the Norbulingka and Potala palaces. In Switzerland, I was already acquainted with and knew a little about Tibet when I interacted with the Dalai Lama. But somewhere at the back of my mind, the awestruck teenager continued to linger.

'Come, let's get back into the car again,' I heard Srongsheeshi say, breaking into my reverie. Gazing out of the jeep, I bade farewell to the Norbulingka Palace for the last time. The vehicle moved along the approach to a valley. A question that had been simmering in my mind could no longer be kept from rising to the surface. 'Why did you persist in referring to the Dalai Lama as "Dalai"?' I asked Srongsheeshi. 'After all, he is the Dalai Lama. A little respect would be quite in order here, don't you think, seeing that you're Tibetan?'

'That's right,' he replied, 'I am, indeed, Tibetan. But I am also a guide and interpreter employed by the Chinese government. Like others of my kind, I have been trained in Beijing, in keeping with their particular norms. We are obliged to abide by them and everything else that has been instilled in us at the Language, Guide and Architecture School in the Chinese capital. You might have heard of our chief secretary, Mr Zhang Huizhen. He is a historian, specializing in Chinese and Tibetan history, and has been to the United States several times.'

'Fine,' I shot back. 'In that case, your qualifications are truly laudable.'

Having left Lhasa behind us, I seemed to breathe free again. The jeep moved noisily ahead along a route that would have been monotonous had it not been for the indescribably beautiful valley it cut through. We passed several small villages on the way and in the distance, the mysterious snowy peaks rose before us. Visible, far away, were houses clinging precariously to the mountainside. Drawing our attention to what he was pointing at, Srongsheeshi announced, 'That is the Ganden Monastery in all its picturesque beauty!'

It was the first time I had set eyes on such remarkable architecture. The beauty that surrounded me on all sides left me quite speechless. Three rockfaces had been put to use in constructing these incredible palatial edifices. As the car drew closer to this architectural marvel before us, my amazement knew no bounds. Captivated as we were by their compelling beauty, we couldn't have been blamed for assuming that these structures, crafted elsewhere, no doubt, by magicians, had been subsequently transported here by winged giants and set down precariously on the mountainsides at a height of 4,300 metres! From the architectural point of view, the Ganden Monastery, also known by various other names, was certainly far more impressive than the Potala. And it was a historical landmark too, thanks to Songkhapa who had founded the Geluk-Pa sect in 1409. Srongsheeshi did not have to utter a word to enhance our appreciation of this place. Like the sunset, the enchanting loveliness of the garden at the Ganden Monastery spoke for itself. While my fellow tourists were busy capturing it all on film, I put my heart and soul into concentrating on all that surrounded me and absorbed its celestial beauty deep within myself. Judith, my German fellow traveller, inquired, 'Didn't you bring a camera with you? Never mind. I will send you a copy of the pictures once we return to Germany.'

'Thank you,' I said. 'You are capturing the scene before you on film. But when you are dead and gone, these pictures will be left behind. I, on the other hand, am absorbing what I see with my very heart and soul, with every bit of life force I have within me. I will allow the memory of every single moment I enjoy here flow through my entire being so that in my next birth, I will be able to savour its beauty all over again. Even when I am reborn in another body, a different physical form from the one I now inhabit, the ethereal manifestation of these moments will be there for me to experience anew.'

'Do you believe in reincarnation?' she asked me.

'I do.'

'You really are fortunate to be an Indian, a Hindu,' was her answer.

The vehicle entered the grounds of the monastery through a huge gateway. Five young ascetics, wrapped in saffron blankets, stood waiting at the parking space nearby, ready to welcome us with a smile. We entered a huge hall. Some distance away, a colossal image of the Buddha bestowed his blessings on us. There were innumerable thangkas on the walls. The adjoining room was a library, full of religious tomes. Multicoloured pictures of the life of the Buddha in its different phases greeted us everywhere. Every single pillar in the hall had been lovingly painted. All the articles used for the rituals of daily worship gleamed as though they were brand new. The care that had gone into the maintenance of this place, the labour that had contributed to its pristine state and the artistic mind that had lent it all its beauty, now clearly visible in the bright light, were amazing to behold.

An elderly monk approached us and we were introduced. He turned out to be the institution's head lama. I prostrated myself on the ground before him as a mark of respect, while the others shook hands.

Very humbly, the lama asked me, 'Are you Indian?'

'Yes, sir,' I answered, 'I am.'

'Our morning prayers and readings from the scriptures are over. The boys have all gone to the dining room for their meal. But I can always send for them and ask them to recite aloud for you. That they should be able to do.'

'Please don't trouble yourself over it,' I begged him.

'Then let us sit down to a meal together,' he suggested.

'I wouldn't mind, but it all depends on Srongsheeshi,' I told him.

'I have no problems about it either,' Srongsheeshi reassured us.

'Do have your meal,' said the lama 'And later, if you can see your way to leaving a donation for the monastery, it will help greatly in its upkeep.'

We agreed. I think this had been included in our programme. We arrived at the college hall and were quite amazed at the absolute silence that reigned there despite the presence of nearly two hundred students. We joined the boys for the meal that consisted of a kind of flour, boiled potatoes and cauliflower curry.

After the meal was over, the head lama began to give us a great deal of information about the monastery. We learnt that the Ganden Monastery was the largest educational institution in the country. In 1959, almost five thousand five hundred monks had lived here, around the same number that resided at the monasteries of Sera and Drepung. Compared to those two monasteries, however, the standards followed here at Ganden were much higher. In fact, the spiritual and educational mentors for the Dalai Lama were chosen from this monastery. Ganden also stood out from other religious institutions of its kind in that the head lama here was not selected on the basis of his past incarnations, but on his eligibility as the most erudite and able candidate among all the lamas in the monasteries of Tibet. The chief of Ganden had to be a truly worthy man.

I was quite absorbed in the head lama's lecture to us, but my companions were eager to take photographs and record their impressions of the daily regimen here so that they could preserve them for posterity. It was imperative for them, when they returned home, to have concrete evidence in the form of photographs to substantiate all the stories they had to tell. 'The market is overflowing with books on Tibet,' they declared. 'Here, all the material one could want is available. The trick is to know what to choose. We have come to see, to witness everything first-hand as far as possible.'

So, Srongsheeshi was forced to rise and go looking around the monastery. History, it seemed, was dispensable as far as these visitors were concerned.

The unfortunate part was that the head lama knew neither English nor Nepalese. 'I have a question,' I told him. 'Apart from education and religion, what else attracts an average tourist like me on a pilgrimage to Tibet?'

'Visitors come to this huge monastery to see the Lord Buddha, just as you have done. This is followed by a tour around the Linkhor, similar to the one undertaken by devotees around Kailashnath.'

Interpreting the conversation for me, Srongsheeshi added at once, 'It is for the purpose of trekking at Linkhor that we have come here. There are about twenty locals waiting for us. We will enjoy ourselves while they accumulate good deeds.'

Ganden stretched over a vast area. It was not merely a monastery, but rather, a monastery-cum-village. A great many temples, bridges, chorten and stupas stood about the place. Ascetics milled around in large numbers. It was all so beautiful. And then I got a rude shock.

Having seen some new constructions around the place, we were stunned to come upon a huge pile of rubble, similar to the kind found at the site of a natural disaster like an earthquake. We came to an abrupt halt. Without missing a beat, Srongsheeshi launched into an explanation. 'Chinese soldiers did not attack this place in 1959,' he volunteered. 'But in 1966, the People's Liberation Army suddenly launched an assault. All the houses of this principal monastery were destroyed in the bomb attack. Almost half the village was reduced to rubble. It is heartening, however, to think of the way all the ascetics and villagers and almost everybody from Lhasa's Tibetan community raised funds and contributed generously to ensure that the historical Ganden Monastery would rise again. However, despite all such efforts, the ancient art form that was once manifest in this monastery, could not be replicated. The

Chinese government is trying very hard these days to encourage
Tibetan art and culture for the purpose of restoration.'

Without being a first-hand witness to the scars left by the
destruction, it was impossible to believe that such unspeakable acts
could be perpetrated. If Tibet had become a part of China, I
mused, the destruction of Tibet implied that China too was
similarly affected. What connection a cultural revolution could
have with all this destruction was beyond my comprehension.

I had been in a comparatively better frame of mind after
leaving Lhasa, but now, despondency clouded my mind once
again. Perhaps, trekking at Linkhor would make me feel better? I
urged Srongsheeshi, 'Come, let's be on our way.'

Trekking here involved going around the Ganden Monastery
over a mountain path. To one side lay the ruins of the temple, a
scene of devastation. But without moving an inch from this
vantage point, one could look around and enjoy the most
breathtakingly lovely vistas. However much the Chinese soldiers
might cause wanton destruction in the name of the Cultural
Revolution, I thought, there was no way they could despoil the
beauty that lay all around us.

After conferring together, the head lama and Srongsheeshi
informed us that since the Germans were particularly keen on
trekking, the guide would move ahead with them and ensure that
they took some video photographs from the platform in the
distance. Later, they would take the jeep and drive down to Sha
where they would be camping out. The driver would pick them up
subsequently and stop by so that I could join them. There was
another problem. I had not brought a sleeping bag. Although
Srongsheeshi was carrying an extra one, the jeep's driver would
apparently need it. That region was bitterly cold right through
the year.

I was quite happy with the way things had turned out. I had
wanted to spend the night at Ganden and the Almighty had heard
my prayers. The head lama knew that I hailed from India and he
too, had been keen that I should spend the night in their company.
'You may go ahead,' I reassured Srongsheeshi, 'it will be no bother
for me at all.'

The guide went ahead with the others, leaving me in the
company of eight young trapas.

The Ladakh Valley and the Lamayuru Monastery bore a strong resemblance to Tibet's Ganden Valley and monastery. As we walked around the religious institution, gazing at the magnificent beauty of our surroundings, the group of trapas moved ahead at a rapid pace. One of them, a boy who was not quite as sprightly as the rest, fell back to walk alongside me. After exchanging introductions, I came to know that his father had some sort of a business in Lhasa and frequently travelled to Kathmandu for the purpose of buying and selling goods. Having accompanied his father on such trips on a number of occasions, the boy was familiar with some Nepalese words and we managed to conduct a conversation of sorts. Since the path we had taken was a popular pilgrim route, prayer flags were visible everywhere.

Walking for almost an hour, we arrived at a small patch of level land situated at an elevation, the highest point in the area. It was only too apparent from the human skeletons and bones scattered around the place that this was the cemetery. As I had observed during my first visit to this country, the custom of cremation was not prevalent here owing to the extreme scarcity of firewood. Burial too, was not an option in ground so unyielding. Enough labour was never available to dig the stone-hard soil where not a blade of grass grew during the winter months. Nothing short of a bulldozer would have done! A strange tradition had, therefore, evolved out of such limitations: corpses were dismembered and the pieces strewn around in this area for birds of prey to feed on. The view from the Heavenly Platform, as it was known, was stunning. But there was no place for one to stand and enjoy it and the wind had a vicious nip to it. We were forced to turn back along the same path, clambering our way down while holding onto the stone wall running alongside for support.

By the time we returned to the monastery, nearly three hours had gone by. The head lama was waiting outside for us. There was another man with him who also spoke Nepalese, had a smattering of Hindi and could even manage a few words of English. Here, unless one held some sort of government post, people were generally not forthcoming about their names. I did not ask for an introduction and it soon became apparent that he was to be my interpreter during my conversation with the head lama.

They led me directly to a small room adjoining Shakyamuni's

temple where the light that streamed in from a tiny window was sufficient for me to have a look around. As soon as we sat down, a trapa brought the three of us some tea in a kettle. I was told that the room had been prepared for my use. Mattresses made of grass had been laid out and a couple of blankets had been provided for spending the night there. Tea was served in bamboo glasses, after which the head lama asked me directly, 'Have you brought any pictures of His Holiness the Dalai Lama as a gift for me?'

'No,' I answered, 'I have been forbidden to carry pictures of the Dalai Lama.'

'Oh, yes! That's right,' he laughed, 'those who give such pictures and those who receive them are both criminals. Despite that, people still smuggle them in and we too, accept them clandestinely. By the way, have you actually seen the Dalai Lama in person?'

'Yes, indeed,' I replied. 'I have had the privilege of an intimate conversation with him.'

This greatly enthused them. They reached out to touch me, then carried their hands to their hearts, as if drawing some great blessing from my person into their own. This they did several times. Then followed innumerable questions in rapid succession, beginning with how the Dalai Lama was keeping and going on to whether he would stay in India during his next incarnation or return to Tibet. I was in no position to answer them and did, in fact, have very little to offer by way of information. But the mere fact of being able to put those questions to me appeared to offer him great consolation.

Just before sunset, the gong sounded for dinner and we all rose to our feet. Dinner was a kind of hotchpotch mixed with cauliflower and boiled potatoes. It tasted heavenly. As soon as the meal was over, the boys left for their rooms. Even after all these years, there was still no electricity in the monastery and inevitably, the old ritual prevailed of going to bed right after dinner and prayers.

The head lama would not leave me right away, but accompanied me to my room himself so that I should not be inconvenienced in any way. Setting down a candle and a matchbox beside the bed, he said, 'I brought these up from my office so that you wouldn't face any problems in case you had to get out of bed at night. If you wish to use the toilet, you had better go outdoors. Although the toilets used by the boys are clean enough, you might find it difficult to make your way there in the darkness. But remember, we are looking forward to many more stories of the Dalai Lama.'

Now it was my turn to say, 'I have said much to you. Now, I am eager for replies to a few queries of my own. I would be deeply grateful if you could answer them. But please don't feel bound to do so. If silence is your response to any of my queries, I will understand that it was an inappropriate one.'

He seemed agreeable to my suggestion. 'Is the Ganden Monastery exactly the way it used to be in the past?' was my immediate question.

'No,' he replied, 'there can be no comparison with the past. In the era of the Dalai Lama and Panchen Lama, this was one of the world's largest religious research centres and the place to which men came in quest of a spiritual mentor. In the past, there used to be between five and six thousand permanent residents. These days, there are no more than four hundred.'

'Are these four hundred inmates receiving the same standard of education that lamas did in that era?' I asked him.

'No, I'm afraid not. The system of education has changed. These days, there is more emphasis on thangkas and mandala art. Initiatives have been taken for translating ancient texts into Chinese. The art of debate is still alive, but there is now a lack of suitable teachers. The truly worthy teachers have all left for either India or Nepal.'

'It will be a good idea, won't it, if old Tibetan texts are translated into Chinese? That will pave the way for Tibetan philosophy to be propagated throughout China.'

I had to go to some trouble explaining my question before it could be properly understood. Nodding wisely, the head lama said, 'That is not possible. Our confidential texts do not lend themselves to translation. I have learned Chinese and can give you a few examples. Judge for yourself.

'*Lo-Chen-Os-Spai*, for one, Valiant Victor (Transcending his knowledge of the Lord of Dharma Amitabha) and '*Eerta-Mgreen*. In Pali, it meant a sign of victory. If these secret documents dedicated to the occult deities are translated, they will lose their power. And that is not the only problem. If what has been recorded in Tibetan and Pali, and most importantly, in Sanskrit, the basic mother language, is translated into Chinese, it will lose its uniqueness.

'Have a look at this monastery. We have lost count of the number of priceless thangkas and wall murals utterly ruined by the bombing. The government in Beijing has brought in many prominent artists to replicate those murals and paint the thangkas again. But the spirit underlying those works is missing. The life force is spent. It would be the same with translations.'

Our conversation was coming along just fine, but the interpreter was not a local and had to return home. He lived in the next village where he had a piggery and poultry farm of his own. With government help, it was doing quite well. The man was, however, shouldering many responsibilities relating to his work and would have to return home. So, we were forced to end our conversation right there. I bade the man a friendly farewell.

The candle had burnt out. The night was mysterious and silent, bringing back memories of the enchanting night I had experienced so many years ago with Rimpoche.

The following morning, I was awakened by the trapas who brought me buns and tea for breakfast. I had not expected such an extravagant meal at the monastery. Once I had eaten and thanked them profusely for all they had done for me, I bade them a warm farewell before being picked up by the jeep that would take me down to the site where the German tourists had camped. The drive was a relatively short one. We pulled up before the camp right next to a mountain cave. As soon as they saw me, my fellow tourists sprang up to greet me as though I were an old friend.

We set out together in the jeep and a forty-five-minute drive brought us to an ancient monastery. Drawing closer, we realized that all the residents were female ascetics! I had not expected to come across a nunnery. I had not even known that there was an old-age home for women in this region. Owing to the wave of destruction unleashed by Chinese soldiers, I had assumed that any such institution would be ground to dust. So, the Naga Women's Ashram, as it was known, was, most certainly, an exception.

We were allowed to enter the temple within the monastery's premises. Those who turned up accompanied by a government guide and vehicle were easily granted permission to enter, while those who came trekking carried letters authorizing them to do so. Private visitors did, however, face problems if they wished to see the place.

A total of eighty-one nuns lived in this monastery. I was still more surprised to learn that twenty Chinese ascetics were among them. Two of the latter were teachers who had spent three years in Kathmandu, studying the Buddhist faith and its historical background. The remaining eighteen had come here to learn about the religion and Tibetan philosophy. Inside the temple were artefacts related to tantra, the Lotus Karma and a huge painting of Mao that covered the entire wall. The Full Moon Festival in Lhasa was followed, I had heard, by another celebrating Mao.

The Naga female monks—not to be confused with the Naga or naked sadhus at the Kumbha Mela in India—ran this monastery. The atmosphere at this institution intended exclusively for women was solemn, as though the women had been forbidden to smile. Inevitably, once they had showed us around the temple and offered us tea, they bade us farewell.

Some distance away was the Sha nunnery run by women. It housed a larger number of ascetics—nearly a hundred and thirty. Most of them were Tibetan, but the administrator herself was Chinese. Their main task was to go to the country's remote mountain regions, educate the villagers and teach them the basics of health and hygiene. Though the recurrent theme in Tibet these days was China, the Chinese government and the Chinese language, Tibetans continued to cling to their own culture and beliefs with great tenacity. The Chinese had resorted to coercive measures, reprisals and inducements to enforce their will. They had also introduced a new system of education, a hitherto unknown cuisine, a different concept of health and hygiene and elements of another civilization altogether. There was also a great number of government projects under way in Lhasa. But it was almost impossible for the Chinese to infiltrate remote Tibetan villages and exert their influence there.

These days, the Chinese were, therefore, in favour of the missionary ruse rather than repression. Making use of Tibetan religious institutions, the Chinese were effortlessly delivering their own message to the Tibetan masses. It wasn't possible for us to observe in detail what sort of responsibilities this women's organization carried out away from urban civilization and political influence. But it was apparent from their conversation that under the garb of nuns, they were all social workers. One would have to concede, of course, that the path they had chosen was a commendable one indeed. The sole task of the Barefoot Doctors was service to humanity. And the one who served humanity was serving God.

If they had so desired, the two German women in our group could well have entered the monastery proper to observe the kind of work being done within it. But our interpreter, a man, was forbidden to enter. Since none of the residents of the monastery knew a word of English, the two German women refused to go in on their own.

After exploring the grounds of the Naga and Sha monasteries, we set off again, travelling north. Leaving the Sharapa Chu Valley behind us, we gradually started ascending the mountain road. The jeep seemed to be under considerable strain, as though pulling our combined weight were causing it immense difficulty. A moment arrived when the vehicle stalled completely. The road was in very poor condition and we would have to trek the rest of the way. But however deplorable the state of the road might have been, the view was exquisite. We moved down to Chek La, located at a height of 5,000 metres. It was here that the trekking would begin.

While the driver remained behind in the jeep, Srongsheeshi accompanied us. Occasionally, he would launch into a spontaneous description of the surrounding landscape. With such natural beauty for our eyes to feast on, conversation was minimal. After walking along in this manner for half an hour, we turned a bend and were met by a still more beautiful sight—that of the Miggi Valley. I was amazed to pick out a house in the distance. What a wonder that was! Who could have constructed a house in this remote area, I asked. How had they managed to and for what purpose? Srongsheeshi informed us that what we were looking at was the Reiting village. The big house visible from here was the Samdrup Nunnery, generally known as Samdrup Ling. It was the third women's monastery in the region and surrounded by four mountains that had served to safeguard it from all marauders and foreign invasions. The three women's monasteries struggled to cherish and keep alive the precious art of the thangka by using all the means at their disposal.

The odd thing about being in the mountains was that distances could not be gauged at all from any given vantage point. So, it took us nearly an additional hour and a half to reach the Samdrup Ling. The cheerful welcome accorded to us by its residents seemed to relieve us of our weariness in an instant. A thick mattress had been laid out for us to rest on in front of the main temple. The sheer beauty of our surroundings kept us in thrall.

After spinning the prayer wheels outside the temple, we entered it. Facing us was a massive statue of Shakyamuni. The German tourists paused to rest, while I looked around at the amazing sights before me. The Chinese cannons had evidently not wreaked havoc here. Having welcomed us and ensured that we were seated, the nuns left us on our own.

After spending half an hour in the monastery, we made our way to Reiting village, a stone's throw away, and stopped in front of a tea shop. Tea and fried cauliflower were ordered for us. The owner of the tea shop was an authentic Tibetan. His entire demeanour seemed to suggest that he had remained untouched by Chinese influence despite living in a place that was not too far from Lhasa. Arrangements had been made for us to stay in the kitchen of this eatery. My friends, however, would be camping outside.

It was the first time since I embarked on this trip that I had come across a monastery and a village entirely devoid of Chinese residents. The thought gladdened my heart. Perhaps, because these people lived in such a remote spot atop a mountain and hadn't witnessed much progress, I reasoned, they had been spared the experience of being tainted with the Chinese brush.

The next day was given over to trekking once more. We came up to Chek La and boarded the jeep again. We were passing over the Nyechen Tangla, and the average height of the mountains exceeded 7,000 metres. In normal circumstances, we wouldn't have needed to climb such heights, but the lack of navigable roads forced us to do so. We crossed the Lhachen Pass, situated at a height of 5,150 metres. The condition of the roads was truly lamentable here, but the beautiful vistas that lay before us lifted our spirits and diverted our attention from them.

Having passed Lhachen, we arrived at Namtso Lake, its icy blue waters so calm and pristinely beautiful, that we found ourselves at a loss for words. No commentary offered by any guide could have held a candle to the sheer magnificence of this gift from God. Gazing at it in speechless wonder, we drank in the sight and could only manage to murmur, 'This is Tibet, the reason why we are all here!'

The Chinese invasion and all that it had brought in its wake—radical change of policy, political turmoil and bloodshed seemed to be quite remote from and extraneous to the sanctity of Namtso—untouched by it all. Nature in all her bounty had held herself aloof from the death and destruction, the rancour and political machinations of the human world, meditating in its ambience of beauty and calm serenity. No man could ever rob her of her unblemished purity.

'That small patch of land you see in the lake, like an island, is called the Island of Tashi Dorje,' Srongsheeshi told us. 'Below the mountains surrounding it on four sides lies the Nyechen Tangla mountain chain.

'Is there a monastery or chorten beside the lake?' I asked him.

'Not as far as I know,' was his answer. 'But on the way to the island, on the right, there are a number of small caves by the mountainside. There is a small monastery there. I believe sages and other ascetics used to live and meditate there in the past. Now there is nothing there but ruins. However, you do get to see beautiful wild birds with colourful plumage, particularly Siberian cranes, crowding around the lake. They're not visible from this far, though. You have to go closer to the lake. Let us trek till the Tashi Dorji Island. It will take us close to four hours to get there.'

My companions jumped up in joy. This was precisely why they had come all the way. There would be trekking, sightseeing and taking of photographs. Armed with their elaborate trekking gear, they were all set to go. I, on the other hand, did not wish to relinquish this beautiful sight. At which point in the future would I come here again, I mused, if at all I did. There was no certainty about it. None at all. I wanted to linger there and hold on to what was so precious to me, to capture it and imprison it within me, along with the feelings it had evoked, so that I could enjoy it forever.

I turned to the members of my group and told them that I would not be coming down with them.

'Why, it's such a beautiful trek!' they exclaimed in protest.

'It certainly is,' I agreed, 'but if I do accompany you down now, I will lose this beautiful view. I'll stroll around here a bit and then go down to where the jeep is parked. Don't worry.'

Reassured, they all left for the lake. I chose a comfortable perch and continued to gaze at Nature's immortal beauty, more pristine, more pure than I remembered it at Mansarovar or even Samding. Here, there were no hordes of pilgrims, no Chinese army trucks, no human settlements close by. What swept the place was nothing but an ethereal silence. The vibration of the stone shavings periodically wafted across like the sound of music flowing over the hills, stirring inexplicable feelings within me. Realization dawned that the mystery of Tibet was very much alive. It had simply moved elsewhere.

Moments of bliss are sadly transitory. The sun had almost merged with the horizon and I was engrossed in the atmosphere of the place when I was recalled to the real world by voices. My companions had returned. Panting, they collapsed beside me and said, 'You have just deprived yourself of an unforgettable experience! This stretch of the trek is so exciting! You can learn a great many lessons of nature. And you should have heard the cackling of the wild geese! We must come back again for a few days. Had there been enough provisions with us, we would have stayed overnight.'

Back to the jeep again for our next destination—Lhasa. Following the mountains on the west, we stopped at a wayside food stall. Nobody wanted to leave such a serene and picturesque place. But we had little choice. The jeep drove on through scenic mountain terrain. The most spectacular sight here was the snow-capped mountain peaks in the distance. The jeep turned a bend. One had to virtually hug the shoulder of the mountain as one went along. At times, the rear tyre hung free over the edge, scrabbling for a hold in the air and causing small stones and pebbles to plunge into the deep ravine hundreds of metres below. We moved on, courting death at every step. Just before dusk, we stopped at a small village which had a food stall adjoining it. At the sound of the jeep, the villagers came running out and crowded around us.

'Is there anything you need?' they inquired.

'Nothing at all,' we assured them. 'We've just come to see you.' Neither the driver nor I felt tired, but the others were absolutely worn out. A menu of sorts was decided on for dinner which would be served starting with soup.

The Tibetans I had seen so many years ago seemed to have been reborn and were welcoming me again. The villagers hovered around us and listened attentively whenever we spoke. Two rooms were set aside for us. Originally, the plan had been for my companions to camp, but it was so cold at this altitude, that it was deemed sensible to remain indoors. As ill luck would have it, however, the village curs surrounded the jeep and kept barking at it all night. None of us could, therefore, get in a proper night's rest. Early the next morning, after downing cups of chang, we set off again. The day after, we would be making our way back to Lhasa, over the same tortuous and dangerous mountain roads.

We reached the Tibetan capital in the afternoon. It seemed to us as though we were entering a city after a very long interval. Ensconced in the comfortable chair in my hotel room, I tried to console myself that I had achieved as much as I could in the circumstances. I had visited and explored Sha, Reiting, Samdrup Ling and Namtso Sarovar. Despite all the political and social turmoil that Tibet had been through, the mystical beauty of the mountains had not forsaken it. I would remain for another couple of days in Lhasa before returning home. The ten-day journey I had just made had taken me from Lhasa through Samding, Gyantse, Shigatse, Phinesholing, Segar, Rongbuk, Dhingri and Kasa. I would now be making my way to Kathmandu along a direct route that would involve trekking part of the way and be covered for the rest by jeep. And then, I would fly home.

To those who might want to visit the Dalai Lama's country, I would say, 'Please do visit Tibet. Do not ignore the Tibetans simply because of what the Chinese government has done to them. The restoration and survival of the country's religion and culture depend to a large extent on the influx of visitors from abroad.'

Though many temples and viharas are being repaired and renovated for tourists these days, visitors from beyond its borders might, in the foreseeable future, wish to obtain insights into the faith that was actually practised at those religious sites. Tourists from abroad constitute the only link Tibet has with the outside world. Tibetans are urgently in need of the inspiration and energy that the advent of people from the world outside can bring. And, perhaps, the clarion call for freedom will come along the very path that has only just been opened.